Fighting for Status

Fighting for Status

HIERARCHY AND CONFLICT IN WORLD POLITICS

Jonathan Renshon

PRINCETON UNIVERSITY PRESS
PRINCETON AND OXFORD

Published by Princeton University Press, 41 William Street,
Princeton, New Jersey 08540
In the United Kingdom: Princeton University Press, 6 Oxford Street,
Woodstock, Oxfordshire OX20 1TR

press.princeton.edu

Library of Congress Cataloging-in-Publication Data

Names: Renshon, Jonathan, 1982– author.
Title: Fighting for status : hierarchy and conflict in world politics /
    Jonathan Renshon.
Description: Princeton, New Jersey : Princeton University Press, 2017. |
    Includes bibliographical references and index.
Identifiers: LCCN 2016050191 | ISBN 9780691174495 (hardback : alk. paper) |
    ISBN 9780691174501 (paperback : alk. paper)
Subjects: LCSH: International relations—Philosophy. | Balance of power. |
    Great powers. | BISAC: POLITICAL SCIENCE / International Relations /
    General. | POLITICAL SCIENCE / International Relations / Diplomacy. |
    POLITICAL SCIENCE / Public Policy / General. | POLITICAL SCIENCE /
    Government / International. | PSYCHOLOGY / Social Psychology.
Classification: LCC JZ1310 .R46 2017 | DDC 327.101—dc23 LC record available at
    https://lccn.loc.gov/2016050191

British Library Cataloging-in-Publication Data is available

This book has been composed in Sabon Next LT Pro

Printed on acid-free paper. ∞

Typeset by Nova Techset Pvt Ltd, Bangalore, India

Printed in the United States of America

1 3 5 7 9 10 8 6 4 2

To my favorite, my fiancée,
Michelle

Contents

Illustrations

Illustrations

Tables

Acknowledgments

I think that the popular image of book writing is that one locks themselves away in archives or offices for several years, and then emerges—bedraggled—with a polished manuscript ready for printing. That may capture the process sometimes (at least the bedraggled part) or for some people, but it does not come close to describing my situation. I absolutely could and would not have finished this project without the help of those listed below, making this effort far more reliant on others than most would imagine, and certainly more than I predicted. I am also sure to accidentally omit some who deserve thanks, too, for which I apologize.

This book, like most first books, started as a dissertation, and so I'd like to begin by thanking the members of my committee: Steve Rosen, Iain Johnston, and Rose McDermott. Steve served as the chair of my committee, and I was lucky to have an adviser who was so open to new approaches and methods. I always enjoyed our talks and left his office full of ideas. Iain was a great mentor to me throughout graduate school, and was always up for a helpful chat about my work or career. Despite being located in another state, Rose was available for a discussion, or to read and provide comments on work that I wasn't sure about (and there was a lot that I was unsure about in graduate school) whenever I needed it. She was, of course, particularly helpful in thinking through how experimental research would fit into my project. The translation of that last sentence for any nonacademics reading this is: she talked me out of a lot of bad ideas. Needless to say, all of my advisers endured many, many questions (and requests for letters of various kinds), and did so with good cheer. Not all graduate students are lucky enough to have advisers who are so helpful and whose working style fits with their own.

The lab experiment reported in chapter 3 was conducted at the Harvard Decision Science Laboratory in Cambridge, Massachusetts. It was conducted as part of a larger project, Leadership Decision Making, under the direction of Jennifer Lerner. I want to thank Jenn for inviting me to be a part of this wonderful and exciting project, and Nicole Otchy for making sure everything associated with the project actually worked and ran as it was supposed to. It certainly wouldn't have if they had let the inmates run the institution. Many other people contributed to the project or collaborated in some way, and in turn enriched the experimental work in chapter 3, including Irving Dominguez, Mark Edington, James Gross, Yoel Inbar, Eric Mattison, Chris Oveis, and Ting Zhang,

Several organizations supported the book project financially over the past several years. I would like to thank the Belfer Center for Science and International Affairs for hosting me as a predoctoral fellow at the Harvard Kennedy School, and the many students and professors who attended those workshop, offering fantastic advice and comments. A special thanks to Susan Lynch, Steve Miller, Sean-Lynn Jones, and Steve Walt, who do a wonderful job running a successful and helpful seminar series and fellowship program. During the project's development, the US Institute of Peace (and US taxpayer) brought me to Washington, DC, for two helpful conferences. Those conferences were greatly enriched by my smart and thoughtful colleagues in the Jennings Randolph Peace Scholar program.

I want to extend a special thank you to the Miller Center of Public Affairs at the University of Virginia, which was generous enough to fund my research through the Governing America in a Global Era fellowship program. Brian Balogh, who directs the program, has done a fantastic job creating a fellowship that truly leaves students better off than it finds them; the content of the "dream mentor" program more than makes up for the slightly cheesy name. It was through that program that I was paired with Bill Wohlforth, who has been a wonderful mentor. A huge thank you to Bill, who read and commented on many drafts, invited me to a stimulating conference (which produced a wonderful book that he coedited), talked with me in depth at many stages of the project, and basically did whatever he could do to help me. I certainly didn't expect to come out of the Miller Center fellowship with a mentor, but I am grateful that I did.

The Institute for Quantitative Social Science at Harvard, Tobin Project (through a National Security Graduate Fellowship), Smith-Richardson Foundation (through a World Politics and Statecraft Dissertation Fellowship), Program on Negotiation at Harvard Law School (through a Next Generation Grant), and Mind/Brain/Behavior Initiative at Harvard University all provided additional financial support.

I received support for my entire graduate career from both the Department of Government and Graduate School of Arts and Sciences at Harvard. Needless to say, without that support over the many years, this project would not have gotten far. A special thank you to Thom Wall, the department administrator for GOV. "Department administrator" does not come close to adequately describing what Thom does. Without him, the department (and particularly the graduate students) would just fall apart. Despite being accosted by students basically every minute of every day, Thom is unfailingly generous with his time, and extraordinarily nice even when he should have been throwing things at us.

I think my experience in graduate school was the same as most: while we present our work every once in a while, and meet with advisers to make sure we are on the right track, much of the day-to-day work involves pestering friends to read something we just wrote or discuss an idea we just had. I'm lucky in this respect to have had great friends, all of whom helped at every stage in the project, from the initial idea to the final draft. More specifically, thank you to Matt Blackwell, Andrew Coe, Jenn Larson, Rich Nielsen, and Iain Osgood. Jane Vaynman and Vipin Narang deserve particular thanks, as excellent friends, but also as those who were forced to endure the brunt of this; they may be the only people as excited as I am that this book is complete.

I would also like to thank a host of collaborators and friends. Both Dustin Tingley and Arthur Spirling provided advice on the dissertation and job market at critical times. Though both are extraordinarily productive and busy, they were always generous with their time, and I stopped into their offices or e-mailed them with questions countless times. In every case, they helped me, and this manuscript (and my work in general) has benefited tremendously from their thoughtfulness and rigor. My work with Allan Dafoe and Paul Huth has greatly informed my thinking on both status and reputation, much to my benefit (and this book's). Allan, in particular, was a model of precision in thinking through the thorny conceptual issues that formed the basis of our review article. Josh Kertzer has been an excellent coauthor and friend, providing feedback whenever asked, making helpful suggestions, and generally playing into the stereotype of the unbelievably helpful and friendly Canadian. All these colleagues and friends have made this work better, and this process more enjoyable.

Once I arrived at Wisconsin, I found that I had a lot more help and support than I could have reasonably expected. My colleagues and friends—Rikhil Bhavnani, Mark Copelovitch, Helen Kinsella, Andrew Kydd, Noam Lupu, Lisa Martin, Ellie Powell, Nadav Shelef, Erica Simmons, and Alex Tahk—have all been wonderful, and I'm grateful to have been in such a supportive and fun environment while I completed the book. I especially want to thank Jon Pevehouse—for reading and commenting on so many versions of so many chapters, and answering so many questions about the book process—and Jessica Weeks, who provided wonderful insights into the framing of the experimental chapter early on. My thanks also go the University of Wisconsin more generally for funding over the past few years, particularly for research assistance and course releases that gave me time to finish the book.

Part of this funding included support for a manuscript workshop. I want to thank the participants who attended the workshop for this manuscript: Richard Herrmann, John Mearsheimer, Elizabeth Saunders, and Bill Wohlforth. Having four scholars of this caliber make a special trip in order to spend a day critiquing the thing you have been working on for years is a daunting prospect; personally, I was terrified. The day ended up being totally unlike what I expected. Rather than scary or intimidating, I found it encouraging and helpful. Every one of these attendees provided thoughtful and useful advice that without a doubt improved the final version of the book. I am in their debt. At the same time as the book manuscript workshop occurred, I had begun to work with Eric Crahan and Princeton University Press. Eric has been a wonderful guide in this process, and he and the rest of the group at PUP have been nothing short of fantastic.

While I worked on the book, I also had lots of help from our wonderful graduate students at the University of Wisconsin at Madison. Katie Robiadek read and copyedited several chapters in advance of the manuscript workshop; Anna Oltman proofread much of the book and provided help with the research for chapter 7. They both did a fantastic job, and I'm thankful to have had access to such talented grads. The biggest debt of thanks goes to Ryan Powers, who worked on every aspect of this manuscript for the last two years. He has contributed in too many ways to count, but the most obvious (and helpful) has been in taking charge of the analyses (and their replication) in chapters 4 and 5. I don't think it's an exaggeration to say that without his help, in both fixing my coding errors, working with me on new analysis, and organizing everything at the same time, the quality of the analyses would have gone down precipitously, and it would still somehow have taken longer.

Now on to what they will surely consider the most important part of these acknowledgments: thanking my parents, Stanley and Judith. Needless to say, they are wonderful, loving parents, and I am lucky to have them around. They both read many sections of this book and often provided helpful comments—sometimes solicited, and at other times against my will. I may have friends who are more relieved than I am that I will stop talking about this book soon, but nobody is more excited than my parents to see this in print.

The last spot in this (esteemed) list goes to my fiancée, Michelle. It is not a surprise that a political scientist who has taken more stats classes than I have and is an expert on moral psychology would have insightful, helpful contributions to make while I was writing. But it was a surprise to me that she was able to make the book process—a long, anxiety-ridden experience—as much fun as it ended up being. I might never wear that novelty T-shirt she made me again, but she is still my favorite person, and it's not even close.[1]

---

[1] The T-shirt was a catchphrase for the book (and maybe author): "What other people think of me matters!"

Fighting for Status

1

Introduction

Of all the misperceptions in international politics, perhaps the most grievous is embodied in the Charter of the United Nations, which declares that the organization "is based on the principle of the sovereign equality of all its Members." A laudatory notion, but one belied by hundreds of years of international politics and human nature itself. The fundamental ordering principle of international politics is hierarchy, not equality. And while guns and tanks are easy to count, far more can be explained by things that we cannot see, hear, or hold. It is ultimately on *status*, not bullets, that "the success or failure of all international policies" rests.[1] But status is more even than the "everyday currency of international relations," because status is also the end goal for political leaders, many of whom are plainly obsessed with investing in, seizing, and defending it.[2]

Smoking gun quotes and tales abound. In a 1952 cabinet memo that foreshadowed the war decades later, British officials argued that the Falklands must be retained, since "public admission of our inability to maintain these traditional possessions would cause *a loss of prestige wholly out of proportion to the saving in money obtained*."[3] Friedrich von Holstein, a German diplomat during the 1911 Agadir Crisis, asserted that Germany must escalate the Moroccan crisis "not for material reasons alone, but even more *for the sake of prestige*."[4] Later, on the eve of World War I, Russian leaders seemed wholly preoccupied with the threat to the regime's status if they should fail to meet the challenge issued by Germany. Russia refused to back down, despite the near certainty that its odds would be far better if it delayed the conflict for one or two years. Czar Nicholas explained this otherwise-puzzling decision to the Russian people by referring to the

[1] Wohlforth 1998, 26.
[2] Gilpin 1983, 31.
[3] Quoted in Wood 2013, 11, emphasis added.
[4] Quoted in Snyder 1991, 78, emphasis added.

need to "protect the honor, dignity and safety of Russia *and its position among the Great Powers.*"[5] This is exactly what Germany wanted, since it had manipulated the situation precisely to play on the czar's concern for status: a 1913 memo from German prime minister Bethmann Hollweg stated that it would be "almost impossible for Russia, *without an enormous loss of prestige* ... to look on without acting during a military advance against Serbia by Austria-Hungary."[6]

Not all tales of status in world politics involve war and peace; some cast world leaders in an almost-petty light. At his coronation in 1804, Napoléon arranged an informal meeting with the pope, who was in attendance. While both were competing for political and economic dominance over Europe, Napoléon got the upper hand by arranging his horse carriage in such a way that the pope was forced to dirty his shoes.[7] At the Potsdam conference in 1945, the leaders of the three great powers of the day—Harry Truman, Winston Churchill, and Joseph Stalin—could not agree on the order they'd enter into the conference room. It was eventually decided that all three should enter simultaneously through separate doors.[8] Vladimir Putin reportedly declined the invitation to a G8 summit at Camp David in 2012 so that he could avoid the humiliation of leaving when the leaders of other nations went to Chicago for a NATO summit to which he was not invited.[9]

While it can be difficult to escape the image of world leaders stuck in a door frame, Three Stooges style, these anecdotes touch on concerns far more serious than they might first appear. Status is valuable, not least because it "confers tangible benefits in the form of decision-making autonomy and deference."[10] Certainly, efforts to gain prestige may sometimes be both costly and risky, but "if they succeed, they can bring rewards all out of proportion to [those] costs by influencing the psychological environment and policies of other decision-makers."[11] Even if status was useless as a currency (and it is not), it would still be sought after for the psychological benefits it confers on its holders. Thus, for leaders, a combination of intrinsic motivation—evolution has ensured that increased

---

[5] Quoted in Lieven 1983, 147, emphasis added.
[6] Quoted in Hewitson 2004, 204, emphasis added.
[7] Morgenthau 1948, 70–71.
[8] Midlarsky 1975, 105.
[9] Larson and Shevchenko 2014b, 274.
[10] Wohlforth 1998, 26.
[11] Jervis 1989, 8.

status makes us feel good—and instrumental benefits—higher status brings tangible benefits in security, wealth, and influence—makes status one of the most sought-after qualities in world politics.[12]

So far, we are on uncontroversial, even staid ground; scholars from every corner of political science, along with their real-world counterparts in the White House (and Kremlin) agree on the critical importance of status. Yet the broad agreement that "status matters" has left us in a peculiar situation. While there is considerable agreement within the political science discipline and foreign policy community that status matters in world affairs, the depth of our understanding has lagged far behind our confidence. For all the bombastic declarations, there is too little in the way of focused research on *how* and *when* status matters. Qualitative work on this subject has been illuminating, but unable to establish patterns across time and space.[13] Similarly, cross-national quantitative research on status and conflict has established an excellent foundation for future inquiries, but has yet to generate concrete, replicable findings on the subject.[14]

Thus, our understanding of status in international politics has been guided by intuition, not evidence, and this has left us with a significant gap. There is still much we do not know about how status affects foreign policy behavior and international outcomes, and what we do "know" is often based on surprisingly little evidence. What we need—and what this book provides—is a systematic investigation into the ways that status concerns affect the behavior of states and leaders, especially as these concerns relate to the propensity for military conflict.

This book begins that process by proposing a theory of status dissatisfaction designed to address the following questions. *When* does status matter: under what circumstances do concerns over relative status overshadow the myriad other concerns that decision makers face in complex international environments? *How* does status matter: what specific outcomes do status concerns trigger, and what strategies do states and leaders use to improve their rank? Finally, *which* types of status are most important? If status is standing in a hierarchy, then leaders may construct a virtually unlimited number of hierarchies based on different attributes (for example, wealth or power) and composed of different groups of competitors. Put more plainly, *who* forms the relevant comparison group for different types of

[12] Plourde 2008.

[13] See, for example, Offer 1995; Markey 2000; Hymans 2006; Wohlforth 2009; Larson and Shevchenko 2010b; Murray 2010.

[14] See, for example, Wallace 1971; Ray 1974; Volgy and Mayhall 1995; Maoz 2010.

states? This book addresses these questions while also shedding light on perennial dilemmas of foreign policy such as how status quo actors can accommodate dissatisfied powers (for example, modern-day China or pre–World War I Wilhelmine Germany) using status-based incentives.

THE CASE FOR STATUS

Status in international politics is *standing, or rank, in a status community.* It has three critical attributes—it is positional, perceptual, and social—that combine to make any actor's status position a function of the higher-order, collective beliefs of a given community of actors. There are two ways in which the term is commonly used. The first refers to status in its most purely positional sense: *standing,* an actor's rank or position in a hierarchy. "Status community" is defined as a hierarchy composed of the group of actors that a state perceives itself as being in competition with. "Rank" is one's ordinal position and is determined by the collective beliefs of members of that community. Since status is based on higher-order beliefs, there is no objective, time-invariant formula for what qualities or attributes confer status. The second meaning of status is as an *identity* or membership in a group, such as "status *as* a major power." Status can thus be "about" belonging to a given group or ranking in a hierarchy, but in either case, positionality is critical.

Status refers to the actual position or identity of a state. While either position or identity might have some explanatory power on its own, my focus is on status *concerns.* Status concerns denote the level of focus on status-related issues, and the likelihood of acting in order to advance or salvage one's status. A concern for status might be sparked by a perceived threat to one's status position or rank, but this is not a necessary condition. In this manner, status concerns are a larger conceptual category that includes "status threats" as one precipitating cause among several. Put slightly differently, status concerns may lead to *status seeking*—behavior or actions undertaken in order to gain status—but may also lead to actions designed to preserve one's current position or slow one's decline (neither of which is accurately captured by the term "status seeking"). Status concerns are orthogonal to status itself, since both high- and low-ranked actors may evince powerful status concerns.

Why focus on status? In justifying or explaining a research program, scholars have several rationales from which to choose. Sometimes the case is made that something is important conceptually or theoretically, while at other times the case is made empirically—it helps explain something— or based on intuition or common understanding ("we all agree this is important"). It is rare that the case can be made on all these levels and more, but such is the case for status.

A Broad Consensus

The "case for status" rests on three pillars, the first of which is the broad agreement that status matters in world politics. This wide-ranging consensus crosses disciplinary and epistemological boundaries, and might truly be said to be one of the few facts on which world leaders and political scientists agree.

The first element of this consensus is the strong belief among scholars that status (in some shape or form) affects outcomes of importance across international relations, including behavior related to international organizations, nuclear proliferation and testing, humanitarian interventions, and international political economy.[15] A recent study summarized its findings by noting that "status seeking and dominating behavior may be as important as raw aggression in affecting the likelihood of international conflict."[16] A related belief follows that status concerns have been *particularly* important to certain countries, such as Russia, Norway, India, China, or France.[17] A hyperbolic, but by no means unusual, statement in this vein is that "[China] may very well be the most status-conscious country in the world."[18]

Policy makers and leaders are, for once, in agreement with political scientists. In government circles, the desire for status is cited as a key factor in nuclear proliferation, the rise of China and Russia, conflict in Syria, and a multitude of other issues.[19] There is also a long history of policy-oriented political scientists encouraging government programs devoted to leveraging what is often seen as a universal desire for status.

---

[15] Hafner-Burton and Montgomery 2006; Levite 2003; O'Neill 2006; Löwenheim 2003; Elkins and Simmons 2004.

[16] Horowitz, McDermott, and Stam 2005, 267.

[17] Mandelbaum 1998; Leira 2015; Miller 2013; Larson and Shevchenko 2010b; Hecht and Callon 2009.

[18] Deng 2008, 8.

[19] Ferguson 2010; Semple and Schmitt 2014; Birnbaum 2014; Landler 2014.

Political scientists will likely be aware of the work of Larson and colleagues, who urge the United States to provide status incentives to Russia and China. They might be unaware, however, that Hans Morgenthau himself made similar pleas over a half century ago (he referred to them as "status bribes").[20]

The case for status is often substantiated via leaders' public and private statements. For example, General Matthew Ridgway wrote to his superiors concerning strategy in Korea that the official US policy was "particularly debilitating to our prestige."[21] David Lloyd George described Britain's position during the 1911 Agadir Crisis in his famous Mansion House speech by forcefully arguing that "Britain should at all hazards maintain her place and prestige among the Great Powers of the world," and that "if a situation were to be forced" on it that required it surrendering "the great and beneficent position Britain has won," then "peace at that price would be a humiliation intolerable" for a "great country" like Britain to endure.[22]

The rationale for giving a place of prominence to status holds no matter which level or actor one places the focus on. For example, a renewed emphasis on leader-specific factors in international relations suggests we should take seriously those factors that affect individual-level decision making.[23] Notably, there is a strong consensus that status is a critically important human motivation and "universal feature of social groups."[24] High-status individuals benefit in real economic terms from the deference (i.e., preferential treatment) shown to them by lower-ranked individuals.[25] High-status individuals also enjoy significant physical and mental health benefits as well as greater access to younger and healthier mates.[26] High-status individuals are even perceived as possessing different "intrinsic" qualities than low-status individuals, who are in turn likely to adopt unfavorable beliefs about themselves to explain their lower ranks.[27] Status positions even affect how we see the world. For example, high-status

[20] Larson and Shevchenko 2010b; Morgenthau 1962.
[21] Quoted in Stueck 1997, 241. For more on prestige issues in the Korean War, see Whiting 1968.
[22] Quoted in Onea 2014, 148.
[23] Hudson 2005; Saunders 2009; Chiozza and Goemans 2011; Colgan 2013; Horowitz and Stam 2014.
[24] Frank 1985; Tetlock 1985; Barkow 1989, Cheng et al. 2013, 104.
[25] Ball and Eckel 1998; Ball et al. 2001.
[26] Singh-Manoux, Adler, and Marmot 2003; Marmot 2005; Adler et al. 2000; Akinola and Mendes 2014; Hopcroft 2006; von Rueden, Gurven, and Kaplan 2011.
[27] Gerber 1996; Ridgeway and Balkwell 1997.

individuals hear louder applause for themselves and use different language when they speak.[28] In short, the tremendous benefits that status confers on individuals who possess it help explain why status seeking is such a fundamental motive for leaders.

The justification still holds, however, if we abstract away from the role of the individual political leader—that is, if we "black box" the state and focus our attention on the international system as a whole. Though the system is anarchic, in the sense of lacking a recognized authority with a monopoly on the legitimate use of force, it is not unordered or "flat."[29] It is in fact ordered, or ranked, on many dimensions, leading Lake to describe international hierarchies as "pervasive."[30] Of course, the most obvious set of status hierarchies in international relations are those based on material capabilities or power. But hierarchies based on moral authority, norms, and international law compliance are prevalent as well. Put simply, even if the system as a whole *is* anarchic, nearly all relationships and interactions within that system are characterized by hierarchy and permeated with patterns of dominance and subordination.[31]

Empirical Benefits

The second pillar on which the case for status rests is its empirical usefulness. Here is where one begins to sense a divergence. On the one hand, scholars have been confident in attributing status-seeking motives to states and leaders. For example, Mastanduno, describing the Cold War dynamic, writes that "U.S. officials worried greatly, some would say obsessively, about the costs to U.S. credibility and prestige."[32] The confidence with which status is pronounced to be driving behavior and outcomes, though, belies the amount of evidence we have in favor of such explanations.

There is far less evidence concerning the impact of status than one would expect, and certainly too little to match our confident declarations. As an example, despite the recent turn toward causal inference in political science, there is no evidence for a causal effect of status on anything related

---

[28] Pettit and Sivanathan 2012; Kacewicz et al. 2014.
[29] Perhaps not as much as commonly believed, however. See Milner 1991; Powell 1994.
[30] Lake 2011.
[31] Lake 2007.
[32] Mastanduno 1997, 57.

to international politics. Even if we relax the high standards typically required to discuss causal explanations, there is surprisingly little empirical work on the subject (though that has certainly begun to change over the last few years). To be sure, there is good research out there (and more every year), but it is typically bound by strict criteria, such as a small group of states or narrow time period. Evidence of status' impact *on world affairs* is thus not causally identified, but nor is it particularly comprehensive or far-reaching.

A second aspect of the empirical justification for status is its potential ability to solve puzzles that would otherwise be mystifying. Why were leaders in Wilhelmine Germany so fixated on status concerns? What is the link between status and war? Why don't more states offer the "status bribes" suggested by Morgenthau, and why do some states not accept them when they are offered? Just as important, what are the methods states can use to gain status, and have those changed over time? No single book can answer all the questions it poses, but this book aims to begin the systematic empirical investigation of the nature and consequences of status concerns.

Synthesis

The third pillar on which my case for status rests is the concept's utility in bringing together myriad approaches to international relations (IR). For constructivists, the perceptual and social nature of status make it a natural focus. Lebow provides one of the strongest arguments in this vein, stating that for several hundred years, "honor and prestige were even more important than security and wealth," and in a later work declared prestige to have been the driving motive in 62 percent of the wars fought since 1648.[33] A related literature on status has drawn extensively from Social Identity Theory to examine how rising powers such as Russia and China have attempted to maintain and increase their status.[34]

Nevertheless, the most obvious illustration of status' wide appeal is that consensus on its importance crosses traditional paradigmatic lines in IR. It is to be expected that those scholars inclined toward constructivist or social psychological explanations would embrace status. What is more surprising—and informative—is that realists, despite their focus on

---

[33] Lebow 2008, 284; Lebow 2010c, 171.
[34] Larson and Shevchenko 2003, 2010a, 2010b, 2014a.

material power and force, seem equally convinced that status matters. Status, along with cognates such as "glory" and "recognition," figured prominently in the work of the "big three": Thomas Hobbes, Niccolò Machiavelli, and Thucydides.[35] The father of the realist paradigm, Morgenthau, argued that the desire for "social recognition" was a potent one in both domestic and international politics.[36] A recent summary of this stated that "all realists share a pessimistic worldview that posits perpetual struggle among groups for security, prestige and power."[37] This perspective is shared, even more surprisingly, by those in the rationalist tradition, where one scholar argued that status "is important even within a strategic approach ... since states may use it to judge quality or they may bandwagon, choosing who to support depending on what they expect others to do."[38]

Of course, the fact that an interest in status can be found across theoretical paradigms in IR does not inherently make the concept more useful. In this case, however, the wide variety of extant approaches to status helps in two specific ways. First, it provides prima facie evidence for the importance of status. That such a wide variety of approaches within political science—not to mention throughout the social and behavioral sciences—have coalesced on this concept acts as a powerful signal of its import.

More than a signal, however, each approach adds something to a broader theory of status in international relations. From strategic approaches, we are sensitized to the instrumental utility of status in IR as well as the dyadic nature of interactions in which states bargain over relative rank. From constructivist approaches, we take the focus on the social nature of status and importance of comparison groups, and from realist theories we can incorporate the complex interplay between power and status. A recent debate in political science has brought to the forefront a battle that can be (perhaps simplistically) framed as being between competing paradigms and "simplistic hypothesis testing."[39] A focus on status offers us the chance to eschew both of these by providing a comprehensive theory that cuts across traditional paradigms, mining insights from across the spectrum of modern social science.

A theory of status in IR offers more even than a promise of synthesizing insights from across the various paradigmatic "schools" within the field; it

---

[35] For an overview, see Markey 1999, 2000.
[36] Morgenthau 1948, 73. See also Herz 1951, 1981.
[37] Schweller 1997, 927.
[38] O'Neill 2006, 1.
[39] Mearsheimer and Walt 2013.

also offers us the rare chance to generate a theory that has clear implications across levels of analysis. This is both unusual and valuable. Unlike many important concepts in IR, status concerns can be theorized at multiple levels of analysis rather easily. At the highest level, I follow in a long tradition of imagining the international system as characterized by multiple status hierarchies composed of shifting groups of state actors. Status is an attribute that states possess, and their rank helps to structure the relationships and interactions that take place within the system. Yet status is somewhat unique in its clear implications and relevance at lower levels of analysis. Because leaders are typically assumed to identify with the status concerns of the states they represent, we can analyze status concerns at the individual level.[40] This is in stark contrast to concepts like reputation, where there is a clear disjuncture between leader and state reputations.[41] What we are left with is a theory that has clear and direct implications at levels ranging from the international to the psychological. This is a valuable attribute in theory building insofar as it aids in both scope and complexity.

WHAT WE KNOW ABOUT STATUS IN IR

Historically, status has enjoyed a privileged place in the study of IR, though one full of contradictions. It is consistently invoked by scholars from different "tribes" within IR (which is itself unusual enough), while at the same time eliciting either pleas for more attention or frustrated accusations that it is "ultimately, an imponderable."[42] It is a subject in which scholars can confidently declare that there is firm evidence for the importance of status in international politics, while in the next breath decry its neglect in theories of IR. Is status truly the "everyday currency" of international politics, or is it so elusive that we should abandon hope of ever truly understanding it?

Though status has figured prominently in foundational IR theories that are inherently wide ranging, a great deal of focus has traditionally been put on the relationship between status and war. This stems from the central importance of status in the writings of those classical or early modern political theorists who are often credited as "founding fathers" of realism, such as Hobbes, Machiavelli, and Thucydides. A recent reinterpretation

[40] Wohlforth 2009; Midlarsky 1975, 141.
[41] Renshon, Dafoe, and Huth 2017.
[42] Dore 1975, 206; Dafoe, Renshon, and Huth 2014; Wight 1979, 79; Gilpin 1983, 33.

of those works ascribes the prevalence of war as resulting from our "psychologically prickly" nature, which is inflamed "by even trivial slights to our glory."[43]

Because of—or perhaps despite—its central role in theory, status has played a prominent role in empirical studies of international conflict. The most notable idea among these works is that conflict arises from status "inconsistency," which is a disjuncture between the status the international community attributes to an actor and the status they actually deserve.[44] Throughout this research program, attributed status was measured using the number of diplomatic representatives received whereas achieved status—what countries would feel they "deserved"—was measured as military and industrial capacity.[45]

Findings in this tradition were mixed. Some found that greater inconsistencies were associated with the onset and severity of international conflict while others found either no relationship or a negative relationship between status inconsistency and war.[46] More recently, some have argued that these mixed results might be explained by temporal shifts in the relationship between status inconsistency and conflict. For example, status inconsistency might predict war in some historical periods and peace in others.[47]

Despite the popularity of the idea waning over time, it is fair to say that the "abandonment of the idea may have been premature."[48] In fact, no analysis to date has examined the complete international system over the entire span of time for which data exist. Rather, studies have focused on either a subset of states or a specific window of time. And while some studies examined the overall levels of status inconsistency in the international system and their relationship to levels of international violence, all other works examine status inconsistency for individual states. This means that we have little sense of whether the mixed results are the "fault" of the general intuition, specific theory (based on frustration and aggression, as discussed later), or the multiple and conflicting ways it has been tested. Thus, what appear in table 1.1 to be "failed" replications are

---

[43] Abizadeh 2011, 298.
[44] Galtung 1964. This notion has also been popular in other fields, and linked to outcomes as disparate as negative health outcomes and voting behavior. Jackson 1962; Lenski 1967.
[45] Singer and Small 1966.
[46] Wallace 1971, 1973; Ray 1974; East 1972.
[47] Gochman 1980; Volgy and Mayhall 1995.
[48] Werner 1999, 713.

TABLE 1.1
Previous Research on Status Inconsistency.

	Domain		Dependent variable	Independent variable	Finding
	Temporal	Spatial			
Wallace 1971 & 1973	1820–1964	"Central system" (N = 26)	Amount of conflict in system in a given year	Status inconsistency (aggregated)	**Positive** relationship between status inconsistency and war, lagged 15 years
Doran, Hill, and Mladenka 1979	N/A	United States, Japan, and Finland	Threat perception	Status inconsistency (individual)	**Positive**: in a survey of individuals from 3 nations, status "disequilbrium" was a significant predictor for feelings of threat
Midlarsky 1975	1870–1945	All states	War involvement	Mean status inconsistency (state) over 75-year period	**Positive** relationship between status inconsistency and war involvement
Maoz 2010	1816–2000	All states	Conflict involvement (monadic and dyadic) and amount of conflict in system in a given year	Status inconsistency (state, dyad, and system)	**Positive** relationship between status inconsistency and war involvement at monadic, dyadic, and system levels
Gochman 1980	1820–1970	Major powers (N = 9)	War involvement	Status inconsistency (state)	**Mixed**: status inconsistency associated with conflict for some states in some time periods

TABLE 1.1
Continued

| | Domain | | | | |
	Temporal	Spatial	Dependent variable	Independent variable	Finding
Volgy and Mayhall 1995	1950–87	All states	Amount of conflict in system in a given year	Status inconsistency (aggregated)	**Mixed**: positive relationship between overall levels of status inconsistency in international system and international violence during period 1950–64, but negative relationship during period 1964–80
Ray 1974	1816–1970	European powers (N = 10)	War involvement	Status inconsistency (state)	No relationship
East 1972	1946–65	All states	Amount of conflict in system in a given year	Status inconsistency (aggregated)	**Negative** relationship between overall levels of status inconsistency in international system and international conflict

actually an agglomeration of different research designs, hypotheses, and subsets of data.

Thus far, much of the interest in the hierarchy of IR has focused on the ability of those at the top of the pyramid—the hegemons—to construct institutions that solidify and preserve their privileged place.[49] In the particularly important cases of power transition and hegemonic war theory, for example, status has been accorded crucial role in theory, but mostly neglected by empirical efforts. Gilpin, Organski, and Kugler have all argued for the importance of prestige as one of the central benefits denied to rising powers by the reigning hegemon, who "locks in" a hierarchy of prestige that may no longer accurately reflect the balance of capabilities.[50] Since not all rising powers desire to change the structure of the entire international system, a key question for this theory is, Which states are "satisfied" (and how can we tell)?

In these works, one observes the tendency to discuss "power," "rank," and "hegemony" in an expansive manner that incorporates notions of status, material capabilities, intellectual innovation, reputation, or moral authority, but to operationalize these hierarchies narrowly as direct outcomes of aggregate military capabilities or national wealth. In fact, thus far, "satisfaction" with the system has been measured through second- or third-order implications, such as similarity of alliance portfolios.[51] But these measurement strategies do not truly reflect the theory suggested by power transition scholars. Revisionist intentions follow in this theory from a situation in which a rising power is denied the benefits they deserve based on their objective power and resources (because the hierarchy of benefits has been "locked in" by the current hegemon). Self-consciously focusing on status and prestige, and more important, *disentangling* them both conceptually and empirically from the others mentioned, is thus a necessity for understanding the dynamics of the international system, above and beyond any interest in individual decision making.

---

[49] Vayrynen 1983; Lemke and Werner 1996· Kugler and Lemke 1996.

[50] Gilpin 1983, 1988; Organski and Kugler 1980. See also Geller 1993; Lemke and Reed 1996; DiCicco and Levy 1999.

[51] Signorino and Ritter 1999. This practice has been extended in recent work by Efird, Kugler, and Genna (2003) and Lemke and Reed (1996, 1998), who have refined the measure of alliance similarity in similar attempts to infer satisfaction with the status quo. Other methods—such as diplomatic history, intuition, or informal panels of experts—are more promising but likely better suited toward smaller-scale efforts such as comparative case studies. See Wallace 1982; Geller 2000.

Related work can be found in research on the acquisition and demonstration of both conventional and nuclear weapons.[52] On the former topic, Eyre and Suchman incorporate status into a constructivist theory based on the "highly symbolic, normative nature of militaries and their weaponry," though they find mixed results in the empirics.[53] More recently, Gilady has convincingly argued that decisions to purchase aircraft carriers cannot plausibly be explained with reference to strategic necessity, and are better understood in the framework of status and symbolic significance.[54] Speaking about status and symbolic significance, Sagan invokes prestige concerns as part of his "norms and identities" model, and traces how it affected the French decision to pursue nuclear weapons and Ukrainian decision to give up its nuclear arsenal.[55]

More recently, a growing literature on status in IR has drawn from Social Identity Theory (SIT).[56] In several works, Larson and colleagues have used SIT to explore strategies that great powers (particularly Russia) use to maintain and increase their status, such as by emulating the practices of higher-status groups.[57] This body of literature is particularly valuable in the attention that it focuses on social comparison.[58] Predictions are that to maintain a positive social identity, states will either emulate or compete with higher-ranked states, or otherwise reframe status achievement within a new hierarchy or based on a new dimension.[59]

There is also significant research on status as a cause of war. "Prestige politics," for example, figured prominently in Kagan's discourse on the origin of major wars. Specifically, Kagan argued that political leaders often

---

[52] O'Neill 2006.

[53] Though their theory incorporates the notion of status, the actual finding is a correlation between membership in intergovernmental organizations (IGO) and acquisitions of conventional weaponry. Their hypothesis was that IGO membership would have a relationship with "high-status" weapons such as supersonic aircraft, but the relationship was found to hold even with items that possessed low symbolic significance, such as armored personnel carriers and propeller aircraft. See Eyre and Suchman 1996, 86, 105–9.

[54] Gilady 2002, 2004.

[55] Sagan 1996. See also Quester 1995; Levite 2003. Prestige has also been used to help explain both Pakistan and India's decision to pursue nuclear weapons while others have argued that the Non-Proliferation Treaty has eliminated much, if not all, the prestige previously associated with obtaining nuclear weapons. See Ahmed 1999; Perkovich 2002; Glaser 1998, 120.

[56] Tajfel 1981, 1982.

[57] Larson and Shevchenko 2003, 2010b.

[58] Clunan 2014.

[59] Larson and Shevchenko 2010b, 67.

see prestige as a critical interest worth fighting to preserve.[60] Lebow has proposed a grand theory of motives for war in which he finds—based on his codings of wars from 1648 onward—that desire for greater *standing* accounts for over half of all international conflict.[61] In a similar vein, Wohlforth has proposed a theory of great power status competition that predicts more "status conflict" (wars whose motivating factor is competing for primacy in the status hierarchy) in multipolar than in bipolar or unipolar systems.[62] Related work has focused on the dynamics of status recognition, anxiety, and immobility.[63]

Finally, status has been the focus of recent experimental work on the decisions of political and military leaders, and an analysis of how states balance the trade-offs involved in seeking both status and power through formal military alliances.[64] These and other studies enumerated here represent a shift toward more detailed examinations of how status operates in world politics.[65]

Four Pathologies

Where does this leave us? Although the efforts I described represent a useful beginning, we are on less than solid ground. A survey of the literature reveals four pathologies common to theories of status in IR.[66] While these issues are likely a sign of the relative "youth" of status research in IR, that is all the more reason to shine a light on them in hopes of furthering the research agenda in the years to come.

The first is IR's collective fixation on major powers. There are, naturally, reasons to focus on the most important states in the system. Most previous research on status, however, has excluded smaller states. In some cases, such exclusions have resulted from the limitations of data or computing power (earlier quantitative work on status inconsistency falls into this category). In

---

[60] Kagan 1995.

[61] Lebow 2008, 2010a, 2010b, 2010c.

[62] Wohlforth 2009.

[63] Greenhill 2008; Wolf 2011a; Murray 2012; Onea 2014; Ward 2015.

[64] Renshon 2015; Renshon and Warren 2015.

[65] See also a small but growing literature on the determinants of status. Neumayer 2008; Kinne 2014.

[66] A less common problem is that of hyperbole. For example, even those sympathetic to the general argument might be skeptical of the notion that status was the dominant motive in 58 percent of wars, while security concerns account for only 18 percent. Lebow 2010c, 127.

many cases, the scope is narrowed implicitly by utilizing a research design (such as measuring status seeking via purchases of aircraft carriers) that selectively includes wealthier and more powerful countries. In other cases, scholars simply argued that status did not matter as much to lower-ranked powers.[67] Early research on status in IR, for example, simply argued that only "central" powers would be affected by status concerns.[68]

Of course, some theoretical mechanisms might be different for major powers, as Wohlforth argues is the case.[69] The overall result, however, is the same: an overemphasis on major powers at the expense of all other states in the system. This pattern has begun to shift slowly in recent years, with works examining regional powers (such as China and Russia) or even "small states" such as Norway, but the overall emphasis in the literature remains unaltered.[70] Major powers *are* important, perhaps even disproportionately so. But by focusing nearly exclusively on great powers, scholars have skipped the critical step of theorizing how status concerns work on a more general level that is common to all actors.

A second pathology concerns the general reluctance to incorporate insights on status from related fields, such as economics, psychology, and biology. In addition to a basic case for the importance of status and reputation, research in other fields provides a viable source for the generation of new hypotheses or answers to empirical puzzles that are observed in IR. Too often, theories of status start and stop with the notion that states (or leaders) pursue status, but fail to address critical related questions such as: *When* does status matter most? *How* are status comparisons made? Of course, there are exceptions that have helped propel status research forward by drawing on sociology or economics, but these are not yet the norm.[71]

Of course, it's not advisable to simply pluck answers from other fields and insert them into the context of world politics; it is not always obvious how research on status in small-scale hunter-gatherer societies or chimpanzee hierarchies relates to world politics. Yet there is a substantial amount of untapped (from the perspective of political science) work on status from the field of psychology and behavioral economics that may

---

[67] Ibid., 74.

[68] Wallace 1971, 24. See also Gochman 1980; Gilpin 1983.

[69] Wohlforth 2009.

[70] On regional powers, see Cline et al. 2011. On smaller states' status concerns, see Neumann and de Carvalho 2015.

[71] See Gilady 2002; Pu and Schweller 2014.

prove useful in cases like this. For example, Frank's observation that "status is local" suggests something about the nature of comparisons that might be applicable to international politics.[72] Perhaps states make "targeted" comparisons to specific reference groups rather than simply compare themselves with the population of states as a whole. These reference groups might be formed by common history, shared culture, strategic interests, religion, and so on.

Even when political scientists have learned from other fields, we have oftentimes generated new problems. A third pathology concerns the difficulty in constructing IR theories using models and assumptions—borrowed from other areas of research—that are difficult to translate into the realm of world politics. IR research on status that is based on the foundational assumptions of SIT is but one example of this. Work in this tradition has been focused and useful, but its predictions have proven difficult to test systematically in IR. For example, experimental findings on social comparison and "which of many possible identity-maintenance strategies they [states] will choose" have been difficult to operationalize in the context of world politics.[73] Other recent work has suggested that IR scholars have misinterpreted the traditional distinction in SIT between *individual* and *collective* responses to status frustration as well as potentially overlooked novel identity-maintenance strategies that may be unique to the political domain.[74] While it is unfair to criticize social identity theorists for some of these issues—it would be unusual for a paradigm to *not* generate some controversy or have drawbacks—it does help make the case for a "bigger tent" in status research moving forward.

The final pathology concerns the tendency to see status seeking as, well, pathological. More specifically, it is the noted tendency of IR scholars to view status-related behaviors as irrational or noninstrumental.[75] A typical example is Abizadeh, who sees status as central to the origins of war, but only because of our "fragile, fearful, impressionable" natures that are easily subject to "manipulation" and can "become irrationally inflamed by even trivial slights to our glory."[76] Of course, status-seeking or status motives may in some cases be nonrational, but relying on this assumption has

---

[72] Frank 1985. See also Heffetz and Frank 2011.
[73] Wohlforth 2009, 36.
[74] Ward 2015.
[75] For example, Eyre and Suchman 1996; Gilady 2002, 2004.
[76] Abizadeh 2011, 298.

all but blinded us to the strategic rationales for acquiring status.[77] This is problematic insofar as it has created a separation between research on status and the dominant rationalist paradigms in political science. This siloing off of status has been to the detriment of both "sides," because status research should take the strategic logic of status seeking more seriously, while rationalist-flavored IR theories that already invoke status concerns should do more to integrate these concepts into their empirical work.

THIS BOOK'S CONTRIBUTION

My earlier review of the state of status research can be summed up by noting the general agreement among policy makers and scholars concerning the importance of status. This agreement is balanced by the pathologies I noted as well as several outstanding issues. Specifically:

1. We lack a full understanding of what factors make status more or less salient to political leaders or states.
2. Despite its popularity, we have relatively few overarching theories to guide us in understanding how status works in world politics, and how it might be connected to international conflict and cooperation.
3. The perceptual nature of status has precluded its direct measurement.
4. There is little evidence for a *causal* link between status and traditional IR outcomes (such as conflict behavior or incidence).

This book innovates on all these fronts. First, my theory gains traction on the issue of what factors make status concerns more or less relevant for leaders by switching focus to status concerns that vary systematically and are generated within "status communities" of peer competitors. While previous work has noted that status is relative, it has failed to ask: Relative to *whom?* Instead, most other research has assumed a competition of all against all, setting up difficult-to-imagine status contests between, for example, Mongolia and the United Kingdom. Thus, one notable advancement of my theory is its treatment of these *reference groups*, long cited as one of the key elements of status by virtually every other field in the social sciences, but severely neglected in IR.[78] This also helps to address what I earlier

---

[77] O'Neill 2006.

[78] As always, there are exceptions that focus on some sort of targeted comparison, such as regional power competition, but these are not the norm.

described as the "collective fixation" on major powers: since all states compete with groups of (relevant) peer competitors, status concerns are no longer confined to the most powerful states.

Second, my theory of status dissatisfaction provides a comprehensive explanation for how status is linked to international conflict. States seek status commensurate with their abilities because it is a valuable resource for coordinating expectations of dominance and deference in strategic interactions. And rather than an instinctual, frustrated response following a "failed bid for status," the initiation of conflict is better conceptualized as one way for states to alter the beliefs of other members of the international community. Previous theories have relied on "frustration" or unthinking aggression, presupposing a degree of irrationality that is both difficult to prove and misleading. Moreover, such assumptions underemphasize the *strategic nature of status seeking* in world politics that is consistent with both psychological and rationalist accounts of IR.

Third, I noted that the perceptual nature of status has largely precluded its direct measurement. This book contributes on this front through innovative large-N measurement strategies as well as by triangulating status and status concerns through multiple methods. Status concerns, for example, are measured using leader statements and writings in the case studies; experimental manipulations in the lab and survey experiments; and status "deficits" (divergences between status accorded a state and what they deserve) in the large-N chapters. All three methods provide valuable leverage; experimentally, we are able to *directly manipulate* the status concerns of our subjects. In the cross-national section, I improve on the traditional method of status measurement, which typically involves counting the number of diplomats hosted (the more diplomats a country receives, the higher their status ranking). I use cutting-edge network analysis methods to incorporate two key facts about status: that actors gain more from associations with higher- rather than lower-status actors, and that actors compete not against all other states in the system but rather against local "reference groups" composed of peer competitors. These large-N measures of status are supplemented and cross-validated using process tracing in several case studies that show the influence of heightened status concerns on foreign policy decision making.

Finally, I have noted that the methods employed thus far have made it difficult to assess the *causal* importance of status in world politics. Previous research designs have generated associations in large data sets that may be driven by omitted variables or case studies in which we must take the potentially "cheap" talk of leaders as gospel. While careful statistical and case study research can address the influence of potential confounders—and this book does both—it is simply not enough on its own. Given the importance of the subject, we must utilize all the tools we have at our disposal, including experimental methods, which have significant advantages in detecting causal relationships and testing hypotheses related to causal mechanisms. This book addresses this shortcoming through the use of several experiments designed to test hypotheses about status and political decision making at the micro level. In doing so, I present the first experimental evidence on the effects of status concerns, using subject groups composed of high-level political and military leaders along with a laboratory experiment that relies on real financial incentives and is framed around a narrative of war and peace.

STATUS DISSATISFACTION

Status dissatisfaction is a state-level theory. The primary actors are states, and it is *attributes of the state*—its level of status concern and the composition of its status community—that are the primary explanatory factors. To the extent that leaders enter into the theory, their status concerns are assumed to mirror those of the state. Though the theory sketches out microfoundations at the individual level, the overall theory is not one of leaders' decision making. Leaders, in the broader theory, are endogenous to the status concerns of the state, and their individual-level attributes—for example, whether they served in the military or came into power through "irregular means"—are irrelevant.

Status in international politics is *standing or rank in a status community*. It is positional (relative, not absolute, values are most salient), perceptual (based on beliefs), and social (the beliefs that matter are those higher-order, collective beliefs about where a given actor "stands" relative to others). While status most often refers to rank in a hierarchy, in some cases it may be used to discuss an identity ("status as ... "), in which case it might be thought of as something akin to a club good. Even in those cases, positionality is critical.

The first way in which status dissatisfaction departs from previous work is in its motivating puzzle. In a review of status as a motive for war, my colleagues and I noted: "If there is one feature of ... status that scholars are in agreement upon, it is that leaders, policy elites, and national populations are often concerned, even obsessed, with their status."[79] Despite this agreement, many theories begin with the puzzle, "Does status matter", or "Do leaders care about status?" But these questions and their answers do not provide much in the way of inferential leverage. Even if we stipulate that status matters, or that states or leaders care about their position in a hierarchy, or all prefer higher rather than lower status, all we have done is—in the language of statistics—added a constant to our model. If we seek to understand something that varies, and we do here, then this can only be a first step. This suggests an important move in our theory building: we must first focus on variation in preferences for status. To do so, I propose a focus on status *concerns*. And if our focus is on variation in concern for status, we are best served by theorizing the systematic and predictable ways in which heightened concerns are triggered.

One of the first things we learn about status—even in this book—is that it is positional, and that relative amounts matter. But relative to *whom*? Earlier works on status in IR have tended to either ignore this question, focus exclusively on the hierarchy composed of major powers, or place all states in a de facto global hierarchy. None of these solutions are optimal, and the latter is acceptable only if we believe the global hierarchy to be the most salient community for all states. Given the difficulty of imagining small island nations in the Pacific focused on a status competition with the United Kingdom—and following recent work throughout the social sciences on the importance of reference groups—I propose a new rule of thumb: even internationally, status is local.

Thus, the oft-cited maxim that status is "positional" is true but incomplete. Status is positional, but for that to mean anything, we need to know something about the "status community" to which the actor belongs: the reference group that actors see themselves as belonging to and competing against. In theory, actors can compare their status to a multitude of targets along an almost-infinite array of dimensions, but in practice the most important comparisons will be along dimensions that are salient aspects of national identity (for example, region, major power status, or religion). This has important implications for our research design and theory: status communities will be more salient as the number or importance of shared attributes increases. Thus, my innovation is to identify status communities *other than the global system* that are relevant to states. I operationalize this broadly in two ways. The first, deductive approach constructs status

[79] Dafoe, Renshon, and Huth 2014, 381.

communities that are based on attributes of states that are widely viewed as important, such as geographic region. The second approach is inductive and uses the foreign policy choices of states—primarily their diplomatic, trade, and alliance partners—to sort them into groups of peer competitors. This latter approach also allows those groups to evolve over time as states move up (or down) and out of different reference groups.

Given proper boundary conditions—the composition of the "status community"—for the status concerns of states, the next step is to identify how those concerns might vary systematically. I propose that status concerns will be heightened when actors believe they are being accorded lower status than they deserve. This then requires an account of how some actor, i, develops beliefs about how much status they deserve. My theory of status dissatisfaction focuses on the critical role of expectations that underlie many of the most important comparisons that we make.[80] Evidence from the individual level is corroborated by scholarship in IR, such as power transition theory, in which conflict results from an aspiring hegemon being denied the benefits that they expect. This literature also provides one helpful way of proxying expectations in the domain of international politics: "asset levels" of other attributes, such as power or economic capacity.

We now have an account of who states compete against (status communities), when status concerns are likely to be triggered (when status < expectations), and where actors' expectations about their own status comes from (asset levels of other important attributes, such as military power). But what happens when those status concerns are triggered—when states are dissatisfied with their status position? Research on the related topic of "status inconsistency" has coalesced around an answer: states dissatisfied with their status, desirous of shifting their position in a hierarchy, might try and fail to change that position—how exactly is not specified—and after failing to gain status, "engage in conflict and violence."[81]

In this formulation, states that are dissatisfied resort to violence only *after* failing to change the status quo—that is, out of frustration. But positing that states act out of "frustration" or "anger" presents two serious problems. First, it is a rather weak mechanism by which status might be linked to war. It presupposes an irrationality (acting out of frustration rather than

---

[80] Friedman 1957; Novemsky and Kahneman 2005; Koszegi and Rabin 2006.
[81] Volgy and Mayhall 1995, 68. See also Gochman (1980 10, 119), where he speaks of states "venting" their "frustrations." On the role of "negative feelings" and "anger" as mechanisms, see Midlarsky 1975, 110.

strategic interests) that obscures the more likely way that status concerns might relate to conflict: because states can expect to profit from higher status and because status is positional (and thus other states can be expected to be reluctant to cede status voluntarily), violence may be one way of *achieving* higher status as opposed to a last resort after having failed to do so. Second, it attributes individual-level emotional states ("frustration" and "anger") to state actors, confusing the levels of analysis even further while also playing a role in de-emphasizing the strategic rationale for violence I described earlier.

In contrast to previous explanations, I propose a new way forward based on an understanding of how status operates in international politics. Because an actor's status position is based on the collective beliefs of their community, states seeking to change their status position must alter others' *beliefs*. Not all interactions, however, are capable of affecting beliefs about status. Because status is a perceptual construct, our cognitive limitations affect the ease with which we can move up or down in a hierarchy. Chief among these restrictions is that beliefs are updated sporadically—not continuously—and then only in response to large events. Rather than continuously updating their beliefs in response to every interaction, large or small, actors change their beliefs only when they are "hit over the head," or "shaken and shattered into doing so."[82]

Because beliefs about status require some consensus in the international community, there are three requirements for a "status-altering event." First, it must be highly visible (i.e., public). This is because status is based on collective beliefs: events that change perceptions of status must be visible to all potential observers. The second requirement—that the event be dramatic or highly salient—is implied by the basis of status in collective beliefs. Because political leaders and their advisers face severe constraints on their time and attention, they cannot pay attention to everything that happens in the world. Dramatic events, in which lives are lost, for instance, are more likely to be able to compete for the attention of multiple actors in the system. Finally, because status requires a shared consensus on a given state's "standing" in the relevant community, the event must convey unambiguous information. Taking these conditions into account, status dissatisfaction theory predicts that states are likely to initiate violent military conflicts to shift beliefs about where they stand in a given hierarchy.

---

[82] Shleifer 2000, 113; Stoessinger 1981, 240.

In the chapters that follow, I elucidate the theory in further detail and begin the process of amassing evidence. In providing evidence, it has become common for scholars to either incorporate additional levels of analysis or different methodologies. This book does both by combining state-level data (in a cross-national research design) with qualitative and historical accounts as well as experiments. In the experimental components of the book, the focus shifts so that the primary actors are individuals. While the theory of status dissatisfaction is a theory of state behavior, I use experimental methods to test the second-order implications of the broader theory at another level of analysis.

In fact, the rationale for the focus on the individual level is much the same as the rationale for incorporating qualitative/historical research and experiments into the project. First, both help me investigate a potential mechanism suggested by status dissatisfaction: if the theory is right, status concerns should vary systematically, and when triggered, cause individuals to increase their value for status. Put simply, once an actor's status is threatened, or once they decide a situation requires defending or increasing their status, they should be willing to pay far more to keep x amount of status than they would be had those concerns not been triggered.[83] This suggests that once status is threatened for leaders, they will become increasingly willing to expend resources to save it. This, in turn, suggests that status concerns should have strong implications for a class of decisions related to the escalation of commitment.

Status dissatisfaction theory predicts a greater tendency to "throw good money after bad" once status concerns are heightened. Note that this is *not* "sunk costs bias," which implies cognitive bias or errors in judgment. Without information on the value of the status sought by the actor, we have no way of knowing whether the increased expenditure of resources represents biased judgment or a sound investment. We know only that such behavior is more likely when status concerns are triggered. This hypothesis, a "microfoundation" of status dissatisfaction theory, is best suited to verification in the controlled environment of a lab experiment, but also provides implications that are testable in the qualitative record.

In principle, one could imagine this being examined with quantitative data sets in a cross-national design, but in practice the available data (even, for example, the LEAD data set) do not address the objects of interest in

[83] Pettit, Yong, and Spataro 2010.

this theory.[84] Because the mechanism I referenced that links status concerns to conflict is inherently psychological in nature—remember, psychological does not mean "not strategic"—qualitative and experimental methods are uniquely suited to providing evidence that helps us to evaluate the overall theory.

In addition to helping assess potential mechanisms, a research design that incorporates both experimental and qualitative methods makes it easier to establish and validate the *causal* effects of status concerns. It's obvious how experiments do so, given that their defining feature is the random assignment of experimental treatments that (if the study is properly designed) rule out confounders. Qualitative research helps in much the same way. For example, it's important to establish that heightened status concerns lead to conflict initiation rather than the other way around. In cross-national designs, we can address this in some ways (for example, by lagging the independent variable), but without fully ruling out alternative causal paths. Chapter 6—along with the illustrative cases in chapter 7—help to corroborate this basic causal chain by showing that Germany's status concerns originated before the strategy of conflict initiation versus as a result of it. Such investigations also aid us in establishing important assumptions of the theory, such as the notion that leaders will be aware of, care about, and respond to shifts in the status of their country as distinct from their own personal status.

PLAN OF THE BOOK

Chapter 2, "Status Dissatisfaction," outlines my theory of status dissatisfaction by providing answers to basic questions surrounding status in world politics (for example, what types of status are most important? What strategies do states use to maximize or salvage their status?), and clarifying the relationship between status and conflict. In place of the traditional focus on status seeking or preferences for status, I examine status *concerns* that vary over time and context. This is critical because while preferences for higher status can be taken as a constant, the level of concern over relative status is not. Building on this fact provides far greater analytic leverage in examining the effects of status in world politics than previous approaches have been able to offer.

[84] Horowitz, Stam, and Ellis 2015.

Status dissatisfaction theory provides a comprehensive explanation for how status is linked to international conflict, beginning with the critical issue of how states make status comparisons. In particular, it focuses on how states sort themselves into "status communities" of peer competitors. Thus, one notable advancement of this theory is its treatment of these reference groups, long cited as one of the key elements of status by virtually every other field in the social sciences, but mostly neglected in IR. Finally, the theory provides an explicit link between status dissatisfaction—a heightened concern for status triggered by status deficits within a given status community—and conflict. Previous theories have relied on "frustration" or unthinking aggression, underemphasizing the strategic nature of status seeking in world politics. States seek status commensurate with their abilities because it is a valuable resource for coordinating expectations of dominance and deference in strategic interactions. And rather than an instinctual, frustrated response following a *failed bid for status*, the initiation of conflict is better conceptualized as one way in which states seek to alter the beliefs of other members of the international community.

Three major concerns emerge in chapter 2. First, there is no empirical support for a *causal* link between status concerns and outcomes related to international conflict: the associations found in qualitative and large-*N* work cannot rule out the influence of unobserved variables, which impact both the likelihood of war and the measure that is often used as a proxy for status—diplomatic representation. Second, the social and perceptual nature of status has precluded both precise and direct measurement, leading to a reliance on proxies such as diplomatic representation and success in the Olympics. Finally, we have scant information on what factors make status concerns more or less salient to political leaders.

In chapter 3, "Losing Face and Sinking Costs," I use experimental methods to test the behavioral microfoundations of status dissatisfaction theory, focusing on the three gaps in our understanding enumerated above. In particular, I use two simultaneously fielded experiments to provide direct evidence on the foundational tenets of status dissatisfaction theory: that status concerns vary predictably in response to contextual and dispositional factors, and that once triggered, those concerns raise the value that actors are willing to pay for increased status. The chapter also provides and tests additional mechanisms that link status concerns to international conflict through individuals' willingness to escalate their commitment to a failing course of action. In our observational data, a common issue is that status concerns might sneak their way into "both sides" of our equations, making any effect of status concerns difficult to disentangle. In these experimental studies, I prime status concerns irrelevant to the decision process that subjects are engaged in, helping me to cleanly isolate the effect of status concerns while also providing what is likely to be a lower bound on the effects of status in political decision making.

In study 1, I replicate and extend a well-known sunk costs experiment that asks subjects to make a hypothetical investment decision. In study 2, I introduce a newly developed experimental paradigm—the "Island Game"—to provide a behavioral measure of escalation, using real financial incentives, and framed around a narrative of war and peace. Study 2 utilizes a unique sample of political and military leaders from the Senior Executive Fellows (SEF) program at the Harvard Kennedy Schools as well as a group of demographically matched control subjects to address common concerns about external validity in IR experiments. This chapter also begins the work of investigating other factors that might exacerbate status concerns, particularly social dominance orientation (SDO) and power. I find that individuals high in SDO—that is, subjects with stronger preferences for hierarchy—are most affected by status concerns and correspondingly more likely to exhibit patterns of biased escalation. And while the fear of losing status impedes decision making and increases the tendency to "throw good money after bad," power aids decision making by buffering high-power subjects against the worst effects of status loss.

Chapter 4, "A Network Approach to Status," tackles the challenge of how we should think about and measure status in the realm of international politics. Directly addressing the role of status in international conflict requires wading into the messy world of observational data, whether quantitative (in this chapter) or qualitative (in the last two chapters). Doing so requires us tackling thorny issues of measurement. This issue is even more pressing when the concept of interest (status) is both perceptual and social.

In this chapter, I describe how we can use the tools of network analysis to sensibly infer international status rankings. I innovate by incorporating universally acknowledged aspects of status that have thus far been ignored, including the notion that status is more efficiently gained from higher (rather than lower) status actors. And while diplomatic exchange data are often used—in one form or another—to examine international status, I provide the first ever cross-validation of the data, using a combination of alternative data sources and historical research. In doing so,

I provide insight into the sources of status. I find that there are many "paths to status" in world politics; states can manipulate their international standing through both normatively good and bad actions such as greater international engagement and nuclear proliferation. Finally, I use cutting-edge "community detection" techniques to operationalize *local* reference groups. This allows us—for the first time—to directly measure states' reference groups, the "status communities" to which they belong, using data on the nature and intensity of diplomatic representation.

Chapter 5, "Status Deficits and War," provides empirical evidence drawn from a large-N statistical analysis of the relationship between status dissatisfaction and international conflict at several degrees of intensity (ranging from crises to interstate war). First, I examine a direct implication of my theory: Does conflict serve as a status-altering event? In fact, no matter how one measures it, victory in conflict pays status dividends. This is true whether a state initiates or is targeted, whether the comparison category is losing, drawing, or not being involved in conflict at all, and holds across time periods, regime type, and size of state. I then turn to the link between status deficits and conflict initiation, and find that controlling for other important factors, states that are attributed less status than they are due based on material capabilities are overwhelmingly more likely (than "satisfied" states) to initiate militarized disputes at every level of intensity.

This chapter also presents unique data on which comparisons are most salient in motivating international conflict (for example, Who do powerful states compare themselves to? Are South Africa and the United States likely to compare themselves to similar groups of countries?). I show that the types of comparisons that are made—who the "reference group" is—have important implications for how status concerns are manifested in international politics. In addition to making war more likely, dissatisfaction over status changes the very nature of conflict. I show that dissatisfied states choose different targets than otherwise-similar but "satisfied" states. In particular, they disproportionately select into conflicts against lower-power but higher-status states.

In examining the impact of status deficits on international conflict, I also consider several potential objections. First, I show that far from being a "remnant of the nineteenth century," the impact of status deficits on war does not change significantly over time. Another potential objection revolves around the notion of norms that may have developed over time in some status communities, prohibiting the use of violence to attain greater international standing. I show that even among communities with extremely low absolute levels of violence, status deficits predict the initiation of conflict.

While the quantitative chapters carry important advantages, their primary drawback is the possibility that the statistical associations found might be spurious, driven by endogeneity stemming from either measurement error or omitted variables. While careful statistical modeling can address some of these concerns, the addition of carefully selected case studies helps protect against spurious correlations, provides insight into causal mechanisms, and helps to tease out further implications of the theory not observed in the cross-national data.

In chapter 6, "'Petty Prestige Victories' and Weltpolitik in Germany," I unpack the "black box" of the state by investigating whether and how status concerns motivated German decision making during the years, 1897–1911. Seen in light of my status dissatisfaction theory, Germany's "world policy," often derided by historians as blundering or reckless, is cast a new. German leaders, driven by the strong belief that they weren't accorded the status they deserved, formulated a grand strategy intended to raise their international profile through the instigation of major and minor international crises designed to coerce status concessions from Britain, France, and Russia. I demonstrate that the policies associated with *Weltpolitik*—primarily the constant initiation of international crises, and pursuit of a large navy and mostly worthless colonial territories—may instead be seen as policies designed to coerce other states into ceding status to Germany. This chapter both fleshes out the empirical results from the laboratory and large-N chapters while shedding light on the long-term origins of World War I.

Despite the strong evidence on the importance of status concerns in Wilhelmine foreign policy, several open questions remain relating to the generalizability of status dissatisfaction theory. To that end, this last empirical chapter, "Salvaging Status: Doubling Down in Russia, Egypt, and Great Britain," examines three separate sets of decisions:

1. Russia's decision to aggressively back Serbia in the 1914 July Crisis
2. Britain's decision to collude with Israel and France in launching the 1956 Suez War
3. Gamal Abdel Nasser's 1962 decision to intervene in the Yemen Civil War (and continue to escalate through the rest of the decade)

I broadly corroborate the patterns found in the Weltpolitik case while highlighting the plausibility of several new mechanisms. These cases also help to make the critical point that status concerns are not confined to European countries, great powers, or states in the pre–World War I era. No single system of government, culture, or people has a monopoly on status concerns and the link between sharpened status concerns, and international conflict is robust. And where Wilhelmine Germany's status concerns led to a policy of aggressive conflict initiation and brinksmanship, the minicases examined here show the other side of status concerns: state behavior designed to salvage or defend status rather than increase it.

2

Status Dissatisfaction

Political scientists, pundits, and leaders all evince strong beliefs that status matters. Yet this conventional wisdom—really, a hunch—that status matters only gets us so far. In fact, this widespread consensus has obscured a broader and more critical problem: we lack a nuanced understanding of many fundamental questions related to status in international politics.

My theory of status dissatisfaction provides answers to these questions. In place of the traditional focus on status seeking or preferences for status, I examine status *concerns* that vary over time and context. This is critical because while preferences for higher status can be taken as a constant, the level of concern over relative status is likely to vary. Building on this provides far greater analytic leverage in examining the effects of status in world politics than previous approaches have been able to offer.

Another notable advancement of this theory is its treatment of reference groups, long cited as one of the key elements of status by virtually every other field in the social sciences, but oftentimes neglected in IR. While previous work has noted that status is relative, it has failed to ask, Relative to *whom*? Instead, most works have assumed a competition only among great powers, or of all against all, setting up unrealistic status contests between, for example, Nauru and the United States. In contrast, my theory suggests—and my empirical results support—a strong emphasis on how states group themselves into "status communities" of peer competitors. Status dissatisfaction is thus shorthand for a heightened concern for status triggered by status deficits within a given status community.

The theory also provides an explicit link between status dissatisfaction and conflict. Previous theories have relied on "frustration" or unthinking aggression, presupposing a degree of irrationality that is both difficult to prove and misleading. Such assumptions underemphasize the strategic nature of status seeking in world politics, consistent with both psychological and rationalist accounts of IR.[1] States seek status commensurate with their abilities because it is a valuable resource for coordinating expectations of dominance and deference in strategic interactions. And rather than an instinctual, frustrated response following a *failed bid for status*, the initiation of conflict is better conceptualized as one way that states seek to alter the beliefs of other members of the international community.

STATUS DISSATISFACTION AND ITS CONSEQUENCES

What Is Status?

Status in international relations is *standing or rank in a status community.* Its three critical attributes—it is positional, perceptual, and social—combine to make any actor's status position a function of the higher-order, collective beliefs of a given community of actors. Even more broadly, it might be described as an attribute of a *social role*—an umbrella definition large enough to accommodate the dual meanings of status.[2] The first—and likely most common—meaning of status is in the purely positional sense: *standing* or *rank* within a given status community. "Status community" is defined as a hierarchy composed of the group of actors that a state perceives itself as being in competition with. "Rank" is one's ordinal position within that hierarchy and is determined by the collective beliefs of members of that community.

Even when the emphasis is on *rank*, "social role" helps describe the dynamic, since the rank itself is important only insofar as it clarifies what rights, obligations, and patterns of *deference* from others the actor should expect as well as how the actor is expected to behave with respect to others in dominant or subordinate positions. The second meaning of status is as an *identity* or membership in a group, such as "status *as* a major power."[3]

---

[1] For an example of this, see O'Neill 2006.

[2] See definition in Dafoe, Renshon, and Huth 2014, 375. This accords with the definition in Larson, Paul, and Wohlforth (2014, 7), which sees status as "collective beliefs about a given state's ranking on valued attributes" that might be manifested in international politics as either membership in a "defined club of actors" or "relative standing within such a club." This definition complements the one used here because both see status as reflecting collective beliefs about where a given state *stands* (or ranks) with respect to comparison groups, and both agree that it can be about belonging to a given group or ranking in a hierarchy, but that in either case, positionality is critical. Broad agreement with this conception of status can also be found in Wood 2013.

[3] As in Murray 2010; Larson and Shevchenko 2010b; Volgy et al. 2011. A review of the relevant literature in fields such as political science, sociology, and economics suggests

It is this second meaning of status that has inspired some to argue that it is either not zero-sum or is better conceptualized as a "club good."[4] Even if we think of status as an identity or "membership in a group," however, its positional nature is still critical. First, the status associated with becoming a member of group is to a large extent fixed, and thus every additional member of the group inevitably lessens the value associated with it (being a "major power" becomes less meaningful the more major powers there are); this is the classic definition of "zero-sum." Additionally, membership in the group still relies on the notion of positionality, only the unit of observation has changed. In these cases it is about the relative position of members and nonmembers of the group, or perhaps the relative rankings of different groups to which they might belong.

This clears up at least some of the confusion relating to status: one set of scholars use it to refer to rank or standing in a hierarchy—emphasizing its

---

varied answers. Status might be collective beliefs about a given state's ranking on valued attributes (Larson, Paul, and Wohlforth 2014); public recognition of eminence, and hence an assessment of relative position (Markey 2000, 55); one's position in a social hierarchy (Frank 1985; Congleton 1989; Ridgeway and Walker 1995; Quint and Shubik 2001; Heffetz and Frank 2011); a "reputation for power" (Nicolson 1937; Morgenthau 1948; Gilpin 1983); recognition by others of one's strength (Carr 1937); esteem or credit accorded by others (Herz 1951); the demonstration effects of institutions and practices in the international system (Fordham and Asal 2007); or a costly signal of nonobservable qualities (Rege 2008). The disagreement evident in these many definitions obscures some important patterns. For instance, economists and modern sociologists tend to agree on defining status as one's rank in a hierarchy. While economists are agnostic with respect to the determinants of that rank, sociologists often argue that it is a function of deference, respect, social influence, and honor (Ridgeway and Walker 1995; Lovaglia and Houser 1996). Political scientists in the realist tradition tend to see status as merely a reflection of power (though not all of them; see Herz 1951), while others view it as collective beliefs about where a given state ranks on valued attributes. This last meaning comes closest to my definition, emphasizing, as it does, the importance of collective beliefs about where a given state "stands" relative to others.

[4] Clunan 2014, 376; Lake 2014. Such a definition would, for example, imply that new members could be admitted into a high-status group (such as the UN Security Council) without taking away prestige from the other members. Rather than an argument against positionality, this is merely a special case of positionality in which the group/club is large enough that the addition of only one member wouldn't *noticeably* detract from the prestige of membership. What if two new members are added? Or twenty? What if the group is small to begin with and several new members are added? At some point—and based on a function that includes the number of new members and original size of the group—the admission of actors into a club does obviously detract from the other members' status. Of course, it might only injure the current members of a relatively large club slightly to admit one new member (and thus, on balance, might be worth the cost). That, however, does not constitute evidence that status is not positional,—only that it is sometimes difficult to detect a small marginal effect in some real-world environments.

positional nature—while others—for example, those influenced by SIT—use it to denote identity or group membership.[5] Those definitions are not as different as they appear and are both critical elements of international status. One solution is for scholars to specify what the status is for—that is, Status *as what*? Many types of status are possible, including position derived from following international law, leading the development of international norms, or identities derived from being in a particular club (for example, "status as a major power") or having a particular role (for example, "status as defender of the Slavic people"). We can also assume, though, when these aspects are not specified, that the scholars are referencing default meaning of status: standing within the global status hierarchy.

ATTRIBUTES OF STATUS: POSITIONALITY AND PERCEPTION

Several other features of status are key. First, it is *positional*. This is, in fact, what any undergraduate learns in their introductory economics courses and conforms to its common usage. It makes little sense to speak of two actors—say, Australia and Japan—as both "having status." Without specifying what *sort* of status is being referenced, we default to the "fundamental unit" of status: rank. And status as rank is not about "having" versus "not having"; it concerns how *much* we have relative to others (which "others" exactly matter will be a topic we turn to soon).

Status is also *perceptual* in the sense that it is based on beliefs. There is no "objective" or "natural" status hierarchy, nor are there immutable characteristics that confer status. In later chapters, for example, I show that the "sources of status" in international politics have changed as beliefs about valued attributes have shifted in different areas of the globe. In the international system, some attributes—for example, European great powers' possession of colonies in the nineteenth century—were once great markers of

---

[5] One other source of terminological confusion regards the use of "status" as opposed to "prestige." Larson, Paul, and Wohlforth (2014, 16) define prestige as "public recognition of admired achievements or qualities," and note that it is similar to status in being relative, but does not connote ranking in a hierarchy. Similarly, Dafoe, Renshon, and Huth (2014, 6) argue that although the terms are often used interchangeably (and indeed, are often linked) and both have normative components, prestige differs in that it is generally more under the control of the actor than status: "Actors can seize, acquire and invest in their reputation and prestige. Status, on the other hand, is more often regarded as a function of the community." While these two works have traced out subtle distinctions between the two concepts, I follow Wohlforth (2002, 4) and Wood (2013) in noting that many IR scholars use these concepts interchangeably, but that "status" fits better conceptually while tying it to past large-*N* research on the subject.

status, but are no longer so. What is considered "high status" can thus shift over time or in different settings. Some associated features, such as wealth, may be longer lasting, but they are not necessarily permanent. Status is thus ideational or nonmaterial. Yet material objects (such aircraft carriers) can become markers for status, and the status hierarchy, once formed, is capable of exerting tremendous consequences in the material world.[6]

But whose perceptions matter? O'Neill suggests one elegant way of thinking about this when he asks us to imagine a "hierarchy of beliefs."[7] The 0th level of beliefs is the objective situation, such as the number of nuclear missiles possessed by the United States. First-order beliefs are one actor's beliefs about another actor (more specifically, beliefs about how an actor will behave in a particular situation, or beliefs that another actor possesses a certain quality or trait). Carrying the example forward, China's belief about whether a US president would use those nuclear missiles in a crisis over the Taiwan Strait would be a first-order belief. First-order beliefs do not require agreement among a group of actors, nor do they require knowledge of what any other actor believes or thinks. Second-order beliefs are beliefs of one actor about the beliefs of another actor or group of actors. For example, if China believes that Russia believes the United States to be high status, this would be a second-order belief.[8] For O'Neill, *prestige* is located at this second level of beliefs.[9]

While it is reasonable to view status as a second-order belief, status is not *one* actor's beliefs about *one* other actor. Rather, status describes *many* actors' beliefs about what many other actors also believe. At this level of higher-order beliefs, it is probably easier to think of these beliefs as "common" or "shared beliefs," with the addendum that they are not just convergent but also shared (and that the actors know that they are shared). It is at this level that beliefs about status reside, since they rely on shared agreement among a community about where each actor stands in some hierarchy.

[6] Ball and Eckel 1998.

[7] O'Neill 2006; see also Dafoe, Renshon, and Huth 2014, 374.

[8] This is similar to a common definition in sociology: first-order beliefs are "what an actor personally thinks," second-order beliefs are "what an actor thinks specific others in the situation think," and third-order beliefs are "assumptions about the beliefs or perspective of the 'generalized other' in society." See Ridgeway and Correll 2006, 433.

[9] O'Neill 2006, 8. In that account, an actor has status with a group for a certain quality if: [a] the members generally believe that they generally believe that the actor has the quality; [b] they generally believe that they see the quality as desirable; and [c] they generally believe on account of the considerations in [a] and [b] that the party holds power within the group.

But what exactly is "shared agreement"? Unanimity is certainly not necessary, and is a condition unlikely to obtain in reality. There was something less than consensus regarding European great powers in the pre–World War I era, for example. German leaders certainly saw themselves as part of that group, but the behavior of England and France suggests sharp disagreement on that issue. A more realistic definition is that status hierarchies exist when most actors believe that most other actors share beliefs about the composition and ordering of a given hierarchy.[10] *The higher the proportion of actors in a given community who hold these shared beliefs, the more powerful the status hierarchy will be in governing the relations of the actors of whom it is composed.* Note that disagreement over the hierarchy in its more limited sense—who defers to whom in a given interaction?—is likely to be far more common than disagreement over which strata of the status hierarchy any given actor resides in. In other words, consensus on who belongs where is highest at the lowest resolution, and lowest at the highest resolution.

REPUTATION, HONOR, AND AUTHORITY

One vexing problem throughout social science is the conflation of related terms and concepts. Honor and reputation (not to mention "authority" and "power"), for example, are often used interchangeably with "status," especially in political science.[11] This problem has been exacerbated by the varying understandings of these terms in different historical eras and cultures, complicating our ability to use historical quotations as evidence; when Lyndon Johnson referred to the United States' "national honor," what exactly did he mean?[12]

The conceptual underpinnings of status I outlined help us to hone our understanding by both clarifying the concept and separating it from related concepts, such as reputation, honor, and authority. Honor is a belief concerning the virtue of some other actor or behavior, following both Nisbett and Cohen ("reputation for strength and toughness") and O'Neill (the fact of an individual possessing some positive characteristics).[13] This

---

[10] Ridgeway and Correll 2006.

[11] See, for example, Nicolson 1937; Morgenthau 1948; Singer and Small 1966; Gilpin 1983.

[12] Quoted in Dafoe and Caughey 2016, 344.

[13] Nisbett and Cohen 1996, xv; O'Neill 2001. There are other definitions, such as that of Kagan (1995, 8), who sees honor as including "deference, esteem, just due, regard, respect or prestige." Such a definition is too expansive to be useful in clarifying and separating related concepts, however.

also fits in with our intuitive understanding in that we believe others to "be honorable" or believe that certain actions are honorable (in the sense that they confer honor on those who perform them). Honor is also similar to status in that both are social characteristics, and thus both involve and require the beliefs of third parties.[14]

Honor, however, is distinguished from status by one important characteristic: status is a positional concept, while honor is not. This can be illustrated by constructing a simple definition of honor such as "honor requires that one never tells a lie." In a group in which all members are honest, then all have honor (or "are honorable"). If a new person joins the group and forswears lying, then they too are honorable and have acquired honor without in any way affecting the rest of the group's honor. This is in contradistinction to status, which is relative: everybody in a group cannot possess the most status. Even in extreme cases, such as when there are two powerful actors—such as the Soviet Union and the United States during the Cold War—eventually, in any given interaction, one actor will be forced to defer to the other. Of course, as was true in that example, the two actors in question might not agree on the status hierarchy (and the question of who *should* defer), but that, among other factors, is exactly what the conflictual nature of their relationship resulted from: the necessity of sorting out the "pecking order."

A similar problem concerns the relationship between status and reputation. Reputation is often used interchangeably with status, especially in political science.[15] Reputations are judgments about an actor's past behavior that are used to predict future behavior.[16] "Reputation" is in reality a shorthand for a more complete description. Actors do not simply have *a* reputation. Rather, they develop reputations for a *specific quality, characteristic, or behavior*. One might have a reputation for resolve, cowardice, "bandwagoning," and so on. In political science, reputation tends to be employed as a shorthand for "reputation for resolve."[17]

---

[14] Though in fact this can conflict with our intuition that honor is a personal trait (one's "sense of values"), and one that specifically does not require others to know how and whether we have acquired honor. O'Neill (2003, 230) thus distinguishes between "personal honor" (an intrinsic trait or value system) and "social honor" (which is the concept I refer to here). See also Dafoe and Caughey 2016.

[15] See, for example, Nicolson 1937; Morgenthau 1948; Singer and Small 1966; Gilpin 1983; Tang 2005; Prosser 2008.

[16] Miller 2003.

[17] Guisinger and Smith 2002.

TABLE 2.1
Disentangling Status, Authority, Honor, and Reputation.

	Perceptual	Second-order belief	Positional	Requires legitimacy
Reputation	✓	Sometimes	X	X
Honor	✓	✓	X	X
Authority	✓	✓	✓	✓
Status	✓	✓	✓	X

Another way of putting this is that status is distinguishable from reputation in that status is *inherently* social. Reputations can form in interactions with only two actors, while it makes little sense to talk about status with fewer than three actors. More to the point, a status hierarchy cannot form with only two actors.[18]

A final concept intrinsically related to status is authority. Lake sees authority and status as two different types of "social power."[19] Authority is, quite simply, "rightful rule," implying that when one state exercises authority over a subordinate actor—by, for example, ordering them to take an action they would not otherwise take—the subordinate actor has the *obligation* to comply.[20] Critically, the possession of authority carries obligations as well. While the subordinate actor is obligated to comply or defer, the relationship is two-sided: the dominant state possesses authority partly by virtue of its willingness and ability to provide social order.[21]

Status and authority quite obviously share a number of features. Both are positional (or as Lake puts it, "relational") in that neither concept makes sense without reference or comparison to other actors.[22] One can no more have authority in isolation than one can have status. Both are also higher-order social beliefs in that they rest on shared, collective understandings (in this way, both are intersubjective). But status, unlike authority, is not bound by the concept of legitimacy. Subordinate states need not recognize the higher status of other actors as "rightful," whereas such recognition is required for the exercise of authority. Moreover, whereas authority binds both dominant and subordinate actors—the subordinate actor is obligated

[18] Of course, once formed (with $n > 2$), a status hierarchy can impact dyadic interactions.
[19] Lake 2014, 247.
[20] Lake 2007, 50.
[21] Lake 2007, 54.
[22] Lake 2014, 249.

to comply while the dominant actor is obligated to provide social order—status binds only subordinate states in a given relationship.

Another question concerning status is where it originates—that is, Where does status come from? There may be multiple hierarchies in international politics, each one based on different valued attributes. After all, if there are "security" and "economic" hierarchies in international relations, there are surely those based on many other attributes, including moral authority, compliance with international norms, quality of living, and so forth.[23]

Status in those many hierarchies generates the expected deference behavior in those contexts. Thus, status in a hierarchy based on observance of human rights norms gives Norway and Sweden rights and privileges, *but only in those situations in which that status is relevant*. Neither country can cite its human rights record as rationale for deference in other, unrelated arenas.

In fact, if we were to examine status based only on the statements of leaders, we'd be led to believe that there were dozens of hierarchies operating simultaneously in international relations. This, however, is entirely consistent with Frank's observation that actors strategically select their field of competition.[24] Leaders who see their states as excelling on a particular dimension will be likely to frame their state as dominant within a hierarchy based on that dimension, not along other ones on which they fall short.

There are two different types of status hierarchies: general and particular (or "issue specific"). Particular status hierarchies are based on what are essentially single attributes (e.g., norm compliance, human rights, or development). There may be many of these *particular* status hierarchies, but status within them is useful only in limited contexts. Much as I advised scholars to specify what sort of status they mean (e.g., status *as* a major power), those wishing to refer to particular hierarchies must specify them—for example, status in a hierarchy *based on moral authority*.

The default status hierarchy is general, not particular. General status is multi- rather than unidimensional. It is based on a constellation of factors that shift over time, though some remain important for longer stretches. When we discuss status without specifying any particular kind, it is general

[23] Lake 2011.
[24] Frank 1985.

status to which we refer. When we speak of German leaders who (in 1908) "sought higher status," we are referring to a generalized hierarchy of importance in international politics. Thus, while actors in international politics *may* have status for all sorts of traits or behaviors, and in constantly shifting reference groups of peer competitors, we can also safely assume that there is an overall status hierarchy in international politics that serves as our default notion of "international status."

STATUS ↔ POWER

John F. Kennedy is quoted as asking (to his confidant Arthur Schlesinger), "What is prestige? Is it the shadow of power?"[25] Thus, a final definitional question is whether status *is* in fact, multidimensional, as I argue, or simply a reflection of power.

This latter conception of status reflects the standard position of realist theory, which by and large sees status as a "reputation for power." Even when realists *do* argue for notions of status to accompany more traditional measures of power, they often mean that in the sense of Herz, who sees status as "the subjective ... factor" of power.[26] Morgenthau similarly discusses a "policy of prestige," though that boils down to nothing more than the demonstration of power.[27]

In its most narrow sense, this objection is empirical in nature: we should be able to determine if our measure of status is simply a noisy proxy for power. Chapter 4 does just this and shows that status is not simply reducible to power; power is but one determinant of international status, and its contribution to a state's rank is different for different types of states and changes over time.

In its broader sense, however, the question is better framed like this: What is the relationship between status and power? While IR scholars have typically limited their discussions of power to crude proxies such as military capacity (aided by the wide availability of Correlates of War (COW) data), most sensible definitions of the concept are similar to Holsti's in emphasizing its relational nature: "Power [is] the general capacity of a state to control the behavior of others."[28] In this sense, anything that aids a state

[25] Schlesinger 2002.
[26] Herz 1981, 186.
[27] Morgenthau 1948, 52.
[28] On COW data, see Maoz 1989. On power as relational, see Holsti 1964. Similar definitions abound. For Singer (1963, 20), for example, "power is the capability to influence."

in influencing or affecting the behavior of other actors can be viewed as increasing its power. Military capabilities are certainly one attribute capable of accomplishing this, but so are many other factors, including a reputation for following through on commitments, wealth, moral authority, charisma of leaders, and (of course) status. Status contributes to power (in its broader sense) by clarifying who in a given relationship is expected to defer and to what degree. It is a social, immaterial power brought into force by the coherence and strength of collective beliefs.

The relationship between status and power does not end there, though. There are attributes—such as wealth or military capabilities—that contribute to power (as many scholars have already recognized), but also to status. Great wealth, for example, contributes to one's ability to influence the behavior of other actors (through bribes and financial leverage), but to the extent that wealth is widely perceived as a valued attribute, it would also give one a high-status rank. In this sense, power and status might be said to have common ancestors.

Status Is Relative, but to Whom?

I noted that status is positional good. Nothing is too novel there, but this is the beginning, not the end, of a complete definition of status. Status may be relative, but *relative to whom?* Left implicit in most IR research on status are the types of comparisons that are being made. Earlier works noted that a state's position in a hierarchy was important, but stopped short of specifying *which* hierarchy we should examine. Instead, states were often placed in a de facto global hierarchy such as the "central system."[29]

This is acceptable to the extent that one assumes the global hierarchy to be the most salient structure for all states. In the context of world politics, however, such a perspective would imply some odd things about the preferences of states. Do small island nations in the Pacific care about a struggle for relative status in eastern Europe? Did major powers in the 1800s (primarily located in western Europe) care about the jostling for relative standing that took place on the periphery of the system? In the context of

---

See also Baldwin 1979. There are outliers, however. Gilpin (1975), for example, called military capabilities the "ultimate form of power." For a somewhat-different approach, see Barnett and Duvall 2005.

[29] Singer and Small 1966.

this book, the case studies examined speak loudly and clearly: countries are hypersensitive to position with respect to peer competitors, and more or less oblivious to the fights over rank that take place among and between all other nations. Thus, we find that Egyptian president Gamal Abdel Nasser initiated and escalated a conflict in Yemen to preserve his status among the grouping of states that he viewed as peers: other Arab, Muslim, and nonaligned states, and *not* because he aimed to supplant the United States or Soviet Union (or even necessarily saw those states as belonging to the same group as Egypt).

In fact, decades of research have demonstrated that actors are most likely to use as reference groups others that are similar to them on important dimensions rather than all other actors. Or as Frank put it:

> We come into the world equipped with a nervous system that worries about rank. Something inherent in our biological makeup motivates us to try to improve, or at least maintain, our standing against those with whom we compete for important positional resources. *A critical feature of this motivating mechanism, often too little emphasized, is that it is much more responsive to local than to global comparisons.*[30]

This is as true in world politics as it is for salary comparison: *even internationally, status is local.* Thus, the oft-cited maxim that status is "positional" is true but incomplete. Status *is* positional, in the sense that it matters what level of status an actor has relative to other actors, but it doesn't tell us anything about the relevant "status community," the reference group that actors see themselves as belonging to and competing against. In theory, actors can compare their status to a multitude of targets along an almost-infinite array of dimensions. The literature on social comparison is voluminous, but some important lessons can be distilled: the most significant comparisons will be on dimensions that are widely regarded as important (for example, size of house or salary on the individual level; economic or military capability on the international level), and the comparisons will be made against some salient reference group.[31]

This has important implications for our research design and theory: status communities will be more salient as the number or significance of shared attributes increases. Again, the logic is straightforward: a hypothetical IR scholar at a research institution is more likely to see other IR

---

[30] Frank 1985, 7–8, emphasis added.
[31] Huguet et al. 2001; Falk and Knell 2004.

scholars at similar institutions as their reference group rather than broader groups that share fewer attributes in common (for example, political theorists at similar institutions, or IR scholars in think tanks). Thus, one innovation of this research is to identify status communities *other than the global system* that might be relevant to states. And while there are many candidate possibilities, in later chapters I operationalize this in two ways: regional geographic hierarchies, and status communities composed of peer competitors that states sort themselves into and reveal by way of their foreign policy choices (for example, diplomatic, trade, and alliance partners).

For Whom Does Status Matter?

One final concern is *whose* status is at stake, the country's or the leader's? Status dissatisfaction is a state-level theory. The primary actors are states, and *attributes of the state*—its level of status concern and the composition of its status community—are the primary explanatory factors. To the extent that leaders enter into the equation (for example, in the case studies examined in the book), their status concerns are assumed to mirror those of the state. In fact, a vast empirical literature on minimal groups and identity formation suggests that threats to group status are likely to be felt by individuals just as strongly as if it was a threat to their personal status position.[32] This is unsurprising given the critical importance that group identity has for personal self-esteem, especially when group identity is primed or salient (such as it is likely to be for political leaders acting in their official roles).[33]

In contrast to the empirical literature I've cited, identity in international politics is in many ways a simpler proposition: "decision-makers' identification with the state is generally a given."[34] Similarly, Midlarsky maintains that "decision makers acting for their countries internalize the status inconsistency of their respective nation-states."[35] Status dissatisfaction assumes the same, and uses the historical record in chapters 6 and 7 to corroborate this assumption. It is of course possible to imagine situations

---

[32] Ellemers, Spears, and Doosje 2002.
[33] Mercer 1995.
[34] Wohlforth 2009, 26.
[35] Midlarsky 1975, 141.

in which the status concerns of leaders would differ from those of the state. If, for example, a leader's *personal* status was under threat (perhaps during an election) or lower than the leader saw themselves as deserving, such concerns might be orthogonal to those of the state. Such situations are not covered by status dissatisfaction theory and are best thought of as potentially competing explanations, as discussed later in this chapter.

WHERE DO WE LOOK FOR EVIDENCE OF STATUS CONCERNS?

While this account of whose status concerns matter is rather straightforward, scholars often want an answer to what is commonly referred to as the "levels-of-analysis" problem.[36] This "problem" is actually a bundle of distinct issues relating to ecological inference (inferring individual preferences or behavior from aggregate data), assumptions about the aggregation of preferences (using data from a "lower" level of analysis to explain state- or system-level outcomes), the unit of analysis where measurement takes place, and whether a given empirical test "matches" the relevant theory exactly or provides microfoundations (i.e., testing out microlevel implications of higher-level theories).[37]

In fact, status is conceptualized and measured at varying "levels of analysis," often within a single research project. The confusion that sometimes results from this stems from the additional complexity of status concerns, which require specification of the reference group (*"who* is threatening the status of the actor?"*) as well as whether it is group or individual status that is at stake (*"whose* status is threatened?"). This is compounded by an extra layer of complexity based on where the researcher looks for evidence—a decision based in many cases on data availability.

Table 2.2 categorizes some extant works on status in IR based on *whose* status is relevant. As it makes evident, many extant theories of status concerns in IR are "pitched" at a variety of levels. While the most well-known status research, including status inconsistency as well as more recent research, uses quantitative designs aimed at analyzing state-level outcomes, a closer look reveals that the overall picture is far more eclectic.[38] In fact, some either directly concern individual and/or group-level phenomena, or have indirect implications for that level that are amenable to experimental tests in addition to the more standard quantitative IR setup. More to the

[36] Singer 1961; Buzan 1995.
[37] King 1997.
[38] See, for example, Maoz 2010.

TABLE 2.2
The Level at Which Status Is Implicated in Past Research.

	Whose *status is relevant?*
Galtung 1964	Unclear (goes back and forth)
Markey 1999, 2000	Individual
Wolf 2011a, 2011b	Individual
Lebow 2008	Individual
Onea 2014	Individual and group
Doran, Hill, and Mladenka 1979	Individual and group
Wohlforth 2009	Individual and group
Volgy and Mayhall 1995	Group (anthropomorphization of the state)
Wallace 1971	Group (anthropomorphization of the state)
Larson and Shevchenko 2014a	Group (anthropomorphization of the state)

point, many previous state-level quantitative efforts are based on theories designed to explain individual-level behavior.[39]

As for *whose* status is threatened, a fair reading of the IR literature suggests that it varies considerably. Wohlforth's concern, for example, is "whether Great Powers care about status," but the underlying theory is targeted at the group level, and much of the evidence relies on perceptions of key elites.[40] Larson and Shevchenko use the same group-based theory (SIT) to focus on "*states'* concerns about their relative status," but evidence is again drawn from individual actors' perceptions of key events and trends.[41]

While IR scholars sometimes consider these "group-level" theories, data are drawn from the *individual level,* and the theoretical framework is based on the assumption that individuals' status goals will be transmitted through collective identity to group behavior and threats to the group's status will be transmitted the opposite way—to the individual. An example of this

[39] For example, status inconsistency theory is almost always measured at the state or system level, while the theory underlying it (based on the "frustration-aggression" hypothesis) is individual level (Miller 1941). In a representative work, Volgy and Mayhall (1995, 68) describe a theory in which status inconsistency is measured at the system level for practical purposes, but that matters only insofar as it is "salient for decision makers." Theories of hegemonic war and power transition differ from this because they take place almost wholly at the state and system level. Even these "state-level" theories, however, often implicate individual-level phenomena, such as perceptions of threat or credibility. See, for example, Organski and Kugler 1980.

[40] Wohlforth 2009, 34–35.

[41] Larson and Shevchenko 2010b.

dynamic can be found in the foundational work on the "minimal group paradigm," in which psychologists measure the effect that being in a group (which is based on trivial or imaginary differences) has on how *individuals* behave.[42]

So what does this mean for the current project? First, this brief overview has suggested the importance of paying close attention not only to the "levels of analysis" problem, broadly speaking, but also to how these issues are manifested in status research. Second, the history of status research in IR is more eclectic than it is given credit for being. Despite the strong association with quantitative IR and state or system-level outcomes, many of the ideas and much of the evidence is drawn from other levels of analysis.

As for where our empirical examination should focus, state-level theories are most appropriately tested with state-level data. To that end, we must devise measures of status and status dissatisfaction at that level to test the theory described here. As an additional matter, however, we might do as so many methodologists have prescribed: use the theory of status dissatisfaction to generate additional, testable implications at other levels of analysis. In this case, the theory suggests that the state's status will be felt by individuals at the same level of intensity, and lead to specific patterns of behavior at both the state and individual levels.

Why Do We Seek Status?

Do actors value status as an instrumental or intrinsic good? In some cases, status may be pursued in the expectation that higher status will provide tangible benefits in the future, such as by signaling competence or providing access to power and resources.[43] Evidence comes from the laboratory, where even weak and artificial inductions of "high status" provide significant material benefits to its holders. High-status participants, for instance, are more likely to receive higher offers in both dictator/ultimatum games and simulated negotiations.[44] Additionally, there may be explanations from evolutionary biology that help to elucidate

---

[42] Turner, Brown, and Tajfel 1979.
[43] Huberman, Loch, and Onculer 2004; Plourde 2008.
[44] Ball and Eckel 1996, 1998; Ball, Grossman, and Zame 2001.

the larger sense in which status is instrumentally valuable, such as a costly signal of other characteristics.[45]

This account of status as instrumentally beneficial has been influential in IR, and Morgenthau concisely notes this point of view: "prestige... [is] rarely an end in itself," but instead "one of the instrumentalities" used to pursue other goals.[46] Dore writes: "Prestige counts, in such a view of the world, but only instrumentally; prestige is the way you gain the coercive or deterrent advantages of power without actually having to use it. ... [P]restige, then is not an end in itself, but only a means to economy in the use of power."[47]

Summing up the advantages of status for states, Wohlforth observes:

> In addition to deterrence, governments also care about deference.... High status confers tangible benefits in the form of decision-making autonomy and deference on the part of others concerning issues of importance to one's security and prosperity. The higher a given state's status, the more other states adjust their policies to accommodate its interests.... [T]he success or failure of all international policies, however grandiose or mundane, is crucially dependent on status.[48]

In other cases, we think of status as an "end" in the sense that individuals pursue greater status solely for the psychological benefits associated with its possession. Early social scientists such as Thorstein Veblen saw status as an "intrinsically valued social good," and some in IR have taken a similar position.[49] Much of the work on status in international relations has focused on status as an "end" in the sense of leaders pursuing status for its own sake. Some of these studies are informative on the individual case level, but are unlikely to offer generalizable explanations of how status motivates behavior in world politics.[50] This is mostly because focusing solely on status

---

[45] Henrich and Gil-White 2001; Plourde 2008. It is "costly" in these accounts because one must invest resources to attain it, such as buying a Tesla car rather than an old station wagon, thus signaling wealth along with a number of other attributes.

[46] Morgenthau 1948, 77.

[47] Dore 1975, 202–3. Jervis (2012, 338) provides a similar take when he notes that "status and prestige do appear in some accounts, but usually in an instrumental way, something akin to resolve."

[48] Wohlforth 1998, 26.

[49] Veblen 1899; Lebow 2008, 2010c; Markey 2000; Murray 2008.

[50] Two good recent examples include Markey 2000; Murray 2008.

as an end in and of itself often leads one to see status-seeking behavior as "irrational."[51]

In reality, actors may pursue status for either or both of these reasons. Enough evidence has been compiled to assert that actors sometimes pursue status for the intrinsic psychological benefit that it confers. This does not mean that actors do not also sometimes pursue status because they believe it will confer direct benefits in the near future (or even indirect benefits in the long-term). In fact, to the extent that high status is evolutionarily adaptive, status might be "instrumental" (in the broader sense) even when actions provide no discernible material benefit to the actor seeking increased status.

One's perspective on this issue is likely to be constrained in some way by the choice of empirical strategy. Large-N studies that use proxies for status or status seeking—as in chapters 4 and 5—are likely to find it extremely difficult to disprove the possibility that status was sought instrumentally. Qualitative work offers more promise in this regard, but disentangling the different motivations for status is likely to be incredibly difficult even with access to the documentary record. Educated guesses are more likely here than concrete findings with respect to the motivation for status seeking.

DO WE *NEED* TO KNOW THE MOTIVES FOR STATUS SEEKING?

Setting the specific question of motives for status, a larger question is, Does it matter what the motives are? If we stipulated that status was sought *only* instrumentally, in pursuit of other ends, how would that affect how we think about status?

This question is far less important than commonly believed. First, as a rule, such objections are often unfalsifiable: What evidence would one have to provide to *prove* that an action—ostensibly taken in pursuit of status—was not designed to use that status to achieve other ends years or decades after the fact? Such an argument rests ultimately on an article of faith among scholars of different schools that states and leaders *must* be pursuing a given end goal, such as power or security. If they are found to be pursuing some other goal, such as status, then that is only more evidence in favor of their theories! After all, such motivations *must* be in pursuit of the larger (and *obviously* more important) goal of greater power or security.

Even if status were sought instrumentally, that in itself would not obviate the need for theories to explain how status and status concerns

---

[51] As in Markey 2000, 54.

operated in international politics. If, in fact, *everything* is sought only in pursuit of the larger goal of power or security, why then theorize anything else to begin with? The example of resolve illustrates the dynamics I have in mind. Few would argue that human beings intrinsically desire a reputation for "standing firm." Instead, it is commonly believed to be instrumentally useful for gaining access to resources and deterring challenges from other actors. Yet it is also widely seen as a crucial factor in international conflict, and a number of theories have proliferated to explain how these inferences develop, when its effects are visible, and how concern for it varies by context and leader characteristics.[52] Thus, one might believe status to be sought only instrumentally, but still see enormous value in understanding how concerns over relative position affect international conflict.

This is particularly important given the prospects for demonstrating that status concerns are *solely* intrinsic in world politics. As Wohlforth notes, "Cumulating research shows that humans appear to be hardwired for sensitivity to status and that relative standing is a powerful and independent motivator of behavior."[53] If high status is evolutionarily adaptive, however, status might be "instrumental" in the broader sense even when actions provide no discernible material benefit to the actor seeking increased status.[54]

This is, if anything, further evidence that an exclusive focus on the dichotomy between the instrumental and intrinsic benefits of status is unlikely to be fruitful. The key then is not "proving" that status is not useful for other purposes (it almost certainly is) or sought to provide long-term benefit (again, it probably is) but rather using the theory of status dissatisfaction to generate unique and testable hypotheses that help to explain patterns of conflict that cannot be accounted for by a simplistic focus on power, security, or wealth.

IS STATUS SEEKING IRRATIONAL?

Another related objection concerns the irrationality of status seeking. There are extant theories of status in international politics, whether self-described or tacit, that acknowledge the importance of status, but see it largely as a manifestation of pathology or irrationality. Murray, for example, argues

---

[52] Renshon, Dafoe, and Huth 2015a; Weisiger and Yarhi-Milo 2011; Kertzer 2016.

[53] Wohlforth 2009, 29. See also Harsanyi 1976.

[54] The notion that status is adaptive is supported by others as well. See Henrich and Gil-White 2001; Plourde 2008.

that Germany's naval ambitions during the Weltpolitik era were driven by concerns over status and identity, and can thus be considered "irrational."[55] Forsberg, in his study of Russia, echoes this sentiment, arguing that "status concerns may give rise to behavior that is typically depicted as emotional or irrational."[56]

So, is status seeking irrational? Or must it be? Status in this book is very much about perceptions, beliefs, and psychology as well as the socially constructed nature of hierarchy in IR. Because of that, it fits neatly with a constructivist and political psychology "take" on IR. But invoking beliefs and perceptions does *not* require invoking the irrational or biased nature of individual psychology.

Two points are relevant here. First—and similar to the debate about instrumental versus intrinsic motivations for status—the debate about the rationality of status concerns is a bit of a red herring. Scholars who describe status seeking as irrational use this as shorthand for arguing that actors pursue status even when doing so comes at the expense of other (often-material) values. This, however, is not "irrational," or if it is, stretches the term so far as to be useless. This simply suggests that status, like honor, reputation, credibility, or other ideational constructs, is something that political actors care about and are willing to pay costs to gain (this is entirely compatible with a rationalist approach).

Moreover, given the wide body of evidence now compiled that demonstrates the tremendous value of status, it seems a strange starting point to *begin* by assuming the irrationality of status concerns. Doing so is both unnecessary and misleading because it underemphasizes the strategic nature of status seeking in world politics—one consistent with both psychological and rationalist accounts of IR.[57]

There is, in fact, considerable evidence that high status confers benefits on its holders.[58] As a result, we need only make the rather-weak assumption that states and individual leaders pursue higher status because there is an expectation that it is instrumentally valuable. This then implies that status also fits rather neatly within the rationalism/strategic paradigm. O'Neill

---

[55] Murray 2010, 680, see also 671.

[56] Forsberg, Heller, and Wolf 2014, 263—though, on the next page, they seem less sure. Larson, Paul, and Wohlforth (2014, 27) provide another example of scholars who walk a fine line in assessing the rationality of status concerns: "No matter how irrational or petty they may seem, status concern cannot be evaded because they are inherent to human preferences."

[57] For an example of this, see O'Neill 2006.

[58] See, for example, Ball et al. 2001; Akinola and Mendes 2014; chapters in this book.

writes that "[Prestige] is important even within a strategic approach to international relations since states may use it to judge quality or they may bandwagon, choosing who to support depending on what they expect others to do."[59] More broadly, status "informs patterns of deference and expectations of behavior, rights and responsibilities."[60] As I show, status-oriented behavior does not have to be irrational, as was presumed too often in the past. Status is a valuable resource, and conflict can be status enhancing, so states deprived of the status they believe themselves to deserve may well turn to conflict (among other strategies) to attain their goals. Thus, although this is not a self-consciously rationalist theory, it fits in easily with such approaches insofar as they take into account non-material stakes or preferences, such as other work on prestige, reputation, or honor.[61]

When Does Status Matter Most?

Smoking gun quotes related to status are abundant in scholarly works.[62] Summing this up, my colleagues and I wrote, "If there is one feature of … status that scholars are in agreement on, it is that leaders, policy elites, and national populations are often concerned, and even obsessed, with their status."[63] Recall that "status" refers to the actual position or identity of a state. But knowing that leaders have strong preferences for status does not provide much in the way of inferential leverage; if all actors cared about status all the time, it couldn't explain much of the variation in international behavior. Of course, all actors do not care an equal amount about status, but we must know *when* status moves up the list of priorities.

This suggests two equally important steps in our theory building. First, we must focus on variation in *status concerns*: the level of focus on status-related issues, and likelihood of acting in order to advance or salvage one's status. The second part of this implication follows naturally from the first. If our focus is on variation in concern for status, we are best served by theorizing the systematic and predictable ways in which heightened concerns are triggered. I suggest that those concerns will be especially

---

[59] O'Neill 2006, 1.
[60] Dafoe, Renshon, and Huth 2014, 374–75.
[61] O'Neill 2006; Guisinger and Smith 2002; Dafoe and Caughey 2016.
[62] See, for example, Jervis 1976; Jervis and Snyder 1991; Markey 2000; Press 2005.
[63] Dafoe, Renshon, and Huth 2014, 381.

sharp when actors experience "status deficits" (a status ranking that falls below a level set by expectations), and that those expectations will be viewed through the prism of "local" comparisons to some salient reference group.[64] Status concerns may lead to "status seeking"—behavior or actions undertaken in order to gain status—but may also lead to actions designed to preserve one's current position or slow one's decline.

THE MISMATCH BETWEEN EXPECTATIONS AND REALITY

While there are several candidates for events that might trigger heightened status concerns, I focus on one of the most generalizable: the divergence between the status accorded an actor and what they believe themselves to deserve.[65] The deleterious effects of a mismatch between status expectations and that which is actually accorded has a long history in the literature, and has found substantial empirical support.[66] Such a theory, however, requires both evidence that actors are able to assess the status that is accorded to them by the community with a minimum of bias or error, along with an account of how they develop beliefs about how much status they deserve.

On the former point, it would be problematic if, for example, all actors believed themselves to be ranked near the top of a hierarchy. And indeed, a quick reading of the literature on positive illusions—the collection of biases that include overoptimism, overconfidence, and the illusion of control—might provoke some concerns: individuals *do* seem to fall prey to overconfidence and overestimation biases.[67] Yet "status considerations offer an important exception to predictions made by the theory of positive illusions."[68] In groups where there is some interaction (even among near strangers), there are severe social penalties for "status self-enhancement" that include expulsion and sanctioning. In several studies, psychologists found that their subjects were quite accurate in perceiving the status they were accorded in groups (including both objective and subjective elements

---

[64] Of course, status concerns might be heightened through other mechanisms as well. The last section of this chapter discusses some potential alternative mechanisms for triggering status concerns.

[65] Other potentially useful candidates for events that might trigger status concerns have been suggested in the literature, but are narrower in scope. Wohlforth's (2009) is a good example, as it is a useful lens for examining status concerns but only relevant for great powers.

[66] Lenski 1954, 1967; Zhang 2008.

[67] Johnson et al. 2006; Deaves, Luders, and Schroder 2010.

[68] Anderson et al. 2006, 1094.

of that status), and that this was not moderated by gender differences or other factors.[69]

In fact, individuals seem to be just as good at judging where they stand as they are at determining where others do—both difficult tasks that require inferring the mental states and interactions of numerous other actors.[70] Some attributes of status (for example, strength or wealth) are easily visible and accounted for, while others are unobservable—for instance, "toughness," "influence," or "quality"—and must be inferred through patterns of deference and dominance behavior. Despite the complexity of these calculations, humans (as well as other species) are quite skilled at inferring status rankings as well as dominance and deference behavior, even from an early age.[71] While our motivation for accuracy might be to avoid social punishments, our ability to be accurate likely derives from the evolution of our cognitive and neural architecture, which has developed to help us interpret myriad, subtle cues related to status.[72]

STATUS EXPECTATIONS

If actors are fairly accurate in discerning where they stand relative to other actors, how do they develop beliefs about what they deserve? Status dissatisfaction theory focuses on *expectations*—what actors believe they "deserve"—which are then filtered through the lens of a comparison to the most salient *reference group*.

Why are expectations so important in setting the level against which actual status is compared? There are in fact any number of possible comparisons that political actors might make. The status quo, goals or aspirations, or even past states might set the level against which status comparisons are made.[73] But there are significant gains in concision to be made by modeling comparisons as a function of expectations, which subsume these other categories.

In fact, a significant body of work in psychology and political science has demonstrated the importance of expectations in evaluating prospects, or in this case, comparisons. Expectations are critical to foundational theories of

---

[69] Anderson et al. 2006; Anderson, Ames, and Gosling 2008.

[70] Srivastava and Anderson 2011.

[71] Grosenick, Clement, and Fernald 2007; Mascaro and Csibra 2014.

[72] Marsh et al. 2009; Koski, Xie, and Olson 2015.

[73] Jervis 1992; Berejikian 2002; Heath, Larrick, and Wu 1999; Weyland 1996; Gregory, Lichtenstein, and MacGregor 1993.

micro- and macroeconomics as well as theories of individual decision making, such as prospect theory, an updated version of which demonstrated that more analytic power could be gained by using expectations rather than the status quo as the assumed "reference point" for comparison.[74] In political science, the divergence of expectations from reality has provided explanations for everything from revolutions to US political attitudes.[75]

Further evidence for the importance of status expectations can be found in the power transition literature. Although this research is often framed in terms of material power, a key factor in the initiation of conflict is that aspiring hegemons are being denied the benefits that they expect and deserve based on their material capabilities. Put another way, one source of states' revisionist preferences is that the international "hierarchy of prestige" is out of line with their expectations (which are based on the current distribution of power). In fact, it is this divergence between expected and achieved status, albeit often implicitly, that was the focus of the earlier status-inconsistency research program.[76]

Of course, to say it is expectations that matter only pushes us one level deeper: What are those expectations based on? Or more specifically in the case of status comparisons, how might we plausibly operationalize status expectations? Here we are on firmer ground because a number of theories from both IR as well as individual decision making suggest that actors' beliefs about how much status they deserve will be set by their "asset levels" of other attributes, such as power or economic capacity. For example, power transition theory suggests that wars occur when status does not match up to material capabilities, while earlier work on status inconsistency suggested that it was specifically material or military capabilities that set an expectation level for status.[77] On the individual level, experimental work has corroborated some of these ideas. For example, a disjuncture between status and levels of other attributes (such as high status / low power) is psychologically aversive, and causes both decreased cognitive functioning and increased risk seeking.[78]

---

[74] Friedman 1957. On prospect theory, see Kahneman and Tversky 1979. For recent statements of prospect theory related to expections as reference point, see Koszegi and Rabin 2006; List 2003; Novemsky and Kahneman 2005; Abeler et al. 2011; Pope and Schweitzer 2011.

[75] Davies 1962; Johnson 1962; Niven 2000.

[76] See, for example, Ray 1974; Midlarsky 1975; Volgy and Mayhall 1995.

[77] While military capabilities seem likely to be the most broad and powerful proxy for expectations, other assets (for example, social welfare or normative authority) might be relevant for certain groups of states in certain time periods.

[78] Josephs et al. 2006; Zyphur et al. 2009.

THE TIMELESSNESS OF STATUS CONCERNS

In its more limited sense, this question—when does status matter?—asks whether status concerns might be relegated to a particular historical period. Jervis summarizes this concern when he notes that the "old linkages between standing... and war do seem to have been severed," and "unless wars are justified by self-defense... they now lower rather than raise the country's status."[79] A similar concern is voiced by Lebow in explaining his cultural theory of IR (he places the date for the change around 1945).[80] Wood provides another example, though one that is a bit more qualified. He first states that "the extent to which nations will go to defend their prestige... has changed in the 'post-heroic' West."[81] He notes in the next sentence, however, that "these motivations can still incite advanced liberal democracies to the ultimate in risk and sacrifice," citing Britain's motivations in the Falklands War as a prime example.

This notion suggests that status concerns might have been determinative in the ancient world, or perhaps even as late as the nineteenth century, but have disappeared in the new era of the post–World War II international system. Certainly, as Jervis points out, status concerns seem to be invoked less frequently by leaders. But this might result from norms about how we explain behavior as much as any changes in state motivations. As such, this is largely an empirical question. Qualitatively, it requires an in-depth analysis of cases before and after the posited change. Quantitatively, we can assess the impact of status concern on war *over time* in a systematic manner to examine such a potential boundary condition more thoroughly.

There is no theoretical reason to suppose that status concerns would have diminished in importance. Fundamentally, status should still carry the same benefits as it always did: deference from lower-ranked states, and a combination of valuable instrumental and intrinsic benefits. Thus, the *value* of status is unlikely to have changed. It is, of course, possible that the most efficient method for gaining status has changed over time. We can begin to address this in our quantitative analysis by examining how or whether the status benefits of conflict initiation have changed over time.

[79] Jervis 2012, 342–43.
[80] Lebow 2010a, 490.
[81] Wood 2013, 397.

What Are the Consequences of Status Concerns?

A baseline assumption of this theory is that all states and leaders prefer higher rather than lower status. Where my theory departs from previous work is in its argument that heightened status concerns intensify this preference, leading to a greater focus on acquiring status. But how can this be accomplished? What should we expect actors with heightened status concerns to *do*?

STATUS-ALTERING EVENTS

To answer this, we must ask a more basic question: What types of events are *capable* of changing our status position? Because actors' status ranking is based on the collective beliefs of the community to which they belong, changing their position requires changing the beliefs of other actors. Yet a number of cognitive limitations affect our ability to update beliefs, chief among that they are updated sporadically—not continuously—and then largely in response to big events.[82] For instance, Shleifer has proposed that not only are beliefs slow to change—as a result of "cognitive conservatism"—but that they do so only when actors are "hit over the head" repeatedly with similar pieces of information.[83] Summing up how this process applies to international politics, Stoessinger argues that national leaders will not examine or change their beliefs until they are "shaken and shattered into doing so."[84]

The example of a "rising China" is instructive. In the years since the end of the Cold War, some have made the case that China is representative of slow and steady growth into a world power, and possibly one in direct competition with the lone superpower (the United States). Scholars of Chinese foreign policy and culture, though, have made the persuasive case that whether or not one sees China as a "great power," or even as "rising" at all, depends entirely on what observable indicator is used to measure that progress.[85] Focusing on material indicators such as GDP per capita or alliance portfolios would provide different answers than an emphasis on "influence" or military spending. The reason *why* these authors find evidence of so much disagreement is precisely due to the difficulty (though

---

[82] Deutsch and Merritt 1965; Jervis 1976; Peffley and Hurwitz 1992.
[83] Shleifer 2000, 113. See also Barberis, Shleifer, and Vishny 1998.
[84] Stoessinger 1981, 240.
[85] Chestnut and Johnston 2009.

not impossibility) of "rising" in the international system purely through slow long-term growth.

Of course, the next relevant question is, If beliefs are not updated slowly in response to trends in objective indicators, what types of events might be capable of changing beliefs? Earlier I noted several reasons we might expect some difficulty in the updating of any beliefs, but they pose special challenges for updating status beliefs. Because beliefs about status require some consensus in the international community, there are three requirements for a candidate "status-altering event": it must be highly visible (i.e., public), dramatic or salient, and convey unambiguous information.

The first requirement can be explained by the definition of status. Status is a belief about other actors' beliefs, or in other words, a belief about some shared consensus. Because of that, events that change perceptions of status must be visible to all potential observers. Events that are private or even only partially public are thus unlikely to cause shifts in status beliefs. The second requirement—that the event be dramatic or highly salient—is a necessity because the event must capture the attention of all (or the vast majority of) potential observers. Many events contain or convey information theoretically available to all who might be interested. Still, because political leaders and their advisers face severe constraints on their time and attention, they cannot pay attention to everything that happens in the world. Dramatic events that are widely publicized are more likely to be able to compete for the attention of multiple actors in the system.

And since beliefs about status require some consensus in the international community, events are not likely to change a state's rank unless the action taken accords with shared understandings of what constitutes a valuable attribute or possession. Simply put, actions or acquisitions are more likely to increase status to the extent that there is consensus on the value of those actions/possessions. Nuclear weapons, for example, might have at one point been unambiguously high-status markers, but some have argued that the sign has reversed in recent decades, with current proliferators more likely to be viewed as "rogue states" than "great powers."[86]

Taking these conditions into account, one likely candidate—though not the only possibility—for an event that is capable of changing a state's place in a status hierarchy is the initiation of a military conflict. The initiation of

[86] Glaser 1998, 120.

conflict demonstrates a bundle of attributes, both material (technological prowess, fighting ability, and military and industrial capability) and psychological (toughness, resolve, and honor) that are perceived as valuable. Militarized conflicts—which are public, dramatic, and salient—represent a chance for the international community to simultaneously calibrate its judgments concerning how much international standing a given state possesses (or should possess). Rationalist scholars have argued that war reveals private information on relative strength otherwise unavailable to potential belligerents.[87] I propose a variant on this argument. While war (or militarized disputes in which force is used) does reveal private information about capabilities, it exposes other things as well. The capabilities, along with the behavior of the two opponents and outcomes observed by the international audience, combine to influence the status beliefs of others in the hierarchy.

Of course, the initiation of conflict is not the only candidate "status-altering event." In some cases, the repeated use of such strategies might even be counterproductive because there are probably declining marginal utilities to the status benefits that accrue to belligerents (plus a host of other nonstatus costs the aggressor must pay). If an action or possession is perceived as valuable, and if it is taken/acquired in a public and dramatic way, it should increase actors' status rank. Technological advances (such as advances in space programs) would fit this description, as would the acquisition of "status markers" such as aircraft carriers.[88] Accession to elite "clubs" (such as the "G2" between the United States and China, or UN Security Council) and the ratification of important treaties or alliances are also plausible candidates.

How Do Leaders React to Status Concerns (and Why Should We Care)?

Though status dissatisfaction is a state-level theory, there are still strong reasons to consider its implications at the level of political leaders. Fundamentally, the actual decision unit is ultimately a single leader or group of leaders, which in turn make up the committees, parliaments, departments, and executive branches that govern the state. This fact suggests that one profitable way forward is to generate additional and overlapping support

---

[87] Wagner 2000; Smith and Stam 2004.
[88] Gilady 2002.

for status dissatisfaction theory by drawing out its implications at a different level of analysis. What this means in practice is that we must consider the microfoundations of status dissatisfaction: What actions at the state level are driven by processes at the individual level?

While all states and leaders are assumed to prefer higher rather than lower status, one innovation of status dissatisfaction is to theorize systematic variation in those preferences. Status dissatisfaction thus places the focus squarely on *concern* for status, which is predicted to vary in response to different situations. Once triggered, it is hypothesized that the intensity of preferences for status increases. In effect, heightened status concerns should lead to an increased value for status—a result already obtained in experimental contexts.[89] This, then, is the core behavioral microfoundation of status dissatisfaction and a necessary component of the book's empirical infrastructure; after all, even state-level theories such as this can have individual-level implications or assumptions that can be subjected to empirical scrutiny. In this case, I replicate and extend a recent result from social psychology by showing that status concerns increase individuals' value for status, and that they do so across both a survey and lab experiment, and in populations as diverse as online samples as well as political and military leaders.

BEHAVIORAL MICROFOUNDATIONS OF STATUS DISSATISFACTION

Once on the individual level, two additional opportunities present themselves. For one, we can take advantage of experimental methods to provide the first evidence of a *causal* connection between status concerns and political behavior. I do this by linking a "microfoundation" of status dissatisfaction to behavior on the individual level, and—to make the question more tractable—limit this discussion to implications related to the escalation of commitment to a failing course of action. This class of decisions—when to stop throwing good money after bad—has long been implicated in world politics as a potential cause of conflict and been identified as one of the critical mistakes often made by leaders in world politics.[90] While it is commonly associated with "sunk costs bias," I sidestep

---

[89] Pettit, Yong, and Spataro 2010.

[90] Walt 2010; Jervis 1976; Goldgeier and Tetlock 2001; Kahneman and Renshon 2007. It has been empirically linked to the public's appetite for war irredentist disputes, great power military interventions, international negotiations, and the length of commitment to conflicts like Vietnam. See Boettcher and Cobb 2009; Von Hippel 1996; Taliaferro 1998; Meerts 2005;

the question of whether or not escalation is rational or not; to know whether or not escalation is "biased" would require a full accounting of the value of the status being sought, and we do not yet have answers to that. In fact, this perspective fits in with recent work that calls into question the "irrational" nature of escalation of commitment to failing courses of action.[91] One does not have to believe that it is "irrational," however, to see that it may often result in what appears to be suboptimal decision making, or the proverbial throwing good money after bad.

The primary microfoundation of status dissatisfaction is that status threats increase the value that actors associate with status. Put simply, once an actor's status is threatened, they are willing to pay far more to keep x amount of status than they would be if it had not been threatened in the first place.[92] This suggests that once status is threatened or otherwise engaged for leaders, they will become increasingly willing to expend resources to save it. Within this framework, the increased escalation occurs because concerns about status are raised high enough that they overshadow the increased expenditure of economic resources.

We can also address an additional question that—while not a foundational element of status dissatisfaction—helps to broaden its depth and scope. This second question concerns the individual-level factors that affect variation in how status concerns are manifested. While scholars have often noted when a particular leader seems fixated on issues of status (for example, "Kennedy was... obsessed with prestige"), we have little to guide us in understanding *which* individuals are likely to be most sensitive to status concerns, and *what* contextual conditions will magnify these effects.[93] Possible answers come in two categories: dispositional factors that will affect the extent to which given individuals will be focused on status concerns, and contextual factors that will influence the degree to which any given population will be affected. In the dispositional category, the most obvious candidate is SDO, a popular and validated measure of preference for hierarchy and dominance. Specifically, SDO is a personality variable that measures individuals' preference for inequality among social groups. More to the point, it measures one's comfort level with hierarchy, and the extent to which one believes or desires that their own group "dominate

Staw and Ross 1989. For more examples, see Hudson 2005; Schott, Scherer, and Lambert 2011; Von Hippel 1996; Taliaferro 2004; Meerts 2005; Tetlock and Goldgeier 2000.

[91] On this, see Friedman 2014.

[92] Pettit, Yong, and Spataro 2010.

[93] Vaughn 1987. See also Guzzini 2013, 525.

and be superior to outgroups."[94] High SDO individuals tend to see other people in terms of their group membership (leading to greater tendencies to stereotype), and also see those group boundaries as clear, obvious, and legitimate.[95] And while it was originally developed to study out-group prejudice, SDO has been found to correlate with "valuing power, prestige and status."[96] High-SDO individuals are thus far more likely to be affected by status concerns than their low-SDO counterparts.

One prime candidate for a contextual (i.e., situational) factor is power. A close reading of the literature on status and conflict suggests that the effects of status are almost always conditioned in some way on power. In status inconsistency theory, it is the discrepancy between power and status that is associated with the initiation of conflict. In power transition theory, it is a status hierarchy that no longer coincides with the balance of material capabilities that is most strongly associated with conflict. In Wohlforth's work, it is, conversely, the *balance* of material capabilities that leads to uncertainty about the status hierarchy, which conflict helps to resolve.[97] This suggests a general agreement that power matters *somehow* in moderating the impact of status in world politics, but also considerable uncertainty about the actual relationship between status, power, and conflict.

The specific hypotheses regarding the moderating effect of power are not quite as clear as the general intuition that the two are related. Anderson and Galinsky, for example, find that power seems to induce optimism and risk seeking in most individuals.[98] Yet in the study I describe in chapter 3, power did not operate in a vacuum but rather in conjunction with the prospect of gaining or losing status. Because of this, the work of Inesi seems more relevant.[99] She found that powerful individuals were less sensitive to losses than their low-power counterparts. Power may provide a "buffer" for powerful individuals, who are less likely to be affected by the experimental status manipulation. This is corroborated by other work, which has found converging evidence that power can protect individuals from the "press of the situation." Powerful individuals are, for example,

[94] Pratto and colleagues 1994, 742.

[95] Haslam and Levy 2006; Tausch and Hewstone 2010.

[96] Son Hing et al. 2007, 69. This fits with the original conception of SDO. Pratto and colleagues (1994, 745) noted that "prestige-striving" was "related" or "adjacent" to their core interest in group superiority and unequal group relationships.

[97] Wohlforth 2009.

[98] Anderson and Galinsky 2006.

[99] Inesi 2010.

less likely to allow outside influences to change their stated belief, while less powerful subjects exhibited impaired "executive functioning" in memory, inhibition, and planning tasks.[100]

SUMMARY OF THEORETICAL EXPECTATIONS

Microfoundations

Status dissatisfaction predicts that concern for status is not constant but instead varies systematically in response to a number of situational and dispositional factors. Further, it predicts that once triggered, heightened status concerns raise the value of status for those actors. This is the most basic behavioral microprocess on which the state-level theory is built. In the context of the experiments described in chapter 3, affirmative evidence would come in the form of an increased "willingness to pay" for higher status among those in the *status threat* conditions. An alternative hypothesis (and disconfirming evidence for status dissatisfaction) might be that individuals subjected to status threats would come to value status *less*, rather than more. Such a finding would be difficult to reconcile with my theory, but would be consistent with a broad body of work on cognitive dissonance, with the reasoning being that individuals whose status is threatened might comfort themselves with the notion that status is not particularly valuable anyway.

As an additional factor, we must take into account the subject population to which we wish to generalize, and specify that we expect to find evidence of these processes not just among Internet samples or college students but also among high-level political and military decision makers. There is no reason to suspect that—unconditioned by any other individual-level factor—political leaders would evince notably different base levels of status concerns.

Next, we can turn to the *causal* effect of status concerns on political behavior. Recall that the focus here is on one particular aspect of decision making: the escalation of commitment to a failing course of action. Status dissatisfaction suggests that increased status concerns will trigger an increased value for status. We can thus predict that status concerns will lead to increased escalation of commitment in pursuit of higher status, concurrent with decreased value for monetary resources (i.e., increased

---

[100] Galinsky et al. 2008; Smith et al. 2008.

sunk costs). If we instead find that individuals with heightened status concerns risked a lower or equal amount of money—real or hypothetical— in escalation tasks compared to subjects in other conditions, this would be disconfirming evidence for this aspect of status dissatisfaction theory.

Of course, any consideration of status in political decision making must contend with the argument that policy-relevant implications can rarely be drawn from main effects alone. Put more directly, we can almost never hold "all else equal" in the real world, so our theories and research designs must be robust enough to offer insight into how concepts interact with relevant real-world factors. To that end, I argued that status concerns interact with both dispositional and situational factors to influence behavior.

In the former category, I proposed SDO as the personality characteristic most likely to influence status-related behaviors. SDO can be characterized as one's preference for (or comfort with) dominance and hierarchy, and is a stable individual difference that affects a host of beliefs and behaviors. Because of that, I propose that high-SDO subjects will be particularly susceptible to the deleterious effects of status concerns.

I proposed power as one of the situational variables most relevant to the examination of political decision making. Nevertheless, the expectations regarding the moderating effect of power are not quite as clear. The most likely case one could make from previous research on the subject is that power should act as a psychological "buffer," protecting subjects from the negative consequences of status threats. Conversely, less powerful subjects are likely to feel the "press of the situation"—in this case, the status threat—more deeply, leading to greater impairment than their high-powered counterparts.

These can be summarized as follows:

H1 (systematic variation in status concerns): *Preferences for status will vary systematically in response to situational contexts, with increased status concerns leading to increased value for status.*

H2 (status concerns and escalation): *Status threats will increase escalation relative to control condition.*

H3 (status concerns and SDO): *The effect of status threats will be highest for subjects high in SDO.*

H4 (status concerns and power): *High-powered subjects will be protected against the worst effects of status threats.*

Status and International Conflict

Next, we must establish a foundational assumption of the theory that violent interstate conflicts—public, dramatic, and salient—will serve as "status-altering events." If this is true, we should expect to see evidence that conflict—and particularly victory in conflict—should provide status boosts to the victor or initiator. The "null" here is that conflict would have no effect on status ranking, or perhaps depress status rankings as other states withdraw diplomats in protest of the initiator's belligerence. For conflict to be "status enhancing," however, states must reveal capabilities (military or otherwise) in conflict that provide new information on where they should stand in a given hierarchy. Notice that this is accomplished not necessarily by victory—since one could in theory defeat a weak foe and reveal nothing new about capabilities, or lose "valiantly" to a more powerful state—but rather by exceeding the expectations of observers. This suggests that we must take additional care in our research design.

We should expect to see evidence that states experiencing status deficits initiate conflict at a greater rate than "satisfied" states. Thus we should expect to see that states with larger status "deficits" (how dissatisfaction is operationalized in the large-N chapters) are more likely to initiate conflicts than otherwise-similar but "satisfied" states. Building on decades of evidence in cognate fields, the theory also posits that more "local" or fine-grained reference groups are likely to be more salient to states, and in turn have larger consequences for conflict behavior. To that end, we should see evidence that status deficits within the detected status communities are better predictors of conflict behavior than deficits within either regional reference groups or the global hierarchy. Finally, if conflict is in fact status enhancing when states exceed observers' expectations, then we should see evidence that dissatisfied states target the states that suit those purposes best. In particular, they should focus on targets that give them the best chance of prevailing and/or exceeding observers' expectations.

These can be summarized as follows:

H5 (winning status): *Exceeding expectations in conflict will increase the initiator's status rank.*

H6 (status deficits and war): *Status deficits will be associated with an increased probability of war and militarized interstate dispute initiation.*

H7 (status is local): *Status deficits within detected communities will be better predictors of conflict behavior than deficits within regional or global hierarchies.*

H8 (targets of status aggression): *Dissatisfied states will pick fights that are most likely to provide the status benefits they seek (namely, against states they believe they can defeat).*

COMPETING AND ALTERNATIVE THEORIES

Alternative explanations fall along a continuum, from true competing theories to "null" hypotheses that simply predict no findings in favor of status dissatisfaction theory. Given the number of methodological approaches I use in the book, a full discussion of these alternatives is most appropriate within each empirical chapter, since the precise form of the alternative explanations will often depend on the method employed. For example, in chapter 6, one alternative explanation for German foreign policy is that it was motivated by commercial interests in domestic society, while in chapter 5, one might argue that the effect of status deficits are context dependent and no longer a factor in the twenty-first century. I deal with both these explanations in detail there as well as others that are more targeted. Here I provide an overview of three broad schools of thought that provide competing accounts of how status operates in world politics.

Power Transition Theory

The most obvious competing theory for status dissatisfaction—certainly the one that comes to mind most quickly—is power transition theory (or the related theory of hegemonic war).[101] In fact, the connection between status dissatisfaction and power transition theory has been remarked on by others as well. Geller writes that

> power transition theory ... bears strong resemblance to Galtung's structural theory of aggression.... The dissatisfied challenger in power transition theory is almost certainly a rank disequilibrated state. This challenger is the

[101] Gilpin 1983.

second most powerful state in the Great Power system ... but enjoys few or no benefits from the status quo, and arguably is not accorded the prestige its power warrants.[102]

Power transition theory argues that the international system is characterized (most of the time) by one dominant power that shapes the international order and receives a disproportionate share of the spoils. Patterns of unequal growth, however, eventually lead some states to rise in power to the point where they are capable of challenging the dominant power for leadership of the global system. The prevailing international system will eventually begin to break down because the dominant state will no longer be able to impose its will and the rising challenger will demand changes to the system so that it more accurately reflects their growing power. If the rising power is dissatisfied with its place in the system, power transition theorists argue that the point where the two powers (dominant and rising) achieve rough parity is when war is most likely.[103]

In some ways, status dissatisfaction and power transition theories are complementary. For example, both see prestige as a key factor in international politics. And though power transition scholars do not use the language of status "concerns," it is easy to see that their focus is indeed on variation in those concerns—a significant innovation compared to arguments about whether status "matters." They see those status concerns as being "triggered" for rising powers denied the benefits commensurate with their newfound capabilities by a hegemon who has locked in their spoils in the international system.

And in fact, the theories generate (almost) overlapping predictions, though those of power transition are more narrowly bounded. Power transition theorists argue that war is likely when power transitions occur between a formerly dominant hegemon and a rising power dissatisfied with its position in the international system. Status dissatisfaction theory

---

[102] Lemke 1997, 33n5. See also Galtung 1964.

[103] Organski 1958; Organski and Kugler 1980. Gilpin's (1983, 1988) theory of hegemonic war is similar in many respects. Like power transition theory, it identifies differential rates of growth as a key determinant of conflict and argues that the most likely timing for outbreaks of wars are when rising states achieve rough parity with the dominant hegemon. Differences from power transition theory are modest and subtle. For example, Gilpin "clearly self-identifies as a realist," while Organski and his associates "contrast power transition theory with balance of power theory ... and, in fact, explicitly reject the realist label." See DiCicco and Levy 1999, 679. For practical purposes, we can address them simultaneously.

makes a similar prediction, though without the necessary condition of a power transition between two states. Similarly, status dissatisfaction does not make any predictions regarding the target of the aggression, while power transition theory predicts that the rising power is likely to initiate against the hegemon (both theories see the dissatisfied state as the initiator of conflict).

While there are some areas in which the two theories complement one another, there are clear divergences as well. Power transition theory focuses on the status concerns of rising states powerful enough to challenge the dominant hegemon in the international system—a select group of states never likely to number more than a handful. As a result of that, the theory is narrower in scope than status dissatisfaction, which argues that status concerns are relevant at *all* levels of the international system. Such a theoretical move is made possible by another stark difference between the two theories: while power transition theory focuses on the international hierarchy, status dissatisfaction explicitly theorizes the multiple "local" hierarchies that states see themselves as being members of.[104]

Finally, the two theories diverge in how they operationalize key concepts. Status is crucial for both theories, and in power transition theory, it is one of the benefits denied to rising powers by the dominant hegemon that has "locked in" a hierarchy of prestige that no longer reflects material capabilities.[105] Since not all rising powers desire to change the structure of the system, though, a key question for this theory is, Which states are "satisfied (or revisionist)," and how can we tell?

Thus far, "satisfaction" with the system has been measured through second- or third-order implications, such as similarity of alliance portfolios ("tau-b" or "S").[106] One significant drawback to these measurement strategies is that they do not reflect the reality of "dissatisfaction" in the international system. Alliance similarity may *reflect* satisfaction (though the evidence is decidedly mixed so far), but it is at best a consequence and not a cause of dissatisfaction. In any case, the formation of alliances is complex

[104] A variant of power transition theory focused on minor powers has made a similar point, but it represents a relatively isolated departure from mainstream power transition theory. See Lemke and Reed 1996.

[105] Geller 1993; Lemke and Reed 1996; DiCicco and Levy 1999.

[106] This practice has been extended in recent work by Efird, Kugler, and Genna (2003) and Lemke and Reed (1996, 1998), who have refined the measure of alliance similarity in similar attempts to infer satisfaction with the status quo. Other methods—such as diplomatic history, intuition, or informal panels of experts (Wallace 1982; Geller 2000)—are more promising, but likely better suited toward smaller-scale efforts such as comparative case studies.

enough that it is difficult to ignore the many confounding factors that are likely to prevent it from reliably serving as a proxy for dissatisfaction.

Moreover, these operationalizations do not truly reflect the theory suggested by power transition scholars. In this theory of conflict, the accordance of prestige is considered one of the prime benefits that is supposed to accrue to the hegemon.[107] Revisionist intentions follow in this theory from a situation in which a candidate hegemon is denied the benefits they deserve based on their objective power and resources. Thus, we should find that states with revisionist preferences have less status than they deserve based on their material capabilities. In other words, the measure of dissatisfaction developed in this book is likely to be a better operationalization of dissatisfaction—in the sense that the measure is both more direct and more closely tied to the theory—than those used by power transition theorists for testing their own theory.

Domestic Politics

While there is no large, coherent body of work on domestic politics and status, a number of prominent theories touch on the subject. Levy, in describing the "diversionary theory of war," notes the "tendency of peoples ... to support assertive national policies which appear to enhance the power and prestige of the state [and] may lead decision-makers ... to embark on aggressive foreign policies, and sometimes even war as a means of increasing or maintaining their domestic support."[108]

Other prominent theories of domestic politics and international relations make similar claims. Snyder notes that German leaders often "resorted to superficial prestige strategies, such as seeking dramatic foreign policy success in crisis showdowns to improve their governments' popularity."[109] In a broad sense, Van Evera's reflections on self-glorifying myths perpetuated by elites makes the same point: war is more likely when elites and ideologues perpetuate chauvinist myths to either divert attention from domestic political problems or increase support by castigating an out-group.[110]

---

[107] Geller 1993; Lemke 1997.
[108] Levy 1988, 666.
[109] Snyder 1991, 101.
[110] Van Evera 1994.

These various approaches have in common a concern summed up by Rosen: "Political leaders talk constantly about prestige and status. Is it just talk?"[111] As Rosen hints at, it is beyond dispute that leaders persistently invoke status and prestige concerns to justify their actions. Yet one might be concerned that, for example, evidence of status dissatisfaction exists only in the public record as a tool used to mobilize domestic coalitions or score electoral victories.[112]

This alternative explanation implies a particular empirical strategy. In qualitative work, justifications and explanations provided by leaders are useful, but we must take caution not to overinterpret status concerns invoked in public speeches to either domestic or international audiences. More compelling evidence would come from private letters, diaries, or conversations in which leaders had no incentive to misrepresent or distort their true beliefs and motivations. Quantitatively, it suggests the need for objective measures of status rather than a reliance on the content analysis of public speeches.[113] While there are benefits to content analysis of public speeches, there is no reliable way to disprove the "cheap talk" hypothesis in contexts where leaders can be expected to attempt to maximize support for their preferred policies.

Other Status-Based Approaches

Finally, it is worth considering potential competing theories that are self-consciously focused on status. Two are of particular note because of their historical impact on security studies as well as their direct relevance to the current work.

POLARITY, STATUS, AND WAR

Wohlforth offers a system-level theory of status and war that begins with the observation that

> even capabilities distributions among major powers foster ambiguous status hierarchies, which generate more dissatisfaction and clashes over the status quo. And the more stratified the distribution of capabilities, the less likely such status competition is. Unipolarity thus generates far fewer incentives

---

[111] Rosen 2007, 17.

[112] Putnam 1988. In a variant of this argument, it might be used as a tool to symbolically tie one's hands internationally. See Fearon 1997.

[113] As in Miller 2013.

than either bipolarity or multipolarity for direct great power positional competition over status. Elites in the other major powers continue to prefer higher status, but in a unipolar system they face comparatively weak incentives to translate that preference into costly action.[114]

Here we can see a theory that both complements and diverges from status dissatisfaction. Critically, both (status dissatisfaction and Wohlforth) eschew the question "does status matter?" in favor of an approach that examines systematic variation in status concerns. Both also use advances in social psychology over the last several decades to generate testable predictions that are examined through a combination of quantitative data as well as close study of leaders' perceptions and beliefs. It is after this, however, that they diverge.

In the broadest sense, the theories are pitched at different levels of analysis. Wohlforth's theory of status competition is a system-level theory whose critical explanatory factor is the concentration of capabilities in a given system. Status dissatisfaction, by contrast, focuses on state- and dyad-level interactions (though both mine the historical record for evidence of leaders' beliefs). And while both theories focus on systematic variation in status concerns, they come to different conclusions about how those concerns are triggered—in status dissatisfaction, through a divergence between expectations and reality; and in Wohlforth's theory, through an equal distribution of capabilities among great powers.

Finally and critically, while status dissatisfaction operates on a "lower" level of analysis (the state level), it is broader in scope. Unlike other extant theories of status concerns, it is not constrained to focus only on major powers, while Wohlforth's, for example, is self-consciously a theory of "great power war." Great power wars are of course incredibly consequential, and come to mind far more easily than skirmishes or conflicts along the periphery. While the impact of major powers on the number and intensity of violent conflicts is disproportionate, it is not as strong a case as scholars commonly believe. Of the 139 interstate wars initiated by states and coded by the Correlates of War project, 53 percent (73) were initiated by nonmajor powers, and 43 percent (60) of the wars involved no major powers at all. Thus, one innovation of status dissatisfaction is a theory that not only includes the myriad smaller states in the system but also generates a mechanism (local comparisons) that allows

---

[114] Wohlforth 2009.

that theory to scale up to the great power level and down to the level of states that most previous theories have until now neglected.

The "status inconsistency" paradigm is the body of work most likely to be linked to status dissatisfaction theory. The theory has several variants, but can be summarized as follows:

> Countries may diverge on a number of status dimensions which are considered salient for decision makers. For example, a country may rank relatively high on economic and/or military capabilities (i.e., achieved status) but may be accorded little prestige (i.e., ascribed status) by the international community. Under such conditions... it is plausible that a nation's decision makers would evidence a strong desire to change the status quo, and *failing to do so, to engage in conflict and violence*.[115]

The theory that much of this work was based on—"frustration-aggression"—was borrowed from psychology, as is evident from a slightly different version of the theory: "under certain conditions, national decision-makers who are exposed to conditions of extreme frustration or uncertainty may react in ways which facilitate the onset of international aggression."[116]

While both status inconsistency and status dissatisfaction focus broadly on the divergence between expectations and reality, there are several notable differences. One significant difference concerns the respective theories' scope. As with other works noted in this section, much of the research on status inconsistency focused exclusively on major or great powers, ignoring the vast majority of the system.[117] Those works that did examine the entire population of states placed them in one enormous hierarchy, implying that all states were in constant competition with all other states—a notion that is difficult to believe. In contrast, one innovation of status dissatisfaction is to explicitly theorize the presence and formation of local hierarchies.

Perhaps the most significant difference, however, concerns the comprehensiveness of the respective theories. Status inconsistency theory is set up to test a hypothesis vaguely based on psychological research from the

---

[115] Volgy and Mayhall 1995, 68, emphasis added.
[116] Midlarsky and Midlarsky 1976, 373. See also Miller 1941; Haner and Brown 1955.
[117] For example, Gochman 1980.

1950s, which was controversial at the time and never particularly well founded in the empirical record. States—or leaders, since it is often not clear which—are seen as experiencing frustration at being denied the status they feel they deserve. Following that, it is hypothesized that they change the system (how?), and if that fails, "engage in conflict and violence." In other words, the most popular incarnations of the theory rest on states "lashing out" in frustration. In contrast, status dissatisfaction provides a concrete mechanism that links status concerns to war, grounded in a theory of how status operates in world politics. Status is linked to war not through irrationality and frustration but instead because highly visible conflicts serve as a viable strategy for states to change the community's beliefs about where they rank relative to others.

RESEARCH DESIGN

Most previous works on status utilize a single methodological framework in their research design. In doing so, they gain the advantages associated with that particular method, but are generally unable to offer a comprehensive picture of how status operates in international politics. Taken individually, each of these methods has advantages and drawbacks. Content analysis assumes that leaders' public speech is not strategic; patterns uncovered in case studies may be limited to particular historical eras or episodes, and quantitative analysis relies on proxies for status and status seeking that are not always entirely plausible (such as performance at the summer Olympics).[118] Even experiments, largely used in cognate fields to study status (such as psychology or economics), typically use subject pools and outcome measures that are far removed from international politics.[119]

Yet these limitations—prominent when relying on a single method— can be ameliorated through a carefully planned research design that relies on multiple methods.[120] Why multiple methods? The drawbacks or weaknesses inherent in each method are far more limiting in isolation. This point is perhaps more obvious if we reframe the question from "working

---

[118] See Miller 2013; Offer 1995; Markey 2000; Wohlforth 2009; Eyre and Suchman 1996; Gilady 2004; Rhamey and Early 2013.

[119] Loch, Huberman, and Stout 2000; Pettit and Lount 2010.

[120] Similar to Lieberman's (2005) call for "nested" research designs, though even that guide to mixed methods considers only the integration of case studies with quantitative research, ignoring the role of experiments.

with different methods" to advantages gained from using multiple methods and sources of data.[121]

Generally, scholars who work on status have used a particular method and single source of data (the source may be narratives of a particular case, a large-N data set, etc.). The limitations thus come not *just* from using a particular method but also because they rely on a single source of data. Inferential leverage—our ability to learn and draw conclusions from data—is far greater with *multiple sources of information that are* (as much as possible) *unrelated to one another*. No magic occurs when combining methods that inherently make an argument more believable. The value that comes from incorporating different methodological frameworks obtains only insofar as doing so allows for an increase in the "diversity and amount of observable implications."[122]

These comments regarding methodologies and data sources are perhaps even more important when investigating the effects of status concerns on foreign policy behavior. This is because the notion of status (a state's "standing" in the international system) is elusive, and by definition involves leaders' perceptions and beliefs. Because we cannot measure status directly, a mixed-method and multiple-source approach provides the best hope of triangulating the effect of status concerns on political behavior. Each method allows us to generate and test different (and diverse) implications of status in world politics. This is possible only in a book-length work, however, where space is available to definitively triangulate status and its effects in a cohesive, plausible manner.

To that end, this book employs a combination of case studies along with quantitative, large-N designs and experiments (both lab and survey) that test the implications of my theory at multiple levels of analysis. Each additional method involves significantly different measurements and outcomes, thereby increasing our confidence in the ability to draw inferences regarding status—a notoriously ephemeral concept. Additionally, each method has different strengths that allow for testing subtly distinct and overlapping sets of hypotheses as well as implications drawn from my theory. While the differing measures of status increase confidence in the theory's validity, the different methods allow for the construction of a far more subtle and deep theory, able to shed light on the dynamics of status at multiple levels of analysis and across time periods.

[121] As suggested by King and Powell 2008.
[122] Ibid., 10.

3

Losing Face and Sinking Costs

Earlier chapters highlighted three major concerns that emerge from a review of the literature on status and conflict in world politics:[1]

1. There is no empirical support for a *causal* link between status concerns and international conflict; the associations found in qualitative and large-N work cannot rule out the influence of some unobserved variable (such as a decline in trust) that impacts both the likelihood of war and the measure that is often used as a proxy for status (diplomatic representation).[2]

2. The social and perceptual nature of status has precluded *direct* measurement, leading to a reliance on proxies such as diplomatic representation and success in the Olympics.

3. We have little information on what factors make status concerns more or less salient to political leaders.

Answering this last question requires switching our focus from the effects of status itself (for example, the possession of high or low status, or a particular identity) to *relative concern* for status; only that is likely to provide variation that can be exploited in theory building and hypothesis testing. And by experimentally inducing such concerns in a laboratory, we can address the first two issues listed above, gaining significant leverage in isolating a causal effect of status concerns on political behavior as well as shedding light on factors that moderate its impact.

Of course, providing behavioral microfoundations for understanding how status operates in world politics necessitates careful operationalization and research design. This is especially the case for experimental IR, which often relies on "convenience samples" of undergraduates or, increasingly, online Mechanical Turk (MTurk) workers. And while questioning the use

---

[1] Parts of this chapter draw on work previously published as Renshon 2015.
[2] Maoz 2010; this work.

of first-year college students as subjects is no longer a novel complaint, it is still a valid one in some cases. Asking the typical sample of undergraduates to act "as if" they are political leaders can be problematic, since doing so can in some cases exacerbate their own biases.[3] Moreover, highly experienced elites may be more likely to adhere to traditional tenets of rational decision making, thereby making studies that use undergraduates potentially misleading for the purposes of extrapolating to world politics.[4]

This chapter presents two simultaneously fielded experiments focused on the escalation of commitment to a failing course of action.[5] This class of decisions has long been implicated in world politics as a potential cause of conflict, and has been empirically linked to the public's appetite for war, irredentist disputes, great power military interventions, international negotiations, and the length of commitment to conflicts like Vietnam.[6] In study 1, I replicate and extend a well-known sunk costs experiment that asks subjects to make a hypothetical investment decision. In study 2, I introduce a newly developed experimental paradigm—the Island Game—to provide a *behavioral* measure of escalation, using real financial incentives, and framed around a narrative of war and peace.

In the broader theory, status concerns are generated by the situation that states find themselves in, and leaders are presumed to take on the status concerns of the state and act accordingly. In those situations, the status concerns are both a component of the decision process or situation, and instrumentally useful. For example, in Nasser's decision to escalate Egyptian intervention in Yemen in the 1960s (see chapter 7), the intervention engaged his and Egypt's status, and status was both part of the motivation for acting and part of the goal. To the extent that status concerns are present on both sides of an equation, it makes disentangling their effect nearly impossible. To get at this, I construct the sort of difficult test that is only possible using experimental methods: I experimentally manipulate status concerns that are *unrelated* to the escalation decision to isolate the effect of status concerns on behavior. To the extent that this generalizes to the political domain, the effects of status concerns should only be more

---

[3] Kertzer and Renshon 2015.

[4] Hafner-Burton, Hughes, and Victor 2013; Carnevale, Inbar, and Lerner 2011.

[5] Study 1 was in fact fielded after the date of study 2, but before the data from study 2 were available for analysis.

[6] See Boettcher and Cobb 2009; Von Hippel 1996; Taliaferro 1998; Meerts 2005; Staw and Ross 1989. On escalation being implicated as a cause of conflict, see Goldgeier and Tetlock 2001; Kahneman and Renshon 2007.

powerful once the status engaged is related to the actual decision process (and not "incidental," as it is here) and we allow it to be instrumentally useful (as it cannot be in these experiments).

Both studies use an identical "status threat" treatment that asks subjects to think and write a short essay about a time in their lives when they faced the prospect of gaining or losing status.[7] The symmetry of the two studies—both use the same experimental treatment, and both focus on escalation outcomes—allows for easier interpretation of the results as well as the traditional benefits that accompany replications. In the first two sections of this chapter, I provide an overview of the use of experiments in political science and describe the logistics of the two studies. Then I offer direct evidence on two foundational tenets of status dissatisfaction theory: that status concerns vary predictably in response to contextual and dispositional factors, and that once triggered, those concerns raise the value that actors are willing to pay for increased status.

This chapter also begins the work of investigating other factors that might exacerbate status concerns. I begin this process by focusing on two key factors that have a strong claim to importance in moderating the impact of status concerns in politics.[8] The first quantity, SDO, is a dispositional characteristic that describes individuals' preference for dominance and hierarchy, and is a particularly important precursor for political beliefs and individual decision making.[9]

The second factor, power (here operationalized as a combination of the "feeling" of power and objective authority over subordinates), straddles the line between a situational and dispositional variable. Power is cited by a large number of conflict scholars as a factor in international conflict that operates in tandem with status. In fact, virtually every systematic theory or empirical analysis of status and conflict has relied to some extent on an interaction with power, whether it is a material distribution of power that no longer accords with the hierarchy of prestige, or leaders' beliefs that they are not ranked as highly as they deserve to be based on material capabilities.

In study 1, I rely on a convenience sample of MTurk respondents who exhibit the expected variation in levels of SDO. Because we have strong

---

[7] Experimental treatment is borrowed from Pettit, Yong, and Spataro 2010.

[8] Other candidates include cultures of honor, past history, power distributions, and biological predispositions. See Nisbett and Cohen 1996; Dafoe and Caughey 2016; Miller 2013; Gilpin 1988; Volgy and Mayhall 1995; Newman, Sellers, and Josephs 2005; Mehta and Josephs 2010.

[9] Pratto et al. 1994.

prior beliefs that our theoretical interest is in high SDO individuals—who are likely to be disproportionately represented in positions of authority— we can simply use the convenience sample and subset the high SDO populations that are of primary interest. With respect to the subjective and objective concepts of power under investigation in study 2, however, we have little evidence to guide us. In order to address that uncertainty, this experiment uses a sample of political and military leaders drawn from the SEF program at the Harvard Kennedy School, along with a group of demographically matched control subjects from the Boston area. This provides natural variation on power within and between groups that should address some of the typical concerns about external validity in IR experiments as well as allow for the testing of more subtle inferences derived from the literature on status, power, and war.

POWERFUL ELITES: EXPERIMENTATION IN IR

One notable benefit of the experimental approach is that it is uniquely suited to investigate how status concerns affect individuals at the microlevel. Yet, doing so in this case requires reconsidering some of the standard operating procedures of experimental political science—which often rely on subject pools composed of college students—and experiments that are abstract and hypothetical. While some of these issues can truly be cause for concern, or at least caution, other fears are largely overblown. Below I provide an argument for how to understand the debate surrounding "external validity" in the context of experimental political science.

External Validity and Sample Selection

External validity—the degree to which a given result is generalizable to alternative contexts, populations, and measurement strategies—is not a property of *individual* experiments: "external validity follows, as replications across time and populations seek to delineate the extent to which . . . conclusions can generalize."[10] Two related concerns are relevant here. The first—whether "methods, materials and settings of the research are similar to a given target environment"—asks if we can generalize outside the lab to

---

[10] McDermott 2011, 28.

other settings. The other, more common concern in political science is in assessing "the approximate truth of the inference or knowledge claim for observations beyond the target population studied."[11]

It is this latter concern, about generalizing to alternative *populations*, that is most prominent in critiques of experimental political science. Simply stated, it goes as follows: laboratory studies (and even survey experiments) that use "convenience samples" of undergraduates cannot tell us much about elite decision making. This critique has been influential and many political scientists use a "simplistic heuristic" in which student samples prevent generalization to other contexts.[12]

These concerns are neither unique to political science nor particularly new. Psychologists have long worried that conducting the majority of the field's research on college students would yield conclusions that lacked clear external validity. As early as 1946, psychologists were lamenting that "the existing science of human behavior is largely the science of sophomores."[13] Concerns over this "narrow data base" have not changed a great deal in the ensuing years.[14] In the context of IR, this dilemma is highlighted by recent work finding that asking students to "act as if" they were leaders simply caused them to act more like themselves.[15]

As a productive response to these concerns, social scientists have taken to replicating findings using different populations, though the results have been mixed. For example, one study found that professional traders were just as likely as "laypeople" (even more in some circumstances) to exhibit biased overconfidence.[16] In other cases, results were either moderated or wholly different. Weather forecasters, for example, who receive immediate and unambiguous feedback, do not exhibit overconfidence and are reasonably "well-calibrated."[17] Other research has found that different populations, such as political officials and military officers, seem to employ different decision strategies.[18]

---

[11] Morton and Williams 2010, chap. 7. Bundling these two concerns together, as I do in places in this chapter, is conventional in IR contexts, but also fits more closely with standard definitions, such as offered by Campbell and Stanley (1963) and McDermott (2002b).

[12] Barabas and Jerit 2010; Kam 2007. See also Druckman and Kam 2011.

[13] McNemar 1946.

[14] Sears 1986; Gordon, Slade, and Schmitt 1986.

[15] Kertzer and Renshon 2015.

[16] Glaser, Langer, and Weber 2005.

[17] Tyszka and Zielonka 2002.

[18] Mintz, Redd, and Vedlitz 2006.

Political scientists, too, have gradually begun to recruit more elite subjects, such as military officers, and have found significant differences between those samples and the standard student pools.[19] Fehr and List, for example, found that CEOs were both more trusting and more trustworthy than students in experimental settings, while another study found that Indonesian civil servants exhibited different patterns of beliefs and tolerance for corruption than Indonesian students.[20]

Logistical problems have slowed this useful area of research, however, as scholars have found it difficult to find a suitable number of "special subjects." Moreover, virtually no experiments have used high-level political decision makers. Even an article titled "How Politicians Make Decisions: A Political Choice Experiment" used professors with doctorates in economics as surrogates for political leaders.[21] This is flattering for professors, but common sense suggests that they may not be the best stand-ins for high-level political and military leaders.

Of course, it is neither necessary nor desirable to use *only* political leaders as subjects, both because logistical problems make this approach extraordinarily costly, and because in many cases, concerns about external validity and generalizing are either overstated or premature.[22] But while "special subjects" are not necessary for every political science experiment, they may be particularly useful when the target population differs on attributes that are *theoretically relevant* for a given study, such as experience, familiarity with the decision context, or age.[23] This is often the case in IR, where it is obvious that we must address the significant differences that separate undergraduates and Internet samples from real-world leaders. An analogy can be made here to omitted variable bias in large-N work: we know that our statistical models are incomplete, but what matters is whether that incompleteness is correlated with something that is relevant for the model.

So what are the implications of this stance for the current studies on SDO and power? In fact, we have strong theoretical and empirical reasons to believe that high SDO individuals will be disproportionately represented in positions of authority, since SDO theory predicts that high

---

[19] For studies that employ military officers, see Mintz 2004; Mintz, Redd, and Vedlitz 2006. For more on the differences between elite subjects and student pools, see Hafner-Burton et al. 2012; Hafner-Burton, Hughes, and Victor 2013.

[20] Fehr and List 2004; Alatas et al. 2009.

[21] Fatas, Neugebauer, and Tamborero 2007.

[22] For a similar argument, see McDermott 2002a.

[23] Hafner-Burton, Hughes, and Victor 2013; Mintz 2004; Horowitz, McDermott and Stam 2005.

SDO individuals will be most comfortable in roles that enhance the existing hierarchy. Previous work has found that high SDO individuals disproportionately select into careers that include the police/FBI, criminal prosecutors, or managers, but political leadership positions represent an obvious extension of the logic.[24] This is buttressed by empirical work, such as the finding that high SDO individuals are more likely to obtain leadership positions in the lab, and was summed up in a recent study noting that "such individuals seek social, political and economic status at all costs ... strive—indeed, disproportionately self-nominate—for leadership positions."[25] Here, because we have strong priors about the distribution of SDO in leadership positions, we can simply focus our attention on high SDO individuals in the general population.

With respect to power, the issue is more complex. SDO is a distinct concept—one that has been replicated countless times, and has gained widespread acceptance as the preferred measure for a specific cluster of beliefs that centers on a preference for hierarchy and dominance. Power is a muddier concept, and might refer to any number of things at varying levels of analysis. Certainly, at the objective level, and in comparison to the general population, political leaders will—almost by definition—have more power (in the sense of ability to influence events or control resources). In fact, despite all the many differences—age, experience, or regime type—among political leaders, they are all far more powerful as a general rule than any undergraduate in a lab. Yet, there is a large component of power that is situational and relative: in any given interaction, i might have power over j, even though in other circumstances, j has power over k, l, and m. Power is also a psychological state, however, and as such, we must be careful to consider both objective and subjective indicators of power.[26] These facts suggest that a leadership sample would be particularly useful, since we know little about the distribution of subjective power mind-sets among leaders and elites.

Experimental Realism

A second, related concern often invoked in response to IR experiments is that *even if* we were able to use high-ranking political leaders as subjects,

[24] Pratto et al. 1997, 39.
[25] Anderson and Summers 2007, 111–12. See also Altemeyer 2003; Son Hing et al. 2007.
[26] Anderson, John, and Keltner 2012.

they would behave differently in the lab than they would in real-life situations. There are two reasons why this might occur: either subjects would not truly engage in the task in the lab, and so we would not observe the actual decision process as it would happen in the real world, or other factors in the real world (and unaccounted for in the experiment) might induce different results.

On the former, the lack of "high stakes" in the lab (compared to the Situation Room) is the factor most commonly implicated as preventing us from learning from experiments. Empirical work on this subject is nonetheless relatively clear: stakes don't change the dynamics observed by experimenters dramatically in most instances, and to the extent they do, it is the inclusion of moderate stakes (compared to no financial incentives) that make a difference, not marginally increasing stakes that are already present in the experiment.[27] This is, in fact, exactly why both experiments described in this chapter incorporated (moderate) monetary incentives.[28]

On the latter question, it is always possible that there are other factors (for example, emotions, time pressure, stress, or group dynamics) unaccounted for in an experiment that might make a difference in the real world. It is worth remembering here that external validity is built up over time by replication and extension, and that any given experiment can only do so much without losing the very advantages that experimental methods and randomization provide. Buttressing our confidence, there is a long tradition of experimental results generated by "trivial" tasks in laboratory settings that generalize to people in the "real world" operating in much more complex situations. This is the case with aggression, anchoring, and prospect theory, and more recently, in political science with negative advertising and turnout as well as findings related to immigration and Medicare.[29] These results stand as testament to Verba's warning that "the experimental model does not need to 'look like' the real world. What is important is the question of whether it operates like the real world in the respects that are relevant to the study at hand."[30]

---

[27] Camerer and Hogarth 1999; Holt and Laury 2001; Hertwig and Ortmann 2003.

[28] The relationship between incentives and performance does not appear to be entirely monotonic when incentives are extremely high. See Ariely et al. 2009.

[29] See Anderson and Bushman 1997; Enough and Mussweiler 2006; Camerer 2004; Ansolabehere, Iyengar, and Simon 1999; Barabas and Jerit 2010. See also Levitt and List 2007.

[30] Verba 1964, 502. See also Kelman 1965, 598.

The "Levels of Analysis" Problem in Status Experiments

In chapter 2, I provided an extended reasoning for the best way to think about the "levels of analysis problem" in the context of status research in IR. It is not necessary to recapitulate the reasoning at length, so I confine myself here to explaining how this particular chapter fits into the broader argument.

In earlier chapters, I demonstrated that research on status in IR has (necessarily) implicated a number of levels of analysis, from the individual to the group. This chapter follows a similar logic. I ask subjects to consider a decisively *social* event ("losing status in the eyes of your peers"), but measure its impact at the individual level. Additionally, it is the status of the individual that is threatened—a decision that was taken in order to benefit from a tested and validated instrument used in published research. To the extent that many IR theories of status already implicate the status of individuals, this design poses no issues for interpretation. Nevertheless, because some theories do implicate a combination of group and individual status, I rely on the explicit claim of Wohlforth and others who use SIT that threats to group status are transmitted to individual leaders so perfectly that we can use psychological theories of status to understand how that individual will react to these threats.[31] If this is wrong—if, for example, a threat to the group's status at magnitude x is felt by the leader as a threat to their own status at some level below x—then the results of these studies would represent an overestimate of the effect for situations in which individual status was not threatened, but group status was. I return to this issue in the discussion of the results, where I propose extensions that more directly address potential differences between group and individual status threats.

This research is thus well suited to provide "microfoundations" for theories of status in world politics, many of which rely on individual and group-level mechanisms, and all of which hold at least some testable implications at the individual level. As for the relevant level for analyzing power in IR, it is obvious that power in IR is typically a state-level characteristic, often measured as state capacity. As noted earlier, however, a great many influential works, recognizing that our measures of power are necessarily filtered imperfectly through the perceptions of individual leaders, have focused precisely on those individuals' beliefs. Thus, to the extent that

---

[31] Wohlforth 2009, 37.

TABLE 3.1
Overview of Samples.

Study	Location	Sample	N
1	Online	MTurk	705
2a	Laboratory	Political/military leaders	77
2b	Laboratory	High-education Boston/Cambridge residents	62

material constraints affect behavior through the instantiation of *beliefs about power*, it follows that we should take advantage of the laboratory setting to precisely measure those beliefs. Previous experimental work has leveraged the precision inherent in experimental methods to measure power at the individual level (as individual capacity or probability of winning, for example).[32] I provide an even finer-grained measurement of this important concept by measuring *beliefs* about power at the individual level.

THE STUDIES

Two studies were fielded for this endeavor with three distinct samples (see overview in table 3.1). Study 1 was fielded on MTurk in fall, 2011. A total of 705 subjects were all paid $1 for their participation as well as entered into a lottery drawing for an additional $25 prize, contingent on following the instructions carefully. In the sample, the mean age was thirty-four, a majority were female (60 percent), highly educated (> 50 percent had at least a four-year college degree), and liberal (with a mean score of 42, on an ideology scale anchored by "extremely liberal" at 0 and "extremely conservative" at 100).[33]

Study 2 (a and b) took place at the Harvard Decision Science Laboratory in fall 2010. The seventy-seven adults in the "leadership sample" were members of the SEF program at the Harvard Kennedy School, and were overwhelmingly male (76 percent) and highly educated (75 percent had postgraduate educations). SEF members are typically high-ranking government employees and military personnel who possess the rank of GS14 or GS15 (for civilians), and O-5 and O-6 in military grades, and generally include members of every branch of the US armed forces as well as representatives from other agencies, such as the Federal Emergency Management

---

[32] Renshon, Lee, and Tingley 2016.
[33] Summary statistics describing the study 1 sample are contained in the online appendix.

Losing Face and Sinking Costs • 85

Agency, Department of Energy, Department of Defense, and Department of State as well as several foreign governments.[34] Often the members of the military sent to the SEF program are being screened for promotion to "flag rank" (O-7 or above). The "control population" comprised sixty-two adults from the Boston metropolitan area.[35] To the extent possible, they were matched to the leaders on demographic attributes, and a comparison reveals that this goal was largely accomplished.[36]

Procedures

In both studies, subjects completed a brief demographic questionnaire following the consent process. In study 1 (but not 2), this included the SDO instrument ($\alpha = 0.93$).[37] Because study 1 was an online survey, subjects were presented with an "attention gate" following the demographic questionnaire.[38]

Following the demographic questions, subjects in both studies were randomly assigned to one of three conditions in an autobiographical essay task. Participants in the *status threat* condition were asked to spend several minutes imagining and writing about a situation at work in which they might lose status in the eyes of their peers.[39] They were further instructed to focus on how they would feel when they were worried about losing the status, but had not actually lost it yet. Subjects in the *status gain* condition were asked to spend several minutes imagining and writing about a time

---

[34] There were not enough foreign nationals to draw meaningful inferences about cross-cultural variation, so they were excluded from the analysis.

[35] While the control group was paid a $5 show-up fee, leaders were not. We were advised that such small compensation for their time would be insulting to SEF members and thus depress participation. Once the study began, the incentives for both groups were identical, and included payment from the escalation task described below.

[36] The gender distribution was similar (80 percent male compared to 76 percent for leaders), as was the distribution of age ($M_{leaders} = 48.5$, $M_{controls} = 51.0$) and education ($M_{leaders} = 4.8$, $M_{controls} = 4.5$, scaled from 1 [high school] to 5 [postgraduate or professional degree]). They also scored similarly on the cognitive reflection test ($M_{leaders} = 0.8$, $M_{controls} = 1.0$), a common proxy for cognitive ability scaled from 0 to 3 (Frederick, 2005), and Wechsler (1997) adult intelligence scale ($M_{leaders} = 34.9$, $M_{controls} = 32.3$). Distributions and additional summary statistics describing the samples used in Study 2 are in the online appendix.

[37] See online appendix.

[38] As suggested by Berinsky, Margolis, and Sances 2013.

[39] The status manipulation was borrowed from Pettit, Yong, and Spataro 2010. The full text of the essay instructions are contained in the online appendix.

at work when they might gain status, and subjects in the *neutral* condition were asked to think and write about a typical day at work.

MEASURES OF ESCALATION

The outcome measure in both studies was the expenditure of resources in an "escalation task." "Escalation of commitment" problems represent a class of decisions in which actors must decide whether to cut their losses and walk away, or "double down" in an effort to recoup past losses.[40] Decision making in these situations is often described as "biased," since tenets of normative rationality suggest that it shouldn't matter what costs were already paid, only whether future costs are worth the expected gain.[41] I refrain from using the language of "bias" or "irrationality," since in many cases, the status engaged in an escalation decision makes the precise accounting of costs and benefits extremely difficult. In these experiments, however, we can at least note that the status engaged (and threatened) is not directly relevant to the decision process, helping us to remove status benefits from the "left-hand side" of the equation and isolate its effects on behavior.

In world politics, the tendency to fixate on sunk costs has been implicated as one of the critical mistakes often made by leaders.[42] Unfortunately, the proclivity is as persistent as it is pernicious, proving to be surprisingly resistant to de-biasing.[43] Even replacing individuals, while intuitively appealing, does not always work, as individuals often seem to go to great lengths to justify the actions of those they replace, triggering the same escalation tendencies that the change in personnel was designed to avoid ("vicarious entrapment").[44] For example, even after replacing President Lyndon Baines Johnson with a campaign *premised* on cutting losses in Vietnam, Richard Nixon found it extremely difficult to actually halt the

---

[40] The literature on this class of problems in psychology and economics is voluminous, and focuses on sunk costs, mental accounting, emotions, prospect theory, and self-justification. A full review is outside the scope of this work, but see Staw 1981; Bazerman, Giuliano, and Appelman 1984; Wong, Yik, and Kwong 2006.

[41] On the potential "rationality" of escalation in IR, see Bowen 1987; Friedman 2014.

[42] Staw and Ross 1989; Taliaferro 1998; Kahneman and Renshon 2007; Boettcher and Cobb 2009; Walt 2010; Goldgeier and Tetlock 2001.

[43] Renshon and Renshon 2008, 527–28. Children are more likely to exhibit the normatively rational behavior associated with ignoring sunk costs, but this does not provide much in the way of practical advice for politicians. See Arkes and Ayton 1999.

[44] Gunia, Sivanathan, and Galinsky 2009.

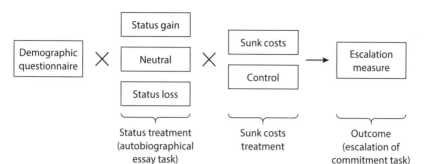

Figure 3.1: **Study 1: Experimental Design.**

US escalation of commitment.[45] Critically, this class of decision problem is one with obvious applicability and relevance to domestic as well as international politics.

In study 1, the main outcome task was a survey instrument designed to measure the escalation of commitment. It asked subjects to "play the role" of the undersecretary of defense for acquisition in the Department of Defense who was tasked with making an allocation decision between two departments (services and manufacturing) in a fictional company that had applied for a federal grant. Subjects were presented with a basic spreadsheet showing profits/losses for each division over the last seven years, and asked how much of the $20 million available they would like to allocate to each division. In the *sunk costs* condition, there is additional text that describes an earlier allocation decision that the subject was responsible for, in which all available funds were invested the "services" department of the same company. The difference between the investment in satellite services in the *sunk costs* and the *control* version of the experiment thus provides a measure of sunk costs.[46] The entire experimental design is a 3 (*status threat / status gain / neutral*) × 2 (*sunk costs / no sunk costs*), fully-crossed, between-subjects design and is depicted in figure 3.1.[47]

The measure of escalation used in study 1 is a modification of one standard in the literature in which subjects are asked to allocate resources between two departments or groups, with a condition in which they are

---

[45] Welch 2005.

[46] The entire text of this instrument is available in the online appendix.

[47] All subjects took part in other, unrelated studies during the sessions that generated the data used in this chapter.

told they are responsible for past investment into one of those groups.[48] The advantage of using a variant of this design is that it allows for easy, direct comparability to previous results. Its use over two to three decades also provides added confidence in the validity of the instrument itself.

On the other hand, there are potential drawbacks as well. Most notably, the design in study 1 (and in fact, most experimental designs in the escalation literature) is both hypothetical and far removed from the domain of politics. An additional (potential) concern is the notion that subjects have no "skin in the game," as they are paid the same amount no matter what decision they make. While many studies have demonstrated the relevance of these sorts of hypothetical tasks for real-work decision making, this still represents a potential issue that is best addressed through the type of replication of studies pursued in this chapter.[49]

A NOVEL, BEHAVIORAL MEASURE OF ESCALATION

In order to remedy these problems, I developed a new experimental protocol—the Island Game—for study 2 that provides a *behavioral* measure of escalation using real money, and framed around a narrative of political decisions relating to war and peace. Participants were endowed with $10 in the form of a hundred "units" of soldiers (each valued at $0.10) and control over 50 percent of the island, which is visually represented by a drawing of an island divided equally into two colors. Each turn, they were asked if they would like to end the game and cash in their units, or allocate a number of their units to try to capture more of the island (capturing the whole island netted a $200 cash prize for the subject). If they chose the latter, they were asked how many units they would like to allocate in that particular turn. They could allocate a maximum of fifteen units or however many they had left (whichever was lower).[50]

The amount of the island captured each turn was determined by a weighted function such that in each turn they had a small probability of capturing the whole of the remaining territory (and thus the grand prize) and a larger chance, weighted by the number of units they allocated, of capturing smaller pieces of territory. Each round comprised one turn by the participant and one by the computer (which could also capture a small

---

[48] See, for example, Bazerman, Giuliano, and Appelman 1984; Moon 2001.
[49] Kühberger, Schulte-Mecklenbeck, and Perner 2002.
[50] Full instructions are contained in the online appendix.

bit of territory). The algorithms determining outcomes in the game are weighted such that—at the end of the computer's turn—the subject was always in a worse position than at the beginning of the turn. Put simply, as long as subjects continued to play the game, they were pushed back into worse and worse strategic positions, steadily losing territory on the island (no subject won the "grand prize" of $200). This is critical because we wanted to structure the game so that everyone had a similar experience: that of losing ground.[51] The game ends when the participant "walks away" (keeping whatever money is left) or runs out of units to use.[52]

While the scenario was made as realistic as possible, we do not need to count on the subjects feeling as though they were really making decisions about war and peace ("mundane realism"). Rather, the decision was designed to mirror, in its essence, the types of decisions that political leaders face on a daily basis: whether to continue investing resources in what appears to be a lost cause or walk away. This strategy maximizes "experimental realism," and takes advantage of our ability to isolate and identify causal factors in the lab.

The structure depicted in figures 3.1 and 3.2 allows us to estimate a causal effect for status concerns on escalation, but it is worth noting that the outcome itself has nothing to do with status. This structure is analogous to the way in which researchers have used the "carryover" effects of emotions to properly isolate their causal effects: status concerns triggered by thinking about a situation that might happen in one's own life carry over to affect what should be an unrelated decision regarding escalation in the Island Game.[53] It is with this structure, and *only* with this structure, that we are able to properly isolate the causal effect of status concerns on behavior.

---

[51] In order to avoid deception, subjects were given purposely vague instructions that they would be interacting with "another player." The focus on escalation of commitment to *failing* courses of action required that subjects lost ground in every turn, unfortunately precluding the use of real dyadic interactions.

[52] That subjects were not specifically prohibited from interacting following the experiment might constitute a weak accountability induction. Accountability can reduce "sunk costs" effects in some cases (Simonson and Nye 1992)—though this would likely reduce estimates of escalation across the board—but can have unpredictable effects, not all beneficial; for example, it makes a difference whether actors learn of the need to account for their actions pre- or postdecision. In the latter case, accountability can increase escalation, while in the former it can attenuate it, but even then only under specific conditions. See Lerner and Tetlock 1999.

[53] In psychology, see Lerner, Small, and Loewenstein 2004. In political science, see Renshon, Lee, and Tingley 2015.

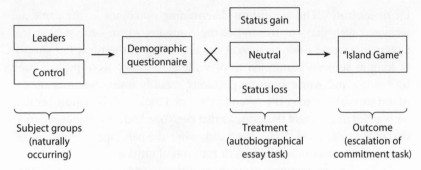

Figure 3.2: **Study 2: Experimental Design.**

SYSTEMATIC VARIATION IN STATUS CONCERNS

The first priority in these experimental studies is to provide direct evidence on a key tenet of status dissatisfaction theory: preferences for status are not constant but rather vary systematically in response to both situational and dispositional factors, and once triggered, increase actors' value for status. In order to provide compelling evidence on this key assumption, I designed both studies in such a way that they would be comparable: both studies used the exact same "autobiographical essay task" to trigger status threats and both contained the same three experimental conditions (*status threat, status gain, neutral*). This research design should give us additional confidence in the results, as we are replicating across both samples (online, Boston residents, and leaders) and experimental setups (online survey and laboratory).

Immediately following the experimental prime, I asked subjects to "think back to the short essay you wrote a few moments ago. Try to recall what you were feeling and thinking as you wrote the essay. At the time of the experience you recalled in your essay, how much did you value having: status/influence/respect/prestige?"

The results of this are depicted in figure 3.4 for both studies. They strongly suggest that status concerns vary systematically in response to context, and that threatening status causes actors to attach higher values to its possession. In study 1, online MTurk participants valued status more in the *status threat* condition than in the *neutral* condition—a jump from 3.3 to 4.9 on the scale, equivalent to a 48 percent increase in the value they attached to status.[54] In study 2, the leaders in the *status threat* condition

---

[54] $t(489) = -11.58$, $p < 0.001$. I focus here on the comparison between *status threat* and *neutral* since there are no strong hypotheses concerning behavior in the *status gain* condition.

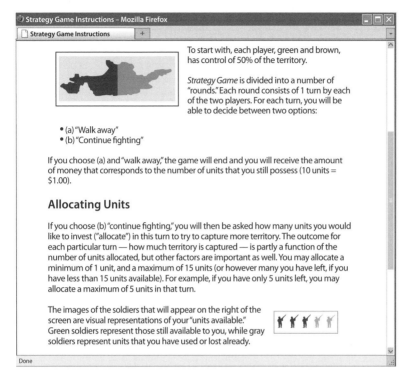

Figure 3.3: **Screen Capture of Island Game Task.**

valued status more highly (5.2) than in the *neutral* condition (4.5)—an increase of 15 percent.[55] Among Boston residents, the pattern was much the same: an increase from 4.5 to 5.4, a 20 percent increase in how much value they attached to possessing status.[56]

Across samples, studies, and lab contexts, we thus find strong support for our first hypothesis: preferences for status are not constant, nor are they random. Instead, they vary predictably in response to situational context. When subjects recall a time in their lives when their status was threatened, the value they attach to status shoots up.

Of course, we must be careful extrapolating from the lab, but several features make this task easier. First, as is often the case, real-world status threats are likely to affect people far more deeply than my experimental prime: a watered-down, IRB-compliant shadow of the type of experience

---

[55] $t(38) = -1.9$, $p < 0.05$.
[56] $t(34) = -1.9$, $p < 0.05$.

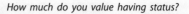

How much do you value having status?

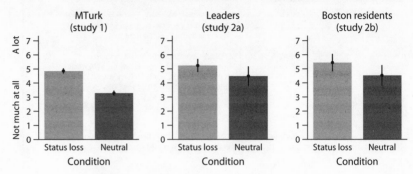

Figure 3.4: **Systematic Variation in Status Concerns across Samples and Studies.**

that people have in the real world. Second, we often have to imagine how our experimental results would replicate if we were able to use a sample of actual political leaders. In some cases, it is argued, the effects would be far weaker, under the hopeful logic that "leaders are more rational / less biased / not human beings." In this case, we can bypass at least some of these concerns through our sample of leaders, who by and large exhibit the same susceptibility to status threats that online and in-person convenience samples do.

STATUS CONCERNS AND ESCALATION

Next we turn to the question of whether and how status concerns affected escalation directly, unmoderated by any dispositional or contextual factors. While there is no extant literature on this exact question—does the threat of status loss lead to the escalation of commitment to a failing course of action?—the theory of status dissatisfaction provides some potential insight. My theory predicts that status concerns raise the value of status, which in turn should lead to greater escalatory behavior, so long as escalation (and victory, unlikely as it may be) has the chance to raise or salvage an actor's status. In the political world, status benefits do accompany victory, though in lab and survey experiments that link is likely to be significantly weaker.

I found that the threat of losing status increased the value of status to participants—a result that has been replicated with different populations by psychologists.[57] If the status threat manipulation increased participants' value for status in study 2 and to the extent that "winning" the Island Game might be expected to increase their status (given that they likely anticipated discussing it with fellow participants following the study), we would expect increased expenditure of resources for those in that experimental condition. In this framework, the increased escalation occurs because concerns about status are raised high enough that they overshadow the increased expenditure of economic resources. In this narrative, the "value for status" is the key causal mechanism, and it is through a rise in that value that behaviors change as well.

Other explanations are possible, however. Others have found that highly aversive states (such as having power without status or focusing on financial difficulties) impair cognitive functioning.[58] High-status groups faced with the prospect of losing status, for example, exhibited the physiological symptoms associated with threat response, which decreased functioning (in comparison to low-status groups that faced the prospect of gaining status).[59] Under this framework, it is the "nonrational" escalation of commitment that is the focus. If status threats are aversive enough to impair cognitive functioning—by consuming precious mental resources that cannot then be utilized to combat decision-making biases—we would again expect them to lead to greater escalation of commitment. This premise relies on the folk theory that greater cognitive effort necessarily correlates with less "biased" judgment, though this is not always the case. In fact, escalation of commitment is notoriously difficult to attenuate, although it is unclear if cognitive effort and attention might accomplish that goal.

Finally and perhaps most important, a large literature has demonstrated the significance that being in a "loss frame" can have on risk acceptance.[60] In fact, this is one of the most popular of the many explanations for the sunk costs effect.[61] The intuition behind this is that the shape of an actor's value function (concave in domain of gains, and convex in the domain of losses) implies that once losses are sustained, further losses do not add nearly enough extra disutility to outweigh the value from a large gain, unlikely as it may be. This is exacerbated by the certainty effect, which

---

[57] Pettit, Yong, and Spataro 2010.
[58] Fast, Halevy, and Galinsky 2011; Mani et al. 2013.
[59] Scheepers 2009.
[60] Kahneman and Tversky 1984.
[61] For the foundational works on this, see Thaler 1980; Arkes and Blumer 1985.

magnifies the psychological salience of certain losses (relative to what they "should be" if our decision weights correlated more perfectly with actual probabilities), increasing the desire to avoid defeat and the tendency to take greater risks to do so. Thus, we would expect subjects exposed to the prospect of losing status to escalate more in the main outcome task relative to those in either the neutral or gain conditions.

While these theoretical and conceptual works all suggest that the threat of status loss should lead to greater escalation, they present three different mechanisms linking the status threat to increased escalation: increased value for status, impaired cognitive functioning, and prospect theory / increased risk taking. The first explanation is the one most consistent with the theory of status dissatisfaction, since the other two imply cognitive impairment or bias that does not feature in my theory. Of course, more than one mechanism may influence behavior simultaneously, and the experimental designs used in this book cannot definitely "prove" the dominance of any one of these potential causal pathways

In study 1, the escalation task used is based on differences in the investments made by subjects in the *sunk costs* and *control* condition. Because "escalation" here relies on a between-subjects manipulation, we must estimate models that include an interaction term for *status threat* × *sunk costs*.

Figure 3.5 displays the results of this graphically, using first differences.[62] There is some ongoing debate about the extent to which including pretreatment controls in regression analyses of experimental data biases the results, though the consensus seems to be that this bias is "negligible" for $N > 20$.[63] The bars and associated confidence intervals represent the effect of the *sunk costs* manipulation by *status threat*.[64] In the *control* condition, sunk costs had no discernible effect (though it is estimated to be negative, the real

[62] Tables in the online appendix display the results of this analysis, both with and without demographic controls.

[63] Freedman (2008), for example, suggests that bias is likely when $N < 500$, while Green (2009) uses simulations and replications to demonstrate that the practical effect of such bias is "negligible" for $N > 20$. This makes little practical difference for the results in this case, and I present models with and without controls in the appendix.

[64] In study 1, the escalation task used is based on differences in the investments made by subjects in the *sunk costs* and *control* conditions. While the difference between the two conditions was in the predicted direction (greater investment of resources in the *sunk costs* condition), the difference was rather small on its own and not statistically significant ($p = 0.11$ using a one-sided t-test). The weakness of this experimental treatment might be due to the manipulation itself, which comes at the end of a rather long block of text. This is rarely optimal, but perhaps especially problematic in MTurk samples, where recent research suggests

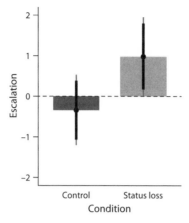

Figure 3.5: **Study 1: Status Concerns Increase Escalation** Points indicate effects of *sunk costs* manipulation in *control* and *status threat* conditions. Y-axis represents escalations (in millions of dollars). Gray and black lines indicate 95 and 90 percent confidence intervals, respectively.

takeaway is that it is not significantly different from zero). In contrast, the *status threat* increased escalation by $1 million—a difference of about 10 percent over the baseline investment. This provides some preliminary evidence on the link between status threats and escalation.

In study 2, the setup was slightly different. In that context, escalation could be measured directly by money expended in the Island Game (and thus did not depend on interacting the experimental status prime with a sunk costs condition). In fact, just as in study 1, those in the *status threat* condition did escalate, on average, more than their counterparts in the *neutral* or *status gain* conditions (by about 6 percent), though these differences were not statistically significant.[65]

Across the two studies, we thus find suggestive evidence for the link between status concerns and escalation. Experimentally induced status concerns did have a direct effect on the escalation of commitment,

---

that "buy-in" from subjects is more difficult to achieve. See Krupnikov and Levine 2014. Study 2 also contained a sunk cost manipulation, for an unrelated study. Unlike the rest of the study, however, the sunk costs treatment was not piloted, and appeared to have little effect. It was most likely overshadowed by other parts of the instructions, which resulted in no main effect of the *sunk costs* condition. Results discussed are unaffected by controlling for the sunk costs condition or interacting that condition with any of the other main variables of interest, so we collapse across the *sunk costs* and *no sunk costs* conditions to gain statistical power.

[65] Escalation by condition can be seen in online appendix materials.

leading to an increased tendency for subjects to "throw good money after bad." Yet, this link was substantively smaller (and not statistically significant at conventional levels) in the lab compared to the online— and hypothetical—version. The next section provides evidence that the link between status concerns and escalation is both substantively large and statistically significant, masked only by the moderating effects of both power and SDO.

Dispositional Roots of Status Concerns

So far I have provided direct evidence on a key tent of status dissatisfaction theory—that status concerns increase actors' value for status—and begun to explore one extension of that finding—namely, that the increased value can result in increased escalation of commitment. This section continues that extension by turning to the dispositional roots of status concerns examined in study 1.

While scholars have often noted when a particular leader seems fixated on issues of status, we have no general theory of *which* individuals are likely to be most sensitive to status concerns.[66] My theory of status dissatisfaction—focused as it is on systematic variation in the concern for status—provides a starting point by exploring on the dispositional roots of status concerns in politics. I hypothesize that individuals whose ideological beliefs are focused on status and hierarchy will be more susceptible to threats to their status position. I measure subjects' SDO—a popular and validated measure of preference for hierarchy and dominance—and randomly assign them to different levels of status threat. Because we have strong reason to believe that high SDO individuals will be disproportionately represented in leadership positions, I focus on those individuals in the analysis, finding that they are far more sensitive to status threats than average or low-SDO individuals.

SOCIAL DOMINANCE AND STATUS

SDO is a personality variable that measures individuals' preference for inequality among social groups. More to the point, it measures one's comfort level with hierarchy, and the extent to which one believes or

---

[66] Vaughn 1987. See also Guzzini 2013, 525.

desires that their own group "dominate and be superior to outgroups."[67] High-SDO individuals tend to see other people in terms of their group membership (leading to greater tendencies to stereotype), and also see those group boundaries as clear, obvious, and legitimate.[68] A wide body of literature has found stable difference between genders (men tend to exhibit higher SDO than women), and this difference has even been cited as the basis for the other well-known differences between the sexes in political attitudes.[69]

Fundamentally, SDO captures beliefs about power, dominance, and inequality. It can thus be aptly described as a coherent set of ideological beliefs. And as social psychologists have demonstrated, ideology can be understood as "motivated social cognition" in which ideologies predict a host of motivated thoughts and behaviors, and are themselves shaped by basic motivational drives, such as uncertainty reduction and threat management.[70] Therefore, individuals who differ in abstract, ideological beliefs will also differ on other dimensions, such as sensitivity to emotions and other stimuli.[71] One of these dimensions is in their response to threats. While related concepts such as right-wing authoritarianism predict passive deference to authority figures, SDO predicts more active responses. As colorfully put by Altemeyer, high-SDO individuals "see the world as *dog eat dog* and—compared with most people—are determined to do the eating."[72]

Because SDO is, at its heart, about individuals' feelings and beliefs concerning hierarchy and domination, much of the work on this subject has focused on status. High-SDO individuals are more likely to associate status with competence, for example, and more likely to view dominance hierarchies favorably even when they are illegitimate.[73] Status threats are also important here, since they exacerbate SDO's influence on behaviors toward others (particularly out-groups). For example, high-SDO individuals offered less help to out-group members than did low-SDO individuals, and this pattern was starker when group-status was under threat.[74] Relatedly,

---

[67] Pratto et al. 1994, 742.
[68] Haslam and Levy 2006; Tausch and Hewstone 2010.
[69] Sidanius, Pratto, and Bobo 1994; Pratto, Stallworth, and Sidanius 1997.
[70] Jost and Amodio 2012.
[71] Sherman et al. 2015.
[72] Altemeyer 1998, 75. See also Jost et al. 2003.
[73] Levin et al. 2002; Oldmeadow and Fiske 2007.
[74] Halabi, Dovidio, and Nadler 2008.

threats to group status "activate" preferences for inequality, though just in high-status individuals.[75]

This brief overview of SDO, in concert with the earlier discussions of status threats and escalation, allows us to generate some preliminary hypotheses to guide the analysis. Because SDO is based on a belief in the importance and legitimacy of status hierarchies as well as the strong desire to be dominant, those who endorse social dominance beliefs—our "high-SDO" subjects—are likely to be affected by the *status threat* manipulation to a much greater extent than low-SDO subjects. Put simply, the effects of *status threat* on escalation will be greater for high-SDO subjects (compared to low SDO).

HIERARCHY, STATUS, AND ESCALATION

Investigating this directly, however, requires some care. Because escalation in study 1 is itself based on differences between treatment conditions, this requires us to include a three-way interaction (*status threat* × SDO × *sunk costs*) as well as all lower-order interactions. The results of this analysis are displayed in online appendix materials. This table displays a clear pattern in which SDO increases the impact of the *status threat* treatment on escalation (the three-way interaction), as compared to *neutral*, *status gain*, and both conditions combined (though only the latter two are strongly statistically significant). But even though two of the terms are dummy variables, interpretation is never straightforward for models with this many interactions.

Figure 3.6 plots the marginal effects of SDO on escalation by *sunk costs* (color) and *status* (panel) conditions. The left panel shows the effects of SDO on escalation for the *control* and *sunk costs* conditions. Here, it's clear that regardless of the sunk costs manipulation, SDO—preference for hierarchy and dominance—had no effect on investment in the experimental scenario. The right panel, however, shows how that changes once subjects are exposed to the *status threat* condition. Here, increased SDO is strongly associated with higher escalation (escalation is the difference between the two lines, or in effect, the difference between investment in the *control* and *sunk costs* conditions).

How do my results compare to other, comparable studies? One comprehensive cross-cultural study found that the mean SDO among samples from Canada, Taiwan, Israel, and China was 2.77 ($SD = 0.87$).[76] I observed

---

[75] Morrison and Ybarra 2008; Morrison, Fast, and Ybarra 2009.
[76] See Pratto et al. 2000.

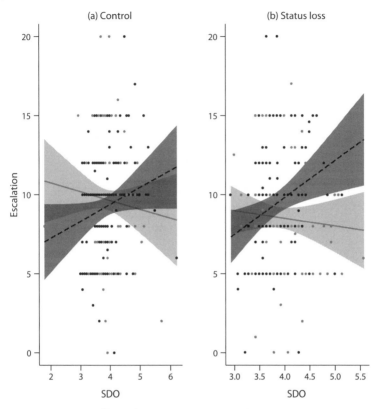

Figure 3.6: **Study 1: Effect of SDO on Escalation, by Status Condition** *Control* condition is in light gray, while *sunk costs* is in dark gray (- - -). Points indicate partial residuals, and bands depict 95 percent confidence intervals. Plot created in **R** with `visreg`.

higher SDO scores in my sample ($M = 3.9$, $SD = 0.49$), though this seems to be consistent with higher SDO scores among MTurk workers.[77] If we simply estimate the effects of the *status threat* treatment on subjects who were +2SD from the mean, we find when treated with the *status threat* manipulation, high-SDO subjects escalated 20 percent more than low-SDO subjects; when *not* exposed to the *status threat* treatment, however, high- and low-SDO subjects exhibited nearly identical patterns of investment.

What does this tell us about status concerns in international politics? First, we should consider the sample used here: an online MTurk panel that

[77] Kteily, Ho, and Sidanius 2012.

is overwhelmingly better educated and older than most student samples as well as one that exhibited higher levels of SDO than traditional off-line samples. In some ways that we can measure, this MTurk sample differed in important ways. For example, political elites tend to be older than the mean age in this sample, and the gender distribution in political circles is likely to be less well balanced than this sample. These demographic differences, however, can be controlled for statistically. There are surely other differences as well, though we must keep in mind that only differences that are *theoretically* relevant should be considered (so, for example, it wouldn't matter that leaders are taller than the average citizen unless one has a theory of how height interacts with either status threats or sunk costs).

There is some consensus that leaders are likely to be higher in SDO, and this prior knowledge allows us to use a convenience sample of MTurk workers while focusing in on the effects among a subgroup that is similar to leaders along a dimension that matters for our theory. Here that theory predicts that the dimensions on which leaders are likely to be more extreme is precisely the one that is likely to exacerbate the effect of the *status threat* treatment. To examine this, I randomly assigned differing levels of status concerns using an autobiographical memory task that is, compared to the force of status concerns in the real world, rather weak. Unsurprisingly, among many of the subjects, the *status threat* treatment did increase escalation, but only marginally so. Yet, in the group that was most similar to leaders, the high-SDO subjects, *status threat* had a much greater effect, increasing escalation by a substantial amount.

Contextual Moderators of Status Concerns: Power

Where study 1 focused on the dispositional roots of status concerns, study 2 investigates the relationship between status and power. Both studies use the same *status threat* treatment, but in many other ways, the second study improves on and complements the first. Study 1 used a standard escalation of commitment task that centered on a hypothetical business reinvestment decision. In contrast, study 2 introduces a new *behavioral* measure of escalation in a simulated wargame that is framed around a narrative of war and peace. Study 2 was conducted in a lab, greatly increasing our experimental control, and subjects' decisions had real economic consequences. Finally, in study 1, I used an online sample of MTurk workers and focused on those who were similar to leaders on the critical dimensions of SDO. In study 2, I use a unique sample of political and military leaders drawn from the SEF program at the Harvard Kennedy School. And in order to leverage this sample as much as possible, I compare them with a group of "control" subjects from the general population, matched on demographic attributes to the leaders.

POWER IN POLITICAL DECISION MAKING

A close reading of the literature on status and conflict suggests that the effects of status are almost always conditioned in some way on power. In status inconsistency theory, it is the discrepancy between power, and status that is associated with the initiation of conflict. In power transition theory, it is a status hierarchy that no longer coincides with the balance of material capabilities that is most strongly associated with conflict. In Wohlforth's work, it is, conversely, the *balance* of material capabilities that leads to uncertainty about the status hierarchy, which conflict helps to resolve.[78] This suggest both a general agreement that power matters *somehow* in moderating the impact of status in world politics, but also considerable uncertainty about the relationship between status, power, and conflict.

Of course, actually examining the moderating impact of power requires some additional conceptual work. IR work implicates "power," but empirically is only able to measure hypothesized determinants of power (for example, coarse proxies such as COW's Composite Index of National Capability [CINC] score).[79] In fact, despite its centrality to theories of politics, there is little agreement about the conceptualization or measurement of power. One oft-used conceptualization relies on the notion of "power as influence."[80] In this sense, power is neither solely material nor social, but both. It is the "ability of actors to secure the desired outcomes or prevent the occurrence of undesired ones."[81]

This conceptualization suggests possible ways of operationalizing power in the lab. In dyadic, or *k*-adic interactions, the relative levels of "power" can be incorporated into the structure of the experiment, such as by changing the odds of winning a showdown with another player.[82] In these cases, power is operationalized at the individual level, but we are

[78] Wohlforth 2009.
[79] Singer 1988.
[80] Baldwin 1979.
[81] Maoz 1989, 240.
[82] As in Renshon, Lee, and Tingley 2016.

still relying on a hypothesized connection between actual power (odds of winning) and *perceived* power (how players interpret those odds). This implies that we can play to the strengths of experimental methodology by focusing on the way that actual material power affects decision making: through the instantiation of low- and high-power "mind-sets" that, in turn, affect judgment and behavior. The status-based theories of conflict listed above, which also implicate material capabilities and involve psychological mechanisms, implicitly assume that those capabilities—whether it is a balance, imbalance, or declining or rising power—are assessed and filtered through leaders' perceptions. In fact, this dovetails with much of the more subtle realist works in IR, which emphasize subjective assessments of power and threat over the objective balance of capabilities.[83]

So what are the consequences of power mind-sets for judgment and decision making? Despite an explosion of studies on this question, social psychological research does not suggest a clear answer. In some cases, power can have salutary effects, such as by facilitating goal-directed behavior.[84] Yet some of its effects are harder to pigeonhole as beneficial or pernicious, and are simply context dependent. For example, the powerful tend to be less influenced by situational factors (such as situational cues) and less affected by loss aversion.[85]

But negative effects abound as well. Power can lead to overconfident decisions and economic losses as well as impel subjects to discount advice, leading to an overall decrease in accuracy compared to their less powerful peers.[86] It has destructive implications for social relations, as it is associated with the objectification of others and prejudice toward out-groups.[87] Finally, it can exacerbate other common decision biases—for instance, by increasing illusory control over events and outcomes.[88]

This study centers on the escalation of commitment, but the evidence for this class of decisions is also unclear. Power increases risk taking, but this tendency is moderated by an individual's power motivation (how much they care about increasing power).[89] In fact, high scores on the power motivation scale predict more *conservative* decisions rather than

---

[83] For example, Wohlforth 1993.
[84] Magee, Galinsky, and Gruenfeld 2007.
[85] Galinsky et al. 2008; Inesi 2010.
[86] Fast et al. 2011; See et al. 2011.
[87] Gruenfeld et al. 2008; Guinote, Willis, and Martellotta 2010.
[88] Fast et al. 2009.
[89] Anderson and Galinsky 2006; Maner et al. 2007.

riskier ones. These findings are buttressed by research in neurobiology showing that powerful individuals who have relatively high levels of basal testosterone (T), generally associated with the pursuit of status and power, were more conservative than their high-T, low-power counterparts.[90] In other words, there is no clear prediction as to how power should affect escalation tendencies in the present study.

Power on the individual level can be operationalized in a variety of ways. In some cases, power was manipulated directly through priming (in much the same way that status is in this book).[91] In others, power was conceptualized and measured as a stable individual difference measure (for example, the "sense of power" scale described by Anderson and Galinsky).[92] Some works use both approaches in combination to triangulate the effects of power.[93]

We built on these approaches by constructing two measures—one objective, and one subjective. This follows from the observation that power is composed both of individuals' actual authority (their ability to control outcomes and other actors) and their own sense of power, and these dimensions of power require separate measurement.[94] In IR, measurement issues force us to focus almost exclusively on the former aspect, measured indirectly and somewhat crudely as state capacity, despite our awareness that the relationship between actors' "material capacity" and their ability to control outcomes (let alone their "sense of power") is neither monotonic nor linear.[95]

To capture this distinction, and as part of a long-term project on leadership and decision making, our research team constructed two additional measures—again, one objective, and one subjective.[96] Previewing later results, I found that both objective measures (that serve as a stand-in for "capacity") and more subjective measures (that more closely align with individuals' feelings of possessing power and authority) are closely correlated in this study, and that both have similar effects. This operationalization of power will be novel for most quantitative IR scholars, but focusing on the perception and feeling of power as experienced by individual leaders has a

[90] Ronay and Von Hippel 2010.
[91] Guinote, Willis, and Martellotta 2010.
[92] Smith, Wigboldus, and Dijksterhuis 2008; Anderson and Galinsky 2006.
[93] For example, Fast et al. 2011.
[94] Anderson, John, and Keltner 2012.
[95] For more on this, see Maoz 1989, 247.
[96] These scales are discussed in more detail in Sherman et al. 2012, 2016.

long tradition in both theoretical and empirical work.[97] One of the defining statements of neoclassical realism argued that "foreign policy choices are made by actual political leaders and elites, and so it is their perception of relative power that matters, not simply relative quantities of physical resources or forces in being."[98]

LEADERSHIP AND POWER MEASURES

The first measure of power (*leadership group*) was binary, and indicated whether the subject was part of the SEF course at Harvard Kennedy School or a matched control. Even though there are reasons to believe that members of the SEF cohort are typical of the "elite leaders" of IR theory, not every subject will be a future general or cabinet secretary. In other words, some of the "control" subjects may in fact be leaders in real life (and less likely, vice versa). This implies that we should account for variation within—and not just between—the two different groups. To address this, we constructed both objective and subjective measures.[99] This dichotomy follows from the observation that power is composed of two elements— individuals' actual authority, and their own sense of power—which are not always in accord with one another (though they were highly correlated in this sample).[100]

The first—the *objective authority scale*—was a composite of questions measuring how many people were subordinate to (or managed by) the subject over the course of their career. Table 3.2 depicts a powerful group of political and military leaders, combined with a control group that is significantly less powerful than the leaders. The second—the *subjective power position scale*—was designed to capture the subjects' subjective evaluation of how powerful they are in their daily lives.[101]

One concern would be a lack of within-group variation, leading us to simply remeasure our rougher, group-based measure. Figure 3.7 shows the distributions of both scales by membership in the leadership group. They demonstrate two important patterns. First, as one would expect, leaders generally score higher on both scales. Importantly, however, the

---

[97] On the perception of power in IR theory, see Morgenthau 1948. For an example from empirical IR, on declining power *as experienced* by Mikhail Gorbachev during the late 1980s, see Brooks and Wohlforth 2006.

[98] Rose 1998, 147.

[99] For more on our measure of power, see Sherman et al. 2012, 2015, 2016.

[100] Anderson, John, and Keltner 2012.

[101] More information on the scales is contained in the online appendix.

TABLE 3.2
Summary Statistics for Objective Leadership Scale All numbers are means calculated from raw scores, without transformations.

	Leaders	Controls
How many people do you manage?	48.6	7.2
How many people are subordinate to you?	344.2	9.2
What is the maximum number of people that you have managed?	175.1	69.2
What is the maximum number of people that have been subordinate to you?	566.4	65.3

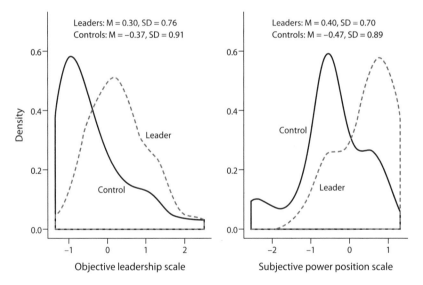

Figure 3.7: **Power Measures by Leadership Group Membership.**

distributions do overlap significantly, capturing the low-power members of the leadership group (some of them may in fact have jobs that resemble midlevel bureaucrats more than they do elite decision makers) as well as the high-power members of the control group.

HYPOTHESES

Earlier, I provided several reasons to expect that status threats would have a direct effect on escalation, increasing the tendency to throw good money after bad. A reading of the literature on SDO furnished relatively clear expectations on how preference for hierarchy might moderate that main effect. Unfortunately, the expectations regarding the moderating effect of power are not quite as clear. Anderson and Galinsky, for example, find that power seems to induce optimism and risk seeking in most individuals.[102] Yet in our study, power did not operate in a vacuum but rather in conjunction with the prospect of gaining or losing status. Because of this, the work of Inesi seems more relevant.[103] She found that powerful individuals were less sensitive to losses than their low-power counterparts. This suggests that power may provide a "buffer" for powerful individuals, who are less likely to be affected by the experimental status manipulation. This is corroborated by other work, which has found converging evidence that power can protect individuals from the "press of the situation." Powerful individuals are, for example, less likely to allow outside influences to change their stated belief, while less powerful subjects exhibited impaired "executive functioning" in memory, inhibition, and planning tasks.[104]

THE MODERATING INFLUENCE OF LEADERSHIP AND POWER

While there were no statistically significant main effects of the status threats on escalation in study z, the manipulation checks make it clear that the treatment did impact subjects' beliefs and feelings. Next, I analyze escalation in more detail by investigating the moderating effect of power. Because the nature of this work deals with political decision making, and even more specifically with high-level decisions related to war and peace, one natural line of inquiry is how our high-power subjects (the "leadership" sample) fared in the task compared to control subjects. Or more generally, we might ask, Does power help or hurt decision making?

I estimated several regression models to shed light on how leadership affected the tendency to escalate in the primary decision task. These models include the primary manipulation (*status threat*), and a measure of power plus the interaction term. In addition to the three observed measures of

---

[102] Anderson and Galinsky 2006.
[103] Inesi 2010.
[104] Galinsky et al. 2008; Smith et al. 2008.

power—*leadership group, objective authority*, and *subjective power position*—
I modeled power as a latent variable using polychoric factor analysis
(only one factor was produced).[105] All visualizations are based on linear
regressions, and those shown in the appendix also include controls for
state-trait anxiety, Positive and Negative Affect Schedule, gender, age, and
education, and whether or not the participants served in the military.[106]
Though the dependent variable is not normally distributed, alternative
specifications using generalized linear models yielded identical results (see
tables in appendix).

Whether power is conceptualized as membership in the "leader" sample,
authority at one's job (whether measured objectively or subjectively), or
even an underlying factor, the interaction term is significant (moderately
so for the rougher, group-based measure, and highly so for the latter three,
more fine-grained measures of power). This suggests strongly that the effect
of status concerns on escalation depended on individuals' level of power.
Substantive effects can nevertheless be difficult to determine in regression
tables, especially when considering interaction terms and conditional main
effects. To more clearly illustrate this pattern, the moderating effect of
leadership is plotted in figure 3.8.

Figure 3.8 plots first differences using CLARIFY: differences between
the expected value of an outcome measure (escalation) at two different

---

[105] All models control for the number of rounds played in order to rule out the alternative
explanation that subjects simply played longer because they enjoyed playing the game.
The advantage of this method is in keeping all observations but statistically modeling the
length of playing time, while the potential concern is that it may result in a form of
posttreatment bias. These worries, however, are somewhat assuaged by regressing the
treatment on the number of rounds played. The results were not significant under any
specification, ruling out the possibility that part of the treatment's effect "flowed through"
the number of rounds played. The distribution of rounds played was highly skewed, with
> 95 percent of the observations between zero and twenty-one, and several outliers who
played as many as sixty-three rounds. An appendix presents results in which those few outliers
are dropped and the number of rounds played is no longer controlled for statistically. The
substantive interpretation of the results does not change, but this modification slightly affects
the levels of statistical significance for some covariates, particularly for the coarser measure of
power (leadership group).

[106] On the anxiety scale, see Marteau and Bekker 1992. On the Positive and Negative Affect
Schedule, see Watson, Clark, and Tellegen 1988. As in study 1, including controls does not
alter the results, though models without controls can be found in the online appendix. There
were too few women in the sample (twelve in the control sample, and eighteen in the leader
sample) to draw strong conclusions about any gender effects, but gender was controlled for in
all models. Results remain the same in terms of direction and statistical significance if confined
to males only.

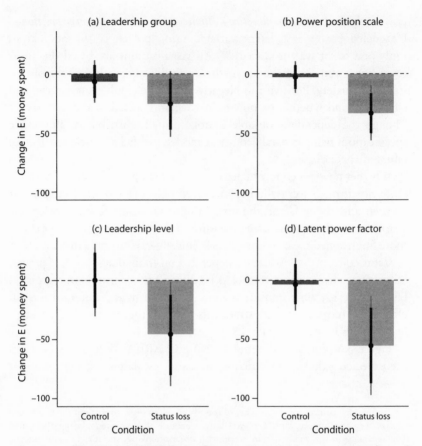

Figure 3.8: **The Moderating Effects of Power** Plotted values represent—for each condition—the change in expected value of outcome measure (money spent) switching from control to leader, mean to max values on subjective power position scale, objective authority scale, and latent power factor. Wider, black lines are 95 percent confidence intervals while thinner, grey lines are 99 percent confidence intervals.

levels of an independent variable (power).[107] In this case, figure 3.8(a) shows the expected change in escalation if we switch from *leader* = 0 to *leader* = 1, or more plainly, from a subject recruited from the general Cambridge/Boston population to an SEF leader. Figures 3.8(b), (c), and (d) show the expected change in escalation if we switch from the mean value on

[107] Tomas, Wittenberg, and King 2003.

the *subjective power position, objective authority,* or *latent power factor* scales to a high value.

This allows us to ask, How did leadership moderate the effect of status concerns on escalation? In fact, power—no matter how it was measured—greatly aids decision making by buffering subjects against the pernicious effects of status threats. These plots were produced by modeling the difference between outcomes—at two different levels of the independent variable—in the *control* condition and then comparing it to the difference between the expected outcomes under the *status threat* condition. This is thus a relatively easy way of visualizing differences in differences. By comparing the first differences for the *control* and *status threat* conditions, we get a visual representation of how power and leadership moderate the worst effects of the status threat treatment.

As figure 3.8 shows, power—no matter how one conceptualizes or measures it—has no detectable effect in the *control* condition. In other words, power doesn't seem to produce the overconfidence found by some other recent works, nor does it improve decision making when acting "on its own" (there are slight differences in means, but none are statistically significant).

Significant differences emerge in the *status threat* condition, however, Where power and leadership had no discernible effect under the control condition, once status is threatened, power is strongly associated with better outcomes, particularly less escalation of commitment to what is clearly a failing policy. Powerful subjects, whether measured by *leadership group,* (subjective or objective) authority at work, or as a latent factor, invested significantly less money in the Island Game. Or in other words, once status is threatened, power seems to buffer individuals against the deleterious effects of the social threat.

While figure 3.8 is helpful in depicting the moderating effects of power, it cannot disentangle two competing explanations. Either

1. low power is increasing the effect of the status threat,
2. or the status threat is triggering some psychological mechanism for high-power individuals that leads to less escalation than expected.

In other words, did high power lead to below-average amounts of escalation (and better outcomes than even those not faced with the status threat), or did it merely prevent the "extra" amount of escalation that would be caused by the status threat if individuals were low in power? Figure 3.9 sub-divides groups (within each experimental condition) based

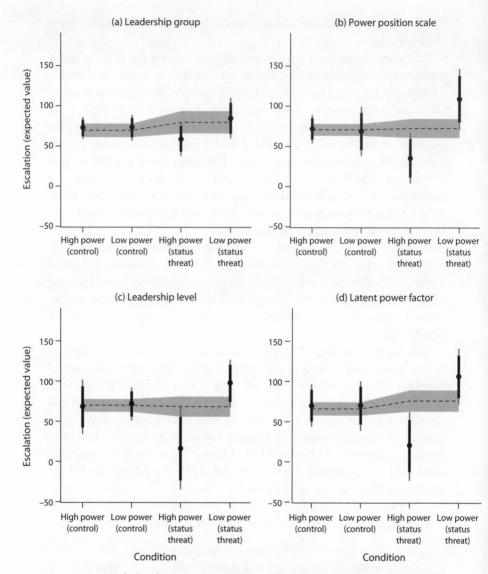

Figure 3.9: **Escalation by Status Condition and Power** Plotted values represent—for each condition—the expected amount of escalation in each condition at high (*max*) and low (*min*) levels of power. As before, (a), (b), (c), and (d) represent different ways of measuring power. Dotted lines and shaded area represent the averaged amount of escalation expected for each condition plus 95 percent confidence intervals. For point estimates, wider, black lines are 95 percent confidence intervals while thinner, gray lines are 99 percent confidence intervals.

on levels of power to look more closely at its moderating effects. We are also controlling for as many individual-level characteristics as we can in order to preempt the concern that one of those characteristics covaries with high/low power.

For each condition, estimates are presented for high (*max*) and low (*min*) levels of power. The dotted horizontal line, along with the shaded 95 percent confidence band, represents the average amount of escalation for the *control* and *status threat* conditions, respectively. Each point estimate (with wider, black vertical lines representing 95 percent confidence intervals and thinner, gray lines indicating 99 percent confidence intervals) represents the change, within the appropriate treatment condition, of switching from average amounts of power to high or low power.

As is evident, in all four plots, escalation—for both high- and low-power individuals—in the *control* condition is virtually indistinguishable from the average. It is in the estimates for the *status threat* condition that new patterns become visible. Focusing on figure 3.9(a), we can see that low-power subjects (here that would mean subjects from the general population) in the *status threat* condition escalate a bit more than average, but not significantly so. Similarly, high-power subjects (the political and military leaders) in the *status threat* condition escalate a bit less than average, but the estimates still overlap a bit using 95 percent intervals. This fits with earlier results and common sense, all of which suggests that there is likely to be a fair amount of variation even within the "leader group" such that group membership might be a noisy way of measuring power.

For more nuanced analyses, we turn to the plots in figure 3.9(b), (c), and (d), which use the power scales described earlier. Here, patterns for the *control* condition are the same: just about average, irrespective of power "condition." But a new pattern emerges when looking at the *status threat* conditions. Here we can see some (tentative) evidence that the moderating effect of power is not working by inoculating subjects against the worst effects of status threats or increasing the effect of the status threat for low-power individuals but rather by doing both simultaneously.[108] Put simply, within the *status threat* condition, low power increases the tendency to escalate commitment while high power decreases that same tendency. High power, under these circumstances, emerges as a key element of high-quality decision making.

---

[108] Overinterpretation of barely overlapping confidence intervals is not advisable as they do not necessarily imply that the estimates are not significantly different.

DISCUSSION

The broad conclusion of both of these studies is that we can identify a real causal relationship in which status concerns, randomly assigned, led to a greater escalation of commitment—an outcome with obvious political ramifications. This occurred in the lab and in a survey experiment, among the general population as well as elite political and military leaders, when the task was hypothetical and when "good" decision making was incentivized. This fits neatly with extant work on status—as well as the theory advanced by this book—in that it serves as an empirical microfoundation for theories of status in IR.

The second implication of these findings relates to whether the effects of status concerns we observe in the real world of IR are likely to be stronger or weaker than the results described here. In the experiments described, status concerns were *unrelated* to the decision process or outcomes. That is, status was not engaged by either of the experimental games nor could the "pursuit of status" be a plausible explanation for subjects' behavior. It was because of this design that we were able to isolate the effects of status, but neither of these conditions are likely to hold in international politics. Political leaders will often face situations where the status concerns are situationally relevant (and thus stronger than the treatments I used) and public, and in which their behavior has the potential to gain or salvage status that is both intrinsically valuable (as it is in the lab) and instrumentally useful (as it is not in these studies). This suggests that any effects of "pure" status concerns that I found are likely to be a dramatic underestimate of their true effect in politics.

The last broad implication of these two studies is that the causal effect of status on the escalation of commitment can be moderated by both situational and dispositional factors: on the one hand, that effect can be attenuated by power, which serves to buffer or insulate subjects against the threat of status loss. On the other, subjects for whom dominance and hierarchy were particularly important—high-SDO subjects—were *most* susceptible to the effects of status threats.

There are two complementary implications of these findings. Given the finding that high power buffers subjects against the worst effects of status threats, it's natural to ask if the implication of this is that political elites (since they are "high power") would be shielded from the threat of status loss along with its attendant effects on judgment and decision making. This would contradict previous findings and, I believe, be a misinterpretation.

Because power is relative, not all leaders in all situations will be in a high-power mind-set that would buffer them against status threats. In fact, a brief glance at the IR literature suggests many occasions in which leaders have become convinced—sometimes correctly, and at other times not—that they led a state in decline.[109] My finding simply suggests that actors in a low-power mindset might be particularly vulnerable to status threats.

This leads naturally to the second implication, concerning both SDO and power, which is that we often observe situations in which states and leaders have heterogeneous responses to status threats (whether they are the kind envisioned by status inconsistency theory, power transition theory, or something else). More broadly, this fits in with the advice of Hatemi and McDermott to take heed that "not everyone reacts to the same stimulus the same way."[110] Put simply, there are many cases where conflict initiation (as an example) is predicted, but not observed. This chapter suggests that leaders' mind-sets and ideologies might provide an important clue as to why we see such wide variation in responses to similar situations. Why, for example, was Kaiser Wilhelm so focused on status threats during the Weltpolitik era when Germany's objective situation, both in terms of status and material capabilities, hardly warranted such concern? Power concerns as well as a fixation on issues of dominance and hierarchy might provide one clue to this and other historical puzzles (explored in more detail in chapter 6).

Simply referring to "states and leaders" as the above section does elides some of the trickier questions regarding levels of analysis. I manipulated status concerns at the individual level in order to test their effects, inherently social and peer referent in nature, on individual behavior. For much of the work on status in IR whose center of gravity lies between the individual and the group, this result provides an important empirical foundation. For the first time, we can cleanly identify a causal relationship between status concerns, experimentally manipulated, and outcomes of interest to scholars of international conflict.

Of course, one key question, posed by a recent review article, is, "Status in the eyes of whom?"[111] Or in other words, who is the reference group? Earlier works noted that a state's position in a hierarchy was

---

[109] See, for example, Levy 1987; McKeown 1991.
[110] Hatemi and McDermott 2012, 21.
[111] Dafoe, Renshon, and Huth 2014, 375.

important, but stopped short of specifying *which* hierarchy we should examine. Instead, states were all placed in a de facto global hierarchy.[112] And whether one believes the relevant actors to be states or leaders, it seems clear that reference groups are a good deal more targeted and purposeful than previously suggested. Or as Frank put it, status is local.[113] Experimental setups such as this one allow us to elicit beliefs about status within the relevant peer group, but building on this will require more explicit theories about how actors define their reference groups. This is not a trivial problem, and it has in no way been "solved" by the psychological literatures that IR scholars have drawn from. In later chapters, I develop some preliminary intuitions about how states select reference groups.

SUMMARY

Many current research programs in IR invoke status as a key factor in theories of IR and foreign policy. Yet they have been subject to significant limitations inherent in the methods used, and thus are unable to provide evidence of a causal association or even precise measurement of status itself. More generally, our intuition that status matters *somehow* has not been matched by the construction of explicit theories of status or empirical work identifying the precise causal mechanisms through which status concerns operate. I argued that this impasse could be resolved through a focus on the "microfoundations" of status, which I see as combining precise measurement of status itself alongside the identification and testing of specific hypotheses and causal relationships.

I reported the results of two experiments in which status concerns were randomly assigned prior to an "escalation of commitment" task. In the second study, I used a unique sample of political and military leaders as well as a group of demographically matched control subjects from the general population. These subjects are in many ways among the most plausible ones yet used in laboratory political decision-making experiments. Importantly, they are also closer to the decision makers envisioned by IR theories on the critical dimension of power. This provided valuable inferential leverage in investigating the role of power in moderating status threats.

---

[112] See, for example, Singer and Small 1966.
[113] Frank 1985.

Moreover, they offered an important empirical benefit: had I used only the "control" subjects, this would have led to an overestimate of the causal effect of status concerns. I found evidence that power—no matter how it is measured—provides a strong buffer against the otherwise-deleterious effects of status threats, but that high-SDO subjects were particularly vulnerable to those same status threats.

4

A Network Approach to Status

The preceding chapter demonstrated some of the advantages of an experimental approach to the study of status in IR. I was able to precisely measure and manipulate status concerns in a way that would not be possible using alternative research designs.[1] Moreover, the random assignment of status concerns provided leverage in estimating a *causal* effect of status concerns. More broadly, the experiments described helped to provide evidence on a fundamental assumption of status dissatisfaction theory (status concerns → higher value for status) while shedding light on potential mechanisms (e.g., escalation of commitment) by which those same status concerns might be linked to international conflict.

No method is perfect, however, and experiments have their trade-offs as well. Though many of the concerns about external validity levied against experiments in IR are either overblown or misguided, some real issues remain. Among the most important thing missing from experimental approaches—even those in this book—is a *direct* connection to outcomes in the realm of international politics. We can extrapolate, of course, but this alone is a poor substitute when the ultimate goal is to explain international conflict.

Directly addressing the role of status in international conflict requires wading into the messy world of observational data, whether quantitative (in this chapter and the one that follows) or qualitative (in the last two substantive chapters). Doing so provides significant benefits in that we are able to speak directly to the concept of interest, but requires us to tackle thorny issues of measurement. This issue is even more pressing when the concept of interest is perceptual, precluding us from, for example, simply counting the number of nuclear weapons a state possesses or the distance between capital cities.

---

[1] Parts of this chapter and the next draw on work published as Renshon 2016.

This chapter describes my method for measuring status and begins by thinking through the requirements of such a measure, referring back to the core theoretical aspects of status described in chapter 2. And while I use a conventional data source—the exchange of diplomats between sovereign nations—I present a series of innovations designed to tie the measurement and analysis more closely to the theoretical concept of interest. I first correct a long-standing shortcoming related to the diplomatic exchange data set: there is little evidence that diplomatic exchange is in any way related to leaders' actual beliefs about status. Despite the common use of these data to measure international status, we have been on relatively shaky ground thus far. To address this, I turn to historical sources, and show that the sending and receiving of diplomats has always been suffused with notions of prestige, and considerations of status are high among the list of factors considered by elite decision makers who allocate diplomatic resources. Next, I use two alternative data sources—official diplomatic visits by the US president and mentions by the president / secretary of states in the *New York Times*—to cross-validate the measures of status generated by the diplomatic data.

In the next section, I demonstrate how we can use social network analysis to address three significant problems in the measurement of status. First, all countries are equal: representation from smaller states "counts" as much as representation from more powerful ones. I use PageRank network centrality measures to account for the fact that diplomats sent by more important states confer more status to host countries than those from low-ranking ones. This approach closes what had until now been a vast disconnect in the literature between our measurement of status and its theoretical conceptualization.[2]

An even bigger disconnect exists with regard to the "relative" nature of status. Of course, we are all taught that status is relative, but relative to whom? Virtually every other approach to status in IR has assumed that there is one international hierarchy, composed of all states in the system. In this unlikely world, Bolivia is embroiled in status competition against the Soviet Union while the United States expends resources to fight off challenges from Bermuda. I use the novel method of community detection to empirically derive the "status communities" into which states sort themselves. The advantage of such an approach is that it uses actual patterns of real-world interactions to inductively derive communities composed of

[2] Highlighted by Ward 2014.

peer competitors rather than relying on arbitrary groupings (for example, those based on geography) that might not correspond to the groupings that leaders see as most significant. In doing so, I address the third problem with status measurements thus far: all levels of diplomatic representation are counted equally. Despite fine-grained data on the level of diplomatic representation, most previous efforts have collapsed these into binary form. I show how we can use these highly relevant data to weight diplomatic connections and derive more sensible status communities.

Finally, the chapter provides insight into the sources of status in world politics. First, I establish that status is not the mere reflection of military capabilities. It is instead multifaceted, and states may take advantage of numerous "paths to prestige." For example, though "good citizenship" (in the form of international governmental organizations [IGO] memberships) in the international community increases states' status ranking, so too do behaviors associated with "bad actors," such as nuclear proliferation and the number of economic sanctions in effect. Moreover, there are aspects of status that are largely out of any given country's control; the number of years since state formation is a robust predictor of status ranking, suggesting that states that appear early are best able to ensure a high place in their community's status hierarchy.

STATUS BY THE NUMBERS

In thinking about how to operationalize status for a large-N analysis, the first step is to consider what we know and what we don't know about status as well as some basic requirements for statistical analysis. The basic definition of status requires that we find a measure that is *social*. Because status is premised on the aggregated beliefs of a particular group, an ideal measure would capture this social aspect of status. Additionally, our current understanding of beliefs is that they are often "sticky"; that is, once set, they are difficult to shift even in the presence of disconfirming information.[3] In other words, the status measure we utilize should be responsive to changes in circumstances, but should not be overly sensitive to daily or weekly events, since beliefs are unlikely to be updated that quickly. It would be a poor indicator that continued to reflect status hierarchies of decades

---

[3] See, for example, Deutsch and Merritt 1965; Anderson, Lepper, and Ross 1980; Carretta and Moreland 1982; Anderson 1983.

ago, but so too one that moved in accordance with the weekly vagaries of international politics. Put another way, it should be difficult to drastically change one's position in a status hierarchy, yet not so difficult that such events don't occur with at least some regularity in the system.

There are also a number of requirements that are more practical in nature. Ideally, the measure would be relatively inclusive. Certain behaviors or possessions undeniably confer status, but may not be feasible for many states. An example of this is the possession of aircraft carriers, which has been used as an example of a "prestige symbol."[4] On its face, this seems perfectly reasonable, since "for a nation that has always felt profoundly insecure, nothing makes more sense than a spanking new aircraft carrier as a symbol that it has made it."[5] Such a measure is profoundly limited, though; few countries can afford the "luxury" of an aircraft carrier. Even China has only recently and at great cost procured its first carrier (a "vintage" Soviet model bought by a private Chinese citizen from Ukraine).[6]

Moreover, this and other similar examples point toward a larger problem: the conflation of status *markers* and evidence of status *seeking*. Conditional on some level of economic capacity, any state may purchase an aircraft carrier, but—even if we set aside motives related to security entirely—this is just as likely to represent a behavior designed to gain status rather than a marker of its possession. The purchase of conventional arms falls prey to the same problem.[7] These operationalizations may serve as useful behavioral measures of how much a given group of actors care about status, but they come loaded with strict boundary conditions and powerful alternative explanations. It's difficult, without extensive historical analysis, to entirely discount the role of security motives. Moreover, it would be desirable to find a measure of status that is not bound to a particular geographic location, time period, or subset of states.

This leads to another requirement for our hypothetical measure: it should relate to an attribute that is a *temporally stable* marker for status. Some behaviors may only be associated with status during particular time periods. For instance, we would hardly use possession of colonies as an indicator of status in 2009, but such a measure would certainly make sense

---

[4] See, for example, Gilady 2002.
[5] Kristof 1993, 70.
[6] Holmes 2015.
[7] Eyre and Suchman 1996.

for 1900. Witness the comment of a French statesperson at the turn of the century: "To remain a great nation, or to become one, you must colonize."[8] Similarly, nuclear weapons or even space programs would constrain us to small subsets of time and subpopulations of states.[9] In the case of nuclear weapons, for example, there is a strong argument to be made that nuclear testing—once seen as legitimate and a symbol of great power status—is now perceived as dangerous and illegitimate (though I don't find much evidence that this is the case).[10]

Finally, because status is at its heart a social concept predicated on the aggregated judgments of many actors, we would want our status measure to reflect the judgment of the entire system. Status is not dyadic, and requires $N > 2$ in order to conform to our conceptualization of status from previous chapters. In other words, it is not enough that one state holds another in high esteem, or conversely that one state holds another in low regard. What is required is a measure that aggregates each actor's beliefs so that the end result is a ranking that can be said to reflect the community's judgment about where each actors "stands" in relation to all the other actors.

Status and the Beginning of Quantitative IR

How well have previous attempts fared in capturing international status? The first efforts began in the 1960s as part of the COW project. Singer and Small took advantage of the 1815 Regulation of Vienna, which divided diplomats into three categories: ambassadors, envoys, and chargé d'affaires.[11] In this original and influential coding scheme, ambassadors were counted as three "points": ministers, minister residents, or envoys as two points, and chargé d'affaires as one point. Scores were then standardized in order to compare across time periods.

This (relative) standardization provided leverage to compare across time periods and geographic regions. For Singer and Small, this also provided the best available measure of status, which they saw as a "rank or reputation attributed to an individual or a group by others in the same social system." Though it "may correlate with certain inherent and objective properties,

---

[8] Quoted in Joll and Martel 2007, 219.
[9] Nayar and Paul 2003, 54.
[10] Sagan 1996.
[11] Singer and Small 1966.

capabilities or skills," it need not.[12] Their discussion of the choice to use diplomats as an index of status is worth quoting in full:

> No matter how we look at it, the decision about the rank of a diplomatic mission must reflect—and, in a subtle fashion, combine—almost all the considerations affecting the sending nation's foreign policy as well as its relations with the host nation. In a sense, no multidimensional combined index could be expected to tap, in so effective a synthesis, the factors which blend into the sum total and rank of all the missions in a given capital. Further, even though the empirical trace is not always as clear and visible as one might desire, it is no more elusive and ambiguous than are many of the other phenomena that students of international relations must eventually, observe, measure and record. Moreover, it not only has the virtue of providing an indication of the importance that one nations assigns to another, but it is also easily susceptible to the combinatorial procedures by which we can ascertain the relative importance that *all* nations in the system attribute to any one of its members at a given time.[13]

Of course, despite their best efforts, there were difficulties with using both the rank and number of diplomatic missions hosted by a given country. Though they had a strong intuition that the rank of diplomats sent *should* matter, idiosyncrasies in the diplomatic process made that impossible to operationalize at times. For example, in the nineteenth century, only European major powers were "allowed" to send and receive ambassadors, injecting potential bias into an entire century's worth of data. Moreover, how were they to decide what counted as a state (rather than, for example, a protectorate) to begin with? Singer and Small decided on a two-pronged system, whereby actors were counted as states if their population exceeded five hundred thousand people and they met the "diplomatic recognition criteria."[14] For the years 1815–1920, this latter condition was satisfied as soon as an actor received diplomats from the "two most prestigious and active nations," France and Britain, which served as "legitimizers." Following that historical period, the COW team relied on historical consensus as well as a population requirement.

Several things are worth nothing at this point. First, it is hard to fully capture how influential this early effort was. For one, few quantitative

[12] Ibid., 238.
[13] Ibid., 241.
[14] Ibid., 245–46.

scholars of IR are aware that the entire basis of the COW data set—literally, which actors "count" as a state—is based on data on diplomatic representation gathered for this early project. Moreover, the procedure for measuring and inferring international status developed in this project was kept, virtually unchanged, for several decades. Second, this early effort was far ahead of its time in many ways. The authors noted, for example, that the status of the *sending* state should matter, so they applied an "iterative weighting" procedure such that each his nations' weighted score would be the sum of scores of all the sending nations for that year. In the end, however, the authors discarded the procedure as providing results too close to the more basic and less computationally intensive counting scheme. I would add that such a method suffers from the fundamental flaw of how to assign initial weights; that is, in 1816, there were no status scores from the previous year, so what values do we start with? This is discussed in more detail in the following section.

Singer and Small's method for measuring status was used largely as is for the next fifty years or so. Wallace is illustrative of this trend.[15] He simply counted the number of diplomatic missions in a given state in a given year and normalized that by year to account for changes in the number of states in the system. This pattern continued unabated for decades with some minor alterations, such as incorporating events data into the traditional measure that counted the number of diplomatic missions.[16]

One recent work has questioned this standard operating procedure, suggesting that more appropriate methods of quantitative analysis (such as social network analysis) be used to construct measures of diplomatic status.[17] In fact, such efforts had already been under way.[18] But, a serious drawback (for our purposes) is that both of these works conceptualize and measure status as centrality within the trade, alliance, and IGO networks rather than diplomatic networks. The logic behind this decision is that there are likely to be multiple dimensions of status.[19] It does not necessarily follow, however, that measures such as trade or alliance centrality would be *more* likely than diplomatic centrality to pick up on status relations; if anything, these other networks seem far more likely to

[15] Wallace 1971.

[16] On the continuation of the pattern, see Volgy and Mayhall 1995. On the use of events data, see Corbetta, Volgy, and Rhamey 2013.

[17] Ward 2014.

[18] For the most prominent and serious examples of this, see Maoz et al. 2007; Maoz 2010.

[19] Maoz et al. 2007.

be determined almost entirely by other considerations, such as security or economic concerns. I return to these questions in a later section when I use a combination of quantitative and archival data to cross-validate the diplomatic status measure.

Of course, not all attempts to measure status have been purely quantitative in nature. Content analysis would seem a possible candidate for this type of research question, yet it confronts a number of critical problems. Miller, for example, examines discourse within the United Nations to illustrate differences between colonized and noncolonized countries (the latter are hypothesized to fall victim to "postimperial ideologies" associated with a fixation on status issues).[20] While such a research design might be feasible for a study focused on a discrete time period or set of countries, it is unclear what type of language we might take as a *universal* sign of status concern. Different cultures and different time periods would likely have different ways of expressing status concerns. Or one might confront the opposite problem. One might easily imagine a situation in which status concerns were *so* important to the decision makers involved that they don't even need to mention it aloud because of the assumption that others will interpret their words through the same basic framework.[21]

In many cases, concern over relative status is measured via statements of political leaders. Two problems, though, make the credibility of such evidence difficult to assess.[22] First, the varying meanings of status, reputation, and honor throughout history (and across cultures) make the use of such quotations problematic; leaders may not mean the same thing that contemporary scholars do when they use language related to status and prestige. Further, leaders face strategic incentives to both provide rationales for their actions as well as marshal support from the public. This makes it difficult to evaluate whether stated reasons—even those provided in private to other leaders—reflect "true" beliefs. Of course, such objections are hardly novel, and scholars typically address them via detailed qualitative accounts and consideration of alternative explanations. The best of them utilize economic and military data alongside data on beliefs of the key actors.[23] Yet the resources required to do such work strongly suggests that this is not the best avenue for a cross-national investigation of status and conflict.

[20] Miller 2013.
[21] For this and other problems related to content analysis, see Larson 1988.
[22] See discussion in Dafoe, Renshon, and Huth 2014.
[23] Such as in Wohlforth 2009.

A NETWORK CENTRALITY APPROACH TO INTERNATIONAL STATUS

I follow the convention of using the diplomatic exchange data set to generate a measure of status. Though it is less familiar than other "standard" COW data sets, the diplomatic exchange data have seen increased use in IR research in recent years.[24] These data were originally compiled by Singer and Small as part of the COW project.[25] Data are available for the years 1817, 1824, 1827, 1832, 1836, 1840, every five years between 1844 and 1914, every five years between 1920 and 1940, and every five years between 1950 and 2005.[26]

The diplomatic exchange data—an example of which is provided in figure 4.1—include indicators for whether i sent diplomats to j and whether j sent diplomats to i in a given year. Codings are as follows:

0 = no evidence of diplomatic exchange
1 = chargé d'affaires
2 = minister
3 = ambassador
9 = other

Codings of "9" can indicate interest sections, interests served by another country, address (with no further information), and so on. Everything other than the actual raw data, however, represents a series of innovations designed to more closely align a cross-national measure of status with its conceptual foundations.

Because there are many possible ways to use diplomatic exchanges to generate status hierarchies, we might ask, Why is the *receipt* of diplomats more important for status than the overall number of links (or number of reciprocated exchanges)? This logic can be made clear by imagining a country, i, that had sent diplomats to twenty-three other states and thus was connected to every state in the system. Another country, j, sent no diplomats, but received diplomats from all twenty-three states in the system. Which one should we consider to be higher status? Intuitively, diplomats *received* are more directly related to status since state i sending diplomats to j tells us little about how much j values i, but something

---

[24] See, for example, Gartzke and Jo 2009; Fordham 2011; Kinne 2014.

[25] Singer and Small 1966; Small and Singer 1973. Updated in Bayer 2006.

[26] The original collectors of the data suggested that researchers who require annual data either use the diplomatic exchange data from the last available date until the next observation, or interpolate the missing years; see Small and Singer 1973. The latter method was chosen in this case.

TABLE 4.1
Sample Data from Diplomatic Exchange Data Set.

Country code i	Country code j	Year	Diplomatic representation level of j at i	Diplomatic representation level of i at j	Any diplomatic exchange between i and j?
2	200	1817	2	2	1
2	210	1817	2	2	1
2	220	1817	2	2	1
2	225	1817	0	0	0
2	230	1817	2	2	1
2	235	1817	0	0	0
2	245	1817	0	0	0
2	255	1817	2	0	1

critical about how much i values j, especially when aggregated across a group of states.

This measure has a number of important advantages. First, it is inclusive, covering virtually every state in the system for the years 1817–2005 (excepting, of course, missing data for some country-years). Critically, the sending and receiving of diplomats has some claim to being important across time periods, unlike, for example, the possession of colonies or nuclear weapons. In that sense, this measure of status is less bounded by temporal considerations than alternative measures. It is also inclusive in the broader sense that there are low barriers to entry, and every state can afford to send some diplomatic representation to some countries.

Second, the measure takes into account the aggregated judgment of the international community; in fact, this was the original intention of the data set. In an article accompanying an update to the data set, Small and Singer write:

> The decision to locate, maintain, or abolish a mission of any particular rank in any foreign capital reflected a wide variety of considerations within and between the several governments, and that the sum total of such missions would represent some consensus as to how important the recipient state was to all the theory in the system. In other words, *we treated the numerous and continuing decisions of whether or not to send diplomatic missions to foreign capitals* as a sort of running sociogram, *illuminating each state's relative diplomatic importance* to the membership of the system at large.[27]

[27] Small and Singer 1973, 578, emphasis added.

And while the original data set sought to measure the aggregated status beliefs of the community, I use social network analysis to bring the measure more closely into line with the conceptual foundations of status. In the next section, I explain how I use a measure of network centrality to properly and systematically account for the notion that status is best gained from high-status countries; in other words, that all countries are *not* equal.

PageRank Measure of Status

Generally, work using the diplomatic exchange data set has followed the intuition above, focusing on the receipt of diplomats. So although there are in theory a number of ways one might use such data to construct a measure of international status, in practice it has nearly always been done by counting the number of diplomats sent or received by each state in a given year and transforming that into a ranking.[28]

This neglects one critical aspect of status, however: *who* sends diplomats to an actor matters as much as (perhaps more than) the raw number of diplomats the state receives. In other words, all diplomats are not created equal; a diplomat from the United Kingdom was a greater indicator of status in 1817 than one from Sweden. But how do we operationalize this? Certainly, how much value a diplomat from i has in year t could be based on i's status at $t - 1$, but such a system requires initial starting values, posing a significant problem. To put it another way, if the first year of data is 1816, then how do we know how to weight, for example, Britain's diplomats in that year? We have no data from 1815, so we have to simply assign an arbitrary starting value—a bigger problem than it seems since that initial, arbitrary starting point will heavily influence all the downstream results (path dependence is a powerful thing).

In order to account for the importance of the sending country, I use a network centrality measure of status based on Google's PageRank algorithm. This class of network centrality measure has enjoyed growing popularity as a tool for constructing hierarchies of influence and prestige in varied applications, such as doctoral programs or citation networks.[29] It also follows naturally on efforts to model the international diplomatic

---

[28] See, for example, East 1972; Volgy and Mayhall 1995.

[29] See, for example, Schmidt and Chingos 2007; Maslov and Redner 2008; Ma, Guan, and Zhao 2008.

system using the tools of network analysis and Maoz's efforts to use network measures to construct status rankings.[30]

This measure assumes that each diplomat sent by *j* to *i* is a "vote" for *i*'s importance. The algorithm calculates this by—for every year—picking a random starting point in the system and tracing all the diplomatic connections (based on the receipt of diplomats), repeating this process ten thousand times, and calculating how much time was spent at each state relative to all other states in that year. Because the algorithm will spend comparatively more time at states that receive many diplomats (higher-status states), other states will benefit more from being connected to those higher-status states than lower-status states. In this way, the importance of the sending state is taken into account in a sensible manner. This process is repeated for every year in the data set. The end result is a value [0, 1], which is then transformed into an ordinal rank, since that more closely conforms with our notion of status as inherently positional.[31]

Three possible concerns are of note. First, PageRank might do an adequate job separating low from high-status countries, but a poor job discriminating at the top or bottom of the hierarchy. In response, I note that no state in the data ever receives diplomats from all other states (so it's not the case that states at the top have identical profiles of diplomatic representation, effectively tying them all for first place). In fact, even at the top, there are significant differences. For example, in 2005, the top five ranked countries received 145, 179, 154, 151, and 134 diplomats, respectively. Moreover, the focus on *local* hierarchies should assuage this concern even more, as high-status countries are spread out across both geographic regions and status communities, so that within a given region or community, the differences are even starker than in the global hierarchy.

A second concern is that many states will simply send diplomatic representatives to every other state in the system, which would not generate enough variation to be analytically useful. Yet empirically, states do have limited resources and do not simply send diplomatic representatives to all other states in the system. In fact, diplomatic missions are sent to only

---

[30] See Christopherson 1976; Kinne 2014; Maoz 2010.

[31] PageRank algorithms require a "damping" factor [0,1] in order to deal with nodes that have incoming but no outgoing links. Based on the way the network algorithm works, all the value would end up in these nodes, so a scaling factor [0,1] is added. PageRank centrality is a variant of Eigenvector centrality, which produces equivalent substantive results when tested with these data.

a fraction of states (over the entire data set, the average state received diplomats from only 28 percent of all possible states). Thus, the "numerous and continuing" decisions made by states as to how to allocate their resources diplomatically constitute an "ongoing plebiscite" among all nations in which governments must weigh numerous considerations in their determination of how important it is for them to have a diplomatic mission in each of the other capitals.[32]

A final concern regards what we now think of as "rogue" states. In some cases, influential states might withhold diplomatic representation from some actor, j, while also encouraging other states to do the same. All we would witness would be the diplomatic isolation of j, and thereby infer its relative lack of international status, but is this reasonable? The United States has done this periodically, such as by refusing to recognize the Soviet Union in the 1920s and 1930s as well as China in the 1950s and 1960s. One interpretation is that China's international status score in the 1960s was being "artificially" depressed by the US refusal to recognize it and the pressure it put on its allies to do the same. Another perspective, offered by Small and Singer, is that

> every government is faced periodically with the need to estimate, or re-estimate, how "important" it is to exchange missions with every other one in the system. That relative importance is reflected in its willingness to (a) allocate limited resourced to a given diplomatic bond (b) incur the costs of overcoming domestic or foreign opposition to such a bond and (c) sacrifice one set of attractive bonds in order to maintain or establish another set of more or less equally attractive ones. We might think of those recurrent national choices as constituting a slowly changing and ongoing plebiscite among all the system's members. [33]

In other words, China's status score in the 1950s—rather than being artificially "depressed" by the United States—might represent an accurate ranking to the extent that it takes into account other countries making the trade-off between acknowledging the importance of China or deferring to the wishes of the United States. If international status rankings are indeed based on collective beliefs concerning expectations of dominance and deference in IR, then China's position in the 1950s would represent an accurate depiction, not a distortion.

[32] Small and Singer 1973.
[33] Ibid., 582.

In this section, I've provided an overview of the most common quantitative measure of status, and showed how I improve on it. In fact, the intuitive assumption that diplomatic scores represents a rough measure of diplomatic importance and international status is widespread, as evinced by the persistent use of the data in quantitative work on status. However popular this intuition is, the empirical basis for it is practically nonexistent. In the next section, I use several methods of validation and cross-validation, drawing from archival data and other quantitative data sets, to demonstrate the utility of the diplomatic exchange data as a measure of international status.

Validating the Status Measure

While the diplomatic exchange data have been used consistently since the 1960s to generate measures of international status (and here, for the first time, *local* status), I am not aware of a single project that has sought to validate the measure by comparison to other sources of data or historical data. Note that this is not strictly necessary, as we might find, for example, that the receipt of diplomats correlated well with how leaders thought about relative standing in the international system, even if the receipt of diplomats was *not* consciously linked in their minds to international status. The link would certainly be stronger, though, if we were to find evidence of a connection in the historical record.

I address the issue of "face validity" here by validating and cross-validating the measure using a variety of quantitative and qualitative methods. First, I provide an overview—using primary and secondary sources—of the link between diplomacy and international status. Next, I show how my measure of status compares fares against other potential measures based on data sets of diplomatic visits and mentions by leaders in the *New York Times*.

DIPLOMACY AND STATUS

Diplomacy is suffused with issues of status and prestige. Everything about diplomacy, up to and including the seating charts for official dinners, is influenced by beliefs about where each state stands with respect to its rivals.[34]

[34] Pigman 2010, 21.

Under that general umbrella, however, we can further pin down the link between status and diplomatic exchange by making two related points. The first is that there is strong evidence that the treatment (and behavior) of diplomats within host countries was interpreted by those involved as almost wholly concerned with status, dominance, and deference. For example, in 1618, the Spanish ambassador to London refused to attend holiday celebrations unless his "place" was higher than that of the French ambassador. When the French ambassador did not receive assurances of *his* precedence, he announced his own recall, which was to be followed by an ultimatum and, "possibly, war." In the end, the bluff was called, and the Spanish ambassador retained his precedence, signaling something significant about the balance of power and influence among the three countries.[35]

Decades later, a similar disagreement arose, though with far deadlier consequences. In 1661, a new Swedish ambassador arrived in England, and as per custom, already-arrived emissaries gathered to enhance the pomp of the occasion. In this case, however, the French and Spanish ambassadors refused to give way to one another, leading to a struggle in which fifty people were killed or wounded. Anderson describes this as "the most spectacular humiliation suffered by any major European state" during that era, and though hyperbolic, he may have a point: Louis XIV struck a medal to commemorate his victory in the diplomatic struggle.[36] These two examples are merely some of the more colorful in a series of "endless crises … caused by intended or unintended slights" between diplomats.[37]

The second important point—and the one most relevant to the current project—is that the exchange of diplomats was viewed in large part as a series of signals regarding influence and status.[38] How they are received in host countries and how they behave are aspects of this, but more important still was the how the sending countries apportioned their resources. Even as recently as 2010, the former chief of diplomatic protocol for the United States wrote that the "presence of a diplomatic mission in a foreign country may lend … prestige to both sending and receiving states."[39] During the early years of the American republic, President George Washington sent diplomats at the rank of minister plenipotentiary to France, Great

[35] Jönsson and Hall 2005, 53.
[36] Anderson 2014, 64.
[37] Jönsson 2006, 215.
[38] Barston 2014, 23.
[39] French 2010, 279.

Britain, and Prussia, while reserving the lower rank of ministers resident for Portugal and Spain. In describing this distinction in his seminal history of the US diplomatic service, Plischke writes that it "reflected ... an attitude of differentiating among foreign nations on the basis of their perceived importance to, and the foreign relations interests of, the United States."[40]

Other, similar examples abound. For instance, after the Japanese defeat of Russia in 1904–5, Japan's missions in the West and those of the principal Western powers in Tokyo were "progressively upgraded to the rank of embassies—a move which immensely enhanced Japan's prestige" and cemented its status as a "quasi great power," thereby suggesting that the causal direction was the opposite: the growing importance of Japan led to the elevation of diplomats sent to that country.[41] And in a survey of diplomacy in the modern era, Malone notes that "notions of national prestige have long driven decisions, even by very poor countries, to fund more embassies than seems required or affordable."[42]

But we need not rely on secondary sources here, as diplomats and leaders have not been shy about describing their motives. In testimony before Congress, the director of US consular service explained, "It is prestige we want above all things."[43] In fact, those in charge of the diplomatic services seem positively fixated on issues of prestige that infuse everything from which rung of society diplomats should be drawn to the neighborhood in which the residences should be established. In 1916, the secretary of state (Robert Lansing) pleaded with Congress for nicer facilities in a better neighborhood, arguing that if the United States was forced to move to a different neighborhood, outside the traditional consular area, "the result would be a loss of prestige ... for the United States in its commercial and political relations with China."[44] In 1917, Wilbur Carr, director of the consular service in the Department of State, summed it up aptly:

> We can not go on indefinitely as one of the great world powers, as one of the big nations of the world, and occupy rented property and send our ambassador scurrying about ... while other nations have their whole establishments from year to year well housed and enjoy all the prestige that comes from having well-maintained embassies.[45]

[40] Plischke 1999, 49.
[41] Hamilton and Langhorne 2011, 119. See also Anderson 2014, 109.
[42] Malone 2013, 134.
[43] Quoted in US Congress 1920, 94.
[44] Quoted in Loeffler 1998, 18.
[45] Quoted in US Congress 1917, 87–88.

Even more to the point, there is at least anecdotal evidence the United States and other countries paid careful attention to the importance of other states and adjusted levels of representation accordingly. For example, when the British incorporated the Federal Republic of Rhodesia and Nyasaland in 1953, the deputy assistant secretary of state drafted a memo urging that "the establishment of this new government warrants an elevation in the prestige of our Consulate General," and recommending an increase in rank to "minister," which he argued was "consistent with our representation at such posts as Hong Kong and Singapore." In order to make this case, he focused his memo on the strategic importance of the new federal state, including its mineral reserves and crops.[46] A British member of Parliment, in internal deliberations concerning who to send to the United States following the Civil War, noted that it would be "looked upon as a slight if we did not send to Washington a man of the first rank as a diplomat."[47]

Those concerns evidenced in the above paragraph seem to have been spot-on: host countries were very much aware of the implications of differential levels of representation. In 1876, the United States reduced their level of diplomatic representation in Switzerland as a result of across-the-board cuts in every branch of government. In a report to the Committee on Foreign Relations in 1891, the chief US diplomat in Switzerland wrote, "The failure of the United States to express an interest and sympathy towards Switzerland in less than the highest diplomatic agent is a disappointment to the latter that is frequently discussed." John Sherman goes on to argue that upon the adoption of the Swiss constitution in 1848, Russia and other world powers were all represented by chargé d'affaires, but that since then, all other countries (with the exception of the United States) had adjusted their diplomatic representation to account for the newfound prominence of Switzerland in Europe.[48]

CROSS-VALIDATION USING ALTERNATIVE QUANTITATIVE MEASURES

However much qualitative evidence one amasses to validate a quantitative measure, one is always open to concerns about the selection and representativeness of the data presented. Given the critical importance of my measure of international and local status for the book as a whole, I now turn to alternative means to cross-validate my quantitative measure.

---

[46] Foreign Relations of the United States 1953.
[47] *Papers Relating to Foreign Affairs* 1866, 278.
[48] US Congress 1890, report no. 227.

To do so, I look at two recently constructed data sets relevant to issues of status and ranking in international politics. In particular, I compare the portfolio of diplomats sent by the United States to mentions of foreign countries in speeches made by the US secretary of state, and official state visits / diplomatic travel by the US president and/or secretary of state.

Given that both of these data sources are US-centric, the question to ask is, Does the portfolio of diplomats sent by the United States each year in the data resemble the distribution of mentions of a country by the secretary of state, or bilateral visits by the president / secretary of state? In essence, we can think of each of these actions as indicative of how important the United States sees other countries as being. For example, the US president and secretary of state have limited resources, and cannot visit all the countries in the world, or even a significant subset. They must focus on countries that *matter* and exclude countries that they view as less important. While collecting data on either visits or speech mentions is an expensive, time-consuming endeavor even for one country—let alone every state in the system in every year—we can use the limited data available to corroborate the rankings generated by the PageRank status measure.

To begin this analysis, I first dropped all observations from the Diplomatic Exchange Data that did not include the United States as the sending country.[49] Then, because the diplomatic data have observations only at five-year intervals, I carried forward all values to create a country-year data set. These new observations at years $t + 1, \ldots t + 4$ take values from year t. I merged this data set with data on bilateral visits from the US president and secretary of state (1965–2012) from Lebovic and Saunders along with data on mentions of a given country by the US secretary of state in the *New York Times* (1990–2003).[50]

The results of this analysis are depicted in figure 4.1. For the data on mentions of foreign countries in speeches made by the US secretary of state, I broke these mentions down by the diplomatic status of each country and plotted them by their COW geographic region.

For the data on diplomatic visits, I plotted the percentages of visits to host countries at each level of diplomatic status across each of the COW geographic regions. Each region category includes all strictly bilateral visits

[49] Bayer 2006.
[50] Lebovic and Saunders 2016; Finkel, Pérez-Liñán, and Seligson.

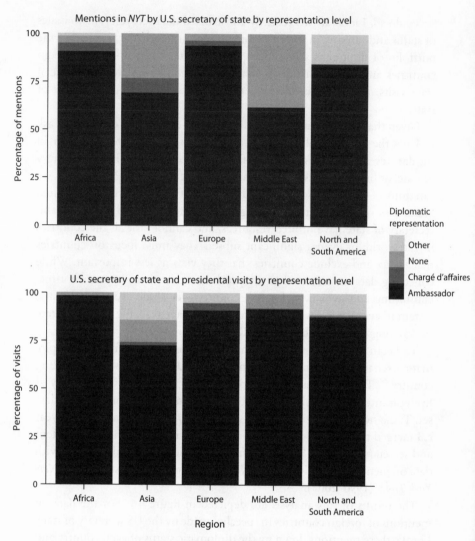

Figure 4.1: **International Status, *NYT* Mentions, and Diplomatic Visits.**

to any country in the region at any time between 1965 and 2003. As is evident, nearly all visits go to countries that host a US ambassador.

As is also evident in both panels of figure 4.1, the diplomatic exchange data set aligns closely with other sources of data that measure the importance of a given country, j, to the United States. For example, the first panel shows that in every geographic region, the vast majority of mentions by the secretary of state go to states that have received the highest level of diplomatic representation from the United States. Across all regions, the average is 83 percent. Similarly, the second panel of the figure shows that nearly all official diplomatic visits by the US president and secretary of state go to countries that host a US ambassador, and not to countries with lower levels of diplomatic exchange (for example, an interest section in another country's embassy).

SOURCES OF STATUS

Is Status Just Material Capabilities + Measurement Error?

The next step after providing reassurance regarding the measure's face validity is addressing potential concerns. Of those, the most significant is likely to be the notion that my measure of international status may reflect only a noisy measure of material capabilities. While recent work would suggest that this is unlikely to be true, more systematic analysis might uncover other patterns.[51] Figure 4.2 plots the correlation between status and power ranks for all states over time as well as subdividing the population into major and nonmajor powers.

As is evident, the correlation between international status and power typically hovers between 0.5 and 0.75, though with considerable variation over time. Moreover, the variation over time differs for different *types* of states. Major powers, for example, see a substantial decline in the correlation between their material capabilities and international status in the twentieth century. Put more directly, status is manifestly *not* just material capabilities. Of course, strength is a factor in determining status, but there are other inputs as well.[52] It is for this reason that there are countries with "normative" or "soft" power, or moral authority, that are high status without being militarily powerful.[53] It is also for this reason that some instruments of hard power or military capabilities are not only not status enhancing but instead actually detrimental in some cases.[54]

[51] Neumayer 2008; Kinne 2014.
[52] von Rueden, Gurven, and Kaplan 2008.
[53] Hall 1997; Nye 2004.
[54] Glaser 1998, 120.

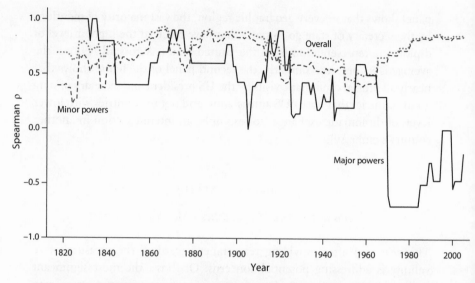

Figure 4.2: **The Changing Relationship between Power and Status** Y-axis depicts Spearman rank correlation between status and power ranks for all states, major powers, and small states, over time.

Paths to Prestige

If the previous section provides some preliminary evidence that status is *not* simply a rough proxy for material capabilities, then what exactly are the sources of status in international politics?

One possibility is that the *fixed characteristics* of a state are responsible for its status position in international politics; these are operationalized here as land area (in square kilometers) and state age (years since the state entered the COW system)[55]. Another possibility is that the *type of government*, whether it is aggressive or dovish, a democracy or dictatorship, may play a part. Here that is operationalized as dummy variables for "democracy" or "autocracy," where "anocracy" is the reference category.[56] Another category is the behavior of states, described here as *good citizenship* in international society and operationalized as the total number of IGOs that a state is a member of in a given year.[57] Of course, bad behavior may be just as

[55] World Development Indicators, World Bank 2014.
[56] Polity IV, Jaggers and Gurr 1995.
[57] Pevehouse, Nordstrom, and Warnke 2004.

influential, so I also include a covariate that measures the number of sanctions in effect in a given year.[58] Finally, a number of *material capabilities* may impact a state's status ranking. Here, I operationalize these through measurement of GDP, military capabilities, and population, and whether or not a state is in possession of nuclear weapons.[59] The last measure is the "composite index of latent nuclear weapons production capability" and is ordinal. The maximum value of seven means a state is currently producing all the materials needed to produce a nuclear weapon in a given year.

Table 4.2 presents the results of an analysis in which the dependent variable is rank in the international system. Because the dependent variable is in the form of rank, a negative coefficient means that a one-unit change in the independent variable is associated with *increased* status for that state. I estimated a country fixed effects (FE) model in order to account for potential correlations between unit-level characteristics and the explanatory variables of the model. FE models do this by removing all variation resulting from time-invariant, unit-level (country) characteristics. Without FE, correlations between omitted unit-level characteristics and the other explanatory variables will cause the model to attribute variation driven by the omitted unit-level variables to one or more of the included explanatory variables, thus overestimating the influence of the covariates in the model. This bias can be pernicious and is especially bad in data like these, where the explanatory variables of interest change slowly over time.[60] Models presented are for two time periods, 1815–1960 and 1961–2001. This particular partitioning was the result of data availability with respect to land area, nuclear capabilities, and GDP.[61]

Several things are apparent from this analysis. First, fixed characteristics—attributes over which states have little control—appear to exert an important effect on states' status ranking. Greater land mass, for example, is associated with greater status, though the effect is not statistically significant. State age is predictive of higher status for the earlier time period, but less status in the years since 1961. In later chapters, you

---

[58] From the "TIES" data, which measures the threat and imposition of economic sanctions. Morgan, Bapat, and Kobayashi 2014.

[59] GDP from Maddison GDP data, Bolt and Zanden 2014; Teorell *et al.* 2015, CINC data from COW, Singer, Bremer, and Stuckey 1972, Jo and Gartzke 2007.

[60] Clark and Linzer 2015. See also Wooldridge 2002, 265.

[61] The addition of these extra covariates for the later time period does not affect the other covariates in the model; sensitivity analysis using the later time period, but without the addition of any covariates, generates substantively identical results.

TABLE 4.2
Sources of Status.

	1815–1960	1961–2001
Fixed attributes		
Land area		−26768.4
		(25076.7)
State age	−0.0218**	0.877**
	(0.00667)	(0.0528)
Government		
Democracy	−1.752**	−2.817**
	(0.383)	(0.786)
Autocracy	0.508+	−2.992**
	(0.274)	(0.647)
Good citizen		
IGO memberships	0.0913**	−0.434**
	(0.0139)	(0.0449)
Number of sanctions in effect (TIES)		−0.724*
		(0.311)
Capabilities		
Five-year change in GDP (USD/100 billion)		2.892
		(6.011)
Five-year change in military capabilities (CINC)	−5.925	−54.79
	(8.570)	(103.0)
Nuclear capable		−1.687**
		(0.319)
Population (millions)	−0.0456**	−0.0510**
	(0.00637)	(0.0108)
Constant	25.24**	276.7
	(0.249)	(219.1)
N	5776	4633

Standard errors in parentheses
$+ p < 0.10, * p < 0.05, ** p < 0.01$

will read of German elites who were convinced that their state had been penalized for arriving on the international scene too late; here we find evidence that their suspicions may have had a basis in reality. States that modernized late do appear to have been artificially held back (at least during that time period).

The type of government also influences a state's status ranking, though here the picture is a bit less clear. Democratic governments were, in earlier time periods, advantaged relative to "mixed regimes" (i.e., anocracies), while in that same time frame, autocratic government were (if anything) disadvantaged and accorded less status. But that pattern has shifted over time. In the years since 1960, both autocracies and democracies have tended to be accorded more status than mixed regimes. In the more recent time period, the "democratic advantage" has only gotten bigger, with democratic status "worth" almost three ranks in the global hierarchy.

States, of course, may pursue policies that gain or cost them in the coin of prestige. Some of those behaviors are generally agreed to be normatively "good," such as engagement with the international community through IGO membership. As expected, in the last forty years—a period that overlaps with an enormous increase in the number of IGOs as well as their importance—membership in IGOs is associated with an increase in standing. During the earlier time period examined, however, the pattern reverses—a finding perhaps driven by the much smaller number of IGO memberships during this period (though the substantive effect size is quite small). Normatively "bad" behavior seems to have an effect as well, though if it demonstrates anything, it shows that bad behavior can sometimes be rewarded.

The last section showed the status was not simply a reflection of material power rather but that those capabilities do matter. Here, a more detailed analysis allows us to disaggregate "capabilities" and discover how its different forms affect a state's international standing. Wealth, for example, turns out to have only marginal effects on a state's standing, and if those effects exist, they run counter to the notion that states may "buy" prestige. If anything, countries seem to grow richer at the expense of their international position. Population, on the other hand, one of the long-standing indicators of power in world politics, is positively correlated with status: states do gain prestige as they grow in size. Similarly, nuclear capabilities seem robustly associated with increasing status. As states go through the stages of "nuclear latency" necessary to approach a weaponized nuclear deterrent, their status grows.

So what does this analysis tell us about the overall profile of a high-status state? First, in earlier time periods, there were in fact distinct advantages that came from early unification, but these seem to have largely worn off in the last several decades. In terms of government, the normative value associated with democratic regimes does indeed contribute to a state's status, and this value has only increased over time. Autocracies, however, are also accorded greater standing; it does pay to be a dictator, at least in this case, and it seems that the worst thing to be is a mixed regime or state that is in some type of transition between regime types. Similarly, behavior matters. Here, though, we can see that both "good" and "bad" citizens are rewarded, suggesting that there are multiple avenues to greater international standing, consistent with our intuition that high-status states may be just as likely to resemble Switzerland as Iran.

Finally, we learn that capabilities matter, but in a more complex way than often suggested; status is not simply a rough proxy for power, and in fact, while some capabilities help, others lead to lower standing. Population, for example, helps: larger states are consistently accorded higher status. Similarly, nuclear weapons are robustly associated with higher status in the data. Military capabilities, however, seem rather inconsequential once other facets of power (e.g., nuclear weapons and population) are taken into account. Finally, wealthier countries gain many advantages from their riches, but status does not appear to be one of them.

DETECTING STATUS COMMUNITIES

Given a measure of status (a network of diplomatic representation transformed into status ranks through PageRank centrality), we can now turn to the crucial question of reference groups. After all, if status is local, then we must ascertain where status concerns lie, and for every state, i, which group of states forms the relevant comparison group. Previous works on status concerns in international politics have assumed that all states are in competition with all other states in one immense global hierarchy.[62] Yet my theory of status builds on the notion that status concerns should matter

---

[62] Though some scholars have analyzed subgroups of states (for example, major powers), those groups were chosen for reasons of data availability and under the argument that status would only matter for "central" powers. Wallace 1971, 24.

most among reference groups, or status communities, in which states have salient attributes in common. How do we find these status communities?

In a perfect world, we could survey leaders of every state in the system, past and present, to ascertain which states they view as peer competitors. Practically, however, there are two broad approaches. The first is to hypothesize salient attributes that might correlate with communities. For example, it is easy to imagine that geography might matter a great deal in determining the reference groups of states. Countries located close to one another would share languages, culture, and history in such a way that makes them obvious comparison groups. This approach is not perfect, though. First, for major powers, it is precisely their global reach and influence that defines them, but this also cuts across geographic boundaries. Major powers are thus likely to see themselves in competition with each other, regardless of geography. But such a measure is problematic for smaller states as well, since plenty of important attributes that might form the basis of status communities might also cut across borders, such as religion, language, and ideologies (for example, Communism or the non-aligned movement).

The second broad approach is inductive in nature and relies on observations of interstate interactions. Earlier, I showed how one can use network analysis methods to provide centrality or authority scores that are more meaningful than simply counting the number of diplomats a state has received. Here, I continue along that track by using formal "community detection" methods developed in network science, which are designed precisely in order to detect underlying communities of actors "in a way that is both methodologically rigorous and produces results that are substantively meaningful."[63]

Broadly speaking, a community is "a group of nodes with more and/or better interactions among its members than between its members and the remainder of the network."[64] Whether the interactions are, in fact,

---

[63] Lupu and Traag 2012, 1023. Community detection is a topic of considerable interest to network scientists, and has been used more recently in political science as well—for instance, in Lupu and Voeten 2012—to identify communities in the network formed by citations to domestic and international case law by the European Court of Human Rights (Lupu and Traag 2012), to detect "trading communities," (Macon, Mucha, and Porter 2012), to detect "voting communities" within the UN General Assembly (Lupu and Greenhill 2014), and to examine the impact of IGO communities on conflict behavior. On the structure of communities within the US Congress see Porter et al. 2005; Zhang et al. 2008. On alliance communities, see Traag and Bruggeman 2009.

[64] Leskovec, Lang, and Mahoney 2010, 1.

more and/or better is measured through the concept of modularity, or Q. Formally,

$$Q = \sum_i (e_{ii} - a_i^2), \tag{4.1}$$

where Q is the proposed community grouping's quality, e_i is the fraction of all edges (connections) that exist entirely within community i, and a_i is the expected fraction of all edges that would exist across communities if edges were assigned to communities at random. As modularity increases, the proportion of edges that connect two actors in a single community (e_{ii}) increases relative to the proportion that would be found if the edges were assigned randomly (a_i).

Modularity thus measures the quality of a proposed network partitioning scheme by comparing the fraction of all network edges (diplomatic connections, in this case) that fall entirely within each proposed community to what would be expected in a network with the same number of nodes (states), but edges assigned at random (with the same total number of degrees for each node). If a particular division gives no more within-community edges than would be expected by random chance, then the modularity (Q) is zero. Values greater than zero indicate "better than random" groupings, and relatively higher modularity values suggest more efficient network partitions.[65]

Choosing one's method of community detection often involves comparing Q values (in this sense, they function similarly to log likelihoods) and combining that with substantive knowledge about the data.[66] I use the Fast Greedy algorithm, developed by Clauset and colleagues as well as Newman, and widely used throughout network science.[67] Weights are an optional feature of such algorithms, and if not assigned, imply that all connections are equal. Here, I weight the edges by the type of diplomatic link, from

---

[65] Newman 2004.

[66] Louvain, another popular method, is used by Lupu and Traag 2012, and functions similarly to fast greedy in that it uses heuristics in order to maximize modularity. Its exact process is, however, slightly different, as described in Blondel et al. 2008. Figure B.1 (in online appendix materials) compares fast greedy and the Louvain algorithm in their weighted and unweighted versions. As is evident, Louvain provides no obvious benefit over Fast Greedy, and weighted versions typically perform worse in the earlier, sparse networks of the early ninteenth century, but better later on in the larger networks of the twentieth century.

[67] Clauset, Newman, and Moore 2004; Newman 2004. In particular, the built-in `fast-greedy.community()` function in the iGraph package for R; Csardi and Nepusz 2006.

one to four, ranging from "interest section" to "ambassador."[68] The Fast Greedy algorithm works by assigning each node to its own community, and then iteratively pairing these communities in a search for the "greatest increase (or smallest decrease)" in modularity. This process forms larger and larger communities with each iteration. Once all communities have been merged into one supercommunity, the algorithm selects the partition that produced the highest modularity.

In order to see how this works, consider a snapshot of the international system in 1817, depicted in table 4.3, noting that some countries (e.g., Germany and Italy) did not exist in their current form yet in 1817 but rather are labeled with their modern state names, as per COW convention. The table is sorted by column (f), the total number of diplomats received by each state in the system. It is worth reminding the reader here that nearly all past works have discarded *all other information except this total.* Columns $(b–e)$ break down the total number of diplomats by type, arranged on a scale from least ("other," which includes personnel assigned to a country's "interest section" hosted by another embassy) to most important ("ambassador"). A country's status rank was determined in the past simply by counting the total number of diplomats received from all other states. Note the potential limitations of such an approach: all countries are equal, so representation from smaller states "counts" as much as representation from more powerful states; all diplomats are equal, so we ignore the different levels of diplomatic representation by collapsing it into a binary form; and there is only one hierarchy, composed of all states, whether in the Middle East, North America, or Europe.

The first issue can be properly accounted for using PageRank measures of network centrality, in which the importance of the sending state is sensibly taken into account. This innovation is depicted in column (h), in which rankings are based on PageRank scores, not simply raw counts of the number of diplomats hosted by each nation. Already we can see that the overall picture changes from the traditional methods, such that some countries ranked high in (g)—Germany, for example—rank rather low in (h). These adjustments result from some states hosting a large number of diplomats from relatively unimportant countries; in this case, Germany's numbers are inflated by a large representation of other Germanic states.

---

[68] For a related example, see Macon, Mucha, and Porter (2012), who weight edges between countries in the United Nations by the number of voting agreements in place between them.

TABLE 4.3
Detecting Status Communities (a Snapshot of 1817).

| (a) State | Number of diplomats | | | | | | PageRank | | (j) Region | (k) Detected Community |
	(b) other	(c) charge d'affaires	(d) minister	(e) ambassador	(f) Total	(g) Rank	(h) Overall	(i) Community		
FRN	1	1	7	4	13	1	2	1	Europe	A
UKG	0	0	9	3	12	2	5	2	Europe	A
BAV	4	3	8	0	12	2	1	1	Europe	B
AUH	1	3	5	3	12	2	6	2	Europe	C
SIC	0	1	9	1	11	5	12	5	Europe	A
RUS	0	0	9	2	11	5	10	3	Europe	A
NTH	1	0	9	1	11	5	11	4	Europe	A
GMY	0	1	9	0	10	8	15	5	Europe	B
SAX	3	1	6	0	10	8	3	2	Europe	B
SPN	1	0	5	3	9	10	14	6	Europe	A
TUR	0	2	4	3	9	10	17	7	Middle East	A
SWZ	1	1	7	0	9	10	16	5	Europe	C
DEN	0	0	8	0	8	13	18	8	Europe	A
PAP	1	0	5	2	8	13	9	4	Europe	C
TUS	2	0	6	0	8	13	7	3	Europe	C
BAD	2	1	5	0	8	13	4	1	Europe	C
USA	0	0	7	0	7	17	20	9	North America	A
ITA	0	0	6	1	7	17	21	6	Europe	C
SWD	0	0	7	0	7	17	19	6	Europe	B
HSG	2	0	4	0	6	20	8	3	Europe	B
HSE	1	0	4	0	5	21	13	4	Europe	B
WRT	0	0	5	0	5	21	22	7	Europe	B
POR	0	0	0	0	0	23	23	10	Europe	A

Notes: Row shading indicate detected status community. States are sorted by rank (total number of diplomats received). AUH = Austria-Hungary; BAD = Baden; BAV = Bavaria; DEN = Denmark; FRN = France; GMY = Germany; HSE = Hesse Electoral; HSG = Hesse Grand Ducal; ITA = Italy; NTH = Netharlands; PAP = Papal States; POR = Portugal; RUS = Russia; SAX = Saxony; SIC = Sicily; SPN = Spain; SWD = Sweden; SWZ = Switzerland; TUR = Turkey; TUS = Tuscny; UKG = United Kingdom; USA = United States; WRT = Wuttemburg.

Even once this adjustment is made, however, the second two issues remain. Here, we can see the advantages of community detection. Column (k) lists each state's detected status community: A, B, or C. These communities cut across regional geographic boundaries, demonstrating the potential advantage of formalized community detection over other approaches. One can see a clear cluster of powerful states in community A (for example, the United Kingdom, Russia, France, and the United States), a cluster of Germanic states in community B (for example, Hesse Grand Ducal, Hesse Electoral, Wuerttemburg, Saxony, Germany, and Bavaria), and Italian regions in community C (for example, Tuscany, the Papal States, and Italy). The structure of the status communities of 1817 are easily visualized in figure 4.3. The algorithm also does well on face validity in other time periods, such as by accurately recovering US–Soviet dynamics during the Cold War.[69]

Now that we have detected the relevant status communities, we can create status ranks *within* the relevant status community for each state, depicted in column (i). For these to represent an improvement over the overall rankings in column (h), we must simply ask. Is Wuerttemburg in 1817 likely to care more about its status in the hierarchy of all states (in which it ranks twenty-second), or in its status community composed of other states that are similar in size, power, culture, and language (where it ranks seventh)? Intuitively, the latter grouping seems more plausible, though confirmation must wait until a later section, when we can more formally test the relevance of the different potential status communities.

Some Descriptive Statistics on Status Communities

I now turn to some of the basic aspects of the status communities generated by the community detection algorithm described above. These descriptive statistics serve a dual purpose, providing substantive content while also functioning as a basic validity check to ensure that the community detection procedure is functioning as intended.

First, I turn to the question of whether international status communities are stable over time. Because communities themselves are generated anew each year, we can't simply ask whether, for example, Britain remained in the "Western bloc" during the Cold War. Instead, I examined the

---

[69] See figure B.2 in online appendix materials.

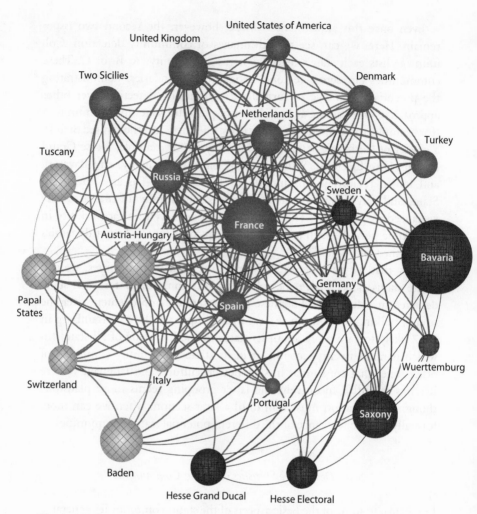

Figure 4.3: **Status Communities of 1817** Edge (TIES) colors represent the community of the sending state, and edge widths (thickness) represent the weight of the TIES (based on the level of diplomatic representation, from one to four). Node size is a function of PageRank status (bigger nodes are more important).

proportion of dyads that changed from being in the same community to being in different communities between year t and year $t + 1$. The results of this analysis are depicted in figure 4.4, and present estimates that either discard or incorporate "new" states (from $t + 1$) into the denominator.

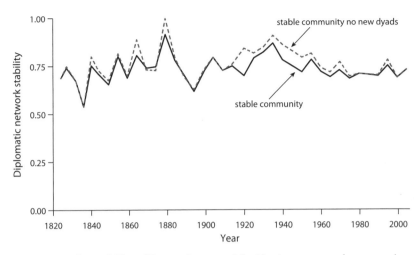

Figure 4.4: **The Stability of Status Communities** Y-axis represents the proportion of states that remain in the same community from one observation to the next.

However one measures it, it is plainly evident that the communities exhibit a fair amount of stability over time, with the most volatility immediately preceding World War I. Given the novelty of my procedures, there is no hard-and-fast rule for what would constitute a problematic amount of turnover within communities. Clearly, we would not expect *entirely* different status communities from one observation to the next, since that would suggest that our procedure was picking up on something far more ephemeral and variable than our quantity of interest. Nevertheless, we should still observe some movement over time, as states do move in and out of each other's orbits.

I now turn to the question of how large these status communities are. Figure 4.5 plots the average size of a status community, measured here as how many states are in a status community relative to the size of the system as a whole. Thus, if the average size of a status community is 0.25, the correct interpretation is that on average, each status community contains 25 percent of the states in the system. That same figure also plots the maximum size of the community in a given year to give the reader a sense of the distribution.

A final question relates to whether we observe an intercommunity hierarchy. That is, do states sort themselves into communities of, for example, high, medium, and low status? As it turns out, there is not a great

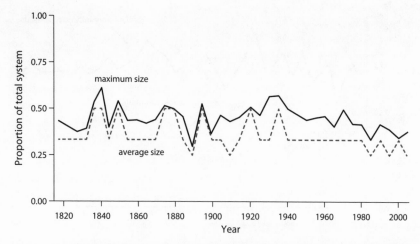

Figure 4.5: **The Size of Status Communities** Y-axis represents the proportion of states in a given community relative to the size of the international system.

deal of evidence for this proposition, as most communities seem to exhibit considerable variation in the status of their members. Several figures in the online appendix materials plot the distribution of status scores (ranging from zero to one) for each community in each year for which there are observations. As is evident, some years might be interpreted as evincing a clear hierarchy between communities, but in others such patterns are difficult to observe. Moreover, there is no clear pattern over time.

SUMMARY

Entering this chapter, I had provided a theory—*status dissatisfaction*—of how concerns over relative status affected decision making and international conflict. In the last chapter, I showed how we could use experimental methods to isolate, measure, and provide casual evidence on the importance of status concerns for judgment and decision making. Taking the theory to the realm of international politics, however, posed several problems relating to research design and measurement that needed to be tackled.

Foremost among these issues was how we could measure status itself. I approached this problem by returning to the core conceptual attributes of status: it is social, perceptual, and relative. After surveying a number of possible methods for measuring international status, I argue that diplomatic exchange between states represents the best foundation for such a measure. In fact, this indicator has been widely used for such a purpose over the past several decades by scholars, who have counted the number of diplomats received by a country to represent "the relative importance that *all* nations in the system attribute to any one of its members at a given time."[70]

But this methodology is not without its faults. In fact, in many ways, the way the diplomatic exchange data set is typically used ignores several key features of status. To address these shortcomings, I innovated along two dimensions. First, I used the tools of social network analysis to account for the fact that not all countries are equal. This allows for my measure of status to more appropriately reflect its conceptual foundation; diplomats sent from the United States in the twentieth century *should* count more than those sent from states such as Bolivia or Mongolia.

Next, I used community detection algorithms to inductively derive each state's status community. This stands in stark contract to previous work, which has largely assumed that status either only matters to major powers or that all states are part of one global hierarchy that is equally salient for all states. Instead, I used data on the rank and number of diplomat exchanges to group states into "local" communities of peer competitors based on real-world interactions. In the next chapter, I continue along this path by using my measure of status and local "status communities" to provide evidence on the link between status deficits and war.

---

[70] Singer and Small 1966, 241.

5

Status Deficits and War

In the previous chapter, I began the process of applying my theory of status dissatisfaction to the realm of international politics. While in chapter 3, I was able to rely on the advantages of experimental methods to measure and manipulate status concerns, applying the theory directly to international conflict posed several problems. First among them, we can no longer rely on random assignment or exogenously manipulated levels of status concerns. In return for giving up such control and precision, however, we gain ground in our ability to investigate how status concerns have affected war and peace in the international system. Even that statement undersells the importance of moving between methods and levels of analysis. Doing so not only allows us to test different implications of the core theory but also builds confidence in the empirical structure of the book through a series of different but overlapping sets of data and evidence.

In chapter 4, I began to tackle the problems of investigating status using observational data on the behavior of states. Though there are many challenges in such an endeavor, one stands above all the others: How do we plausibly and sensibly measure status, a social and perceptual construct? I showed that we could do so by building on a widely recognized data set that captured diplomatic exchanges between states. Yet simply counting the number of diplomats that each state received—as has been the custom for the last five decades—leaves us with a measure that fails to capture most of what is interesting and important about status. I then showed how we could use the tools of social network analysis to address three main problems: all diplomats are counted equally, all countries are counted equally, and all countries compete with all other countries in one immense (and unlikely) global hierarchy. Through a combination of PageRank network centrality measures and novel "community detection" algorithms, I provided one way to address these shortcomings.

Having supplied an overview of my approach to measurement, we can move on to the next stage: applying our newly developed measures of status and status communities to international conflict. First, I establish a baseline assumption of the theory: that the initiation of violent international conflict does indeed bring status benefits to states that pursue this strategy. This is a critical first step, since status dissatisfaction theory is premised on the notion that leaders and states initiate conflict in order to shift their position in a given hierarchy. Yet we have little to rely on—except for the confident predictions of leaders—in demonstrating this link.[1] I provide the first such evidence, finding that initiating and winning a conflict vaults a state up the status ranking, and shifts its place in the hierarchy by seven spots (compared to otherwise-similar states that did not initiate conflict at all).

Following the establishment of conflict as a winning strategy for status seeking, in this chapter I show that status deficits greatly increase the likelihood of initiating conflicts at every level of intensity from low-level disputes to international wars. Switching a state from "no status deficit" to a status deficit one standard deviation above the mean doubles its likelihood of initiating a war or militarized interstate dispute (MID). Following the theoretical predictions, I also demonstrate that even internationally, status is local: status deficits within the fine-grained "status communities" do not change either substantive or statistical significance when I analyze subsets of states that are "satisfied" within other, broader hierarchies. This is not due to the construction of the measure or other issues related to endogeneity: lagging the measure of status deficits by several years produces substantively identical results and so too does controlling for states that initiated conflict after withdrawing their ambassadors (which would otherwise show up in the data as an increased status deficit, but really be driven by an underlying conflict between the two states).

Status deficits do not just change the likelihood of violent conflict occurring; they change its very nature. This happens for two reasons. First, states choose targets strategically; conflicts over status are, in that sense, often "wars of choice." To achieve the ends they seek—increased status in their hierarchy—states target actors they are most likely to defeat, and do so at a higher rate than "satisfied" states. Dissatisfied states also select targets that are commensurate with them in status ranking, demonstrating another implication of the theory: status is most efficiently gained from higher rather than lower status states. Finally, I show that the link between status concerns and conflict has not changed dramatically over time; to the contrary, the relationship is even stronger in recent years than in earlier

[1] Dafoe, Renshon, and Huth 2014.

time periods, despite a common concern that wars over honor and status might be historical relics.

Theoretical Expectations

In chapter 2, I argued that leaders seem to care a great deal about status. It is, in fact, one area where the beliefs of policy makers, leaders, and scholars converge. Moreover, the role of status in international affairs has generated a sizable research program over the years. I contended, though, that knowing that leaders have strong preferences for status, or that status "matters," does not provide much in the way of inferential leverage. A better way forward is to generate theories that tell us *when* status moves up the list of priorities. In short, we must focus on variation in preferences or concern for status.

How Status Concerns Are Generated

The leverage we gain from focusing on status concerns that vary systematically helps us only insofar as we have theories to predict that variation. While there are several candidate explanations for when status concerns might be generated—Wohlforth, for example, suggests an unclear hierarchy—my theory focuses on the role of (unmet) expectations.[2] This focus on expectations builds on a substantial body of literature in psychology and other social sciences suggesting the critical importance of expectations in judgment and decision making.[3]

Of course, to say that expectations matter only pushes us one level deeper: On what are the expectations based? Or more specifically, in the case of status comparisons, how might we plausibly operationalize status expectations? Here we are on firmer ground, in that a number of theories from both IR as well as individual decision making suggest that actors' beliefs about how much status they deserve will be set by their "asset levels" of other attributes, such as power or economic capacity. For example, power transition theory suggests that wars occur when status does not match up to material capabilities, while earlier work on status inconsistency indicated that it was specifically material or military

---

[2] Wohlforth 2009.
[3] See, for example, Niven 2000; Koszegi and Rabin 2006.

capabilities that set an expectation level (though it was not necessarily termed that) for status.[4] On the individual level, experimental work has corroborated some of these ideas; for example, a disjuncture between status and levels of other attributes (such as high status / low power) is psychologically aversive, and causes both decreased cognitive functioning and increased risk seeking.[5]

Status Deficit → War → Increased Status

Once those concerns are generated, how do states react? By far the most popular and well-known research on this question is status inconsistency, which argues that leaders will "evidence a strong desire to change the status quo, and *failing to do so, to engage in conflict and violence*."[6] In this formulation, states that are dissatisfied resort to violence only *after* failing to change the status quo—that is, out of frustration. This is a rather weak mechanism for linking status and war, however, since it presupposes an irrationality (acting out of frustration rather than strategic interests) that obscures a more likely way in which status concerns might relate to conflict. Because states can expect to profit from higher status, and because status is positional (and thus other states can be expected to be reluctant to cede status voluntarily), violence and conflict may be one way of *achieving* higher status rather than a last resort after having failed to do so.

Why would violence bring higher status? To answer this, we must first consider how actors develop beliefs about relative standing in a hierarchy. Broadly, beliefs about where each actor stands in a hierarchy are formed via observation of interactions between a group's members. Some attributes of status (for example, strength or wealth) are visible and thus easily accounted for, while in other cases there are unobservable elements, such as "toughness," "influence," or "quality," that must be inferred through patterns of deference and dominance behavior.

Still, not just any interaction will do if the goal is to shift your position in a hierarchy. Because status is a perceptual construct, cognitive limitations affect the ease with which we can move up or down in a hierarchy.

---

[4] While military capabilities seem likely to be the most broad and powerful proxy for expectations, other assets (for example, social welfare or normative authority) might be relevant for certain groups of states in certain time periods.

[5] Newman, Sellers, and Josephs 2005; Josephs et al. 2006; Zyphur et al. 2009; Ronay and Von Hippel 2010.

[6] Volgy and Mayhall 1995, 68, emphasis added.

Chief among these restrictions is that beliefs are updated sporadically—not continuously—and then only in response to large events. And since beliefs about status require some consensus in the international community, events are not likely to change a state's position unless they are highly public (i.e., visible to all actors in the community), dramatic, or salient (in order to capture the attention of potential observers), and convey unambiguous information. Status requires a shared consensus on a given state's "standing" in the relevant community. Thus, for an event to change status beliefs, it must change all (or the vast majority) of observers' beliefs in the same way.

Taking these conditions into account, one likely candidate—though not the only possibility—for an event that is capable of changing a state's place in a status hierarchy is a military conflict. Rationalist scholars have argued that war reveals private information on relative strength otherwise unavailable to potential belligerents. I propose a variant on this: while war (or militarized disputes in which force is used) does reveal private information about capabilities, it reveals other things as well. The capabilities along with behavior of the two opponents and the outcomes observed by the international audience combine to influence the status beliefs of others in the hierarchy. Militarized conflicts—which are public, dramatic, and salient—are therefore a chance for the international community to simultaneously calibrate its judgments concerning how much international standing a given state possesses (or should possess).

> **H1 (winning status)**: *Exceeding expectations in conflict will increase the initiator's status rank.*

Thus, we must first establish a baseline assumption of the theory: that violent interstate conflicts—public, dramatic, and salient—will serve as "status-altering events." If this is true, we should expect to see evidence that conflict initiation—and particularly victory in conflict—should provide status boosts to the victor/initiator. The "null" here is that conflict would have no effect on status ranking, or perhaps depress status. A state, i, might lose status if norms against the initiation of interstate violence cause initiators to lose status and/or if other states withdraw diplomats in protest of the initiator's belligerence. For conflict to be "status enhancing," however, states must reveal capabilities (military or otherwise) in conflict that provide new information on where they should stand in a given hierarchy. Notice that this is accomplished not necessarily by victory—since one could in theory defeat an extremely weak foe and reveal nothing new about capabilities—but instead by exceeding the expectations of observers. This suggests that we must take additional care in our research design, described in more detail below.

Second, we should expect to see evidence that states that experience status deficits should initiate at a greater rate than "satisfied" states.

> **H2 (status deficits and war):** *Status deficits will be associated with an increased probability of war and MID initiation.*

Who and How Dissatisfied States Fight

Our predictions so far concern *why* status deficits should be linked to war, and *whether* violent conflict does in fact bring higher status. We can now turn to two additional questions related to the nature of the conflicts themselves.

The first question concerns the nature of the target. H1 concerns the link between conflict and higher status. However, if conflict is, in fact, status enhancing when states exceed observers' expectation, then we should see evidence that dissatisfied states target the states that suit those purposes best. Unlike defensive wars, conflicts over status are in many ways "wars of choice." Dissatisfied states, then, will to a greater extent than satisfied states have some ability to consciously select targets. In particular, they should focus on targets that give them the best chance of prevailing and/or exceeding the expectations of observers—namely, against less powerful states.

> **H3a (targets of status aggression—power):** *Dissatisfied states will select targets that give them the best odds of prevailing in combat; thus (compared to satisfied states), they will initiate against weaker opponents.*

> **H3b (targets of status aggression—status):** *Dissatisfied states will pick fights that are most likely to provide the status benefits they seek, particularly, against states ranked higher in status.*

Other dimensions are critical here as well. Consider i, ranked eighth, which wishes to move up in the hierarchy. Seven spots are available above i, but are currently occupied by other states. Whose beliefs need to shift in order for i to move up? There is little evidence to guide us here, but what is clear is that i cannot move up without displacing some state, j, ranked above it. In principle, this doesn't require any interaction between i and j. In practice, however, head-to-head dominance contests between the state seeking higher status (i) and the state it is seeking to displace (j) would be the most efficient manner to move up in the hierarchy.[7] This dynamic can be made especially clear by thinking through how such movement occurs at the top: challengers for dominant (or "alpha") status in the animal world do not pick fights with other subordinate actors but rather with actor they are seeking to displace.[8] Thus we should expect that dissatisfied states will disproportionately target higher-status ones.

Even Internationally, Status Is Local

Thus far, I have provided a brief reminder of how the theory of status dissatisfaction approaches the questions of how status concerns are generated and what the consequences are likely to be for international conflict. I argued that status concerns are triggered when actors' status falls below a level set by their expectations. Nevertheless, unless all states are in competition with all other states, then we must set boundary conditions for this theory.

This task is made more difficult by the fact that previous research *has* assumed that all states exist in one international hierarchy. Previous work has taken to heart the dictum that status is "positional" or "relative," but failed to follow this to the next logical question: Relative to *whom*? Earlier works noted that a state's position in a hierarchy was important, but stopped short of specifying *which* hierarchy we should examine. Instead, states were all placed in a de facto global hierarchy.[9]

This is acceptable only if one believes the global hierarchy to be the most salient structure for all states. In the context of world politics, however, such a perspective would imply some odd things about the behavior and preferences of states. In fact, decades of research has demonstrated that

[7] Mendoza and Barchas 1983; Mazur 1985.
[8] Silk 2002.
[9] Such as the "central system," as defined in Singer and Small 1966.

actors are most likely to use as reference groups others that are similar to them on important dimensions rather than all other actors. Or as Frank put it, status is local.[10]

H4 (status is local): *Status deficits within detected communities will be better predictors of conflict behavior than deficits within regional or global hierarchies.*

In theory, actors can compare their status to a multitude of targets along an almost-infinite array of dimensions. The literature on social comparison suggests that the most important comparisons will be on dimensions that are widely regarded as crucial (that is, size of house or salary on the individual level; economic or military capability on the international level), and the comparisons will be made against some salient reference group. Thus, H4 suggests that status deficits will be most predictive of conflict initiation when they occur within local "defected" communities.

FIGHTING FOR STATUS

I used the EUGene software program to generate a directed-dyad data set of MIDs, both wars and nonwars, from 1816–2005.[11] Only the originators involved on day one of a conflict could be coded as an initiator (this is the most restrictive coding). Control variables used in various models include: share of dyadic capabilities, CINC, distance, contiguity, ongoing MID,

---

[10] Frank 1985.

[11] On EUGene, see Bennett and Stam 2000, 2007. On MIDs, see Jones, Bremer, and Singer 1996. Pre-1993 data is taken from Maoz 2005. The first COW/MID data sets were not dyadic in nature, and so any analysis of dyadic data prior to that must rely on a conversion scheme in order to convert pre-1993 data into directed-dyad form. In these data, pre-1993 data are generated from the Maoz's (2005), dyadic MID data, which have a stricter set of criteria for generating pre-1993 dyads (both options use the same data for post-1993 dyads). The Maoz dyadic data fix a number of problems present in the alternative option, which include but are not limited to: states listed as on opposing sides of a dispute (for example, Japan and Bulgaria in World War I) that never used or even threatened force against one another; incorrect outcomes (for example, Poland listed as winner of the Germany–Poland World War II dyad); and inaccurate levels of hostility (for example, the United States and Hungary were on opposing sides of World War II, and both sides individually reached the highest level of hostility, but never fought each other, which should be reflected in the data). For more detail, see Maoz 2005.

polity, peace years, joint democracy, major power, Syscon (concentration of power in the international system), and alliance type.[12]

The main predictor variable is a measure of the status deficit for a given state in a given year. The inputs to this measure are the status rank (described earlier) and rank on material capabilities, based on a country's CINC score. It is constructed by subtracting the rank on status from the rank on material capabilities, which are then standardized by year. The result is then multiplied by −1 so that positive (negative) numbers indicate greater (lesser) status deficits. This standardization process aids in interpretation of the results as well as allowing for fluctuating patterns in the relationship (the "exchange rate") between status and power—over time. Because both components of the status deficit measure (status and power) are likely to be affected *by* military disputes, all analyses described in the manuscript lag this measure by one year, so that the relationship examined is between status deficits in year $t − 1$ and conflict in year t.[13]

The Status Benefits of Conflict (or, "War Pays")

First, we turn to the question of the long-term effects of conflict on status. There is certainly some anecdotal evidence that leaders *believe* that conflict initiation and victory will bring greater status.[14] Leaders' perceptions are key here, since the theory is reliant on their mental models of how status is gained. Yet there is little empirical evidence to corroborate this relationship between conflict and increased status.

As a first step in this empirical exercise, I conducted an analysis of the effect of conflict involvement and initiation as well as victory on status. Unlike other analyses described in the chapter, this relies on a country-year data set of conflict initiation in which country i is coded "1" if it initiated

---

[12] Polity scores used are "Polity2" variables from the 2010 version of the Polity IV data set; see Jaggers and Gurr 1995. Military capabilities data are taken from Singer, Bremer, and Stuckey 1972. A state's share of dyadic capabilities is defined as $\frac{CINC_i}{CINC_i + CINC_j}$. Contiguity was calculated as "direct contiguity" (level 1: contiguous on land). Distance is measured as "capitol to capitol." Data on alliance commitments were taken from the Alliance Treaty Obligations and Provisions Project; Leeds et al. 2002. Peace years were adjusted for pre-1816 disputes using Werner 2000.

[13] As a general note, however, results do not depend on lagging the IV, and lagging it two or three (or zero) years instead of one produces similar results as well.

[14] Dafoe, Renshon, and Huth 2014, 383–84.

a MID in year t or "0" if it did not (multiple MIDs in a given year by the same country are still coded as a "1").[15]

To examine this, I regressed *change* in status rank on a series of independent variables relating to conflict victory.[16] Figure 5.1 plots the results of the analysis.[17] The models are shown in three versions: bivariate, control models with and without GDP (inclusion of GDP restricts data to the post–World War II period), and dependent variables, including changes in status rank over both five- and ten-year periods after the initiation of conflict.

In fact, we do find support for H1: initiating and winning conflicts provides a boost to status over both five- and ten-year periods following the conflict initiation, relative to:

1. not initiating at all
2. initiating and losing
3. initiating and drawing
4. initiating and losing/drawing

For example, initiating and winning vaults the initiator state 6.7 rankings over states that did not initiate at all, and 6.9 ranks over states that initiated but fought to a stalemate.

The theoretical expectations in H1 relate specifically to *exceeding the expectations of observers* in combat, however, not necessarily winning. Fighting a superior opponent to a stalemate might generate as much in status benefits as defeating an inferior opponent. Moreover, even victory itself is subjective.[18] Many factors—including material changes, achieving goals of war, expectation of participants and observers, and satisfaction with the settlement terms—impact the perception of victory and defeat.

---

[15] While this research design has important advantages, it does present two complications. First, it prevents us estimating an effect of a particular type of conflict on victory, since 13 percent of the data include observations where a country initiated more than one MID in a given year. The second issue is related: a state could initiate two MIDs in a year, win one of them and suffer defeat in another. How to count this? For those countries with more than one MID in a given year, I selected the MID(s) with the highest level of hostilities. In cases where this did not result in a unique MID per country-year, I randomly selected one of the remaining MIDs for inclusion in the sample. The consequence is greater uncertainty surrounding our outcome variable.

[16] Because states sometimes switch communities, and the algorithm provides arbitrary "names" for each community in each year, one cannot follow the progress of a state within a given community. This means that we cannot examine changes in status rank within a given community.

[17] Full results are contained in online appendix materials.

[18] Johnson and Tierney 2006; Mandel 2006.

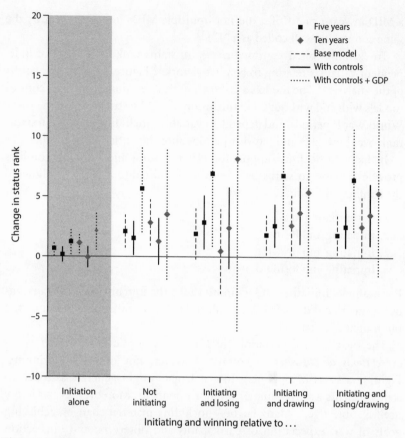

Figure 5.1: **Status Benefits of Conflict Initiation and Victory** Y-axis represents change in international status rank over either five or ten years after conflict. On the far left, in gray, are estimates for initiation of a MID—independent of outcome—relative to not initiating.

We can possibly expect COW's codings to line up with those subjective understandings in expectation, but the relatively small numbers for any analysis of these outcomes (for example, there are only 105 states in the data that initiated and then lost a MID) combined with measurement error (particularly in the cases where a state both won and lost in the same year) suggests that we should not rely too heavily on codings of victory and defeat.

To provide a broader perspective on this, figure 5.1 plots (in the leftmost, gray panel) results for *initiation alone* (compared to not initiating). While the substantive effects are smaller, there is considerably less uncertainty. This fits with the explanation provided in the last paragraph: while "victory" and "defeat" are variable and subjective terms, and multiple MIDs present difficult problems for this design, conflict *initiation* is (compared to these concepts at least) clear and unambiguous. Thus, I find that on average, conflict initiation by itself—regardless of the outcome—provides a status boost to initiator states of 1.0 ranks over five years and 2.7 ranks over ten years. Unsurprisingly, the longer the time frame, the greater our uncertainty: results for a five-year period are consistently and unambiguously statistically significant, while results for the ten-year period are more uncertain. This likely results from the inherent trade-off of examining temporally distant outcomes: a greater chance of things outside the model affecting the results.

It's also worth noting that this finding is not driven by any particular type of state or time frame. Supplementary analyses show alternative plots with different samples, limiting the analyses to major powers, minor powers, the nineteenth century, and the post–World War I, post–World War II, and post–Cold War periods.[19] In all cases, the pattern remains consistent. Minor powers, for example, are no less likely than major powers to gain status benefits from the initiation of (and victory in) conflicts. If anything, the status benefits that accrue to smaller, less powerful states seem larger than those that major powers can expect. "Ceiling effects" might be part of the explanation for this, as powerful states just have much less room for status improvements than their less important counterparts.

Finally, I examined the extent to which these findings are conditional on the initiation of conflict. In status dissatisfaction theory, the critical factor is whether a state exceeds expectations in conflict. Because the theory is focused on the conscious, strategic actions that states take in order to increase their status, the first part of the analysis concentrated on initiation. States that exceed expectations in conflict, though, should receive status benefits whether they set out to shift their status rank or not. Thus, we should also expect to see evidence that the effects described above are not conditional on initiation.

To investigate this, I redid the analysis above, changing the comparison so that "involved in conflict + winning" was compared to the same four categories described above (not involved in conflict, involved and losing, involved and drawing, and involved and losing/drawing). In fact, I find that

---

[19] Reproduced in online appendix materials.

TABLE 5.1
Status Deficits across Initiation Status $N = 1278971$.

	War		MID	
	Mean	SD	Mean	SD
No initiation	0.000	0.995	0.000	0.995
Initiation	0.372	0.836	0.227	0.904

the status benefits of conflict are not conditional on having initiated the conflict. Whether a state has been targeted or has targeted others, victory in international conflict pays status dividends. For example, being involved in a conflict and winning provides a status boost of between three and six ranks over five years compared to otherwise-similar states that were involved in conflict but lost.[20]

STATUS DEFICITS AND WAR

Next we turn to the centerpiece of the theory: the hypothesis that dis-satisfied states will initiate conflicts at greater rates than satisfied ones. A rough approach to addressing this is by simply looking at status deficit scores for states that initiated a MID or war in comparison to those that did not. Depicted in table 5.1, the results are straightforward: states that initiated a MID or war had significantly higher status deficits one year prior to initiation (status deficits must be lagged by one year to account for the possibility that conflict initiation would affect status deficits, rather than the other way around). Of course, while this tentatively supports the case of status dissatisfaction theory, there are numerous drawbacks to stopping our analysis with cross-tabulations.

I now turn to more sophisticated analyses that incorporate control variables to account for potential confounders. Because the dependent variable is binary, the appropriate regression model is binomial logit. And because the vast majority of observations are zeros (that is, there are few conflicts in the data set relative to the number of total observations), I use rare events logit to correct for the noted tendency of traditional logit models to underestimate the probability of events that occur rarely in the

---

[20] See analyses in online appendix materials.

data (the "ones" or wars).[21] Another way of dealing with the bias that typically occurs when rare events are estimated with logit is provided by Firth.[22] Rather than estimating the bias—as King's method does—Firth's method attempts to prevent it from arising in the first place by penalizing the maximum likelihood estimates with Jeffrey's invariant prior. Firth's method can have advantages in some cases, though King and Zeng note that the two methods give answers that "are always numerically very close (almost always less than half a percent [difference])."[23] In this chapter, I present results using rare events logit, though results are close to identical with Firth's method.[24] The reported results use robust (dyad-clustered) standard errors, although encouragingly, analyses using normal standard errors generate virtually identical results.[25]

The main results are depicted in table C.1 (appendix C.1).[26] In all models—from bivariate regressions to those that include a variety of controls as well as squared polynomials of the IV to account for nonlinear effects and a lagged dependent variable to address temporal dependence—the coefficient for status deficit within the detected community is positive and statistically significant.[27] This in turn implies that larger values for that

[21] King and Zeng 2001a, 2001b. This software works by sampling all the events ("ones" or conflicts) and a small portion of the nonevents (zeros), taking into account the actual proportion of ones relative to zeros in the observed data.

[22] Firth 1993.

[23] King and Zeng 2001b, 148.

[24] For results using Firth's method, see online appendix materials.

[25] King and Roberts 2015.

[26] There is substantial disagreement on how one should utilize controls variables in this sort of setup; see Ray 2003. Solutions entail everything from using no control variables at all (Clarke 2005), to a limit of some reasonable number (for example, the "rule of three"; Achen 2002), to those more optimistic about the utility of control variables (Oneal and Russett 2005). I present all results as both bivariate and "full" models that include a reasonable number of control variables as well as showing through coefficient plots the stability of the results when switching the control variables used in the models.

[27] Temporal dependence is a vexing statistical issue for IR scholars using time-series cross-sectional data. In IR, there have been three broad approaches to the problem: including a lagged dependent variable (LDV; Beck and Katz 1996, 2011; see also Achen 2000), cubic splines (Beck, Katz, and Tucker 1998), and the related but simpler solution of including cubic polynomials of peace years (Carter and Signorino 2010). Typically, IR scholars pick a "fix," justify it with appeals to the statistical authorities, and proceed. But this procedure is dysfunctional in the longer-term, since in many cases, adopting the wrong "fix" can lead to significant inferential problems (Wilson and Butler, 2007). More forcefully, Dafoe (2015) demonstrated that the solution for temporal dependence is always dependent on strong assumptions about the data-generating process. The best "fix" is, thus, not at a fix at all but rather to report estimates under a variety of model specifications, as I do here.

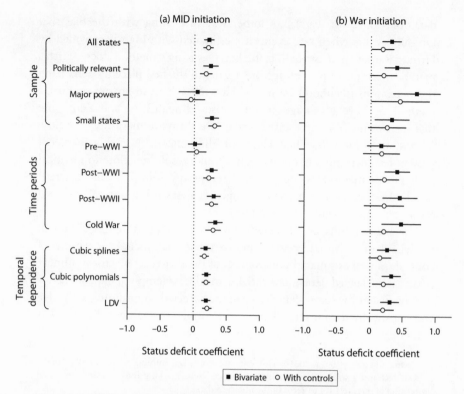

Figure 5.2: **MID and War Initiation Models: Status Dissatisfaction Coefficients**
Plot of status deficit (community) coefficients—and 95 percent confidence intervals—under a variety of model specifications.

measure—in effect, larger status deficits—are associated with an increased probability of war and MID initiation.

The results described above are robust to a wide variety of model specifications. One way to visualize this is through a coefficient plot, here used to depict status deficit coefficients from a variety of different model specifications, including different samples of states, different time periods, and different corrections for temporal dependence. As is evident in figure 5.2, the status deficit coefficient is quite stable in the MID initiation models, remaining positive in all specifications, and highly statistically significant in all but one (where it is only marginally significant; results are highly similar for war initiation models).

That the results are "stable," however, does not tell us much about the effects of status deficits in the real world. To assess this, figure 5.3 plots

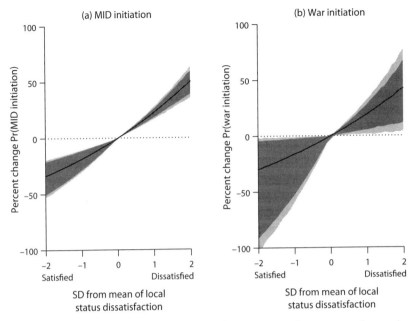

Figure 5.3: **Status Deficits and War** Y-axis represents the percent change in the probability of initiating either a (a) militarized dispute or (b) war. Estimates are first differences—switching only the level of status dissatisfaction while holding covariates at mean or median. Black lines represent estimates, and dark and light gray shaded regions are 95 and 99 percent confidence intervals, respectively. Results are estimates from models two and five in table C.1.

first differences—the difference between pr(DV = 1) at two different levels of the IV—for (a) MID, and (b) war initiation. They answer the question, What is the change in the probability of a state initiating a war or MID if we hold every control variable at some constant (mean or median) level, but switch status deficits from one level to another?

As is easily seen, larger status deficits are associated with an *increased* chance of both MID and war initiation. In fact, the substantive impact of status deficits is rather large, even when compared to other variables commonly implicated in explaining conflict initiation: a state that is switched from "no status deficit" to a status deficit 1 standard deviation from the mean is estimated to be almost twice as likely to initiate a war or MID. This is clear support for our hypothesis (H2) that status deficits are associated with the initiation of violent interstate conflict.

The size of the effects are substantively large as well as statistically significant. Figure 5.4 compares the effects of a change from −1 to +1 standard deviation around the mean for our main variable of interest (status deficit) as well as the control variables (binary variables are switched from 0 to 1). In the plots, the vertical dotted line is centered on the estimate for status deficit, so estimates to the left are smaller in size, while estimates to the right are larger (the plots are ordered from top to bottom by the size of effect in order to ease interpretation).

What do we learn from these plots? For both MID and war initiation, we see that changes in status deficits—effectively switching a state from having "too much" to "too little" status—have relatively large effects in the models compared to other covariates. For example, making a state "dissatisfied" has larger effects on MID initiation than even joint democracy or any type of alliance between states. In the war initiation models, status deficits have larger effects than even whether two states already are involved in a MID as well as many types of alliances, joint democracy, and level of democracy.

WHO GETS TARGETED?

Finally, we turn to the characteristics of the *targets* of status aggression. More specifically, I test the hypothesis (H3a and H3b) that dissatisfied states pick fights with different sorts of states than satisfied states.

To conduct this analysis, I created a dummy variable, dissatisfied, equal to 1 when the states' status deficit was above the mean in a given hierarchy (for comprehensiveness, I include regional and global hierarchies as well as the detected community), and equal to 0 when it was equal to or below the mean. To assess whether a fight was "winnable," I constructed a measure, power differential, that is the difference between i and j's CINC score; positive values indicate that i had greater military capabilities than j, and negative values mean the opposite.[28] Because conflict at time t is likely to affect the power differential between i and j in that same year, I lag power differential one year to better proxy beliefs about the likelihood of winning a conflict. To examine status, I followed a similar procedure, creating a variable, status differential, that is equal to initiator status minus target status (lagged one year). Thus, positive values indicate an initiator

---

[28] Of course, the more powerful state does not always win, but it is difficult to find a better *ex ante* proxy for whether a war was "winnable." Arreguin-Toft 2001.

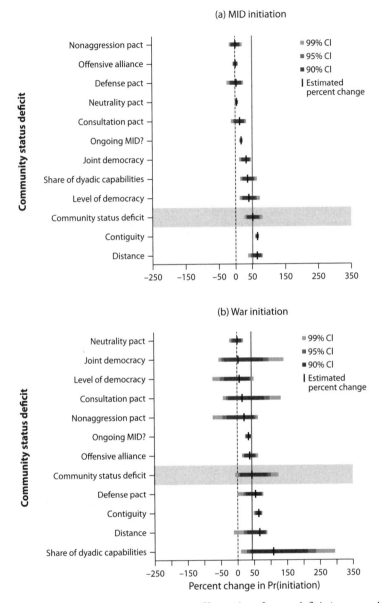

Figure 5.4: **Comparison of Substantive Effects** Plot of status deficit (community) coefficients compared to other covariates in analyses where DV is percent change in probability of MID or wat initiation. Continuous variables are switched from—1 to +1 SD around mean—while binary variables are switched from 0 to 1.

(ranked tenth, for example) targeting a higher-ranked state (such as one ranked first). Negative values for status differential would indicate initiators targeting lower-ranked states.

Using simple t-tests, it is plain that the power differential between initiator and target is greater for dissatisfied states than satisfied ones ($t[2450] = -1.98$, $p < 0.05$). In fact, this pattern persists in all the hierarchies examined—community, regional, and global—and for a variety of operationalizations of conflict initiation (including MIDs, violent MIDs, and wars). As is evident in figure 5.5, differences between satisfied and dissatisfied states targets are significant under all specifications for MIDs and violent MIDs. Moreover, the power differentials for the different groups are substantively significant, as illustrated by the third panel, which plots example dyads along the same y-axis. Dissatisfied states seem to disproportionately target less powerful states than their otherwise-similar (but satisfied) counterparts.

Figure 5.6 displays the results of status differentials. The y-axis scale is actual ranks, so interpretation (aided by the example dyad plot) is rather straightforward. Again, the pattern is clear. Estimates for satisfied states are consistently negative under all specifications, indicating that satisfied states seem to overwhelmingly target lower-status ones. In contrast, dissatisfied states initiate MIDs, violent MIDs, and wars against states that are *higher* ranked in their detected status community and their region. Even in the global hierarchy, dissatisfied states target states whose status is commensurate with their own (negative differential, but not statistically distinguishable from zero). Even a conservative reading of the evidence suggests that while satisfied states clearly target lower-ranked ones, dissatisfied states select targets against relative equals.

This section thus provides support for the notion that status dissatisfaction impacts not only the likelihood of conflict but also the selection of targets. In support of my theory, dissatisfied states pick different sorts of fights from otherwise-similar but satisfied states. First, they seek fights where they are at a greater advantage in terms of military capabilities, thereby giving themselves the best possible chance of accomplishing their goal: perform well in conflict and shift the beliefs of others about where they stand in the hierarchy. Moreover, in contrast to satisfied states, dissatisfied states target adversaries that are relative equals in their status hierarchy. This implication is drawn directly from status dissatisfaction theory, and in fact from the very definition of status. Status is gained more efficiently from higher-status actors, so defeating higher-status states is a far

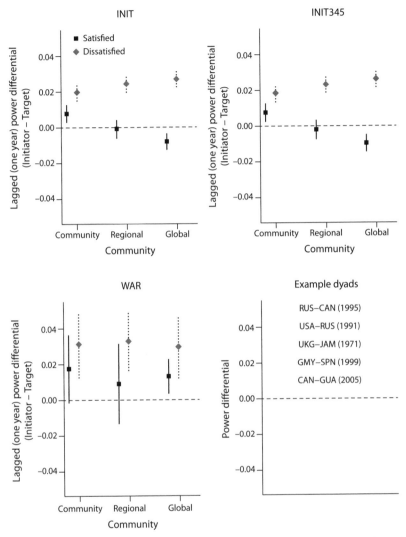

Figure 5.5: **Targets of Status Aggression: Less Powerful** Y-axis represents lagged (one year) power differential between i and j (where i is always the initiator) in terms of CINC score. Plotted estimates represent the means for dissatisfied (♦) and satisfied (■) initiators, with confidence intervals from two-tailed t-tests. Dissatisfied states are those below the mean in community status deficits, and satisfied states are those equal to or greater than the mean. Plots represent different categories of initiation: INIT = initiation of any kind; INIT345 = initiation of violent disputes; and WAR = initiation of wars.

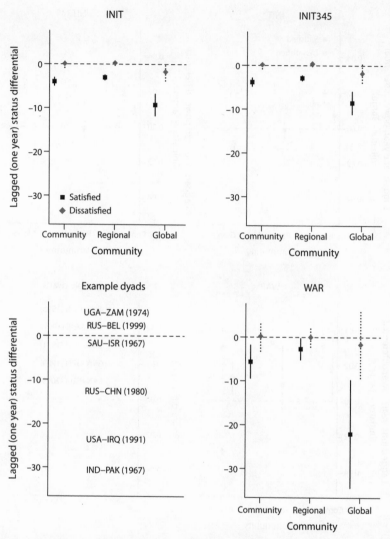

Figure 5.6: **Targets of Status Aggression: Higher Status** Y-axis represents lagged (one year) status differential between i and j (where i is always the initiator) in terms of status rank within one of several communities. Plotted estimates represent the means for dissatisfied (♦) and satisfied (■) initiators, with confidence intervals from two-tailed t-tests. Dissatisfied states are those below the mean in community status deficits, and satisfied states are those equal to or greater than the mean. Plots represent different categories of initiation: INIT = initiation of any kind; INIT345 = initiation of violent disputes; and WAR = initiation of wars.

more efficient means of shifting one's place in the hierarchy than initiating against low-status states. Note that this combination of target attributes (less powerful and relatively equal status) is at least *somewhat* consistent with the predictions of power transition theory, but much broader, this analysis shows how status dissatisfaction impacts states at every level of the hierarchy, not just potential hegemons.[29]

STATUS IS LOCAL

As mentioned earlier, IR scholars have yet to grapple with the "local" nature of status. Typically, previous works assumed that all states interacted primarily within a global hierarchy, and if a smaller grouping of states was analyzed (for example, just major powers), it was under the assumption that those were the only states for which status concerns were likely to impact conflict behavior. Decades of research on status suggest that this view is incomplete, at best.

Earlier, I classified two broad approaches to the identification of reference groups for states in the international system—one deductive, and one inductive. The former approach starts by positing attributes that might define a reference group (for example, geographic region) and proceeds from there. The latter uses data to identify—here through "community detection"—reference groups through real-world interactions. H4 (status is local) states that status deficits within detected communities will be better predictors of conflict behavior than deficits within regional or global hierarchies. Direct tests of this hypothesis are difficult, however, as multicollinearity between ranks in different communities present inferential difficulties.

What is needed is a way to combat this and separate out the effects of status deficits within local communities from those within the global system. To achieve this, I subset the data to examine the effects of status deficits (within detected communities) for only those states that are satisfied within other, broader hierarchies. If my measure of local status provides additional traction, then we should find that even when states are "satisfied" with broader hierarchies, status concerns within their own status community will consistently predict their initiation of violent military conflict.

---

[29] "Somewhat" because power transition is more apt to predict the targeting of lower/equal power states that are *higher* status, since they have "locked in" the hierarchy of prestige.

In fact, I find exactly this. For states that are satisfied within their regional hierarchy, a small shift in their *local* status deficit (from 0 to +1 standard deviation) still nearly doubles their odds of initiating an interstate war (82 percent increase). For states satisfied within the global hierarchy composed of all possible states, that same shift in their local status deficit increases their odds of initiating a war by 62 percent. In both cases, those effects are statistically significant. The pattern is exactly the same when we turn to MID initiation: a small shift in local status deficits increases the odds of MID initiation by either 40 percent (satisfied in global hierarchy) or 47 percent (satisfied in regional hierarchy).

In sum, I find that even for states that are "satisfied" within the larger, global hierarchy, status deficits within their local community emerge as reliable predictors of conflict initiation. This is true even when we subset to states satisfied within their regional, geographic hierarchy (itself a type of "local" hierarchy). Thus, we find initial support for H4: even internationally, status is local.

ALTERNATIVE EXPLANATIONS

Underlying Disputes Cause Both *Status Deficits and Conflict Initiation*

One potential question regarding the findings presented in this chapter is whether the link between dissatisfaction and conflict is driven by factors unaccounted for in the models. For example, the connection between status dissatisfaction (X) and conflict (Y) might be spurious if both are caused by an omitted variable (Z), as in the following causal diagram, in which the dashed line represents the potentially spurious relationship:

$$Z \rightleftharpoons X \dashrightarrow Y$$

In one obvious example, the results might be driven by some an underlying dispute between i and j. Such a dispute might lead j to withdraw diplomatic representation at i, thus inflating i's status deficit and eventually leading to an actual conflict between the two states. In this case, the underlying dispute would be the real cause even though we observe what appears to be a significant association between status deficit and the initiation of conflict.

To address this, I constructed a variable, diplomatic change, that takes on a "1" if j has withdrawn diplomats from i in year $t - 1$ and a "0" otherwise.

Including this covariate in a model for MIDs changes neither the size of the status deficit coefficient nor its statistical significance.[30] Therefore, while there are endless potential omitted variables in any model, this analysis confirms that a significant and plausible one is not responsible for the observed results.

Another version of this concern about endogeneity relates to the construction of the status deficit measure itself. One input into the status deficit variable is a country's CINC score, a "composite index of national capabilities" that includes iron and steel production, energy consumption, total population, urban population, military expenditures, and military personnel. These last two components of the measure are worrisome from the perspective of causal identification. For example, country i might commit itself to a policy building up its military in order to extract resources from other states through armed conflict, but because they were inflating their military power, it would appear as though their status deficit was increasing and leading to war, even though status may not have mattered at all. To address this, I reconstructed the CINC measure without either of the two military components (personnel and spending), and reran the models described in this chapter with this new "modified CINC" score as the input to the status deficit variable. The "modified CINC" covariate correlated with the traditional CINC measure at 0.96. The results of the models linking status deficits to war were unchanged in terms of substantive or statistical significance.[31]

The Link between Status Deficits and War Is a Remnant of the Nineteenth Century

A second class of objections to these results is that the international system has changed a great deal over time. Jervis summarizes this concern when he notes that the "old linkages between standing... and war do seem to have been severed," and that "unless wars are justified by self-defense... they now lower rather than raise the country's status."[32] A similar concern is voiced by Lebow in explaining his cultural theory of IR (he places the

---

[30] When restricting only to wars, this control model's p-value changes from 0.04 to 0.06, though the difference between significant and not significant is not itself always significant. Gelman and Stern 2006.

[31] See analyses in online appendix materials.

[32] Jervis 2012, 342–43.

date for the change around 1945).[33] Wood provides another example, though one that is a bit more qualified. He first states that "the extent to which nations will go to defend their prestige... has changed in the 'post-heroic' West."[34] In contrast, using a different methodology, Gochman found evidence for a relationship between status inconsistency and war among major powers *only* in the twentieth century.[35]

Because such an objection might be based on a number of factors—the number of "poles" in the system or changes in its dynamics, the proliferation of small states with different incentives than major powers, the Cold War, and so on—I addressed it using a flexible methodology that might take into account these different potential mechanisms.[36] First, I estimated models for each decade in the data set (a decade runs, for example, from 1920 to 1929).[37] I also estimated separate models for "geopolitical time periods," including the nineteenth century, the "long nineteenth century" (up until both 1914, and a model that goes until 1918 and includes World War I), post–World War I, post–World War II, the Cold War, and the post–Cold War periods.[38]

The plots suggest little evidence to justify the fears of Lebow and others that the relationship between status concerns and conflict has changed

---

[33] Lebow 2010a, 490.

[34] Wood 2013.

[35] Gochman 1980.

[36] See Waltz 1979; Wohlforth 1999; Volgy and Mayhall 1995; Keohane 1969; Gaddis 1986. A large debate in IR has focused on the related issue of how to "account" for time in our statistical models; Dafoe 2015. These works, particularly prominent ones such as by Beck, Katz, and Tucker (1998) and Carter and Signorino (2010), provide guidance on how to control for temporal dependence. The latter advises interpretation of the baseline hazard, while Beck (2010, 294) declares that "time is not a theoretical variable," and our goal should be "to find variables that lead to duration independence." Without entering into this debate, I note that the question at issue here is subtly different. In effect, I am interested in whether the β for status deficit is different in year t compared to year u, not whether the probability of state i initiating against state j is affected by the time since their last conflict. Thus, traditional time-series approaches are less relevant for this analysis.

[37] For the MID and war initiation models, alliance dummies were transformed into a categorical variable. For the war initiation models, the following variables had to be dropped: joint democracy, ongoing. In some decades, even alliance type would be omitted from the model. So that coefficients could be directly compared, alliance type is not included in any model. The dependent variable does not vary for the entirety of the 1830s, so that decade cannot be estimated.

[38] Figure 5.7 displays the results of this analysis for MID initiation (see analyses in appendix, which display results for war initiation that are highly similar). In both MID and war initiation models, alliance dummies were transformed into a categorical variable.

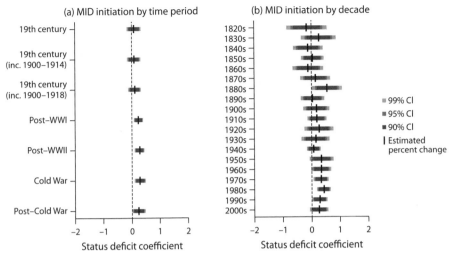

Figure 5.7: **The Effect of Status Deficits over Time** Plots are coefficients on status deficit variable. In the left column, time is divided into periods based on large-scale changes in the international system; in the right column, models are estimated for every decade.

significantly over time.[39] In fact, whether it is measured as a trend "over time" or discretely for different geopolitical time periods, the relationship appears to be growing stronger in recent years.

Supplementary analyses confirm our initial impression.[40] To the extent that any pattern is visible at all, it is that the β for status deficit is *larger* in more recent years, not smaller. Of course, this coincides with an ever-expanding number of states in the system, and thus an explosion of observations. The statistically significant results here might simply be the mechanical result of depressed standard errors from a large number of observations in recent years. The key here is the sign of the coefficient, which is positive in every geopolitical time period, and 84 percent of the decades (sixteen out of nineteen). A conservative conclusion would thus be that the effect of status deficits on conflict initiation is relatively uniform over time, and there is zero evidence that such an effect is confined to the nineteenth century.

[39] Lebow 2010a.
[40] See online appendix materials.

Yes, but This Can't Be True When There Are Strong Norms against Conflict

While the above objection focuses on the changing relationship between status deficits and war *over time*, an additional one combines such an argument with a spatial component. Such an objection would state that the relationship between status deficits and conflict may be true for certain groups of states, in certain time periods, but would be moderated by the development of strong international norms against the initiation of violent conflict.

Some scholars, such as Zacher, have shown the differential development and institutionalization of norms across regions.[41] A large body of literature on the impact of European security institutions makes a similar type of argument: certain groups of countries, in certain time periods, are proscribed from using international violence to further their interests.[42] Such an argument is made explicitly by Florini, who states that it is about both the passage of time and groupings of states: "In the era of trading states and prohibitions against interstate aggression ... war among major powers is no longer the primary means of international change."[43]

Of course, not all scholars agree that norms constrain state behavior. Arguments may be placed on a spectrum from "norms don't constrain states at all" to "norms matter, but states will violate them when they can."[44] And of course, the question of how to examine whether norms "mattered" is complex, since norms are but one factor among many in states' calculations, and some norms simply disappear after a time.[45] This latter point in particular suggests the need for a flexible method of detecting the existence of norms.

In order to examine this, I first sorted states into their "detected communities," as detailed in this and the previous chapter. I then constructed a measure of conflict propensity for each community in each year. This measure simply counts the number of conflicts (wars or MIDs) initiated by member states over the past x amount of years. Measuring it by year allows us to control for long-term trends in the amount of conflict in the international system. Focusing on conflict *initiation* prevents false positives

---

[41] Zacher 2001.
[42] For example, Flynn and Farrell 1999.
[43] Florini 1996, 371.
[44] See Mearsheimer 1994; Shannon 2000.
[45] Legro 1997; Panke and Petersohn 2012.

that would occur if a community had a strong norm against conflict that led to its members being targeted by other states. On the other hand, since we only observe final outcomes (whether or not initiation occurred) and not *direct* evidence of the norm itself, our conclusions must be necessarily tempered.[46]

Because there is little agreement on how long norms take to develop (and this is likely to be different for different groups of states), I estimated models based on conflict propensity as measured over five-, ten- and twenty-year periods. Thus, detected communities in which many states have initiated conflicts in the last x number of years will measure "high" on the conflict propensity spectrum, and communities where conflict initiation is a rare event will measure "low." I estimated models that include covariates for status deficit (in the detected community), conflict propensity, and an interaction term.

Table C.4 (in the online appendix) presents the results of this analysis. The interaction term is not statistically significant in a single one of these models. For ease of interpretation, figure 5.8 presents the results in visual form, showing how the β for status deficit changes over the range of conflict propensity variable.

If one looks closely enough—especially at the bottom row of models, where the interaction term is *marginally* significant—one can see a trend in the direction predicted by arguments about norms: as one moves from left to right, and the norms against violence get weaker, the β for status deficit grows larger (more positive). It seems clear, however, that the key takeaway from these plots is that the estimate for the effect of status deficits on conflict (MID or war) initiation does not change significantly over the range of conflict propensity. No matter how generously one measures the existence of a norm—in fact, even if we allow that they evolve over multiple decades—the link between status deficits and war is just as strong in communities where the initiation of violence is exceedingly rare, as it is for conflict-prone groups of states. This analysis fits well with the arguments of the "norm skeptics" mentioned above: if you squint hard enough, you can find evidence of their impact, but it is not easy or obvious.

---

[46] This is, in the words of Goertz and Diehl (1992, 643), an "external approach" to studying norms.

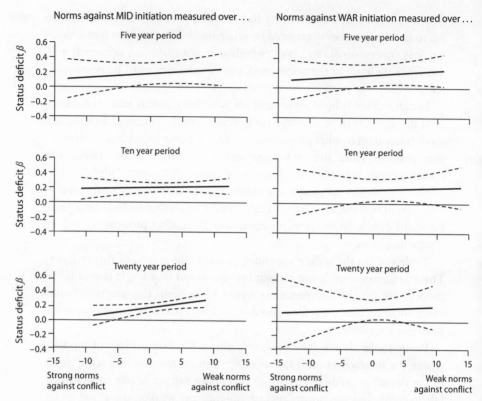

Figure 5.8: **Norms against Conflict Don't Moderate Status Aggression** Estimates and 95 percent confidence intervals indicate effect of status deficits on either MID (left panel) or war (right panel) initiation. Estimates below $y = 0$ (i.e., negative estimates) indicate that status deficits predict more conflict initiation. The x-axis represents the range of conflict propensity for different communities, as measured by the amount of conflict initiated by states within a given community in the preceding five- (top row), ten- (middle row), and twenty-year (bottom row) periods.

Major Powers Are Different

A final concern is that the main results are driven by smaller states in the system rather than major powers. If true, this would be an important scope condition. I showed earlier that major powers do not seem to differ greatly in the status benefits that accrue to them following a successful conflict. Of course, the benefits are lower than they are for smaller states, but major powers also have far less room to move (up).

A related concern might be that link between status deficits and conflict might be dependent on the community detection algorithm employed. I made the case earlier that community detection—the inductive approach that I took throughout these large-N chapters—carries numerous advantages. Among those, we learn how states sort themselves into groups from their actual behavior and expenditures of resources. This is particularly useful since, in many instances, we do not have a deep understanding of how states compose their status communities, and in any case, these almost certainly shift over time.

Yet there is at least one group of states in international politics where we can plausibly claim a strong set of priors about who they see themselves as being in competition with: major powers. For the majority of major powers, it will be *other major powers* that will form the reference group. This might not always be the case—even major powers have regional concerns as well sometimes—but it is likely true enough of the time to show up in the data.

To address this question, I reconstructed the status deficit measure above, but this time specifying the community composed solely of major powers. In other words, status and capability scores were generated as described above, but the status deficit score takes as its input a state's rank within the community of major powers. I measured "major power" in two ways: the more restrictive COW coding as well as a more inclusive measure that allows the top ten most powerful states in year t to be "in the club." In both cases, we are measuring initiation against major and nonmajor powers; the only difference from previous models is that the focus is on predicting the actions of major powers, which are assumed to be concerned with status within the major power community.

From this analysis, we learn two important things.[47] First, the results are broadly consistent with those presented everywhere else in this chapter: larger status deficits predict the initiation of conflict. One significant difference that emerges for this powerful subsample of states, though, concerns the type of initiation that is linked to larger status deficits. For powerful states where we specify other major powers as the reference group, the statistical association between status deficits and MID initiation is even stronger than it is for the sample as a whole using the community detection algorithm. The link between status deficits and war is nevertheless attenuated: estimated coefficients are in the "right" direction, but are less

---

[47] Results are presented in the online appendix.

likely to be statistically signifiant. This is suggestive of the notion that major powers facing heightened status concerns are far more likely to initiate coercive militarized crises than interstate wars.

Thus, major powers are different, but not in the sense that status concerns are not still a critical factor for them. Instead, major powers differ because we are able to use our deeper understanding of their calculations to more closely align our measure of status concerns with empirical reality. Once we do that, we again find evidence in favor of status dissatisfaction: just like other states, major powers initiate conflict when confronted with status deficits and reap the rewards of successful conflict.

SUMMARY

In this chapter, I brought my new measures of status and dissatisfaction to bear on international conflict data. I then found support for a number of implications derived from status dissatisfaction theory. First, I showed that conflict was a status-enhancing strategy, and that winning—and even just initiating—conflict provided a status boost five and ten years down the road. Next, I demonstrated the strong link between status and conflict: status deficits significantly predicted MID and war initiation. Moreover, I showed that these results were robust to a wide variety of model specifications, remaining significant in different samples of states and time periods, with different sets of controls as well as "corrections" for temporal dependence.

I also showed that status dissatisfaction not only increases the likelihood of conflict but changes its very nature, too, and does so in ways that are predicted by the theory. Dissatisfied states target different sorts of states from otherwise-similar but satisfied counterparts in international politics. In particular, they target states that are less powerful (in order to increase the odds of success) and higher status (in order to more efficiently displace higher-ranked states). Dissatisfaction over relative status also changes even the way in which conflicts are fought. Finally, I provided evidence that even internationally, status is local. I presented the first evidence in IR on the nature of status communities and illustrated one way of disentangling their impact from status concerns in other, broader hierarchies.

Of course, this collection of results has left some questions unanswered. While I show *links* between status deficits and conflict initiation, large-N work is always subject to concerns about endogeneity, and causal claims based on such research must necessarily be tempered. Some of these concerns can be addressed in principled ways in a quantitative research design, and to the extent possible, I have done so (for example, by lagging the main predictor several years, or preempting several alternative explanations). Additional confidence, however, can only be generated through convergent evidence drawn from different data sources and methodologies. In the next two chapters, I build on these results through case studies of foreign policy decision making across the majority of the twentieth century.

6

"Petty Prestige Victories" and Weltpolitik
in Germany, 1897–1911

> "...the earlier errors of a Turkish policy against Russia, a Moroccan
> [one] against France, [a] fleet against England, irritating everyone,
> blocking everybody's way and yet not really weakening anyone.
> Basic cause: lack of planning, craving for petty prestige victories. "
> — *Bethmann Hollweg, chancellor of the German Empire (1909–17),*
> *reflecting on* Weltpolitik *to his adviser Kurt Riezler.*

Chapter 2 laid out a theory of status dissatisfaction that set forth several propositions about how status concerns relate to international conflict.[1] In the three chapters that followed, I found support for these propositions at the micro- and macrolevel. Chapter 3 showed conclusively that status concerns lead decision makers to value status more highly, and suggested a casual role for status concerns in affecting patterns of escalation and decision making. Chapters 4 and 5 operationalized the theory at the state level, and showed that states that experienced status deficits were twice as likely as their satisfied counterparts to initiate violent international disputes, and that states received status benefits from initiating and winning those disputes.

Each set of evidence, however, has the drawbacks inherent in the method used to obtain it. Individual-level laboratory studies focus one or two key factors, leaving aside many critical aspects of the environment in which decision makers actually operate, and the nature of cross-national regressions is such that many answers regarding the specific dynamics of the theory remain tentative. This chapter helps address some of these

---

[1] Epigraph from Riezler's diary, quoted in Herwig 1986, 93.

shortcomings by zeroing in on the specific beliefs and actions of German leaders during the Weltpolitik era. These substantiate and illustrate two important findings from previous chapters: the heightened status concerns led German leaders to value status more highly (as in the experiments in chapter 3) and initiate a series of international conflicts (as in chapter 5). We do not see evidence of escalation of commitment in this particular case, though chapter 7 provides several illustrations of this pattern of behavior in other historical cases.

The role of status in this era of German history is much the same as it is throughout the history of political science: oft-remarked on, but little studied. There is nothing new to the assertion that German leaders in the Weltpolitik era cared about both their personal prestige and that of their respective countries.[2] But the assumption that status was important has, ironically, somewhat obscured the actual role that status concerns played in the years leading up the Great War. While many works mention its significance, none explain its role in the development of Weltpolitk, provide a generalizable mechanism by which status concerns lead to conflict, or shed light on the strategic nature of German crisis initiation.

In the case of Wilhelmine Germany, I find evidence in the historical record for several of the most important implications of status dissatisfaction theory. As predicted by the quantitative measures in chapters 4 and 5, German leaders did indeed experience a "status deficit" that led to the development of the grand strategy referred to as Weltpolitik. More specifically, German leaders did not just care about status but also evidenced the belief that they were being deprived of the status they deserved based on their material capabilities. Equally important, their reference group was composed of a small number of peer competitors; for Germany, "local" status referred to standing within a small group of major powers that included France, Britain, and Russia. Finally, German leaders saw conflict and crisis initiation as a viable strategy for rectifying their status deficit.

This case also helps shed light on the dyadic nature of status interactions in world politics. German leaders believed that their status deficit resulted from their relatively late unification as a modern nation-state (a belief consistent with the quantitative evidence presented in chapter 4 on the sources of status). This led to perceptions of its importance lagging behind its quick development as a powerful, wealthy country and major power.

---

[2] See, for example, Markey 2000; Murray 2008; Ward 2012; Onea 2014.

Nevertheless, whatever lag might have existed "naturally" or resulted from the diplomatic strategy of Otto von Bismarck, it was exacerbated through the deliberate strategies of status quo major powers (such as Britain and France) that rightly considered any status gained by Germany as a loss to themselves. In truth, because of its positional nature, any status concession by France or Britain would have been detrimental to their own position, and it is evident that those countries faced a difficult trade-off: accommodate Germany's status demands (and hurt their own status position) or deny them (and risk escalation).

Seen in the light of status dissatisfaction theory, Germany's Weltpolitik policy, often derided by historians as blundering or reckless, can be viewed as a reasonable response to a genuine strategic dilemma: how to acquire status from actors unwilling to cede it voluntarily. As a recent history of the era argues, British leaders "proceeded from the assumption" that their own imperial interests were "vital" and "essential," while German ones were "a mere luxury, the energetic pursuit of which must be construed as a provocation by other powers."[3]

In this chapter, I demonstrate that the policies associated with Weltpolitik—primarily the constant instigation of international crises along with the pursuit of a large navy and mostly worthless colonial territories—may instead be seen as policies designed to coerce other states into ceding status to Germany. Because of the positional nature of status, Germany's gains in that domain negatively affected higher-status powers, which thus had strong incentives to resist Germany's attempts to gain status. Seen in this light, the policies of England and France—which had previously been viewed as wise responses to German aggression—take on a more realistic color. England and France attempted from 1897 to 1911 to slow or stop Germany's rise in international status because it was in their interests to do so, and diplomatic breakdowns (before 1914) occurred primarily because of fundamental conflicts of interest, not intransigence by German leaders.

In what follows, I provide a background to the case study by describing the logic of the case selection as well as how this chapter fits with the large-N measures developed in this book. I then use the quantitative results from previous chapters in concert with the theory of status dissatisfaction to derive theoretical expectations for this particular case. Next, I show how status concerns affected the origins and development of the very idea of

[3] Clark 2012, 145.

Weltpolitik in the late nineteenth century, which at the time represented a significant break from Bismarckian diplomacy. In the last two sections, I trace the effects of status dissatisfaction—exemplified by the policy of Weltpolitik—in both crisis (the Moroccan Crises) and noncrisis situations (the long-term strategic planning of the German Navy).

BACKGROUND AND EXPECTATIONS

Methodologically, this case study is in the spirit of an "analytic narrative" that leverages a well-specified theory to explain behavior and relationships in a historical case of great importance.[4] In this case, one major strength of status dissatisfaction theory is its ability to provide a deeper understanding of some of the most significant aspects of European diplomacy in the years 1897–1911. The strength of the analytic narrative approach is in its distillation of a large number of events to their most theory-relevant aspects. Such narratives also involve testing the theory against competing explanations, so where appropriate, the chapter will present other theoretical perspectives on the events in question, always asking, Which theory provides the best traction on the largest amount of data?

In this section, I provide the background necessary for analytic narratives by first making an argument for the selection of this case that leverages the empirical results from previous chapters. I then outline the theoretical expectations that will guide the narrative throughout the chapter.

Why Weltpolitik?

Methods for selecting cases are myriad in political science, and it can be difficult to reconcile the various rules proposed over the years. Scholars are warned against selecting on the dependent variable, with Achen and Snidal summing up this consensus by noting that the comparative case study method "inherently provides too little logical constraint to generate dependable theory and too little inferential constraint to permit trustworthy theory testing."[5] Needless to say, many have taken the opposite

---

[4] Bates et al. 1998, 2000.
[5] Achen and Snidal 1989, 145. See also Geddes 1990; King, Keohane, and Verba 1994.

position, arguing that selection bias is not as problematic as commonly perceived, and qualitative research can be designed to overcome many of the inferential problems most commonly associated with it.[6]

Encouragingly, more recent work has eschewed the "quantitative-qualitative" divide by framing methodological choices as a series of trade-offs.[7] In this vein, Gerring notes that cases may be particularly useful when the desired inferences are "descriptive rather than casual" and when insight into causal mechanisms is sought.[8] Additionally, when undue weight is not put on a single case to prove a theory, many of these issues may be avoided.[9]

The integration of cases into a larger research design still poses challenges, however. The most comprehensive guidance for such an endeavor comes from Lieberman, who outlines a "nested" approach similar to the one employed here (one important difference is that this book employs experiments in addition to cases and large-N components).[10] In this framework, cases are used following a large-N analysis to provide depth (not breadth) and "answer questions left open" by the statistical analysis. If that statistical analysis is deemed robust—as I argue is the case in this book—then the analyst uses the case(s) to "further test the robustness" of the findings, focusing on the problems of causal order, measurement issues, and eliminating alternative explanations.

As for how those cases are selected, Lieberman's guidance is clear: "Scholars should only select cases for further investigation that are *well predicted* by the best fitting statistical model."[11] So we can now return to the question, Why Germany? Why Weltpolitik? The selection of this country and historical era is guided by two key facts. First, the case is indeed predicted by the theory and statistical models.

While the reign of Kaiser Wilhelm II began in 1888, the development of the Weltpolitik strategy only started at the end of the nineteenth century, and the period of actual crisis initiation covered in this chapter began only in 1905. In fact, no matter which "status community" we focous on— an overall hierarchy of all states, regional geographic groupings, detected

---

[6] See Collier and Mahoney 1996; George and Bennett 2005; Bennett and Elman 2006.

[7] Exemplified by Mahoney and Goertz (2006) in their discussion of the two "cultures" of research in political science.

[8] Gerring 2004, 352. See also Bennett and Checkel 2014.

[9] On this, see the controversy surrounding Eckstein's notion of "crucial cases," discussed in Gerring 2007.

[10] Lieberman 2005. For additional guidance on nested research designs, see Rohlfing 2008.

[11] Lieberman 2005, 44. This is particularly useful given the proliferation of case-selection strategies documented in recent years. For an example, see Seawright and Gerring 2008.

status community, or communities defined by major power status or military capabilites—Germany's average score for this period is positive, indicating the presence of a status deficit (see supplementary analyses in online appendix materials). From 1899 onward, Germany's status deficit increased, first slowly and then sharply. Moreover, the actual status deficits score might underemphasize the salience of those trends for leaders. If German elites were focused on their status ranking as a "dominant indicator," then it would be "dramatic changes" in that indicator—here, a dramatic change from decereasing to increasing status deficit—that would be most apparent to decision makers[12]

Of course, the status deficit indicator depicted here is a function of both status position and material capabilities. As I noted in earlier chapters, this means that an *apparent* status deficit may instead be caused by an increase in military capabilities (or spending), which may be linked to some omitted factor or the dependent variable we are trying to explain. In this case, part of the evidence I present in favor of status dissatisfaction is the Anglo-German naval arms race. If all the information we had available to us was this particular behavior (or dependent variable) and a hypothesis about status deficits causing it, it would be difficult to overcome concerns about enodogeneity: the idea that perhaps the naval arms race caused German status dissatisfaction rather than the other way around. This is one particular advantage of the analytic narrative method. I can show that German leaders' concern for status—and their dissatisfaction—led to the naval arms race, not the other way around. Furthermore, the status concerns evidenced by German leaders—and enshrined in policy as Weltpolitik—were also crucial in causing other behaviors, such as conflict initiation, that are less subject to such endogeneity concerns.

The second fact in favor of selecting the German case—from among a number of cases that are well predicted by the statistical models—is the historical consensus that status was a key factor in German foreign policy during this era. Two implications follow from this. First, the prevailing consensus that status was connected in some way to Weltpolitik mirrors the larger role of status within IR: a strong intuition that it matters combined with a lack of specific theories to explain *how* it does so (aside from one or two exceptions discussed in detail throughout the chapter). Selecting this case thus provides a way of sharpening our understanding of a period recognized for its great historical importance.

[12] See Gartner 1999, 50.

Perhaps even more important, however, the historical consensus that status was a factor in German decision making—combined with the case's fit with the statistical models presented earlier—provides crucial information about how we should interpret the evidence provided. What role does this case have in proving, describing, or investigating the theory of status dissatisfaction? Fundamentally, what sort of "test" is this? While many ways of understanding these issues have been proposed, one simple, useful heuristic comes from Bennett, who describes a series of tests: straw in the wind, hoop, smoking gun, and doubly decisive.[13] Straw-in-the-wind tests increase the plausibility of a given hypothesis, but are not decisive by themselves, providing "neither a necessary nor a sufficient criterion for accepting or rejecting a hypothesis." Hoop tests are somewhat more demanding, since hypotheses must "jump through the hoop" in order to remain viable, so the case alone is not sufficient for accepting an explanation, but is necessary. Given the combined historical consensus and fit with the statistical models, I believe this fits more cleanly into the latter category: a "hoop test."[14] The next section provides an overview of the theoretical expectations for this particular case.

Theoretical Expectations

What type of behavior should we expect if status dissatisfaction theory is a useful model for understanding Germany's "world policy?" There are several predictions that this theory generates for the case of German foreign policy in this period. First, we should see evidence of heightened status concerns on the part of German leaders. Second, we should find evidence of a particular variant of status concerns: status dissatisfaction. That is, we should see evidence that Germany was *dissatisfied* with its status, believing that it deserved more than it had been accorded by other states. Moreover, these status concerns should be *local*, focusing on a select group of peer competitors rather the entire international system.

As to the link with international conflict, our prediction comes in two parts. First, we should see evidence that status deficits led to a strategy of

---

[13] Bennett 2010. See also Van Evera 1997; Collier 2011.

[14] A smoking gun test provides sufficient but not necessary evidence for accepting a causal explanation. That is, failure to find a "smoking gun" would not disqualify a theory, but finding one should lead us to accept it. A "doubly decisive" test both confirms a favored hypotheses while eliminating all others.

conflict initiation. To the extent that we do see conflict initiation, we must provide further evidence that the goal of provoking such a situation was status and not some other good (for instance, valuable colonial territories). To the extent that Germany instigated disputes over objects that have little or no material value—alongside public and private justifications that reference prestige—we can, with appropriate corroborating testimony, consider that as evidence that the real object of bargaining was status related. Second, we should see that the conflict itself resulted from the belief that its initiation would bring with it status benefits.

WELTPOLITIK: A "PRESTIGE-HUNGRY" DIPLOMACY

Above, I noted that we should see evidence that German leaders valued status and pursued it as they would any other important interest (say, security or economic prosperity). We should also see evidence of heightened status concerns during this period, and even further, that their concern for status was driven by a belief that they were being denied their "fair share" of international status. There is ample proof of these beliefs forming the basis for Weltpolitik, the primary purpose of which was to improve Germany's international standing. This section outlines the origins and character of Weltpolitik, with a particular emphasis on the critical role that German status concerns played during this period in influencing the development of Germany's goals.

The Origins and Character of Germany's World Policy

A comprehensive description of Weltpolitik is not a simple matter. One historian famously noted the significance of the fact that decades of "exhaustive research" had "not yet made it possible to say just what the foreign policy goals of Weltpolitik were."[15] Nor is he alone. One German military commander, writing in the 1890s, complained, "We are supposed to pursue Weltpolitik. If only we knew what it is supposed to be."[16]

The architects of Germany's world policy were Kaiser Wilhelm II and his chancellors, Bernhard von Bùlow and his successor, Bethmann Hollweg. The kaiser, however, was the undisputed power behind German foreign

---

[15] Kaiser 1983, 448.
[16] Quoted in Retallack 1996, 79–80.

policy. Article 11 of the German Constitution gave full power to "declare war and conclude peace" to the kaiser (who was also the German emperor and king of Prussia). The only check on his power was the *Bundesrat*, the German Upper House, which was composed mostly of German princes and nobility, and as such would hardly have considered crossing Wilhelm. Wilhelm also had unilateral authority to declare a state of war in the case of a severe security threat to the *Reich*, and was in sole possession of the "power to command" (the famous German General Staff was technically only an advisory bureau).[17]

Wilhelm ascended to the throne in 1888, and by 1896 had succeeded in establishing his own brand of personal rule by dismissing any ministers who opposed his plans for a vigorous foreign policy.[18] Emblematic of this, the following quote is attributed to him on his ascension to power: "The Foreign Office? Why, I *am* the Foreign Office!" And in a letter to the prince of Wales, he insisted, "I am the sole master of German policy."[19]

Because ultimate authority rested with the kaiser, it is worth exploring how he saw the policy of Weltpolitik:

> As my grandfather did for the Army, so I will, for my Navy, carry on ... the work of reorganization so that it may also stand on an equal footing with my armed forces on land and so that through it *the German Empire may also be in a position abroad to attain that place which it has not yet reached* [20]

Bülow was chancellor (a position appointed by the kaiser) from 1900 to 1909, and a chief architect of Germany's foreign policy during that period. His description of Germany's world policy in a speech to the Reichstag summarized it thusly:

> It is the task of our generation at one and the same time to maintain our position on the Continent, which is the basis of our international position, and to foster our interests abroad as well as to pursue a prudent, sensible and wisely restricted international policy, in such a way that the safety of the German people may not be endangered, and that the future of the nation may

---

[17] See Kennedy 1982, 71. While this authority can be claimed for the Weltpolitik era, decision making during the 1914 July Crisis is another matter. There is a fair argument to be made that during that critical time period, the kaiser was largely marginalized. See Clark 2012, chap. 4.

[18] See Geiss 1976, 77.

[19] Quoted in Clark 2012, 178.

[20] Quoted in Williamson and Van Wyk 2003, 77, emphasis added.

not be imperiled ... an international policy based on the solid foundation of *our position as one of the Great Powers of Europe.*[21]

Bülow's remark helps to emphasize the nature of Weltpolitik: a strategy not of world domination but rather of circumscribed aggrandizement, mostly concerned with raising Germany's status internationally *without* resort to war. In fact, Germany's world policy has been aptly described as one of "limited risks and limited aims."[22] While the specific details of the policy are difficult to pin down, there is general agreement that its overriding goals were to improve Germany's position in the world and solidify domestic support at home—themes that were linked together in the minds of German leaders because, in Bülow's words, "only a successful foreign policy can help to reconcile, pacify, rally, unify."[23]

Similarly, Friedrich von Holstein (head of the political department of the Foreign Office) admitted in a private letter in 1897 that "Kaiser Wilhelm's government needs some tangible successes abroad which will then have a beneficial effect at home. Such a success can be expected either as a result of a European war, a risky policy on a world wide scale, or as a result of territorial acquisitions outside Europe."[24] Its actions bear this out, with one historian describing the "conduct of the German government in the years after 1897" as suggesting that "Bülow sought relatively cheap successes that would impress the emperor and German opinion without carrying real risk of war."[25] Historians have coined the term "social imperialism" to describe this strategy, put clearly by Bülow, with his "eye upon the masses," when he wrote to the kaiser, "This ... will stimulate people and navy to follow your Majesty further along the path which leads to world power, greatness and eternal glory."[26]

Often this desire to achieve "world power" status was framed as a struggle against the power that most Germans saw as the dominant state in Europe: England. In one example, Bülow told the budget committee of the Reichstag in 1900 that England had now become Germany's most dangerous foe.[27] More to the point, in 1903, Hollweg described "the

---

[21] Quoted in Hewitson 2004, 161, emphasis added.
[22] Kaiser 1983, 451.
[23] Quoted in Gordon 1974, 217.
[24] Quoted in Kennedy 1973, 609.
[25] Quoted in Kaiser 1983, 450.
[26] Quoted in Kennedy 1972, 138. On "social imperialism," see Wehler 1970, 1985.
[27] Kennedy 1980, 240.

Kaiser's first and basic idea" as being "to break Britain's leading position in the world in favour of Germany."[28]

Several earlier works linked Weltpolitik with the pursuit of colonies and a naval expansion program. And certainly, key German leaders did advocate for both of these policies. In the 1890s, both Bülow (secretary of state until from 1897–1900, and chancellor from 1900–1909) and Alfred von Tirpitz (admiral and secretary of state of the Imperial Navy, 1897–1916) argued that Germany's population and industrial growth "required both a fleet and larger colonial empire."[29]

But an emphasis on colonies and naval expansion conflates means with ends. Colonies and a larger naval fleet were always perceived by leaders as a *means* of achieving their goals rather than being goals themselves. These policies are thus better thought of as a *reflection* of the true goals of German Weltpolitik, not its core. In fact, Mommsen argues that "German 'world politics' was not concerned with concrete territorial acquisitions at all, but only with the prestige associated with Imperial Germany's participation in all affairs concerning its overseas empire."[30] In this, the German belief that colonies would bring increased international standing was typical of the time period. A French statesperson at the turn of the century remarked, "To remain a great nation, or to become one, you must colonize."[31]

One potential concern in these descriptions of Weltpolitik is that we might be overlooking potentially important variation among Germany's leadership. After all, while Wilhelm was the ultimate authority, he had plenty of advisers whose disagreement on other issues is by now well known. Yet on the larger issues of motivations and goals—of what German leaders *wanted*—there was little disagreement. Kennedy nicely sums up this agreement by noting that an "ideological consensus" for Weltpolitik existed: "not that it was a unanimously accepted programme, but that the pursuit of a greater German role in world affairs was regarded as both understandable and desirable by virtually all who had an influence upon external policy."[32] Thus, the important differences (such as disagreement on what kind of navy to build and for what purpose) were in general

[28] Quoted in Ferguson 1992, 730.
[29] Kaiser 1983, 448.
[30] Mommsen 1990, 301.
[31] Quoted in Joll and Martel 2007, 219. Of course, some (but not all) colonies also provided critical material benefits in terms of strategic footholds in important areas of the globe along with economic and financial benefits. This is not to say that status was unimportant but rather to emphasize how difficult it is to sort out a single motive for any pattern of behavior.
[32] Kennedy 1982, 147.

on how best to achieve the ends that most everybody agreed to be the ultimate goal: a greater role in world affairs and improved standing in the international system.[33]

The Roots of German Status Dissatisfaction

Of course, desiring status would have not distinguished Germans from any other state in the nineteenth century. But there was something notably different about Germany's desire for greater status that separated it from other states: while other states desired prestige because (since status was perceived as valuable) every state had a preference for more status rather than less, Germany's status concerns were rooted in a perception that a substantial and unacceptable disjunction existed between what they deserved and what they received. Fischer writes:

> Imperialistic impulses, hunger for prestige, and expansionist desires characterize them all [major powers]. But in sharp contrast to England, France, Russia and the United States, *Germany alone considered her place among the major powers incommensurate with her potential as the most industrialized country on the continent.*[34]

Fischer is effectively classifying Germany as a case of "status dissatisfaction." Fortunately, our access to substantial amounts of material from Germany prior to World War I allow us to delve more deeply into this dissatisfaction. In this section, I argue that there were two core beliefs at the center of Germany's status dissatisfaction, and that these beliefs led not only to a simple dissatisfaction but also to a deep and insistent fixation on status issues. Even Hillgruber—who in other respects paints Germany in a somewhat-sympathetic light—argues, for instance, that "all German statesmen" were "strongly obsessed with the theme of great power prestige."[35]

---

[33] In addition to political and military leaders, scholars and opinion leaders were also very much in favor of Germany pursuing a greater role in the world. For instance, Max Weber in 1895 observed, "The, unification of Germany was a youthful folly ... if it should be the conclusion and not the starting point for a German *Weltpolitik.*" Or the editorial of Hans Delbrück, a moderate historian, in 1899 in the *Preussische Jahrbücher* noted, "We want to be a World Power and pursue colonial policy in the grand manner. ... [T]he entire future of our people among the great nations depends on it." See Howard 1993, 174.

[34] Fischer 1975b, 3, emphasis added.

[35] Hillgruber 1982, 12.

When Joll wrote of the "unspoken assumptions" of political decision makers, he pinpointed a critical problem for political scientists and diplomatic historians: analysis of documents and transcripts of meetings will often miss out on vitally important assumptions held by members of the group in question.[36] This is especially true in the analysis of foreign countries and past generations. Decision makers often operate with a similar basic understanding of the world that may not be voiced aloud. Discussion may center instead on *means*, since the "ends" in question are already agreed on (greater power, security, etc.) and need not be discussed. It is therefore significant that there exists such an abundance of evidence on the matter of German leaders' status dissatisfaction.

The theory of status dissatisfaction implies that we should see evidence that German leaders believed that their country had not been accorded the status it was due, and that this belief affected foreign policy decision making. In addition to theory testing, however, focused case studies are opportunities to further explore the implications of a theory in the context of real-world decision making. In this case, the evidence supports the hypothesis that German leaders (and other elites) exhibited status dissatisfaction, but also sheds new light on the psychological manifestations of that feeling. Status dissatisfaction seems to have been expressed as two distinct subbeliefs. First, German leaders were conscious of their rise to the status of a major power, and believed that their rise was so spectacular (in terms of material capabilities) that they were "outgrowing" Europe and deserved to join England as a "world power." This belief established their expectations concerning what their status *should* have been. In contrast, the second aspect in their constellation of status beliefs was a powerful feeling of having been shortchanged in the race for international prestige as a result of their late arrival in world politics.

OUTGROWING EUROPE?

The first aspect of German status dissatisfaction was a belief that Germany had risen so fast that it should no longer be considered a "European power" but rather a "world power." This was voiced clearly by Wilhelm to the Austro-Hungarian ambassador in the early 1900s: "[Germany has] great tasks to accomplish outside the narrow boundaries of old Europe" and the country's future lay "less in Europe than in the entire world."[37] Similarly,

---

[36] Joll 1968.
[37] Quoted in Kennedy 1982, 158.

on the seizure of Kiachow in 1897, Wilhelm declared that the "German Empire has become a world empire."[38]

And Rohrbach, a political writer in Wilhelmine Germany, added,

Today it is necessary to be clear about the fact that we must stake our claim in the politics of the world and amongst those world peoples by whom Weltpolitik is made, and that we must not allow ourselves to be pushed back into the number of merely European peoples, whose place in the extra-European world is prescribed by the leading world nations, and whose circle we have in fact already outgrown.[39]

For Fischer—who not by coincidence titled a book about Germany *World Power or Decline*—German policy after 1897 was distinct from Bismarck's diplomacy of the 1860s or 1870s. Whereas under Bismarck, Germany had sought *equality* with established European powers, under Wilhelm "she set out consciously and with determination to become a 'world power.' . . . The year 1896–87 thus marks the end of the nineteenth century for Germany. German policy broke away from the old order of the major European powers and entered into the emerging struggle for world power."[40] Similarly, Geiss describes German foreign policy during this period as being motivated by "the German desire to raise the Reich from the status of a continental power to that of a world power."[41] Hillgruber agreed, writing that

behind this feeling stood the demand that the Reich, which had belatedly entered the ranks of the great powers, be considered not only one of the decisive powers of the continent, but equal to any in the world, and be allowed to take its place alongside the established empires.[42]

Even Kennedy, by no means an acolyte of Fischer's, writes, "Such economic expansion also meant that the country was growing out of its European 'skin' and acquiring the early attributes of world influence—booming overseas trade, political prestige abroad."[43]

In fact, this belief that Germany had outgrown Europe was obvious even to outside observers. In 1907, British diplomat Sir Eyre Crowe wrote

---

[38] Quoted in Andrew 1966, 138.
[39] Quoted in Hewitson 2004, 151.
[40] Fischer 1975b, 3–6.
[41] Geiss 1966, 80.
[42] Hillgruber 1982, 2.
[43] Kennedy 1982, 150.

a famous memo in which he assessed the state of Britain's international relations and examined Germany's motivations:

> Germany had won her place as one of the leading, if not, in fact, the foremost Power on the European continent. But over and beyond the European Great Powers there seemed to stand the "World Powers." It was at once clear that Germany must become a "World Power."[44]

Even in the public sphere, the notion of Germany falling behind, of time working against the country, was widespread. Hans Delbrück, editor of the moderate journal *Preussiche Jahrbücher*, wrote that "huge land masses in all parts of the world are going to be divided up. The nationality which comes away empty-handed will, in the succeeding generation, be excluded from the ranks of the great nations which determine the spirit of humanity."[45] And Heinrich von Treitschke, a German historian during the Weltpolitik era, wrote that "it is very easy to imagine that, one day, a country which has no colonies will not be counted amongst the European Great Powers any more, however powerful it might otherwise be."[46]

LATE TO THE PARTY?

The second critical aspect of Germany's status belief concerns the notion that it had lost out because it was a relatively new state. In contrast to the venerable regimes of France, Russia, and England, modern Germany was only several decades old (prior to the 1860s, the German Confederation was a loose agglomeration of principalities). Bismarck had thus only recently succeeded—through a series of military and diplomatic successes—in unifying Germany under the leadership of Prussia. The last series of important territorial acquisitions had taken place after Germany defeated France in the Franco-Prussian War of 1870. This "newcomer status" seemed to weigh heavily on Germany's leadership.

For example, Bülow's principal concern "was that Germany not be left behind in the division of the world's weaker empires." One historian noted that the initial motivation for the German Navy was not to "challenge the British Empire directly, but to make sure that Germany secure[d] its

---

[44] Quoted in Geiss 1967, 29.
[45] Quoted in Hewitson 2004, 148–49.
[46] Quoted in ibid., 156.

rightful inheritance when … [the] 'dying nations' finally expired."[47] In 1897, Bülow famously told the Reichstag, "We do not want to relegate anyone to the shadows, but we also demand our place in the sun."[48]

His successor, Chancellor Hollweg, felt similarly, and used the same metaphor in conversation with the French ambassador Jules Cambon in early 1914: "For forty years, France has followed a grandiose policy. She has acquired an immense empire. … During this time an inactive Germany has not followed her example and today *she* needs a place in the sun."[49] And in an address to the Reichstag in 1911, Hollweg declared, "Belatedly, unfortunately, very belatedly, Germany has joined the ranks of the colonial peoples, let them not then blame us if on this occasion we try to gain whatever we can. … If necessary [Germany] will draw its sword."[50]

This belief came to pervade the German elite in the 1890s. Intellectual Friedrich Naumann stated in 1895, "We Germans are the newest revolutionaries in the European family. … That our nation did this was its well-earned right. … too, wanted after long centuries of misery, to have its place in the sun."[51] Writer Karl Leuthner declared that with respect to the acquisition of colonies, "we Germans [have been] severely disadvantaged and repressed for decades by France and England."[52] A similar belief was voiced in the editorial section of the *Kreuz-Zeitung*, where it argued that Germany enjoyed superiority on the European continent, but also that it had been "artificially held back."[53]

And even had Germany not been a late entrant to the global stage, the policies of Bismarck exacerbated what came to be seen as Germany's most glaring deficit. Bismarck's primary goal—to prevent Germany's diplomatic and military encirclement by rival coalitions of great powers—was attained. But "the Bismarck strategy also exacted a cost. It required that Germany always punch under its weight, abstain from the imperial feeding frenzies in Africa, Asia and elsewhere and remain on the sidelines when other powers quarreled over global power shares."[54]

---

[47] Kaiser 1983, 450. "Dying nations" probably refers to the empires of Portugal, the Netherlands, and Denmark. See Kennedy 1973, 608.
[48] Quoted in Hewitson 2004, 186.
[49] Quoted in Kaiser 1983, 463.
[50] Quoted in Hewitson 2004, 186.
[51] Quoted in ibid., 151.
[52] Quoted in ibid., 153.
[53] Quoted in ibid., 160.
[54] Clark 2012, 141.

THE MOROCCAN CRISES

Having established both a preference for status and Germany's intense status dissatisfaction, this section examines the impact of those concerns on Germany foreign policy during the Weltpolitik era. As predicted by status dissatisfaction theory, a common theme throughout this time period is Germany's tendency to instigate crises (or use them once they appear) in order to bargain over status. And because of the positional nature of status, Germany could not gain more unless it came at the expense of those above it in the hierarchy that it cared most about: the small, exclusive club of major European powers.

One recent work of history notes that Britain, France, and Russia "controlled tokens that could be exchanged and bargained over at relatively little cost to the metropolis." Yet this interpretation fits uneasily with the same author's proclamation that Germany, "pushing to gain a place at an already crowded table ... met with firm resistance from the established club."[55] In fact, those "tokens" were always more valuable for their symbolic significance than their intrinsic attributes. And because highly ranked powers should in general be unwilling to give status freely (since doing so hurts their own interests), the dissatisfied power must either buy or coerce that status from the other powers. In this case, there is abundant evidence that Germany's pattern of crisis provocation is linked closely to its desire to gain international standing. In most cases, the purported object of bargaining had little intrinsic value, either economically or militarily, and yet German leaders went to great efforts to force concessions on these seemingly meaningless issues, all in pursuit of the true value at stake: international status.

Germany in Crisis

German foreign policy from 1897 to 1911 was characterized by a series of crises. In fact, the same could be said for all the European powers, which operated in a perpetual state of crisis readiness. Yet Germany separated itself from its neighbors by its approach to diplomacy and crisis bargaining during this period. Time and time again it resorted to policies of dangerous

[55] Ibid., 142.

brinkmanship in these crises in an effort to gain advantages from other powers. Summarizing this period, Hewitson writes,

> German policy making in the decade before the First World War was characterized by a willingness to contemplate the necessity of an armed conflict on the European mainland. In 1905–6, 1908–9 and 1911–12, different governments used the threat of war, in the belief … that the crises would be resolved diplomatically, in order to gain concessions overseas and in the Near East, or to maintain the Reich's political influence and prestige within the European states system.[56]

What is crucial to understanding this pattern of diplomacy is that while German actions often seem blundering and reckless to historians and political scientists (and on the microlevel, there is surely evidence of this), the rationale for these policies becomes plain once one focuses attention on the true object of bargaining throughout this period: status. It is also significant that—despite the brinksmanship strategies the quote above references—German leaders did not consciously seek war in these crises. Before 1912, Germany faced no serious or imminent threat to its security position and was not ready for war (particularly with Britain; against France alone, Germany might have been prepared to undertake greater risks of actual conflict). Evidence of this comes from many sources, but in one example, Wilhelm told the French ambassador in 1900 that it was crucial for Germany not to be pushed into war with Britain before Tirpitz's fleet was ready.[57] Its strategic vulnerability with respect to Britain (whose navy was far superior) meant that its only hope of gaining the international standing it desired was to provoke crises in which other states would "blink" before Germany or use the threat of a protracted arms race to coerce concessions from Britain (over which the navy was Germany's only leverage). It is to the former strategy that we first turn our attention.

Morocco I: The Landing at Tangier

The first Morocco Crisis occurred in 1905–6, and was triggered by France having extended its political control over the country as part of a diplomatic agreement with Britain. Shortly thereafter (in March 1905), Kaiser Wilhelm

[56] Hewitson 2004, 187.
[57] Kennedy 1980, 239.

made a "theatrical landing" at Tangier, where he visited the Moroccan sultan and promised him support in his struggle for independence, "pointedly" telling the French consul that he "knew how to defend German interests in Morocco and would expect the French Government to recognize that fact."[58] This comment and the kaiser's landing were interpreted by other governments as direct threats, and soon Europe was in the midst of a war panic. For what material prospects did Germany instigate this crisis? One is tempted to suggest that German leaders saw Morocco as valuable for economic reasons, yet in Bülow's own words, German economic interests in Morocco were "trifling and insignificant."[59]

In fact, the trip had been planned by Bülow and Holstein (a powerful diplomat in the German Foreign Office) in an effort to force France to capitulate in a humiliating fashion, and weaken or destroy the entente (an informal alliance between England and France). As in the other crises, Germany's effort to force concessions had a significant status component. Like many German statespeople at this time, Holstein seemed to frame every struggle almost exclusively in terms of status. In a private directive to the press chief of the Foreign Office, Holstein predicted of the international conference to be held on the subject,

> I am afraid that at the conference at Algeciras there will be a tendency on the part of the French, perhaps encouraged, but in any case not prevented, by England, *to put Germany in a position in which it has only the choice between a heavy loss of prestige* in the world or an armed conflict.[60]

At one point, France made overtures suggesting the possibility of a secret face-saving bilateral agreement before the conference. German leaders rejected this proposal, however, choosing instead to convene a public international conference on the issue. The resulting Algeciras Peace Conference of 1906 is often seen as a humiliating defeat for Germany. Germany was isolated, and supported by only Austria-Hungary, while France received exactly what it had wished for (political control over Morocco). Yet that understanding is challenged if one sees the value at stake as status, and not economic control over Morocco. Surely German leaders would have preferred (all else equal) a better result from the Algeciras conference, but the material outcome was not its primary interest in the

[58] Quoted in Craig 1978, 318.
[59] Quoted in Barraclough 1982, 78.
[60] Quoted in Craig 1978, 320, emphasis added.

first place. Its main goal was to force other powers to take account of Germany, and the international conference served that goal no matter the actual outcome of the negotiations.

This also helps to explain German intransigence during the peace conference. Throughout the negotiations, Germany continued its obduracy, refusing to compromise, for as Bülow argued, Morocco had become "a question of honor for us and especially for the Kaiser."[61] German leaders' willingness to take a hard line in negotiations is more understandable when one considers that they could afford to take a risk in the actual negotiations because once at the conference, any additional concessions made by the other powers might be considered a bonus on top of the status rewards.

But Morocco had not *become* a question of status (or honor, in Bülow's words) during the crisis. Instead, status and prestige were the causes of the crisis *from the beginning*. Germany's economic interests in Morocco were minimal, but it had an enormous interest in attempting to prevent England and France from deciding important matters of international diplomacy without regard for Germany. Any bilateral agreement that France would have offered in private, secret negotiations would have been worthless to German leaders, for whom only a public victory would suffice. German policy nevertheless had other, less desirable results. Soon after the crisis ended, the British and French military staffs began talks over how to prepare for a European war in which they would fight together against Germany.[62]

Morocco II: Agadir

In spring 1911, France sent troops into the interior of the country to further consolidate control following a series of uprisings aimed at the sultan of Morocco. The prior agreement (the Algeciras agreement) had given France political control over Moroccan territory, though the country remained nominally independent. German foreign minister Alfred von Kiderlen-Wächter saw in the unrest an opportunity to extract compensation from

---

[61] Quoted in Oppel 1972, 324. For a theoretical distinction between honor and status, see chapter 2. Here, as is often the case, decision makers use the terms rather interchangeably, though the context suggests a concern with status.

[62] Craig 1978, 321.

France for German noninterference in North Africa. Less than a month after learning of France's action in Morocco, Kiderlen (believing that Germany should be seen as acting in a defensive manner) had already contacted German industrialists in order to help concoct a narrative by which Germany might be seen as protecting the German business interests from French encroachment. Shortly after receiving the memorandums that he had requested from German industrialists, Kiderlen sent the gunboat *Panther* to the port of Agadir on July 1, 1911.

Kiderlen's plans involved deploying ships at both Agadir and Mogador, notifying France (and other signatories of the Algeciras agreement of 1906) of the purely defensive motivations for the warships' presence, and informing it that Germany considered the Algeciras agreement void. Meanwhile, the German press was meant to publish stories and editorials that would make it clear that Germany only sought to protect its commercial interests, and held no aspirations to occupy any part of Moroccan territory. This, at least, was the plan.[63]

Events—and reality—conspired to nullify Kiderlen's plans. First, the commercial interests Kiderlen had relied on to serve as a justification for the German military presence began to interfere with political and diplomatic affairs.[64] And despite using the pretext of protecting German economic interests and citizens, Germany managed to send its ships to a port that contained no Germans in the vicinity.[65] Additionally, the diplomatic communiqués that were to be given to the other involved parties in the dispute (including France) the day *before* the arrival of the warship, had in fact only been sent the day of the arrival, on July 1. Finally, the press coverage, which was to have "allayed all fears in either the French or the British mind," had not succeeded.[66]

---

[63] Detailed in Mortimer 1967.

[64] In one example, the Foreign Office ordered a mining assessor for Hamburg-Marokko Gesellschaft named Wilberg to report to Agadir to serve as a welcoming party for the *Panther*, and in particular to serve as an intermediary with the local tribes, to which he was to convey Germany's benign intentions. While the Foreign Office was pleased to receive reports from Wilberg that the gunboat had met a welcoming reception among the local chieftans, it was distressed when it received a series of reports intimating that Wilberg had been discussing the advantages of the German occupation of southern Morocco with various local leaders, and immediately ordered him to "refrain from interference in the political situation." See ibid., 447.

[65] Barraclough 1982, 2.

[66] Mortimer 1967, 449.

Part of the problem for Germany lay in its inability to conduct diplomatic negotiations free of interference from domestic interests. On July 23, Germany communicated to Britain that it had no designs on Moroccan territory, but asked that this information be kept confidential. German leaders could not *publicly* forswear interest in Moroccan territory without alienating the very constituencies (primarily mining-related industries) that they had stirred up in order to serve as a pretext for intervention in the first place.[67] The British press thus continued to publish inflammatory stories hinting at German designs on southern Morocco, and the German press continued to call for more aggressive action and the extension of German influence in northern Africa.

Perhaps unsurprisingly, Britain and France were perplexed by Germany's behavior in the crisis. In fact, the combination of Germany's excessive demands for compensation elsewhere in Africa and refusal to publicly disavow any interest in Morocco itself were so confusing that it had the effect of convincing British leaders that Germany was purposely making unacceptable demands in order to "wreck the negotiation and stay at Agadir"—quite the opposite of the kaiser's true goals.[68] German behavior during the crisis was so baffling that even Kaiser Wilhelm and Chancellor Hollweg were not always certain what Germany's position actually was. At one point, Hollweg was forced to get Kiderlen drunk in order to ascertain whether he intended to go to war or was merely pursuing a policy of brinkmanship.[69]

On October 11, 1911, France and Germany ended the crisis by agreeing to a deal in which Germany recognized French political control over Morocco and renounced its own claims in northern Africa in return for receiving several small pieces of territory in the French

---

[67] Though eventually, even the commercial interests that might have had designs on lands on southern Morocco came to the realization that the land held little value for them. One industrialist who was originally a forceful advocate for increased German presence in North Africa traveled to Morocco during the crisis and returned to Germany disillusioned, finding the land rocky, parched, and unsuitable for either development or colonization. But after working so hard over the summer to persuade Germans of the immense value of southern Morocco, he found few Germans willing to listen to his more realistic assessment of its value. A sample from his reports: "In opposition to the many utterances in the press, [I] have gained an entirely different point of view from my trip. It would have been a disaster had Morocco—the ostensible paradise—been politically acquired. In what unbelievable ways public opinion has been deceived about the economic value of Southern Morocco!" Quoted in ibid., 455.

[68] Quoted in Wilson 1972, 516.

[69] Rohl 1969, 654.

Congo. Perhaps most important, the necessity of involving (and compensating) Germany in matters of colonial affairs in Africa had been established.

How can we explain German behavior in this episode? In one respect, the answer seems simple: Germany provoked a crisis in order to get a share of the economic spoils of colonial Africa, either in Morocco or central Africa. Statements of German leaders belie this motive, however. In fact, German leaders never had any interest in the territory that was purportedly the object of dispute. The recent work of a historian clarifies that "Kiderlen had no interest in securing a German share of Morocco, but he was determined not to allow France unilaterally to impose exclusive control there ... [and] hoped ... to secure an acknowledgement of German rights."[70]

Kiderlen deliberately misled the German press and political parties (including the ultranationalist Pan-German League) into believing that the annexation of southern Morocco was Germany's primary goal in the crisis, and did so in order to convince France of Germany's resolve in the matter.[71] In a government inquiry into the crisis the next year, Kiderlen admitted to fanning the flames of nationalist fervor in order to signal resolve:

> I told him [Heinrich Class, leader of the Pan-German League]: the situation is as follows: we go for compensation elsewhere. But at this stage we cannot say that thereby affairs are settled. Therefore it would be helpful to have a wave of patriotic feeling at home. It will do no harm if you argue in this vein. I would have thought that this is not an offense.[72]

So what was the "compensation elsewhere" to which Kiderlen referred in his testimony? Surely it was not the actual territory that Germany gained in the dispute, since Kiderlen contemptuously described this land as "partly completely worthless, partly almost worthless."[73] Indeed, this was an indirect reference to compensation in the form of status or recognition. Kiderlen voiced Germany's true motivations to an associate in a meeting: "One must remind the French that Germany is still there."[74] More dramatically, Kiderlen was "convinced that Germany's position in

---

[70] Clark 2012, 206.
[71] See Mommsen 1991, 391–92.
[72] Quoted in ibid., 392.
[73] Quoted in Joll and Martel 2007, 145.
[74] Quoted in Hewitson 2000, 594.

the world depended on the outcome of the Morocco crisis."[75] He wrote to his undersecretary, Arthur Zimmerman, that if Germany did not end this crisis having acquired some new advantage, it "shall then be for a long time without political influence in the world."[76] In sum, German leaders sought to "demonstrate that German rights could not be trampled on."[77]

AFTERMATH

By Kiderlen's and the kaiser's initial goals, the crisis had ended successfully for Germany. As Schroeder argues, "Only the Pan-Germans and some ardent colonialists claimed Morocco as a question of vital interest.[78] The kaiser, the Foreign Office, and the bulk of Germany's military, naval, and business leaders saw it as a question primarily of prestige and honor. And that honor had been satisfied, and the prestige retained or even increased, by the objective outcome.

But Germany's diplomatic tactics had snatched defeat from the jaws of victory. Rather than a success, the crisis was widely viewed by the German public as a total failure.[79] Kiderlen's efforts to convince Britain and France of Germany's resolve had done little but confuse leaders in those countries while at the same time convincing the German public that the annexation of southern Morocco was imminent. When Germany gave up claims to southern Morocco (land it had never really desired in the first place), its leaders were seen as backing down in a humiliating fashion.[80] Even other key decision makers, such as Admiral Tirpitz, saw the affair as a humiliation.[81]

The notion of Germany's humiliation in this episode is so entrenched that one still sees references to it in modern scholarship, providing further support for Johnson and Tierney's argument that victory in conflict is often a social construction, and one that in many cases bears only a

[75] Quoted in Fischer 1975a, 73.
[76] Quoted in ibid., 73.
[77] Stevenson 1997, 136.
[78] Schroeder 1972, 337.
[79] Clark 2012, 208.
[80] Kaiser Wilhem apparently earned the nickname "Guillaume le timide" for this episode; see Geiss 1976, 134. This was only one of many nicknames he earned. Kiderlen referred to him as "Wilhelm the Sudden," the German Foreign Office in London referred to him as "His Impulsive Majesty," and Lord Grey in England simply concluded that Wilhelm was "not quite sane." See Kennedy 1982, 161.
[81] Rohl 1969, 654.

slight resemblance to the "facts on the ground."[82] Yet objectively, this was no humiliation at all. While there are aspects of the crisis that suggest chaos within Germany's leadership (for example, Hollweg not knowing precisely what Kiderlen planned at the outset of the crisis), Germany actually succeeded in its goals. The object of the dispute was not market share in Morocco or lands in the Congo but what Hewitson termed the "right of intervention and consultation in world politics."[83] Germany had given up nothing in the crisis, since France had long held de facto control over Morocco and gained the precedent that other major powers could not divide up the world without taking into account the interests of Germany.

ANGLO-GERMAN RELATIONS

While Germany's status dissatisfaction helps to explain its tendency to instigate crises, such as those in Morocco, it also sheds light on a broad array of noncrisis interactions as well. Here I delve into broader patterns of interaction between Germany and its rival, England. I provide evidence that—contrary to most accounts—Germany's naval race was not a dysfunctional attempt to cultivate Wilhelm's personal glory but rather a strategic bargaining chip designed to force England to concede status to Germany.

The Age of Flottenpolitik

The appointment of Admiral Tirpitz as secretary of state of the German Navy in 1897 was a turning point in German foreign policy. During the 1890s, nationalist groups had campaigned for a larger navy, but Admiral Friedrich von Hollmann (Tirpitz's predecessor) had never managed to secure financial support from the Reichstag. In fact, a constellation of interests within Germany—including Pan-Germans, merchants and businesspeople, and the German Navy—lobbied for increased spending on the navy in years before the inauguration of Weltpolitik. But perhaps "most important of all, [by 1897] Wilhelm himself had become almost obsessed with the notion of possessing a large navy."[84]

---

[82] Johnson and Tierney 2006. See also Geiss 1976, 134.
[83] Hewitson 2000, 594.
[84] Kennedy 1980, 224.

Scholars are by and large in agreement on the motivation behind Wilhelm's championing of a great German Navy. Joll and Martel write,

> It is unlikely that German naval building would have been pursued enthusiastically without the Kaiser's personal commitment to the creation of a German battle fleet. This was no doubt partly the result of his own psychology: his emotional need to show himself the equal of his royal British relatives, and his country the equal of ... Britain.[85]

Similarly, Epkenhans argues that Wilhelm's motivations in pursuing a large German Navy were to imitate his cousins in Great Britain and preserve Germany's place in the "Concert of Great Powers."[86] That the fleet was in almost all ways directed at England is beyond doubt. In a private discussion with the Saxon military representative in 1899, Tirpitz noted that "for political reasons the government cannot be as specific as the *Reichstag* would like it to be; one cannot directly say that the naval expansion is aimed primarily against England."[87]

The motivations of Admiral Tirpitz were also significant. Epkenhans writes that Tirpitz also convinced the kaiser of the need to protect German "sea interests" including colonies, and warned that if it failed to do so, Germany would inevitably "decline to the status of a pre-industrial poor farming country."[88] Sea power had important domestic implications as well, since it was hoped it would offer a permanent solution to the "social problem" that threatened the existing political and social order. Joll and Martel summarize Tirpitz's motivation thusly: "Tirpitz himself was primarily concerned with the creation of the navy for its own sake and as a means of achieving a not very clearly defined position as a world power."[89] Tirpitz noted that a great fleet would "maintain Germany's political power position, it would make it easier to keep the peace and it would stave off the danger of serious political humiliation."[90]

And unsurprisingly, Germany's naval ambitions form a key component in past arguments on the importance of prestige in the origins of World War I. Murray is emblematic of this school of thought when she argues that Germany pursued a large navy because its leaders believed that is

[85] Joll and Martel 2007, 141.
[86] Epkenhans 2007, 117.
[87] Quoted in Murray 2008, 139–40.
[88] Epkenhans 2007, 117.
[89] Joll and Martel 2007, 142.
[90] Quoted in Murray 2008, 144.

simply what world powers did.[91] In these arguments, the navy is essentially a "status accessory," and fulfilled a function similar to high-priced cars and watches in modern society. Similarly, Markey asserts forcefully that the development of the German naval fleet can only be explained by recourse to what he sees as Wilhelm's almost pathological fixation on his personal prestige.[92]

Are these convincing explanations for the development of the German fleet? Certainly there are some indications that German leaders saw the navy as a symbol of their international status. Maurer writes that "from the very first navy law in 1898, Admiral Alfred von Tirpitz ... envisioned the establishment of Germany as a world power on equal footing with Britain by the building of a German battle fleet."[93] And perhaps the most damning piece of evidence in favor of the prestige motive in building a great fleet comes from Hollweg himself, who said,

> A really Great Power with a seaboard could not be a *Landrette*: she *must* have a fleet, and a strong one ... not merely for the purpose of defending her commerce *but for the general purpose of her greatness*."[94]

The importance of status is made even more convincing by the lack of a strong security rationale for the fleet.[95] For while Tirpitz envisioned a security rationale for the navy in addition to simply enhancing Germany's prestige, the *use* of the ships negated a great deal of the security benefits of the fleet. To the extent that the fleet was developed to deal with England, it meant stationing ships close to Germany, but the imperatives of Weltpolitik demanded a far-flung navy in which ships were often dispatched to the Far East. And given the option, strength in "home waters" was often neglected by German leaders in order to pursue colonial gains abroad.[96] So while in the abstract such ships might have provided a deterrent effect, the tactics of Weltpolitik frequently undercut those potential benefits.

Moreover, German leaders were well aware that their development of a navy designed to challenge England for supremacy on the high seas was bound to provoke a response in kind by Britain. The reaction of Admiral

[91] Ibid.
[92] Markey 2000.
[93] Maurer 1997, 287.
[94] Quoted in Joll and Martel 2007, 148, emphasis added.
[95] The association of status with large navies has other precedents; see Gilady 2002, 2004.
[96] Kennedy 1974, 53–54.

John Fisher in England was typical of the response, which could not have taken German leaders by surprise: "Germany keeps her whole fleet always concentrated within a few hours of England. We must therefore keep a fleet twice as powerful as that of Germany always concentrated within a few hours of Germany."[97] Even Tirpitz realized that caution was required, lest Germany instigate an arms race or preemptive attack by England (the fear of which was often referred to as the "Copenhagen complex," after the 1807 British bombardment of the Danish capital), while still in the "danger zone" in which England retained naval superiority over Germany. In the words of Steinberg, Tirpitz believed that the risk of provoking England must be taken, "but it could be greatly reduced if German foreign policy and domestic expressions of opinion could be kept under control. Only a pacific and self-restrained foreign policy could provide the right atmosphere to allow Germany's gradual attainment of world power and equality at sea."[98]

While it is true that status played an important role in the development of the fleet, only the theory of status dissatisfaction can explain the dual nature of the fleet. A focus on the desire for greater prestige (in essence, the navy as a status accessory) is partly correct, for there is considerable evidence that German leaders (particularly Wilhelm and his chancellors) saw the navy as a crucial symbol of their great power status, regardless of its material or security benefits.

A focus on the navy as a symbol of prestige, however, falls short in explaining the pattern of naval arms racing that Germany engaged in with England. For even if "any world power had to have a large battle fleet to protect its colonial interests in the world," Germany could easily have produced a large navy to protect its colonial empire (which was not substantial) without overtly provoking England.[99] Yet Germany time and time again refused to compromise with Britain, or even discuss potential naval spending limitations. Status dissatisfaction theory thus sheds light on the navy's dual function: to act as both a symbol of Germany's prestige, but more important, as leverage with which to coerce England into bargaining over relative status.

[97] Quoted in Maurer 1992, 288.
[98] Steinberg 1966, 29.
[99] Murray 2008, 131.

Key to this is Tirpitz's "risk theory," in which he envisioned building a naval force so strong that other powers (specifically England) would not dare risk actual engagements.[100] It was believed that the resultant deterrent power would give Germany advantages in pursuing its world power status through coercive diplomacy. Tirpitz described the essence of the policy in an 1897 memorandum: "England ... [is] the enemy against which we most urgently require ... naval force as a political power factor."[101] Like the Weltpolitik strategy in general, the fleet was designed to gain prestige victories for Germany without resort to war. Rather, Tirpitz and Bülow anticipated that a German Navy would effectively coerce Britain into "giving in" in any diplomatic confrontation.

The notion that the fleet was designed to serve as a "political power" factor as conceptualized in Tirpitz's risk theory is well known. Risk theory takes on a new light when placed in the framework of status dissatisfaction theory, though. The purpose of the fleet was to provide leverage for Germany to use in bargaining with other powers, principally England. But as demonstrated earlier, Germany's goals were—for the most part—status related. When it had leverage in crisis bargaining situations with other powers, it tended to use that leverage for gains that were mostly worthless in material, military, or economic terms. The territory gained in the Congo in 1911 is one example of this, but not the only one.

In fact, the pattern persisted throughout the Weltpolitik era: when Germany actually acquired territories, they were often not useful or materially valuable. Historians have noted that the "extremely limited economic significance" of the territories that Germany managed to acquire in its scramble for empire suggested that the "government did not regard new colonial marks as a really urgent necessity."[102] In 1899, for instance, Germany acquired the Caroline Islands in the western Pacific. These were purchased from Spain as part of the aftermath of the Spanish-American War, yet the Germany Navy saw these islands as "worthless" from a strategic perspective.[103] Bülow described the acquisition thusly to Wilhelm: "This gain will stimulate the people and navy to follow Your Majesty further along the path which leads to world power, greatness and eternal glory." Similarly, the colonial territory that Germany seized from China

---

[100] For an in-depth examination of the relationship between risk theory and the ideas of US naval strategist Alfred Thayer Mahan, see Herwig 1988.
[101] Quoted in ibid., 78.
[102] Kaiser 1983, 449.
[103] Kennedy 1973, 609.

(Kiaochow) has been described as lacking both "strategic" and "economic significance."[104]

Traditional interpretations of Tirpitz's risk theory are thus correct to note that it was designed to force concessions from other major powers, but misspecify the concessions that German leaders actually desired. The political concession they sought to coerce from England was status, not colonies. This is even more evident once one considers the "many failures" of Germany and England to achieve arms control agreements.

Bargaining for Status

To the extent that German naval spending was designed to force England to bargain over status, it largely worked. From almost the beginning of the German naval program, Liberals in Britain were alarmed by the potential costs of an arms race and sought to negotiate with Germany. Lloyd George (then chancellor of the Exchequer) famously told a reporter that "feverish efforts" by Britain to outspend and outbuild its rivals would not work because "if we went on spending and swelling [the navy's] strength, we should wantonly provoke other nations."[105]

But British leaders did not merely pay lip service to these beliefs. In 1906, the Liberals in England unilaterally cut British shipbuilding. By doing so, they hoped that they would be setting the stage to open negotiations with Germany at the Hague Peace Conference in summer 1907. These hopes were dashed when Germany "simply refused" to halt or slow down its naval program. This managed to turn even the Liberal Party (previously dead set against a naval arms race with Germany) toward escalation. Lord Edward Grey concluded, "To make an enormous reduction of our naval expenditure when there was no certainty that it was going to have a corresponding influence on the rest of Europe, would be staking too much on a gambling chance."[106]

In 1908, Britain again approached Germany, this time to begin bilateral arms control negotiations. Germany once again refused to enter into negotiations, exacerbating tensions between the two countries to the point where the chief of staff of the High Seas Fleet actually feared Germany

---

[104] Kaiser 1983, 450.
[105] Quoted in Maurer 1997, 288–89.
[106] Quoted in ibid., 289.

might attack the British ships on their annual summer cruise. That same year, King Edward VII even visited Germany, but still Wilhelm refused to discuss any limits on naval spending or building programs.

Relations slowly improved in 1910–11 as the tempo of shipbuilding mandated by law fell from four ships to two a year. By that time, however, the lack of foreign policy successes had prompted Hollweg to sign off on Kiderlen's ill-fated plans to instigate a Moroccan crisis. The nationalist sentiment unleashed by the failed crisis (or at least the perception of failure in the crisis) allowed Tirpitz to push through another Naval Bill to increase the size of the navy in 1912.[107] In 1912, Grey was pressured into sending British politician Richard Haldane to Germany to negotiate, but the talks soon broke down.

In previous works, the refusal of Germany to compromise is often seen as evidence of its blundering diplomacy: How could Germany have so consistently refused British overtures that might have ended the arms race and perhaps even have prevented the eventual outbreak of World War I? Indicative of this line of argument, Murray writes that "Germany's naval strategy never considered the contingency that Britain would meet Germany's naval challenge."[108]

Yet the issue becomes far clearer utilizing the framework offered by status dissatisfaction theory. In general, discussions of naval arms limitations went nowhere because Britain refused to explore a "grand bargain" without first settling the naval question, while Germany refused to talk about naval spending without a political agreement in place. Kaiser Wilhelm, as the ultimate authority in diplomatic matters, was behind this German strategy, and argued that the price of an arms control agreement with Britain should be a "far reaching political pact" that would solidify Germany's position as a first-rate world power and also solve myriad strategic problems.[109] Among those was Russia, which by 1912 had begun to occupy the minds of German war planners, who sought to use the "naval arms race chip" to coerce Britain into declaring its neutrality in the event of any future conflict between Germany and Russia.[110]

---

[107] Epkenhans 2007, 123.

[108] Murray 2008, 148.

[109] Of course, this negotiating stance did little to reassure Britain. One failure to reach an agreement led George Goschen (British ambassador to Germany) to write, "What we offer them is quite sufficient to show friendliness and that should be quite enough for them if they have no designs upon other people." Quoted in Epkenhans 2007, 124.

[110] Maurer 1992, 287.

Previous scholars have often argued that Germany's refusal to come to an agreement represents an error in judgment on the part of German leaders because their negotiating stance cemented the notion among British leaders that Germany was intent on a "dramatic realignment" of power and influence in Europe.[111] In this vein, Morrow attributes the lack of an agreement to Bülow's "personality" and "insecurity."[112] Status dissatisfaction theory, however, provides a much more compelling explanation: Germany's willingness to compete with England for naval supremacy was its best (and perhaps only) leverage in coercing Britain to cede status that it would otherwise be unwilling to give up. German leaders were not unaware of the reaction they would provoke via their naval policy; they *expected and counted on it.* The political director of the German Foreign Office, Wilhelm von Stumm, wrote in 1908,

> Although I appear to be stating a paradox ... the British anxiety about the development of our fleet may facilitate the conclusion of an agreement. The ... nervousness with which all England watches the growth of our forces at sea, the heavy financial burdens imposed by the attempt to be twice as strong as ourselves ... *these considerations seem to me to show that our naval policy gives us a valuable trump card in relation to England.*[113]

As Schroeder notes, "Even if Germany's encirclement was not a British aim, the 'circling out' of Germany, her exclusion from world politics and empire, *was* Britain's goal in good measure."[114]

Of course, Germany's plans to use the naval race as leverage against England did not work as planned. But this was not the result of poor decision making by German leaders. Britain was simply unwilling to negotiate any terms that might affect its position as a world power, especially if doing so allowed Germany to take its place. Grey wrote of Britain's dilemma, "We cannot enter into a political understanding with Germany which would separate us from Russia and France, and leave us isolated while the rest of Europe would be obliged to look to Germany."[115] And Nicolson argued that Britain must demand from Germany "a real reduction of expenditure on armaments and an undertaking that they will

---

[111] Maurer 1997, 304.
[112] Morrow 1932, 80.
[113] Quoted in Maurer 1997, 294, emphasis added.
[114] Schroeder 1972, 329.
[115] Quoted in Maurer 1997, 292.

not continue to contest our supremacy—in fact ... that they will withdraw the challenge."[116]

Like Germany, Britain was willing to negotiate only on its own terms: the very possibility of conceding anything of importance to Germany rattled British leaders to the extent that when the Haldane Mission broke down, Ambassador George Goschen "rejoiced" and sent his congratulations to Nicolson for his role in frustrating an agreement.[117] Much has been made of the German demand for British neutrality in any war that involved France or Russia. And it is true that Germany often requested "benevolent neutrality" from England.[118] Still, this was one of many German demands, and focusing exclusively on this demand (which seems unreasonable with the benefit of hindsight) obscures the fact that Britain was unwilling to give up anything of importance in negotiations. The breakdown in negotiations came not from unreasonable demands by one side but rather an irreconcilable conflict of interest between one power intent on revising the system and another power intent on resisting.

A final note on this subject is that we should be careful to avoid retrospective indictments of Germany's strategy based solely on outcomes. It is natural to notice that the naval arms race seemed to lead to the war and conclude that Germany's decisions were ill advised. But this was not the only possible outcome, and in fact, there is suggestive evidence that Germany's bargaining strategy worked in some ways (and even came close to dethroning England as the most important power in Europe). Many scholars have noted that from 1912 to 1914, Anglo-German relations improved slightly, but that this improvement was largely the result of cooperation on relatively narrow issues (such as in the First Balkan War) and Germany's growing fear of Russia, and did not solve any of the structural problems at the heart of their troubled relationship.[119] In particular, no progress was made on the issues of alliances or armament limits (naval or army).

Yet this analysis, while true, obscures an important aspect of Anglo-German relations after 1912. Several of the narrow issues on which Britain and Germany cooperated benefited Germany disproportionately. For instance, in 1913, Germany and England devoted considerable efforts

[116] Quoted in ibid., 296.
[117] Ibid., 296.
[118] Woodward 1935; Maurer 1992.
[119] Levy 2014, 150. See also Lynn-Jones 1986, 126–27. This period has been called a "hollow détente." See Crampton 1980.

to negotiations over the future of several Portuguese colonies. The British colonial secretary voiced hope that "Anglo-German relations could be permanently improved if we had 'conversations' leading to an exchange of territory which might give Germany a 'place in the sun.'"[120] This provides some suggestive evidence that British leaders understood that the real object of bargaining was status. But the final agreement (in which Germany gave up virtually nothing in exchange for an increased presence in Africa and more impressive profile as a colonial power) also suggests that Germany's brinkmanship strategy of instigating a naval arms race against Britain for use as leverage might have worked. In 1912, Churchill spoke publicly about the naval arms race and boastfully declared that

> if there are to be [naval] increases upon the Continent of Europe ... we shall have not only to increase the number of ships we build, but the ratio which our naval strength will have to bear to other great naval Powers, so that our margin of superiority will become larger and not smaller.[121]

By 1914, though, the situation had changed drastically, suggesting that the apparent resolve of Britain to spend vast amounts of money to maintain its place as "hegemon at sea" had softened. In other words, it is possible that Germany nearly succeeded in coercing Britain to cede its status as the preeminent naval power. Churchill, in particular, was the driving force in abandoning the decades-long British policy of possessing two capital ships (destroyers) for every one possessed by an opponent. What is striking about the deliberations that surrounded this momentous change in policy is that the only factors that seemed to give pause to British leaders were the potentially deleterious implications for their international standing. The old standard of measurement—how many destroyers a country possessed—was both easy to calculate and favored the British. And yet because of both budgetary reasons (an important factor at that time for the British government) and a belief in a new concept of naval power, they were willing to transition almost overnight to a reliance on smaller ships and submarines.[122] After a review of recent work on British strategy, Williamson and May conclude that for budgetary reasons, "the British navy in July 1914 was on the verge of deserting the command-of-the-sea

---

[120] Quoted in Lynn-Jones 1986, 132.
[121] Quoted in Maurer 1992, 288.
[122] Lambert 1995.

doctrine, which Alfred Thayer Mahan had advertised as the key to Britain's greatness."[123]

While Germany's strategy ultimately cost it far more than it could have imagined, it is striking to note how close it came to achieving its aims. If the July Crisis had ended as other crises had throughout the era, it is entirely likely that Germany would have succeeded in its aim of overtaking (by the generally accepted measure of destroyers / capital ships) Britain as the dominant naval power in Europe.

ALTERNATIVE EXPLANATIONS

Many alternative explanations—often grounded in domestic politics—have been cited to help explain Germany's pattern of behavior during this period.[124] While there are subtle differences in the arguments, they may be summed up by the reasoning that (for example, in the Morocco case) public opinion was sure to turn against the government of Germany if it "allowed events in the Sharif kingdom merely to take course" without gaining some advantage from the episode.[125] And it is true that German leaders believed—as they did throughout the Weltpolitik era—that minor foreign policy victories would help solidify domestic support for the imperial regime. A domestic political explanation falls short in explaining German decision making in the crisis in two important ways, however.

First, it cannot explain the private language used by leaders during the crisis. We might expect German leaders to publicly use language that evokes powerful feelings of nationalism, prestige, honor, and reputation in order to achieve their domestic goals, and in fact, there is some evidence that this occurred (though it happened indirectly, through Kiderlen's manipulation of the press). Yet the language that German leaders used in private was *also* couched in the framework of status. There was, for instance, no strategic rationale for Kiderlen's communications to his secretary that explained that his motivation was to preserve Germany's international standing.

[123] Williamson and May 2007, 343.

[124] Because of the proximity of this time period to World War I, many researchers group them together or focus exclusively on the impact of Weltpolitik on the origins of World War I. I focus here on explanations for German policy and actions during this particular time period rather than the origins of the Great War.

[125] Kaiser 1983, 460.

Second, if domestic political support was the primary factor in Germany's policies during the Agadir Crisis, its behavior is almost entirely incomprehensible. Recall that Kiderlen deliberately manipulated public opinion into expecting an increased German presence in Morocco, yet *had no intention of pursuing this goal.* If public support was the overriding determinant of German behavior, then the government's behavior was self-defeating in a manner that was easily predictable ex ante. Kiderlen's manipulation of the public in this case only makes sense if the motivations were international rather than domestic, and his willingness to risk public outcry (when Germany did not acquire territory in Morocco) suggests a preference for status that *trumped* domestic political considerations.

Economic explanations also fall short in regard to Germany's behavior in the crisis. As is evident, no German leader believed the territory purportedly at stake (in Morocco) or that was gained as compensation (in the Congo) was particularly valuable. And explanations that appeal to the greed or incentives of German industrialists (who might be supposed to favor the German annexation of Moroccan territory) are not congruent with the evidence. In fact, Gustav Krupp (one of the most important and influential industrialists in Germany) was *already a partner in a joint Franco-German commercial venture in Morocco* "and therefore not interested in any change in Morocco's political status."[126]

Another class of explanations involve status.[127] Of these, Murray's may be one of the more prominent.[128] She argues that both the Morocco Crises and policy of *Flottenpolitik* may be understood as efforts on the part of Germany to gain recognition of its identity as a great power. In several important ways, the explanation put forth in this chapter is in accord with Murray's; both see this pattern of behavior as largely about status, and while she frames it as "recognition' of a given status, this is not altogether different from my contention that it is about gaining status. In effect, one of us has emphasized the identity aspect of status while the other has stressed positionality, though making similar broader points about Germany's motives.

Where we differ in important ways is the ultimate *cause* of this status motive. Murray argues that it was "disrespect" and "misrecognition" of

---

[126] Mommsen 1990, 305.

[127] One of these is Ward (2012), who which is largely in agreement with the current analysis, but focuses on the transition from Weltpolitik to a more European-dominated policy in the immediate lead up to World War I.

[128] Murray 2010, 2012.

Germany (by France) that led to the first Moroccan crisis: by attempting to settle the status of Morocco bilaterally with England (via the Entente Cordiale), France had provoked and disrespected Germany, leading to a determined response by the kaiser.[129] While this is possible, I argue that status dissatisfaction provides a more satisfying explanation for two reasons. First, Murray falls into the trap of seeing both Moroccan crises as failures from the German perspective (for example, the Agadir Crisis was "humiliating").[130] Such a perspective is a grave mistake, though, and incorrect if we judge the outcomes with reference to German elites' original goals: to ensure that Britain and France take German interests into account in world affairs. Thus, while it is true that Germany received a "substantially smaller part of the French Congo" than it had publicly demanded, it is unreasonable to interpret outcomes that fall short of their public bargaining position as a failure. Germany did not get everything it demanded, and the crisis did damage the regime in German domestic politics, but it attained its ultimate goal: to acquire "some new advantage" and "remind the French that Germany is still there."

Second and perhaps more important, my theory is more generalizable in the sense that it provides an account of why German leaders were so fixated on status in the first place. In effect, Murray argues that the cause of Germany's behavior was a lack of recognition by France and England that began with the First Moroccan Crisis.[131] But such an explanation misses the development of Weltpolitik, begun nearly a decade prior to the crisis. In fact, it was dissatisfaction over relative status that helps to explain the development of Weltpolitik as well as Germany's reactions to British and French diplomacy during this time period. Moreover, this dissatisfaction is predicted by the quantitative models provided in earlier chapters, demonstrating the benefits of a multimethod approach to triangulating status concerns.

SUMMARY

Starting from almost the moment the first shots were fired in August 1914, a Herculean effort has been made by scholars of all generations and

---

[129] Murray 2012, 138.
[130] Ibid., 144.
[131] Ibid.,

countries to understand the origins of World War I. New archives are found and made use of even still, providing ever more information on the thoughts and actions of the key leaders both in July 1914 and the decades before. But "even well-understood topics, when scrutinized anew, may wear different faces."[132] This chapter has used status dissatisfaction theory to explain a puzzle in the long-term origins of World War I—namely, why did Germany's Weltpolitik policy appear so aggressive and irrational? This is an important question since it is often argued that it was this policy that contributed to the long-term origins of the Great War by provoking the balancing coalition of England, France, and Russia.

Yet I provide evidence of the strategic nature of Germany's world policy, which is most constructively thought of as a policy of instigating (or seizing) opportunities to coerce status quo powers into bargaining over relative prestige. I provided evidence that—in most cases—German leaders had virtually no interest in the material values purportedly at stake in the many crises during the Weltpolitik era. Rather, the object of bargaining was almost always status related, as in the 1905 Morocco Crisis, where Germany created a war panic in order to establish its right to be consulted in colonial matters.

A similar pattern was evident in its relations with England. Previous explanations of Germany's naval program have focused on the navy as caused by either domestic concerns or the desire for a great navy as a sort of "status symbol." I have shown that domestic politics—while it may help in understanding the initial passage of the Navy Bill—do little to explain the manner in which the navy was utilized. Similarly, theories that focus on the navy as a symbol of prestige fall short because they are unable to explain the strategic nature of Anglo-German interactions during this period. In fact, Germany's primary use for the navy was as leverage to coerce (or outspend) England into conceding its place as the dominant sea power of the era. And while the outbreak of war in 1914 tempts one to see the strategy as a failure, we should consider that on the eve of war, British policy had changed to one in which it would unilaterally cease competing against Germany for the prestige associated with naval primacy (as measured by large, *Dreadnought*-style ships).

We entered this chapter with evidence from experiments that concerns over relative status affect decision making, and from large-N analysis that they are associated with the initiation of international conflict. What we

---

[132] Williamson and May 2007, 243.

were missing up to this point was witnessing these associations play out in cases of real-world decision making. To that end, I turned to German Weltpolitik—a case strongly associated with status in the eyes of historians, but still missing a coherent theory to explain what has often seemed to be puzzlingly irrational behavior on the part of German leaders.

Status dissatisfaction theory helps to resolve many of these issues, and I find strong evidence for the theory's implications in a close analysis of Germany decision making and grand strategy. German leaders did prefer higher status, but the driving motivation was the feeling that they had received less status than they deserved, as predicted by status dissatisfaction theory. Moreover, the status competition in which they were engaged was exclusively against a small group of major powers, including England, France, and sometimes, Russia, providing evidence for the notion that status is local. Finally, as predicted by status dissatisfaction theory, German leaders' status concerns led to the persistent initiation of international crises, not out of frustration, but instead because they saw such events as opportunities to enhance their relative standing.

7

Salvaging Status: Doubling Down in Russia, Egypt, and Great Britain

Chapter 6 took my theory of status dissatisfaction to German Weltpolitik, and in doing so, helped to explain what had previously been a historical puzzle: Why did German leaders during the period 1897–1911 persistently and aggressively provoke crises that provided little in the way of material benefits? I argued that German elites' status concerns help to explain this anomaly. These status concerns weren't the result of simply desiring higher status—who wouldn't?—but instead grew out of the specific belief that Germany had been denied its rightful place in the club of great powers; that it was not getting the status that it deserved. In order to remedy this status deficit, German leaders consistently sought out opportunities to provoke international incidents in which they could bargain over status with what they perceived as their peer group: Russia, France, and (especially) England.

Despite the strong evidence on the importance of status concerns in Wilhelmine foreign policy—and their link to the initiation of international conflict—several open questions remain. One set of questions concerns generalizability. The theory of status dissatisfaction makes no ex ante qualifications with respect to historical era (nor do I find evidence of this as a limiting factor in the large-N chapters), but it remains to find qualitative evidence of the link between status concerns and conflict in the modern era, or non-European or non–great power contexts. Finding evidence of such concerns and their link to international conflict in different contexts would not constitute a decisive test of the proposition but instead would help establish the plausibility of status concerns (and their effects) in different contexts.

Another open question relates to the exact mechanism by which status concerns are linked to international conflict. My theory's core mechanism is that states seeking to shift their status position will undertake "status-altering events" that are public and dramatic enough to capture the attention of the international community as well as shift its beliefs about where the state "stands." The experiments described in chapter 3— in addition to providing evidence for a core proposition of the theory— nevertheless suggest another possibility: political elite, doubling down and escalating commitment rather than backing down in the face of a challenge. This potential additional mechanism—escalation of commitment— necessarily requires a conflict already in progress. The German foreign policy described in the last chapter does not neatly fit this, Germany sought to *instigate* new conflicts in order to secure higher status rather than escalating in order to salvage its position. This begs the question: Is there evidence for this potential alternative mechanism in the real world? Are there other potential mechanisms that are suggested by in-depth historical research?

To that end, this chapter examines three separate sets of decisions:

1. Russia's decision to aggressively back Serbia in the 1914 July Crisis
2. Britain's decision to collude with Israel and France in launching the 1956 Suez War
3. Nasser's 1962 decision to intervene in the Yemen Civil War (and continue to escalate through the rest of the decade)

While not selected at random, this "convenience sample" of cases fits well with the theory and empirics presented throughout the book. And as in the previous chapter, all are relatively good fits with the large-*N* measures of status deficits presented in chapters 4 and 5. Egypt, for example, saw its status deficit increase after 1960 and continue to rise throughout the decade-long Yemen intervention. Russia's status deficit was quite high throughout the beginning of the twentieth century, rising to 1.8 standard deviations above the mean in 1912. The United Kingdom's status deficit began to increase (though it was still quite low) in the post–World War II period, corroborating the stated beliefs of British leaders who perceived themselves as being in the midst of a long-term decline.

These cases broadly substantiate the patterns found in the Weltpolitik case—status concerns led decision makers to value status more highly— while highlighting the plausibility of several new mechanisms. These cases also help to make the critical point that status concerns are not confined to European countries, great powers or states in the pre–World War I era. No single system of government, culture, or people has a monopoly on status concerns, and the link between sharpened status concerns and international conflict is robust. The next several sections survey the three "mini cases" listed above, and the chapter concludes with a discussion of how status dissatisfaction fares in the historical record.

"Our Prestige Would Perish": Russian Fears of Losing Status in the July Crisis

In chapter 6, I argued that status dissatisfaction led Germany to seek out issues that it could escalate to armed conflicts in order to bargain over status with other European powers. In the case of Russia, I provide an illustration of how the dynamics work when the dissatisfied state does not actively seek to shift its status upward but rather is challenged and forced to make the decision: respond (and escalate the crisis) or back down? In doing so, I shed light on a perennial puzzle of World War I: Why did Russia—though its leaders had strong incentives to delay war until its military modernization was complete in 1917—unhesitatingly come to the defense of Serbia, *even though it knew such actions would lead to a war for which it was unprepared?*[1] Russia's actions have been described by prominent historians as "belligerent, provocative and ill-designed to keep the crisis in check."[2] I show that this can only be explained by reference to Russian beliefs that "backing down" was tantamount to conceding its status as a major power.

The July Crisis

On June 28, 1914, Archduke Franz Ferdinand, heir to the Austrian throne, and his wife, Sophie, were killed in Sarajevo. There is some irony in the fact that Ferdinand had been a powerful force for peace within the Habsburg Empire, repeatedly clashing with the more aggressive chief of the Austrian General Staff, Colonel Franz Conrad von Hötzendorf; Ferdinand's death both removed an advocate for peace and served as the pretext for war.[3] Preliminary investigations revealed the involvement of a group called the

---

[1] Even if the czar initially believed that the crisis would be resolved peacefully, by the time of his decision, it was obvious that war was an unavoidable consequence of his decision to back Serbia.

[2] Williamson 1988, 812.

[3] Ibid., 805.

Black Hand, known to be associated with Serbian officials, and leaders in Vienna quickly sought retaliatory action against the Serbian government.

Austrian leaders desired a showdown with Serbia, but on no account did they wish for Russia to intervene as a display of Slavic unity. To forestall such an event, they sought German support; after all, aggressive German support had deterred Russian intervention in the past, such as when Austria-Hungary annexed Bosnia in 1908.[4] On July 5, Austria sent Count Hoyos on a mission to Berlin to ask for assurances of German support if and when Vienna acted against Serbia. Franz Joseph needn't have worried, as both Kaiser Wilhelm and Chancellor Hollweg agreed on the need for action against Serbia, and shortly thereafter communicated the famous "blank check," declaring that Austria could count on German support "whatever its decision."[5] Despite having obtained the assurances it desired, Vienna waited more than two weeks, until July 23, before presenting its forty-eight-hour ultimatum to Belgrade. On hearing the content of the ultimatum, the Russian foreign minister Sergey Sazonov accused Austria-Hungary of provoking war ("You have set fire to Europe!").[6] The ultimatum was perceived similarly by other powers. In Britain, Foreign Minister Grey commented that it was "the most formidable document that I have ever seen addressed by one State to another that was independent."[7]

It is safe to say that at this point in the crisis, Vienna wanted a war with Serbia and was willing to risk the involvement of Russia, though it hoped that its alliance with Germany would deter Russian intervention.[8] No Habsburg official believed that Serbia could accept the ultimatum.[9] On July 24, the regent of Serbia addressed a note to the czar begging for his assistance.[10] In response, Russian senior officials met on July 24, and Nicholas joined them on July 25, when he approved the decision to

[4] Joll and Martel 2007, 14.

[5] Quoted in Jarausch 1966, 56.

[6] Quoted in Joll and Martel 2007, 19.

[7] Quoted in Herwig 1997, 25.

[8] Britain's ambassador to Vienna, Maurice de Bunsen, wrote that on hearing that Serbia had not accepted the ultimatum in full, "Vienna burst into a frenzy of delight." See ibid., 17.

[9] And in fact, this was just how Hollweg had planned it. He had known of the content before its delivery and had had ample time to moderate Austria's demands should it have wished to do so. The officials had been informed, for instance, by the Austrian ambassador that "the note is composed so that the possibility of its acceptance is practically excluded." See Copeland 2001, 86.

[10] Joll and Martel 2007, 19.

authorize partial (but not full) mobilization.[11] This decision was made *before* Saint Petersburg knew either the Serbian reply to the ultimatum or Vienna's reply to Serbia. This is important because it allows us to more realistically estimate what factors Russian leaders were faced with in those critical meetings, and what options were open to them. Nicholas also ordered the implementation of a "Period Preparatory to War" to go into effect on July 26; it has been called the "most significant military actions taken by any power" to that point in the crisis.[12]

Russia in July 1914

Before turning to the Russian decision, we must assess both what options were realistically available to Russian leaders in July 1914 and how they perceived the consequences of each action. First, it is possible that given Russia's influence in Serbia, the czar might have coerced Serbia into accepting the entirety of Austria's ultimatum.[13] Instead, there is suggestive evidence of the opposite: that Russia offered support immediately after the delivery of the ultimatum, convincing Serbian leaders that they could afford to provoke escalation by not accepting Austria's conditions in full.[14]

Because Serbian leaders had been informed that anything less than full acceptance would trigger immediate breaking of diplomatic relations (with all that implied for the chances of war), they knew that their stance (accepting most but not all of its provisions) would certainly provoke escalation of the crisis. That they accepted nine out of the ten demands made in the ultimatum, and evinced a willingness to negotiate on the question of an Austrian investigation on Serbian soil, demonstrates the likelihood that Russia might have been successful in convincing Serbia to accept the ultimatum in full.[15]

Russia could also have *threatened* mobilization measures rather than actually implementing them. This would be consistent with a pattern of step-by-step escalation designed to signal how important the value at

---

[11] There is some recent evidence that the partial mobilization orders were sent out on July 24, *before* Nicolas had approved them. See Williamson and May 2007, 369.

[12] Ibid., 368.

[13] Though, as Lieven (2015) points out, it is unlikely that Austria would have found this acceptable and would have probaly have just found a different pretext for a war with Serbia.

[14] Joll and Martel 2007, 19.

[15] Oldenburg 1978, 3.

stake was for Russian leaders. A counterargument to this might be that if Russia believed war was inevitable, then because of the long time that its mobilization would take, it needed to begin it as soon as possible. In this view, any steps toward mobilization can be explained by incentives to preempt German and Austrian attacks. But if Russia truly believed that war was inevitable, then the steps taken later in the crisis make little sense, particularly the reluctance of Nicholas to relent (to the suggestions of his military advisers) and order general mobilization as soon as possible. Because strong deterrent threats would not have precluded either backing down or escalating further, the fact that Russian leaders exerted so little effort in this kind of strategy only indicates how willing they were to immediately ratchet up the level of the crisis and risk the outbreak of war.

Finally, Russia could simply have backed down and allowed Serbia to be "punished" for the assassination. It would not have been a popular decision domestically, since it might have been seen as abandoning "fellow Slavs," but that had not stopped Russia in past crises (in particular during the Balkan Wars) when it had allowed Serbia to be threatened by Austria. And domestically, a long, costly war for which it knew itself to be unprepared was a far greater risk (in terms of increasing the probability of a revolution) than backing down in a crisis, for which there was at least precedent. Indeed, there were some influential Russian elites (such as Petr Durnovo, a member of the State Council and former minister of internal affairs) who feared internal revolution whether Russia won or lost.[16]

Of course, the consequences of those options were not all equally attractive to Russian elites. In fact, Russian leaders were in agreement that they were unprepared for any major war against Germany, even with French support. Domestically, the leaders worried (presciently, it turns out) that war might lead to a revolution internally.[17] Economically, Russia had been crippled by recent workers' strikes and was *less* prepared to finance a war than it had been ten years previously in the Russo-Japanese conflict.[18] Additionally, Russian leaders had serious doubts about the reliability of England as an alliance partner should war break out. Most important, all involved in the decision process in Saint Petersburg knew that Russia had strong incentives to delay any military showdown with Germany or Austria.

[16] Lieven 2015, 306–7.
[17] On this issue, see Lieven 1983; Kennedy 1984, 17.
[18] Kagan 1995, 195.

A 1913 Russian Naval Staff directive had noted, for example, that "what Russia desires in the next few years is a postponement of the final settlement of the Eastern questions and the strict maintenance of the status quo."[19] Even the most aggressive of the Russian decision makers in the July Crisis, Sazonov, recalls that "it was essential for the Russian Government to placate German hostility for a long time to come, by means of all possible concessions in the economic sphere."[20] And while Russia had begun an immense program of military modernization—including strategic railways, an additional five hundred thousand troops, and so on—by July 1914, the program had not even started.[21] On the eve of the fateful meeting of July 24, the minster of war, took aside a deputy of Sazanov's and asked him to pass along the blunt reality that "Even with the support of France we would find ourselves in 1917, and perhaps until 1918, in a position of indisputable inferiority with respect to the combined forces of Germany and Austria. Consequently, we should do everything in our power to avoid war."[22]

So if Russian leaders were aware of their incentives to delay a great power conflict, did they recognize the potential consequences of supporting Serbia? In fact, all Russian leaders understood that the decision to support Serbia by initiating a series of mobilization measures would drastically raise the risks of war, if not practically guarantee it. Recent evidence makes it clear that Russian leaders knew the impact of their mobilization; in an earlier document on the topic of the changing nature of war, the chief of general staff for Russia wrote, "The undertaking of mobilization can no longer be considered as a peaceful act; on the contrary, it represents the most decisive act of war."[23]

Let us now return to July 24, when Russian leaders debated how to respond to the Serbian request for help. Russian leaders probably knew that *Germany's goal was a European war.* And yet at a Council of Ministers meeting on July 24, Sazonov "condemned Vienna for threatening to turn Serbia into a de facto protectorate, denounced Germany for backing Vienna, and argued that Russia had to assist Serbia *even at the risk of a larger war.*"[24] The ministers of agriculture, the navy, and the army all concurred

---

[19] Quoted in Bestuzhev 1966, 96.
[20] Quoted in Williamson and Van Wyk 2003, 116.
[21] Rich 2003, 214.
[22] Quoted in Lieven 2015, 323.
[23] Quoted in Joll and Martel 2007, 19–20.
[24] See Williamson and May 2007, 367, emphasis added.

with Sazonov. On July 25, the British ambassador warned Sazonov that any Russian mobilization would likely provoke Germany to declare war immediately, Sazonov simply replied that because the political stakes were so great, Russia "would face all the risks of war."[25] Moreover, Germany warned Russia on both July 26 and 29 that Russia's continued mobilization would force Germany to mobilize, which would in effect lead to war.[26]

To summarize, Russian leaders by and large believed that their country was unprepared for war, any war risked a revolution that would create chaos and possibly lead to the end of the dynastic regime, and mobilization in support of Serbia would (at the least) risk war with Germany and Austria-Hungary. Yet it is clear that Russian leaders had decided from early on to either (at least) risk or (at most) guarantee war with Germany and Austria-Hungary. It is unnecessary to adjudicate between the two possible beliefs since in either case the same puzzle remains: Why would Russian leaders *take any chance of a military showdown with Germany in 1914, when they expected to be militarily predominant in only two to three years?*

Not a "Second Place" Power

How can we explain the Russian decision to risk war on July 24–25? As noted, there were no direct material interests at stake in Serbia for Russian leaders. Yet what is clear from the limited available evidence on Russian decision making in July 1914 is the crucial importance of status concerns.[27] Here, the meetings of July 24–25 are critical, for it was in those two initial meetings in which Russian leaders made the decision that would guide their policy for the rest of the crisis: to aggressively support Serbia in the face of Austria/German aggression, even if doing so risked a European war.

---

[25] Quoted in Trachtenberg 1990, 127.

[26] Ibid., 127. There is a debate about the extent to which *partial* mobilization was even possible. It probably was not, but for some reason Russian military planners allowed Sazonov and Nicholas to believe it was, until they finally informed them on July 27 of the logistical implications of moving from partial to full mobilization. The crux of the dilemma was that Russia simply had no readily available plans to mobilize only against Austria (and not Germany), as Nicholas wished to do. While interesting as a matter of historical detail, this does not materially affect the argument presented here, since Russian leaders evinced a clear willingness to risk a war in support of Serbia. See Williamson and Van Wyk 2003, 136.

[27] Because of the limited ability of scholars to access Russian/Soviet archives, there has been comparatively little research on Russian decision making during the July Crisis. Two exceptions to this are works by Lieven (2015) and Mcmeekin (2011).

In the first meeting, on July 24, Sazonov admonished the other members of the Council of Ministers:

[Russia] could not remain a passive spectator whilst a Slavonic people was being deliberately trampled down. In 1876 and 1877 Russia had fought Turkey for the liberation of the Slavonic peoples in the Balkans. We had made immense sacrifices with that end in view ... If Russia failed to fulfill her historic mission, *she would be considered a decadent State and would henceforth have to take second place among the Powers ... If, at this critical juncture, the Serbs were abandoned to their fate, Russian prestige in the Balkans would collapse entirely.*[28]

He also argued that Berlin had demanded "from us a capitulation to the Central Powers, for which Russia would never forgive the Sovereign, and which would cover the good name of the Russian people with shame."[29] In the same council meeting, the minister of finance stated that "since the honour, dignity and authority of Russia were at stake," he agreed with the others present on the need to firmly back Serbia, despite the risk of war.[30]

Summing up the available evidence on those two initial ministerial meetings, Kagan writes that

in the ministerial council, where no one had reason to suppress other considerations, it is striking to observe the dominant role of prestige. Russia's material interests in Serbia and the other Balkan states were nugatory, but the Balkans were the place where its power and its reputation were most on display and at risk ... In that sense defense of its prestige *was* the defense of a most important interest, and fear of its loss the most powerful motive for risking war.[31]

Of course, there may be some instances in which states risk war in the present (even if they would fare better in the future) because there is no option to delay the fighting. If, for instance, Germany could act in such a way that would "lock in" its dominance in some structural way, then Russia would have had little choice but to take the risk of fighting even though it was not yet at full strength. But such was not the case in July 1914. Serbian accession to Russian demands would surely have damaged

[28] From the memoirs of the Russian finance minister, Peter Bark. Quoted in McMeekin 2011, 58.
[29] Quoted in Hamilton and Herwig 2004, 110.
[30] Lieven 1983, 144.
[31] Kagan 1995, 196.

the international standing of Russia, because it was seen as the country's "great power protector," but it did not materially affect Russian security.[32] If anything, the "worst case" for Serbia (incorporation of it into the Austro-Hungarian Empire) would only have weakened the Habsburg dynasty, because it would have increased the number of Slavs within the kingdom and posed serious risks (via nationalist movements) to Vienna's domestic stability.

Prestige or status concerns were not the only motive driving Russian decision making. Such a claim would be unreasonable. Aside from other motives, such as avoiding humiliation and the loss of prestige, Lieven notes that "Russian security demanded that this effort [to deal a decisive blow to Russian authority in the Balkans] be resisted even at the cost of war."[33] That is, traditional security motives help to explain quite a bit of the Russian decision, but these issues are not a competing explanation to status concerns. On the contrary, prestige and authority were seen as important both because of their intrinsic value—Russian leaders wanted to maintain their country's identity as a great power—but also because they were thought to have important security implications.

Even McMeekin, who is generally suspicious of Russian motivations in the July Crisis, confesses that the issue of Serbia was important only because of its symbolic value.[34] While he uses that to dismiss the nonmaterial stakes of the crisis, I believe that the national prestige at stake was a key component of Russian decision making, and other Russian statespeople seemed to agree. On July 29, the Russian minister in Sofia argued that in the case of capitulation to Germany/Austria, "our prestige in the Slav world and in the Balkans would perish never to return." On the same day, the Russian minister to Constantinople asserted that backing down "would result in the destruction of our prestige."[35]

Even Czar Nicholas II evinced a similar concern for Russia's international standing. In a manifesto to the Russian people explaining what values were at stake in the upcoming war, Nicholas noted the need to "protect the honour, dignity and safety of Russia and *its position among the Great Powers*."[36] Perhaps even more telling, there is suggestive evidence that both Germany and Austria *expected* the status concerns of Russia to play a key role in their decision making. Austrian prime minister Leopold Berchtold calculated that Russia would "lose prestige" if it allowed Serbia to accept the ultimatum, while if Serbia did not accept, Austria would get the war it had wanted.[37]

But Russia's decision was even more critical for German leaders. Remember that—in order to instigate the war in a way that would maintain domestic stability at home—Hollweg saw the need to force Russia to act belligerently as a pretext for German mobilization. Evidence for German foreknowledge of how the ultimatum would likely affect Russian leaders comes from a 1913 memo written by Hollweg:

> As far as I can judge the situation in Russia, on the basis of information which I have cause to believe is reliable, we can reckon with certainty that the forces, which stand behind the Pan-Slavist agitation, will win the upper hand if Austria-Hungary should get involved in a conflict with Serbia. ... [I]t is almost impossible for Russia, without an enormous loss of prestige, given its traditional relations with the Balkan states, to look on without acting during a military advance against Serbia by Austria-Hungary.[38]

Thus, German leaders intuitively understood how prestige would dominate Russian decision making. Their intuitions seem accurate in hindsight—Russian leaders evinced a clear concern over status in their ministerial meetings—so we must now contend with the most important question: How does status dissatisfaction theory help explain the Russian decision to aggressively support Serbia?

The few previous works on the subject have noted the importance of status to Russian leaders in July 1914, but have mostly stopped at the argument that "status mattered." A few crucial points need to be added to this in order to understand the specific ways in which status concerns affected Russian behavior. First, in this case, Russian leaders' concerns about status emphasized the country's identity as a great power. It was not that they worried that backing down would cause them to lose status relative to peer competitors (though it would) but instead that the consequences of that loss would be demotion from the club of great powers. This might (and probably would) have material consequences as well, but Russian leaders saw these effects largely through the filter of

---

[37] Herwig 1997, 16.
[38] Quoted in Hewitson 2004, 204, emphasis added.

status, though a version of status that focused on identity rather than pure positionality.

Second, as predicted by status dissatisfaction theory, concerns over status—in this case, triggered by a threat to their status, as in the experimental studies in chapter 3—seemed to increase the value of status to Russian leaders. That is, while Germany's decision calculus was dominated by security concerns, Russian leaders saw the conflict as mostly—though not totally—about status. This is important in this case, because as noted, the potential costs of the war (both externally and internally) were extraordinarily high for Russia, and the *material* values at stake were extremely low. Their decision to risk war thus only makes sense if it is understood that there were other values at stake for them (status in particular) in the crisis that dramatically increased the costs they were willing to bear.

Lastly, it is worth remarking on the role of previous behavior in Russian decision making in 1914. Russian dissatisfaction with its international standing was a key factor in determining how it responded to the Austrian/German challenge in 1914. Russian foreign policy had suffered a series of public setbacks in the decade prior to World War I. Neilson argued that Russian diplomacy had "a decade of failure behind it" in 1914.[39] Russia had backed down from challenges in one crisis after another; its extreme military weakness in that period led Nicholas and his advisers to consistently shy away from the risk of war. Neilson contends that for Russian leaders, "being unable to risk war in support of foreign policy goals meant that Russia was temporarily demoted from the ranks of the Great Powers."[40] By 1914, the Russian military situation had improved enough that it was conceivable (though by no means advisable) to risk war through crisis escalation, though Russian leaders had little confidence in their ability to actually win a war against Germany. In other words, while status concerns may have played a key role in Russian leaders' decisions in previous crises, they still backed down because those concerns alone were insufficient to allow them to take the risk of war. Once the military situation had improved sufficiently that a war against Germany/Austria would not be a rout, then status concerns came to the forefront and compelled Russian leaders to risk war in the July Crisis.

[39] Neilson 1995, 109.
[40] Ibid., 107.

"NOT ANOTHER NETHERLANDS": GREAT BRITAIN AND THE SUEZ WAR

The next two sections trace the paths of Britain and Egypt in the 1950s and 1960s, joined forever in the history books by their shared legacy: the Suez Canal along with the eventual nationalization and war that followed. Egypt gained as much as Britain lost in that war, but the overall picture for both countries from that time period is remarkably similar. Both strong, independent countries, secure from foreign invasion or domestic instability, they found themselves embroiled in foreign policy decisions with disastrous consequences. After the smoke from the Suez war cleared, it had "destroyed the Great Power status of England," while Nasser's multiyear intervention in the Yemen civil war proved both costly and debilitating for Egypt, sowing the seeds that led to further military defeat in the Six-Day War; Nasser eventually began referring to the Yemen intervention as "my Vietnam."[41]

In both cases, status dissatisfaction helps shed light on the motives that drove Anthony Eden's and Nasser's decision making. Both cases illustrate what happens when a fixation on status—in Eden's case, this resulted from Britain's long, slow decline; in Nasser's case, from a desire to secure Egypt's status in three reference groups, Arab, African, and Muslim—is coupled with a sharp blow to a regime's prestige.[42] The response in each case was extraordinarily similar, with both leaders actively seeking out opportunities for status-altering events—in one case, the ill-fated Suez War, and in the other, a multiyear intervention in the Yemen civil war. In the latter case, status dissatisfaction helps by explaining not only the initial decision to support Yemeni rebels but also the series of decisions that followed to escalate the conflict once Nasser's prestige had been engaged.

Eden's Status Fixation

Though Egypt and Britain ended the Suez Crisis as enemies, they were not alway so.[43] In 1952, future foreign secretary Selwyn Lloyd reported being "favorably impressed" with Nasser during their first meeting, and

---

[41] Kissinger 1995, 523, quoted in Dawisha 1975, 55.

[42] Podeh 1993, 104.

[43] Some material in this section draws on work published as Renshon 2006, chap. 2. That work, though, dealt with the related theme of preventive wars.

as late as March 1954, Assistant Undersecretary of Middle East Affairs Evelyn Shuckburgh observed that Prime Minister Eden had "come to the conclusion that Nasser is the man for us."[44] Eden, in fact, had been an early advocate of a joint Anglo-American effort to finance the Aswan High Dam, an enormous engineering project designed to regulate irrigation of the Nile and secure Egypt against droughts. The United States was committed to shouldering the bulk of the project's costs, but both members of the Anglo-American alliance saw it as a bulwark against Soviet influence in the Middle East, designed to bring Egypt closer to the Western sphere. Of course, even while championing a project designed to benefit Egypt, Eden was—his permanent undersecretary for foreign affairs recalls—of "two minds, oscillating between a fear of driving Nasser irrevocably into the Soviet Camp and a desire to wring the necks of Egypt and Syria."[45]

On December 14, 1955, Great Britain and the United States made a formal offer to finance the Aswan Dam. Yet a series of events soon conspired to throw the project into doubt. Shortly after the public funding commitment made in December, Nasser rejected US entreaties to facilitate Arab-Israeli negotiations. Then, pro-Egyptian riots broke out in Jordan, leading King Hussein to dismiss General John Bagot Glubb, the British commander of the Arab Legion. Soon after that, in May, Nasser withdrew Egypt's recognition of the government of Chang Kai-Shek and established diplomatic relations with the People's Republic of China, a particularly personal insult to US secretary of state John Foster Dulles, who was deeply committed to Taiwan. Anthony Nutting, a deputy foreign minister, recalled that despite the incentives to "get back on terms with the Arab world ... it was just not practical politics for the [Eisenhower] administration to go ahead and ask Congress to approve so large a loan to Egypt."[46] And so it wasn't; a few days later, Dulles sent for the Egyptian ambassador to the United States and told him that the United States was backing out of the Aswan Dam loan, and the British government soon followed suit. In a symbolic blow, Nasser was informed while attending a meeting in Yugoslavia with Marshal Tito and Jawaharlal Nehru, two leading figures of the "nonaligned" movement. The French ambassador to

[44] Quoted in Lloyd 1996, 15; Shuckburgh 1986, 155.
[45] Quoted in Carlton 1989, 27
[46] Nutting 1967, 44.

Washington, Maurice Couve de Murville, presciently noted: "They will do something about Suez. That's the only way they can touch the Western countries."[47]

"A High-Handed Act of Seizure"

On July 26, Nasser announced the nationalization of the Suez Canal in a public speech in Alexandria. The British immediately condemned the act as a "high-handed act of seizure against an international company," which violated the international guarantee written in the Constantinople Convention of 1888 allowing for free navigation.[48] The truth was a bit more complicated; Nasser argued that since the Suez Canal Company was an Egyptian joint stock company, it could be nationalized without breaking international law, and even British leaders confessed that "as frequently happens in international disputes, both arguments could be supported on legal grounds."[49] If invoking international law was not likely to work, neither was economic pressure; British banks did not hold enough Egyptian assets to "seriously incommode" Nasser's regime.[50] Thus, only one day after the nationalization of the canal, both economic and legal pressure had been ruled out as effective means to resolve the dispute.

Eden is quoted as describing the situation in a cabinet meeting as one in which "Colonel Nasser's action had presented us with an opportunity to find a lasting settlement of this problem, and we should not hesitate to take advantage of it."[51] And in a letter to President Dwight D. Eisenhower, Eden subtly hints at how that might be accomplished: "My colleagues and I are convinced that we must be ready, in the last resort, to use force to bring Nasser to his senses. For our part we are prepared to do so."[52]

Events proceeded quickly. On August 1, Dulles arrived in London to take part in meetings between the United States, France, and Britain. Though there was superficial agreement among the three powers, it quickly became clear that France and Britain were much closer to each other in their positions than either was to the United States. While Dulles spoke of

---

[47] Quoted in Kissinger 1995, 530.
[48] Lloyd 1996, 83.
[49] Nutting 1967, 46.
[50] Gorst and Johnman 1997, 57.
[51] Quoted in ibid., 58.
[52] Eden 1960, 477.

finding a way to make Nasser "disgorge" the canal, he privately warned Eden against "precipitous" military action.[53] Two diplomatic solutions failed in quick succession.[54]

On October 14, Nutting and Eden met with French leaders, one of whom (Albert Gazier, the French minister of labor) cautiously asked Eden what Britain's response would be if Israel were to attack Egypt.[55] Eden replied that Britain "had no obligation ... to stop the Israelis attacking the Egyptians." Eden then asked his secretary to stop recording the minutes of the meeting and encouraged the French leaders to speak openly. Nutting recalls that

> the plan, as he put it to us, was that Israel should be invited to attack Egypt across the Sinai Peninsula and that France and Britain, having given the Israeli forces enough time to seize all or most of Sinai, should then order "both sides" to withdraw their forces from the Suez Canal in order to permit an Anglo-French force to intervene and occupy the Canal on the pretext of saving it from damage by fighting. Thus the two powers would be able to claim to be "separating the combatants" and "extinguishing a dangerous fire," while actually seizing control of the entire waterway and of its terminal ports, Port Said and Suez. This would ... restore the running of the Canal to Anglo-French management.[56]

At a conference a week later in France, the plan was finalized and put in writing (at Israel's insistence) as the infamous "Sevres Protocol." On October 29, Israeli paratroopers were dropped and the Suez War began. The barely concealed pretext contrived at Sevres did not survive for long. After Britain vetoed a US proposal for a cease-fire in the United Nations, US senator Walter George declared that the British were "conniving in an attack against Egypt and are using that as a prearranged pretext. ... It is almost certain that Britain and France are working in collusion with the

---

[53] Nutting 1967, 52; Eden 1960, 487.

[54] First, the "Menzies mission" to Egypt ended with Nasser warning that nothing would induce him to accept a solution that cast doubt on "Egypt's absolute right to run the Canal as an Egyptian national undertaking." Quoted in Nutting 1967, 55. Following that, Egypt spurned Dulles's proposal to form an international "Suez Canal User's Association." Once again, Dulles publicly disavowed the use of force, undercutting the effectiveness of any political pressure that might have induced Nasser to compromise. See Lloyd 1996, 130.

[55] In fact, there is some evidence that Israel had been planning just such a war since at least 1955, though one that was conditional on support from France and Britain. See Levy and Gochal 2001.

[56] Nutting 1967, 93.

Israelis." And so they were. That same day, Anglo-French forces began to attack Egyptian airfields and shortly thereafter reoccupied the canal. The next day, the British chair of the Exchequer informed the cabinet that a run on the pound had been orchestrated by Washington (the currency had lost one-eighth of its value), but that the United States would support an International Monetary Fund loan to prop up the pound if a cease-fire was signed by midnight.[57] The cease-fire was signed, the conflict ended, and the Anglo-French forces withdrew from the canal area. Henry Kissinger later wrote that "by the time the smoke cleared, the Suez Crisis had destroyed the Great Power status of both Great Britain and France."[58]

British Calculations

What led Eden and the UK government to embark on such an obviously reckless and transparent plan? Another way of asking this question is, When Eden described the nationalization of the Suez Canal as an "opportunity to find a lasting settlement of this problem," to which *problem* was he referring?

The first candidate for an explanation—as is often the case when Western powers intervene in the Middle East—is oil. Originally, much of the value of the canal was that it provided easy access for Britain to its empire in India. Even as India became independent in 1948, however the canal had begun to assume importance in a new role. The canal cut the eleven-thousand-mile journey from the Persian Gulf to England down to sixty-five hundred miles and was the conduit through which Western Europe received over 1.5 million barrels—two-thirds of its requirements—a day.[59]

Even Nutting—who resigned his office rather than collude with France and Israel—was in agreement with Eden on the strategic importance of the canal, which was critical for the "life-blood of British industry": oil.[60] Other pathways existed, such as overland routes, but they all presented the same problem: greatly increased costs. As Eden noted later in his memoir.

We estimated that the United Kingdom had reserves of oil which would last for six weeks, and that the other countries of Western Europe owned comparatively smaller stocks. This continuing supply of fuel ... was now

---

[57] Horne 1988, 440.
[58] Kissinger 1995, 523.
[59] Yergin 1992, 480, 580.
[60] Nutting 1967, 10.

subject to Colonel Nasser's whim. ... More than half of Britain's annual imports of oil came through the canal. At any time the Egyptians might decide to interfere with its passage. They might also prompt their allies to cut the pipeline.[61]

And yet whatever the worries of Britain and France, there was another side. In fact, despite the fiery rhetoric and act of nationalization itself, Nasser—conspicuously wary of world opinion—had refrained from any action that might have been perceived as an additional affront. He had, in the words of a British diplomat, "offered no real provocation that would justify the use of force. He had seized an Anglo-French company, but he had not done any injury to British or French lives, nor had he stopped a British or French ship passing through the canal."[62]

At most, we can assume that Eden's post hoc justifications relating to the strategic importance of the canal contain a measure of truth. But that is not the only justification he and other decision makers cited, so even if it is part of the story, it is incomplete. In one National Security Council meeting in the United States, for example, Secretary of State Dulles noted that *"the British and French were thinking in terms of prestige and power,* and not solely in terms of transit through the Canal."[63] A Special National Intelligence Estimate commissioned by President Eisenhower concurred, observing that "the primary significance of [nationalization] is in its political and psychological aspects rather than in the threat it poses to canal operations."[64] To fill in the rest of the picture, we can return to the words of the decision makers themselves. Before that, though, we must start with a snapshot of Britain's place in the world on the eve of the Suez War.

In 1920, the British Empire included Australia, India, Canada, Iraq, Malaysia, Borneo, Papua New Guinea, New Zealand, Sierra Leone, and a stretch of Africa that reached uninterrupted from Egypt in the north down to the tip of South Africa. Yet by 1956, most of these territories were on the road to independence, if not independent already. The "crown jewel" of the empire, India, had been granted independence in 1947, and between 1945 and 1951, Britain had withdrawn from India, Greece, Turkey, and Palestine. In 1951, Iranian premier Mohammad Mossadeq had nationalized the oil industry and thrown out the Anglo-Iranian Oil Company. In Egypt in that same year, King Farouk's ministers had denounced the 1936 treaty

---

[61] Eden 1960, 478.
[62] Nutting 1967, 55.
[63] Office of the Historian 1956, document 72, emphasis added.
[64] Ibid., document 40.

with Britain that allowed for the stationing of British forces in the Suez Canal zone. In fact, in 1954, in an attempt to mollify Egypt, Britain had agreed to withdraw all its military personnel from the Suez Canal base within two years. And finally, on March 1, 1956, General Glubb—chief of the General Staff and commander of the Arab Legion since 1939—was dismissed from his post in Jordan. He had been a respected officer, and his unceremonious removal seems to have been taken by Eden as a personal insult. Nutting writes:

> A few hours later, after the news had reached London, the Prime Minister of Great Britain declared a personal war on the man whom he held responsible for Glubb's dismissal—Gamal Abdel Nasser. ... *For Eden, such a blow to Britain's waning prestige as an imperial power,* capable of influencing men and events in the Middle East, could not be allowed to go unpunished.[65]

In all these instances, Eden had tended to see the issue as one primarily of "standing" and "prestige." In a memo on the wisdom of the partitioning of Palestine following the end of World War II, Eden warned that partition would bring the prospect of "losing to America our pre-eminence in a part of the world which is of great importance to us."[66]

The nationalization of the Suez Canal was not an unexpected blow to Britain's prestige that arrived like a bolt out of the blue; quite the opposite. For Eden—as for many British leaders—it was just the latest in a long series of humiliating public setbacks. In what can be considered an almost-comical act of understatement, Blackwell notes that British policy during this era illustrated "the extent to which emotive considerations of prestige ... coexisted with rational policy management."[67] As it turned out, for Eden, nationalization of the canal was the proverbial straw that broke the camel's back. In his letter to Eisenhower, written shortly after the nationalization, he said plainly,

> We are all agreed that we cannot afford to allow Nasser to seize control of the canal in this way, in defiance of international agreements. If we take a firm stand over this now we shall have the support of the maritime powers. *If we do not, our influence and yours throughout the Middle East will, we are all convinced, be finally destroyed.*[68]

---

[65] Nutting 1967, 17, emphasis added.
[66] Quoted in Kyle 2003b, 22.
[67] Blackwell 2004, 99.
[68] Eden 1960, 476, emphasis added.

While Eden was fixated on the damage to his own prestige (and that of England), he was simultaneously concerned with the status gains that would accrue to Nasser. In other correspondence to Eisenhower, he argued that "if he can get away with this and if he can successfully defy eighteen nations his prestige in Arabia will be so great that he will be able to mount revolutions of young officers in Saudi Arabia, Jordan, Syria and Iraq."[69] Eisenhower was not persuaded, though his response reveals at least that Eden's status concerns were transparent to others as well. The president spends a good portion of the correspondence restating what he takes to be Eden's central concern: "You seem to believe that any long, drawn-out controversy either within the 18-nation group or in the UN will inevitably make Nasser an Arab hero and *perilously damage the prestige of Western Europe, including the United Kingdom.*"[70] Despite this, Eisenhower argues that "this ... is a picture too dark and is severely distorted."[71]

Even if one sees Eden's pleas as strategic—designed perhaps less to reveal Eden's true motives than to convince Eisenhower to aid the United Kingdom—it is notable that such justifications were offered by Eden in private as well. Shuckburgh, Eden's private secretary, reports that on March 3, Eden had thought aloud about the "reoccupation of Suez as a move to counteract the blow to our prestige which Glubb's dismissal means."[72] After the nationalization in fall 1956, Eden was not alone in seeing the issue as one primarily about status. Eden's colonial secretary, Alan Lennox-Boyd, wrote him a private note, declaring that "if Nasser wins or even appears to win we might as well as a government (and indeed as a country) go out of business."[73] Even more memorably, Harold Macmillan asserted that "if Britain did not confront Nasser now, it [Britain] would become another Netherlands."[74]

US diplomatic personnel transmitted reports back to the Department of State throughout the crisis, and their analysis conforms with the private justifications of British leaders cited above. In one telegram, US diplomats note that "[British leaders] foresee a military defeat of Nasser as restoring

---

[69] Office of the Historian 1956, document 181. Note here that while prestige is at issue, it is almost inextricably linked to other issues, such as reputation and strategic concerns.

[70] Ibid., document 192.

[71] Ibid. Though some cabinet members could be seen as disagreeing with Eisenhower. Robert Murphy, deputy undersecretary of state, is recalled by British leaders as saying that "Eden had not adjusted himself to the altered world status of Britain." See Lloyd 1978, 90.

[72] Quoted in Shuckburgh 1986, 341.

[73] Quoted in Kyle 2003a, 117.

[74] Quoted in Horne 1988, 397.

Brit position and prestige in Middle East [and] permitting favorable solution [to] Brit problems with Saudi Arabia, Jordan, Syria, etc. as well as Egypt."[75]

The evidence presented above illustrates several important details related to Eden's status concerns. While "rank" was important, the positional aspect of status is clearly emphasized far less than the identity aspect; in other words, the critical aspect of Eden's status concerns was ensuring that Britain remained in the club of great powers. This also helps to shed light on the reference group, which was clearly a subset of states that could be classified as "major powers." To the extent that smaller, lower-status states are mentioned in the historical record, they are only relevant insofar as they remain under the influence of the higher-status state, Britain.

Yet the positional aspect was critical as well. Recall that one fear that Eden and other British leaders had was not just that Egypt would achieve a victory, but that it would come at England's expense. These leaders seemed well aware that for Egypt to gain status, it must come at the expense of some other actor; in this case, it would have been at the expense of England and France. If anything, this speaks to the fundamental difficulty in disentangling the positional and identity-based forms of status. Rather than being separate, alternative conception of status, they appear to be two sides of the same coin.

"MY VIETNAM": EGYPTIAN INTERVENTION IN THE YEMEN CIVIL WAR

While the Suez debacle had "destroyed the Great Power status" of Britain, it had done nothing but elevate Nasser, both regionally and internationally.[76] The act of nationalization itself was a public relations coup for Nasser and Egypt, and declassified US intelligence documents noted that

President Nasser's nationalization of the Suez Canal Company repre-sents ... a highly effective move to extricate himself from what appeared to be a humiliating setback. ... By accepting arms from the Soviet Bloc in September 1955, Nasser at one stroke elevated himself to a position of extraor-dinary prestige throughout the Arab world as well as at home. ... [S]uccessful nationalization of the canal will greatly increase Nasser's influence in the

---

[75] Office of the Historian 1956, document 158.
[76] Kissinger 1995, 523.

other Arab states and is thus likely to lead to a further erosion of Western prestige and an increased willingness on the part of these states to follow Egypt's lead in relations with the Bloc and the West.[77]

In a National Security Council meeting, President Eisenhower predicted that following the nationalization, "Nasser's prestige would be so high ... that all the Arabs would listen to him."[78] These predictions were made *before* the debacle of Suez War itself, and when the heavy-handed collusion between Israel, France, and the United Kingdom was revealed, it only increased the gains made by Nasser. In attempting to convince the United States to apply pressure to Egypt, Israelis ambassador Abba Eban predicted that should the Western powers "let" Nasser emerge victorious, "increased prestige would cause Nasser to look for new worlds to conquer."[79]

Eban's prediction, however, did not come to pass—at least not immediately. In the aftermath of Suez, and despite its victory, "the Egyptian government did not immediately envisage translating its increased position of prestige in the Arab world into new Arab initiatives."[80] In December 1956, Nasser met for three hours with US ambassador Raymond Hare and passionately declared that his "first priority" in the wake of Suez was to "build up the domestic economy of Egypt." More to the point, he reassured the anxious US official that "preoccupation with foreign affairs" only detracted from "essential domestic reform."[81]

More broadly, in the immediate aftermath of Suez, Nasser realized that his newfound status was a double-edged sword: Arab monarchies (the "royalists") feared his influence would lead to revolution, and the Eisenhower Doctrine had led to economic gains for Egypt's competitors, Jordan, Saudi Arabia, and Iraq. Nasser had been successfully "contained," and his bid for regional hegemony was thwarted, at least for the moment. By 1957, a British official asserted that "Nasser's ultimate aim of achieving hegemony in Egypt's three circles (Arab, African and Muslim) remained unchanged," and that he was "simply waiting for a suitable opportunity to pursue" those objectives.[82]

---

[77] Office of the Historian 1956, document 40.
[78] Ibid., document 72. As it turned out, Eisenhower was right, though not immediately so.
[79] Ibid., document 204.
[80] Jankowski 2002, 86.
[81] Quoted in ibid., 86.
[82] Podeh 1993, 104.

In January 1958, a Syrian military delegation traveled to Cairo to persuade Nasser to lead a union of Syria and Egypt. While exact accounts are somewhat contentious, the balance of evidence suggests that it was motivated in large part by Syrian military officers and Ba'th Party officials who feared a Communist takeover enough to surrender a considerable amount of sovereignty to Nasser and Egypt.[83] Contemporaneous academic accounts note that "Syrian haste" overcame "Egyptian prudence" and that Nasser had "stated more than once that he had not expected the merger to take place so soon."[84] The establishment of the United Arab Republic in (UAR) February 1958 transformed the geopolitical landscape of the Middle East. And while "union with Syria was not his [Nasser's] idea, he was prepared to use it to serve his own ends."[85]

And what ends were those? How can we understand the goals of Colonel Nasser? Noted historian of the Middle East Malcolm Kerr described them as follows:

> If Nasser's leadership has stamped the Egyptian revolution with one identifiable goal, it is to advance Egyptian prestige. Both Nasser's championship of Pan-Arabism and his undoubted desire to raise domestic living standards should be seen as subordinate to this aim ... For yesterday's underdog, and especially for the revolutionary, prestige must be seized from others at their expense.[86]

Other scholars concur, with some describing Nasser's "highest priority" as "his own prestige."[87] Baker, in his study of the Egyptian government under Nasser and Sadat, argued that "the vision animating Nasser's revolution from above crystallized around" five goals, one of which was "the enhancement of Egypt's international standing."[88]

In order to see this in action, however, we must advance several years in the narrative. While the immediate aftermath of Suez saw Nasser's status being "contained," there was no sharp status loss or threat that

---

[83] Ibid., 105.

[84] Parker 1962, 18. Another account noted that the union "took place quite unexpectedly between two States who had never before, through all these moves and maneuvers, proclaimed any such desire—and of whom, ten years ago, one would have said that such an idea could scarcely belong to the realm of the practicable." See Longrigg 1958, 307.

[85] Walt 1987, 72.

[86] Kerr 1967, 66, emphasis added.

[87] Barnett and Levy 1991, 382.

[88] Baker 1978, 43.

would lead directly to a status-altering event. Instead, and as we have seen, Nasser's initial goals were mostly focused on domestic popularity rather than international standing. Even the formation of the UAR—while it did indeed lead to status benefits for Nasser—was mostly reactive in nature; Nasser sensed an opportunity once Syria approached him, but by all accounts was surprised at the willingness of Syria's leaders to—for all practical purposes—abdicate power.

"A Humiliating Blow to President Nasir's Prestige"

The honeymoon did not last long. A series of reports commissioned by the British Foreign Office in 1960 revealed cracks in the facade of Nasser's stature. While his portrait could be seen in shops and cafés throughout the Arab world (often larger than the depictions of the country's ruler), the report concluded that "Nasser's prestige ... has fallen somewhat from the high pinnacle which it reached two or three years ago."[89] Nasser's standing continued to fall, and in 1961 shifted from "relative tranquility to [a situation] characterized by a bitter confrontation between Nasserite Egypt and the status-quo states of Saudi Arabia, Jordan, Syria and Yemen. The catalyst ... was the secession of Syria from the United Arab Republic in September 1961."[90] The secession had followed immediately after Syrian army officers—dissatisfied with their junior role in the alliance—had staged a coup and seceded from the UAR.[91] In short order, Egypt broke off diplomatic relations with Jordan, Saudi Arabia, and Yemen, refused to recognize the new Syrian regime, and initiated a propaganda campaign against all four adversaries.

Despite this, the new Syrian regime survived, and Nasser's political fortunes continued to wane. Materially, Nasser was unhurt, and nobody believed that his rule in Egypt was threatened. Despite the fact that Nasser's domestic political legitimacy was "stable as ever," the "collapse of the union and the consolidation of the new Syrian regime considerably eroded 'Abd al-Nasir's prestige in the Arab world."[92] By 1962, a year after the Syrian secession from the UAR, "the position of Egypt in the Arab world ... was

---

[89] Jankowski 2002, 156.
[90] Dawisha 1977, 205.
[91] A postmortem by a Ba'th Party leader asserted that "the rupture between Nasser and the Ba'th was caused by a certain Egyptian hegemonic view of the union." See Walt 1987, 208.
[92] Podeh 1999, 162.

one of almost complete political isolation." Its roots were obvious to the Egyptian leadership, which "attributed this weakness in Egypt's status to Syria's secession from the United Arab Republic a year earlier, which had been a humiliating blow to President Nasir's prestige and Egypt's pivotal position in the Arab world."[93]

It was against this backdrop that on September 26, 1962, a group of officers in the Yemeni army overthrew the newly appointed imam of Yemen, Muhammad al-Badr. The revolutionaries, known as the Yemeni Free Officers, reflected the style of "republican" revolution that overthrew the Egyptian monarchy in 1952 and that the "Nasserist" ideology promoted in the Arab world.[94] Whether Egypt directly helped orchestrate the coup or merely had foreknowledge of it has yet to be settled, but it responded definitively once the coup occurred.[95] Shortly afterward, Egypt began providing military aid to the republicans, while Saudi Arabia supported the royalists.

Over the next five years, Egypt poured vast military resources into Yemen. Beginning with a few hundred commandos at the beginning of October 1962, Egyptian forces in Yemen grew to roughly seventy thousand by 1965.[96] What started off as military aid provision for a fledgling revolution became a full-scale military intervention that sapped Egypt's military capabilities and is widely considered to have left it unprepared to face Israel in the Six-Day war. It was "an adventure that proved more costly in lives, treasure, and squandered influence than any of Egypt's wars with Israel." The war "crippled the Egyptian economy," "left a permanent scar on society," and "destroyed Nasser's neutralist foreign policy."[97] In the end, Nasser admitted that it had been a "miscalculation; we never thought that it would lead to what it did."[98] Perhaps the ultimate indictment is his later characterization of the Egyptian intervention as "my Vietnam."[99]

[93] Dawisha 1975, 47.
[94] Ferris 2013.
[95] See Mansfield 1969, Ferris 2013.
[96] Ferris 2008, 7.
[97] Ibid.
[98] Quoted in Dawisha 1975, 48.
[99] Quoted in ibid., 55.

"I Beg You to Save the Prestige of the Egyptian Army"

There were, of course, strategic reasons that help to explain Egypt's intervention in Yemen. Primarily, these are geographic; by maintaining influence or control in Yemen, Egypt would have a foothold in a country bordering on both Saudi Arabia (to the north) and the British protectorate, the South Arabian Federation (to the south and east).[100] Indeed, the conflict at times spilled over to both those territories; Egypt bombed two Saudi towns, the British bombed a village in Yemen, and Egyptians used the opportunity to funnel arms to revolutionaries in the South Arabian Federation.[101] There was, as one scholar put it, "undoubted strategic value for Egypt to establish herself militarily" in this region.[102]

Another contributing factor was what appears to be a textbook case of "positive illusions."[103] Egyptian elites explaining the decision noted that "when it was clear in two days that all the people were with the revolution, the UAR gave its full support."[104] Quite obviously, all the people were not in favor of the revolution, and Nasser's misunderstanding seems to have been based on an "almost total ignorance of the social structure and political conditions" of Yemen along with discounting of the "mountainous and warlike Zaidi tribes in the North of the country."[105] On the level of tactical intelligence, a variety of factors conspired in leaving Egypt wholly unprepared for the conflict it was about to enter. Here is just one telling example of these "breathtaking shortcomings": Egyptian commandos "went off to Yemen equipped with maps that would have embarrassed a tourist."[106]

Neither of these potential factors is particularly persuasive, however, let alone a complete explanation for the disastrous Egyptian decision. Strategic reasons might certainly form part of the motivation for Nasser's decision, but this school of thought is decidedly post hoc. There is little to no evidence that Egyptian leaders were particularly concerned about the strategic value of Yemen. Instead, when faced with puzzling

---

[100] Dawisha 1977, 218.
[101] Kerr 1967, 78.
[102] Dawisha 1977, 218.
[103] Johnson 2009.
[104] Dawisha 1977, 215.
[105] Dawisha 1975, 48–49.
[106] Ferris 2013, 57.

decisions, scholars often default to attempting to deduce motives from actions: if Egypt intervened in Yemen, then it *must* have been strategically valuable. There are few things that cannot be rationalized in hindsight. As for the misperceptions and overconfidence, these cannot be more than supplements to a complete explanation. Overconfidence explains why Nasser predicted that the intervention would reap benefits at low costs, but cannot be used to understand what those benefits were. In other words, it provides no insight as to the actual motivations themselves.

For what precisely impelled Nasser to first intervene in Yemen—and later escalate that commitment—we must go back to the Syrian secession from the UAR in 1961. It was that event that appears to have triggered Nasser's status concerns. The definitive history of these events summarizes them by noting that "Nasser apparently took the Syrian slap quite personally, and it was this blow to the president's prestige—and by extension, to Egypt's as a whole—that explains the bitterness of his reactions."[107] International observers were wary of exactly this reaction, and there was worry in the United States even before the Yemen coup that status concerns would impel Nasser toward foreign policy adventurism. A memo from the US director of intelligence and research to Secretary of State Dean Rusk on September 13, 1962 (almost two weeks before the coup in Yemen) stated, "In the wake of his continued failure to stage a comeback in Syria, Nasser probably feels the need for some concrete victory in the war he declared against the 'reactionaries' following the breakup of the UAR."[108]

Even as early as 1961, US intelligence officers were briefing President John F. Kennedy that "Nasser apparently was caught off balance by the Syrian affair, which must have hurt him domestically and in the pan-Arab field. *Consequently we can probably expect some sort of external move by Nasser to restore his prestige.*"[109]

While US intelligence estimates do not have an unimpeachable track record, they were prescient in this case. When Nasser learned of the successful coup in Saana, Yemen, the news "fell upon an Egyptian leadership united mainly by its determination to restore Egypt's position in the

---

[107] Ibid., 27.
[108] Office of the Historian 1962, document 38.
[109] Quoted in Podeh 1999, 268, emphasis added.

Arab world."[110] In fact, countless secondary works cite this motivation as primary as well:

- "The main reason for ... Nasir's 1962 military intervention in Yemen was to improve his position in the Arab world, and his international standing, after suffering the humiliating secession of Syria from the United Arab Republic."[111]
- "Occurring so soon after the Syrian secession, the collapse of the [Yemen] Republic would deal Egyptian prestige, as the leading 'revolutionary' and 'progressive' power ... a massive, even fatal, blow."[112]
- "Gamal Abdel Nasser, still smarting from Syria's secession from the United Arab Republic a year earlier, was determined to restore Egypt's prestige."[113]
- "In September 1961 the United Arab Republic had collapsed after much acrimony between Damascus and Cairo. A year later, the UAR's dissolution still caused Nasser to feel vulnerable, and he believed he needed a decisive political or diplomatic victory in order to reestablish his leadership in the Arab world."[114]
- "[Nasser] probably hoped to ... reaffirm his status as the leading champion of Arab nationalism"[115]

Nearly all secondary sources are in agreement, but more important, primary records from the period—though few exist—make the same case. A memo to McGeorge Bundy, the president's special assistant for national security affairs in 1963, wrote that a "fairly reliable source" asserts that the "real reason" for Nasser's decision is that he "wants a dramatic 'victory' to enhance his prestige in the eyes of the Syrians."[116] And what little firsthand evidence we have suggests the same. Gerges reports that "in the words of an associate of Nasser's," the Egyptian leader "needed an inter-Arab political victory to restore his waning prestige in the Arab arena."[117] Finally, Guldescu claims that "Saudi sources report that at Jedda, Nasser said to King Faisal: 'I beg you to save the prestige of the Egyptian Army.'"[118]

---

[110] Ferris 2013, 49.
[111] Gerges 1995, 292.
[112] Dawisha 1977, 216.
[113] Ferris 2008, 5.
[114] Fain 2001, 132–33.
[115] Little 1988, 511.
[116] Office of the Historian 1962, document 19.
[117] Gerges 1995, 299.
[118] Guldescu 1966, 323.

The bulk of evidence suggests strongly that status concerns formed a large part of Nasser's motivations for the initial intervention. This accords as well with the theory put forward in this book. By many accounts, Nasser was unusually fixated on his own prestige, even before the Suez Crisis, and certainly after it. But that general preference for higher status—as strong as it was—did little to influence Egyptian foreign policy in the years after 1956. Instead, it took a "humiliating blow" to Nasser's prestige, in the form of Syria's secession from the UAR in 1961, to trigger even sharper status concerns. Those newfound status concerns led Nasser to seek out a foreign policy success that might qualify as a status-altering event. When the opportunity was presented to him to intervene in Yemen following the coup, he wasted little time; some accounts portray him as deciding to intervene on the first day following the crisis, after which he allowed several days of faux "deliberation" among his advisers to arrive at the decision he had already made.[119]

An additional advantage of using status dissatisfaction as the lens through which to understand Egyptian decision making in Yemen is that it sheds light not only on the initial intervention but the later escalation as well. In chapter 3, I showed that in a lab environment, status concerns led subjects to throw good money after bad in two separate experiments. We can see that same dynamic at work in Nasser's repeated decisions to escalate Egypt's commitment to the Yemen intervention. In the initial decision, Nasser eschewed an approach based on either indirect aid to Yemeni revolutionaries or overwhelming force. Instead, he chose a middle path that minimized risks but also was least likely to lead to any sort of success.[120] Once committed, however, he found it difficult to disengage. Why? While the initial intervention was designed to improve Egypt's international standing, once his prestige was engaged, the costs of backing down and abandoning his Yemeni allies only grew.

A US intelligence report prepared in September 1963 by National Security Council staffer Robert Komer noted,

> Nasser is trapped in Yemen. It's bleeding him, but *he can't afford either the sharp loss of face in letting go* or (we hope) the risk of confronting us by starting on the Saudis again … Nasser cornered is a dangerous animal, and we want to be mighty careful how we handle him.[121]

---

[119] Ferris 2013, 52–53.
[120] Ibid., 55.
[121] Office of the Historian 1962, document 329, emphasis added.

Other sources agreed. A policy paper prepared by the Bureau of North Eastern and South Asian Affairs a few months later (in December 1963) declared that "further dragging out of the Yemen imbroglio will also erode still more of Nasser's already depreciated prestige in the area."[122] Other recently declassified US intelligence documents indicate that "Nasser's prestige has declined" as it becomes clear that he is "caught in Yemen and cannot extricate himself," and that the "UAR is heavily committed, both materially and in prestige"[123] And by 1965, a Central Intelligence Agency memo noted that "Nasser is in a dilemma in the Yemen. The existing stalemate is a burden on his resources and an affront to his prestige."[124]

In fact, historical works are in agreement that it was Nasser's concerns with prestige that kept Egypt involved in the disastrous intervention for so long. The intervention was so risky precisely because it would "closely tie Egypt's and Nasser's prestige to the eventual success of the republican cause."[125] Once committed, Egypt's "prestige had become involved with the republic's survival" and "withdrawal became impossible."[126] A withdrawal of support would lead to the collapse of the Yemeni republican cause, "which in turn might cause irreparable damage to Egypt's prestige."[127] Nasser, seemingly aware of his predicament, attempted to use status concerns to his advantage. Barnett and Levy report that "Nasser's strategy was to involve the Soviets more deeply in Egyptian affairs" to "ensure that they felt Egypt's defeat was their defeat; that their prestige was bound up with that of Egypt's."[128]

DISCUSSION

After the addition of these three cases to the qualitative evidence presented on Germany's Weltpolitik, what have we learned? In fact, several lessons emerge that allow us to both increase our confidence in some aspects of the theory of status dissatisfaction while refining it and suggesting extensions for future work.

[122] Ibid., document 385.
[123] Ibid., document 381, 97
[124] Ibid., document 360.
[125] Dawisha 1977, 217.
[126] Mansfield 1969, 73.
[127] Dawisha 1977, 217.
[128] Barnett and Levy 1991, 384. The strategy did appear to work, at least in some respects. See Ferris 2008.

The most prominent lesson is that all three case studies surveyed in this chapter show the same link between heightened status concerns and international conflict that was found in the Germany case explored in the previous chapter. Russia, in refusing to back down in the July Crisis, took steps that its leaders knew made war a virtual certainty. Great Britain colluded with Israel and France to launch the Suez War, which killed thousands and helped to destroy the United Kingdom's stature as a great power. Egypt intervened in the Yemen Civil War, and after that initial miscalculation, added to it by slowly escalating over the next several years, growing to a force of roughly seventy thousand Egyptian soldiers by 1965 and degrading its military capabilities to the point that many see the Yemen debacle as responsible for Egypt's humiliating defeat in the 1967 Six-Day War.

While the heightened status concerns examined in these cases are all linked in some way to international conflict—as predicted by the theory—it is worth noting that the type of conflict was different in each case. In the previous chapter, we saw that Germany sought out opportunities during the Weltpolitik era to shift its status by provoking international crises. In these three cases, however, the pattern differed subtly. Russia did not seek out an opportunity to shift its status; on the contrary, the optimal military solution would have been to delay any conflict for several years. In fact, Russia was pushed into a corner by the Austrian ultimatum, and it seems unlikely that—had that not occurred—it would have engaged in a foreign policy that resembled Germany's in the previous years. Egypt, in contrast, *did* seek out an opportunity to shift its status in a manner similar to Germany; there was no military need to intervene in Yemen's internal conflict. Britain also can be said to have sought out an opportunity to demonstrate its international standing through conflict.

The three cases offer additional support for the importance of *local* reference groups. In chapter 6, Germany competed against a small group of peer competitors, including Russia, but primarily England, and France. In this chapter, we see this pattern repeated in all three cases. Russian leaders in the July Crisis were only concerned about their international standing relative to a small group of European major powers, including the Austro-Hungarian Empire, Germany, England, and France. In 1956, Eden and his advisers were focused on ensuring that Great Britain remained in the "club" of great powers, not with their international standing relative to an undifferentiated grouping of other states. Finally, Nasser was quite clearly intent on achieving the status of "regional power" for his country within the Middle East. In this last case, there is specific evidence that Nasser viewed Egypt as competing within three reference groups: Arab, African, and Muslim.[129]

While the cases are similar along key dimensions—the link between status and conflict as well as the importance of reference groups—interesting differences emerge when the causes of their status concerns are examined. In Germany, leaders' status dissatisfaction was formalized into the grand strategy of Weltpolitik, and originated from the perceived disjuncture between the status that Germany had achieved and what its leaders felt they deserved. In the Russian case, there is no strong evidence of heightened status concerns prior to the July Crisis, but once their prestige had become engaged by the public nature of the threat (just as German leaders had intended), Russian leaders found themselves unable to back down. In the British case, the dissatisfaction over relative status was caused by a long-term decline in its status position following two destructive wars and the breakup of its colonial empire.

In both the British and Egyptian cases, however, a "trigger" served to activate the status dissatisfaction and catalyze the conflict initiation predicted by status dissatisfaction. In the former case, it was the nationalization of the Suez Canal—and the public humiliation it engendered—that served as the catalyst. In the latter case, it was Syria's secession from the UAR that activated Nasser's status concerns. Both cases thus suggest something about the importance of public humiliations in triggering status concerns, and illustrate the direct line from those public setbacks to the initiation of violent conflict.

We also find evidence supportive of the additional mechanism uncovered in the two studies described in chapter 3. In that chapter, I used two experiments—including one conducted on a sample of real-world political leaders—to provide evidence for a baseline assumption of status dissatisfaction theory: that status concerns vary predictably in response to contextual and dispositional factors, and that heightened status concerns increase the value of status to actors. Yet both experiments also showed that heightened status concerns led participants to double down and escalate their commitment rather than walk away. While the Germany chapter did not find much evidence of this pattern—Germany was persistent in initiating conflicts, but did not tend to escalate them dramatically during this period—we do here. Russia's decision in July 1914 was a classic choice between escalating the crisis (by backing Serbia) or backing down. In that

---

[129] Podeh 1993, 104.

case, status concerns led directly to the decision to mobilize, risking war and setting in motion a chain of events that contributed significantly to the origins of World War I. In the Egyptian case, too, we see evidence that Nasser continued to double down his commitment in Yemen after finding that his initial "investment" of troops had yet to produce the military victories he expected.

Finally, the cases presented in this chapter also serve to help develop and extend the theory of status dissatisfaction. Despite the fact that status concerns were high in all the cases examined, there are obvious differences in how that dissatisfaction was manifested by the decision makers in each case. In Germany, decision makers evinced a clear focus—in both their words and actions—on gaining greater status. The disjuncture they perceived in their status was based on the perception that they had been artificially held back by two factors: the reluctance of other states to grant them status as well as Germany's relatively late formation as an independent state. Egypt appears to be a similar case, in which Nasser was intently focused on raising Egyptian status, which had been artificially held back by the colonial powers that had once dominated the region. In both those cases, we see that leaders' status concerns were manifested in an active and, in some situations, aggressive foreign policy.

In Russia and Britain, the pattern was different. Russian leaders in 1914 did not seek out opportunities to gain prestige at the expense of status quo powers, and Eden was not seeking to *raise* Britain's status but rather to salvage it. And indeed, in both cases we see that the status concerns were manifested in what was primarily a reactive foreign policy. Russia did not seek out, and certainly would have preferred to avoid, a crisis like that which occurred in July 1914. And Britain would certainly not have wished for the public humiliation of Suez nationalization. But once challenged, their fixation on the status aspects of their respective crises led them to choose—with virtually no real discussion—the most dangerous possible course for their country.

8

Conclusion

I began this book by calling attention to the importance of status—a concept widely acknowledged as a key motivation for leaders in world politics, yet one for which little systematic evidence exists. I've provided a theory that accounts for how status functions—what I have called status dissatisfaction theory—and tested that theory using a variety of approaches, including network analysis, large-N statistical analyses, experiments, and case studies. A common joke in political science is that we persistently lag behind our colleagues in economics, so it's worth recalling Frank's admonition to his fellow economists. He says that

> we have too often neglected fundamental elements of human nature in our study of the ways people behave. The penalty for that neglect has been that we have failed to ask many important questions; and, moreover, that we have offered wrong, or at least misleading, answers to many of the most important questions we do ask.[1]

These outcomes have come to pass. Despite the fact that we IR scholars often take our cue from Hobbes, we have given short shrift to a concept that is at once one of his three fundamental motives for war as well as a universal foundation of human behavior.

A broader issue, however, has been a focus on the wrong questions. While it is understandable—especially at the beginning of a research program, or perhaps out of an unnecessary sense of defensiveness—to make a case that "x matters," we must move on from this evolutionary stage in status research. Focusing on *whether* status matters has diverted attention and resources away from more specific, useful questions. Providing definitive answers to such a question is also nearly impossible without theories that make sense of what status is, offer scope conditions for when it is likely to

[1] Frank 1985, vi.

matter, and answer the question of how it might be linked to the outcomes that IR scholars care most about.

Even if status "matters," it doesn't matter equally for all actors at all times. To address this basic issue, I proposed a focus on status *concerns*. Yet we know little about what factors make status concerns more or less relevant for leaders. *When* do concerns over relative status overshadow the myriad other concerns that decision makers face in complex international environments? Answering this question requires us to begin by theorizing the systematic and predictable ways that heightened concerns are triggered.

In broader terms, status concerns might vary dispositionally (some people might be more sensitive than others to status concerns) or by culture (particular regions or states might be especially attuned to status issues). A comprehensive theory, however, requires factors that vary systematically, not idiosyncratically. To that end, I've concentrated on the divergence between the status accorded an actor and what they believe themselves to deserve. There are several advantages to a focus on this particular combination: it has long been regarded as a potentially important mechanism by which status affects behavior, and there is considerable evidence that the assumptions it is built on (for example, that actors are able to accurately infer where they stand in a hierarchy) are valid.

The second issue for such a theory concerns proper boundary conditions. The first thing one learns about status in an introductory economics course is that it is relative, but relative to *whom*? Earlier IR research on status left implicit or ignored the issue of social comparison; while some of the theories noted that a state's position in a hierarchy was important, they stopped short of specifying *which* hierarchy we should examine. Instead, states were all placed in a de facto global hierarchy. This is acceptable only if we assume that the global hierarchy is the most salient structure for all states. Yet in the context of world politics, such a perspective seems unreasonable for small and large states alike. In fact, decades of research have demonstrated that actors are most likely to use as reference groups others that are similar to them on important dimensions rather than all other actors. Or as Frank put it, status is local.[2]

Thus, the oft-cited maxim that status is *positional* is true but incomplete. Status is positional, in the sense that it matters what level of status an actor has relative to other actors, but it doesn't tell us anything about the relevant "status community," the reference group that actors see themselves

[2] Ibid.

as belonging to and competing against. In theory, actors can compare their status to a multitude of targets along an almost-infinite array of dimensions. I operationalized the local nature of international status in three ways: global hierarchy, regional geographic hierarchies, and status communities composed of peer competitors that states sort themselves into and reveal by way of their foreign policy choices (for example, diplomatic, trade, and alliance partners).

While all actors would prefer higher rather than lower status, there is systematic and predictable variation in *concern* for status, or the level of focus on status-related issues, and the likelihood of acting in order to advance or salvage one's status. In international politics, one significant factor that leads to heightened status concerns is dissatisfaction with one's relative position. This occurs when actors come to believe that they are accorded less status than they deserve within their chosen "status community."

Once triggered, heightened status concerns set in motion a set of consequences at the individual and state level. At the individual level, heightened concern for status—moderated by both situational and dispositional factors—increases the value of status to actors. This in turn leads to greater susceptibility to throw good money after bad. On the state level, heightened status concerns trigger a set of policies designed to return the country to what its leaders see as its "rightful place" or defend its current position in the hierarchy. Because status relies on collective beliefs about where each actor stands relative to other relevant actors, this requires actions that will update the larger community's beliefs. Events that update the beliefs of the larger community with regard to a state's status are status altering. While one can imagine status-altering events that are peaceful or cooperative in nature, a significant portion of dissatisfied actors are likely to resort to armed conflict to alter their position in their chosen hierarchy.

In chapter 3, I used experimental methods to provide behavioral microfoundations for my theory of status dissatisfaction. In that effort, I fielded two studies that examined the impact of experimentally manipulated status concerns on decision making. In both cases, I found strong evidence for a foundational assumption of status dissatisfaction: concerns over status vary systematically in response to situational and dispositional factors, and once triggered, increase actors' value for status.

Study 1 was a survey experiment that investigated the dispositional roots of status concerns. I found that individuals high in SDO—that is, subjects with stronger preferences for hierarchy—were most affected by status concerns, and correspondingly more likely to exhibit patterns of escalation. Conventional experimental protocols (including study 1) face two problems, however. First, measures of "escalation" are typically hypothetical business reinvestment decisions far removed from the realm of world politics. Second, survey experiments, even when they don't rely on "convenience samples" of undergraduates, often use subjects different from political leaders on dimensions that are theoretically relevant.

To address these issues, I conducted a lab experiment focused on status threats and the escalation of commitment. Escalation was operationalized as a new behavioral escalation task using real financial incentives and framed around a narrative of war and peace. In addition, I utilized a unique sample of political and military leaders from the SEF program at the Harvard Kennedy School as well as a group of demographically matched control subjects. This allowed for a more subtle investigation of status concerns that takes into account potential boundary conditions (power) while also addressing typical concerns about external validity in IR experiments. I found strong evidence that the fear of losing status impedes decision making and increases the tendency to throw good money after bad, but that power aids decision making by buffering high-power subjects against the worst effects of status threats.

Following chapter 3, I began the process of applying status dissatisfaction directly to the realm of IR. Doing so required wading into the messy world of observational data, and in particular, tackling thorny issues of measurement. While many "standard" IR variables (such as "power") are tough to measure, status is even more complicated as it is both perceptual and social, requiring us to find a measure of collective beliefs about where every actor stands with respect to every other actor as well as to what "status community" they see themselves as belonging.

In chapter 4, I showed how we can use the tools of network analysis to sensibly infer international status rankings. I innovated by incorporating universally acknowledged aspects of status that have thus far been ignored, including the notion that status is more efficiently gained from higher-status actors rather than lower ones. And while the diplomatic exchange data are often used—in one form or another—to examine international status, I provided the first-ever cross-validation of the data, using a combination of alternative data sources and historical research. I then used cutting-edge "community detection" techniques to operationalize *local* reference groups. This allowed us for the first time to directly measure states' reference groups, the "status communities" to which they belong, using data on the nature and intensity of diplomatic representation.

Next, I put those measures to use. Chapter 5 was a large-N statistical analysis of the relationship between status dissatisfaction and international conflict. First, I showed that conflict was indeed status altering. Winning international conflicts—whether a country initiated one or was targeted by another state—provided a status boost five and ten years down the road. Next, I showed that controlling for other important factors, states that are attributed less status than they are due based on material capabilities are overwhelmingly more likely (than "satisfied" states) to initiate militarized disputes at every level of intensity, from low-intensity MIDs to international wars. This chapter also presented unique data on which comparisons are most salient in motivating international conflict. The types of comparisons that are made—what the "reference group" is—have important implications for how status concerns are manifested in international politics.

In addition to making war more likely, dissatisfaction over status changes the very nature of conflict. For example, dissatisfied states choose different targets than otherwise-similar but "satisfied" states. In particular, they disproportionately select into conflicts against less powerful but higher-status states. In examining the impact of status deficits on international conflict, I also considered and preempted several potential objections. First, far from being a "remnant of the nineteenth century," the impact of status deficits on war does not change significantly over time. Another potential objection revolves around the notion of norms. For example, some communities may develop norms that prohibit the use of violence to attain greater international standing. Even among communities with extremely low absolute levels of violence, however, status deficits strongly predict the initiation of conflict. Finally, I showed that the measurement of status dissatisfaction is not simply picking up states that increase their military spending or withdraw diplomats in the lead up to war.

While the quantitative chapters carry important advantages, their primary drawback is the possibility that the statistical associations found might be spurious, driven by endogeneity stemming from either measurement error or omitted variables. While careful statistical modeling can address some of these concerns, the addition of carefully selected case studies helps protect against spurious correlations, provides insight into causal mechanisms, and helps to tease out further implications of the theory not observed in the cross-national data.

In chapter 6, I unpacked the black box of the state by investigating if and how status concerns motivated German decision making during the years 1897 to 1911. Seen in the light of status dissatisfaction theory, Germany's world policy, often derided by historians as blundering or reckless, is cast anew. German leaders, driven by the strong belief that they weren't accorded the status they deserved, formulated a grand strategy to raise their international profile through the instigation of major and minor international crises designed to coerce status concessions from Britain and France. The policies associated with Weltpolitik—primarily the constant initiation of international crises along with the pursuit of a large navy and mostly worthless colonial territories—may be seen as policies designed to coerce other states into ceding status to Germany. This chapter both fleshed out the empirical results from the laboratory and large-N chapters while shedding light on a critical turning point in the international system prior to World War I.

While there is strong evidence of the importance of status for German leaders in the Weltpolitik era, several open questions remained following that analysis. For example, how generalizable is the theory of status dissatisfaction? Is it bound temporally to the long nineteenth century, or can we find evidence of it in more modern eras? Does status dissatisfaction lead states only to a policy of aggressive conflict initiation, or are there other mechanisms by which it might lead to conflict? Is it strictly a feature of great power politics or Western countries? To examine these questions, chapter 7 looked at three separate sets of decisions: Russia's decision to aggressively back Serbia in the 1914 July Crisis, Britain's decision to collude with Israel and France in launching the 1956 Suez War, and Nasser's 1962 decision to intervene in the Yemen Civil War (and continue to escalate through the rest of the decade).

Chapter 7 thus corroborates broadly the patterns found in the case of Germany's world policy while highlighting several additional mechanisms by which status concerns are linked to conflict. Of these, the most significant is the link between heightened status concerns and the escalation of commitment. While the experimental chapter showed how these dynamics worked in the lab, there is evidence of the same dynamics in the case of

Nasser's escalation in Yemen and the czar's decision to double down in the July Crisis. These cases also help to make the critical point that status concerns are not confined to European countries, great powers, or states in the pre–World War I era.

LESSONS AND OPEN QUESTIONS

While an accounting of each chapter's findings helps place the book's contribution in perspective, it is also instructive to take a step back to examine the themes that run throughout as well as the open questions that remain. Four broad lessons emerge from the theoretical and empirical work in this book.

Status Is Local

I began the book by calling attention to several mismatches between our current understanding of status and the way it had been conceptualized in IR. Among these, perhaps the most important was the notion that even internationally, status is local. While there is an international status hierarchy, far more salient are the many status communities composed of peer competitors into which states sort themselves. This was substantiated by quantitative and historical evidence throughout the book. For example, any understanding of German Weltpolitik must account for the status club that Germany sought to join—composed of a small group of rivals that included England, France, and Russia. Similarly, Nasser's status concerns were not global but instead constructed along regional, religious, and ideological lines—a fact that helps to shed light on how he sought to improve Egypt's ranking (through actions that would be salient within his status community, but not necessarily in the broader community of nations).

While this operationalization of "local" status is indeed an improvement, it is not the final word on the subject, and future work has much to do in bringing our measures into greater alignment with our conceptual understanding. I operationalized "local" status communities, for example, as those inferred by a community detection algorithm. Yet it is possible that some amount of dissatisfaction results not from a disjuncture between power and status *within* a given community but rather from a lack of interactions with the community that one sees themselves as being part of (or aspires to join). In these cases, community detection would fall short by placing a state in the "wrong" status community. While this is certainly an improvement on not taking reference groups into account at all, these still represent a coarse measure of "belonging." Religion, shared history, culture, and ideology are all likely to produce status hierarchies even more finely grained than regional geography or detected communities.

Furthermore, states may see themselves as belonging to more than one community at any given time. The precise algorithm I used in chapters 4 and 5 did not allow for multiple or overlapping reference groups, but it seems likely that these dynamics would occur in international politics. For example, Brazilian leaders will likely have a multifaceted identity that includes a focus on themselves as a "regional power" (status community: South America) as well as a member of the BRIC nations (status community: Brazil, Russia, India, and China). Depending on the time or issue, different elements of identity and status concerns might be triggered, leading not only to different behaviors but also different intended audiences.

There Are Many Paths to Status

One theme that runs throughout this book is the question of how countries achieve high status in world politics. If President Kennedy was right, that prestige is merely "the shadow of power," then the recommendation is straightforward: build up your military.[3] But that simplistic vision of status—as a noisy or lagging measure of capabilities—doesn't seem to fit its multidimensional nature in IR. Material capabilities play a role in status, but they are merely one ingredient rather than the whole recipe.

Moreover, as one would expect for an ideational concept such as status, the role of capabilities shifts over time. This is consistent with an approach (such as the one taken here) that sees status as both social and perceptual; because communities of actors jointly accord status to each other, it is their *beliefs* about what attributes or behaviors are associated with status that matter. Unsurprisingly, those beliefs shift over time and across space so that while possession of colonial territories might have been the sine qua non of "great power status" in the nineteenth century, by the end of World War II, beliefs had shifted and the effect of these same territorial possessions

---

[3] Schlesinger 2002.

had reversed. So too with capabilities: the correlation between capabilities and status has shifted significantly over the last two hundred years. The patterns are also different for different types of states. For example, the correlation between power and status has dropped over time for major powers, while increasing for smaller states.

If capabilities cannot explain all the variation in status, then what can? In another set of analyses, I showed that we can place the "sources of status" into several categories, including fixed characteristics (such as state age), type of government (whether an autocracy or democracy), behavior (whether a state is a "good citizen" or "bad actor"), and capabilities (including possession of nuclear weapons, population, wealth, and military capabilities). The picture that emerges is one of status as variegated, with many different inputs. For example, just as Kaiser Wilhelm worried, states are indeed penalized for late entry into the international system: older states are accorded greater status, and so are larger ones. In status, it seems, there are some things that are more or less out of any leader's control.

Behaviors matter as well, however, and here leaders and countries do have some agency. The fact that both normatively good and bad behavior lead to greater status shows that there is not simply one route to prestige in world politics. Capabilities matter too, though not the ones we typically use in our large-N work in IR. Population and nuclear capabilities were both more predictive of greater status than raw military capabilities or wealth. And while there is a great deal of literature on the virtues of democracy for signaling and military effectiveness, I showed one previously hidden benefit: democratic states are accorded greater prestige in international politics. The flip side of that is that highly autocratic states benefit as well (compared to mixed regimes), demonstrating once again the multidimensional nature of status.

Of course, in addition to the inputs to status mentioned here, the theory of status dissatisfaction makes concrete predictions about the relationship between conflict and status. In particular, since status should be affected only by "status-altering" events that are public, salient, and dramatic, we should expect to find that conflict is itself one route to greater prestige in international politics. War does "pay" in fact in the sense of gaining prestige for the belligerents involved. Initiating and winning a conflict vaults the initiator almost seven rankings over a similar state that did not initiate a conflict and a similar amount over a state that did initiate but fought to a stalemate. Of course, in some cases, merely "standing up" to a more powerful state might come with status benefits, and I find results consistent with this notion: even just the initiation of conflict—independent of outcome—boosts a state's status ranking by three ranks over the course of ten years. Indeed, the status benefits of conflict are not confined to those states that initiate conflict; mere involvement (along with victory) carries the same benefits. And while the inputs to status I mentioned (such as material capabilities) shift in importance over time, conflict seems to be timeless: there are no significant differences in how conflict affects status rankings over time (measured by decade or historical era) or across types of states.

While this lesson helps to place the "sources of status" in perspective, it also spurs questions for future research. For instance, I find that there are status benefits to conflict in the large-N data, and the qualitative chapters corroborate this, at least in terms of leaders' expectations of what would bring their country greater status. Kaiser Wilhelm, for example, clearly saw the initiation of crises as a way to boost Germany's international standing. But the lessons of that chapter suggest a potential shortcoming of such a strategy: while in the short-term, Wilhelm's gambit seemed to be successful, his constant instigation of crises led directly to the formation of a balancing coalition and eventual "encirclement" of Germany that presaged World War I. This suggests that the strategy of conflict initiation (like that of nuclear proliferation) might come with an asterisk: you may gain status, but at the real cost of convincing other countries of your ill intentions. Future work, perhaps formal in nature, might be able to examine these trade-offs in greater detail to determine at what point the pursuit of status costs more than it is worth.

This relates to another broad question: What exactly *is* status worth? There is a large body of evidence on the individual level that suggests some of the benefits of status—strategic, material, and psychological. On the state level, however, I have relied on the generally agreed-on fact that leaders care a great deal about status. But this account leaves out any empirical investigation of what benefits states that seek higher status expect as a result of their increased rank. How do states profit through prestige? One possibility is in the uncountable number of diplomatic interactions with other states, which will exhibit greater deference to the higher-ranked state. Another possibility (though they are not mutually exclusive) is that states seek higher rank in expectation of the rare occasions when institutions and "rules of the game" are established that will structure interactions in the future (such as securing membership in the UN Security Council or regional IGOs).

Status Concerns Are What Count, Not Status Itself

My theory of status dissatisfaction changed the focus from much of the theoretical work that came before, leading to the third broad lesson that emerges from this project: it is not status itself that matters but rather status *concerns*, which exhibit systematic variation that can be captured by our theories. My theory suggested a simple hypothesis: that heightened concern for status would lead to a greater focus on status issues and actors placing a higher value on their prestige. Both experiments, summarized in chapter 3, bear this out: experimentally manipulated status concerns do in fact lead to a higher valuation of status. In other words, focusing more on status leads to a greater willingness to shift resources from other valued commodities in the pursuit of higher status.

The cases examined in chapters 6 and 7 also bear out this dynamic. In no case do we find that status itself—that is, the pure rank component of status—seemed to matter. So yes, we might say that status "mattered," but only insofar as status *concerns* varied over time and place. In the German case, the cause of that heightened concern was transparent: a strong belief—formalized in its public and private justifications for its world policy—that Germany had been denied the status it deserved by other great powers. This provides some corroboration for my operationalization of status dissatisfaction in the large-N chapters as status *deficits* (the disjunction between status accorded and a state's status expectations).

This begs the question, where do those deficits come from? In Germany's case, there is a palpable sense that its leaders saw at least part of the disjuncture as resulting from the country's relatively late unification as a modern state. Indeed, the analyses in chapter 4 suggest that the leaders might have been right because state age does predict greater status. But deficits might also arise from differential rates of growth, as predicted by power transition theorists. If beliefs about status position are slow to update—and everything we know about perceptions suggest that this is likely accurate—then states may improve their "fundamentals" considerably before they are accorded the greater status that they deserve. Another way deficits might arise is from a shift in the behaviors or attributes associated with status. Countries that gained status through a pathway that is no longer associated with increased prestige—such as colonial possessions or a particular ideology—might find that as the sources of status shift, they are no longer accorded the standing to which they had become accustomed.

More broadly, the cases examined in chapter 7 show that status dissatisfaction does not always result from the same dynamics exhibited in the Germany case. In that instance, the heightened status concern could be traced directly to the belief that there was a disjuncture between expectations and reality. This lines up well with the methodology used in the quantitative chapters to operationalize status dissatisfaction. Other countries exhibit different patterns in the qualitative record, however. For example, Nasser's status concerns seem to have resulted not from a disjuncture between his expectations and the status that Egypt was accorded but instead from the shock of humiliation that was caused by the Syrian secession from the UAR. This led to a fierce desire to *preserve* Egypt's standing rather than improve it.

In the British case, Prime Minister Eden and his advisers seemed well aware that their country's standing had declined, and given their personal beliefs about England's importance, we might say that there was in fact a status deficit. Yet the more salient aspect of their status concerns seemed to be a desire to arrest any further decline as opposed to a focus on any disjuncture between expectations and their actual rank. In that case as well, there was a precipitating blow that brought the slow decline of Britain into focus: the dismissal of General Glubb in Jordan along with the nationalization of the Suez Canal by Nasser. Taken together, the events in the British and Egyptian case suggest a role for humiliation in precipitating heightened status concerns.

A final open question relates to additional variation in status concerns. I proposed that individuals higher in SDO would be more sensitive to status concerns than their low-SDO counterparts. But that is unlikely to be the full story. There is likely to be variation by gender as well, for example. The nature of the samples in the experiments did not allow for the analysis of gender, suggesting an obvious route for future research given the likely connection between gender and susceptibility to status concerns.[4] Other candidates include cultures—a hypothesis that dovetails with the famous

---

[4] Rudman et al. 2011.

notion of "cultures of honor" from social psychology.[5] Moreover, status concerns might be generated by idiosyncratic processes that are not as predictable as social scientists are apt to hope; some individuals may indeed be "obsessed" with status even in the absence of any particular cause.

Status Dissatisfaction Leads to Escalation and Conflict, but What Else?

A final lesson concerns the link between dissatisfaction over relative status and international conflict. In the large-N segments of the book, I documented this pattern exhaustively, and found robust evidence that linked heightened status dissatisfaction (operationalized as status deficits) to the initiation of international conflict. Larger status deficits led to a higher probability of initiating conflict at every level of intensity, from low-level disputes to large-scale international wars. These effects were also substantively large; for example, the effect of a moderate shift in status deficits dwarfed the impact of other standard covariates such as whether or not there was already an ongoing dispute, or whether both countries were democratic. This pattern was not simply a remnant of the nineteenth century, and in fact the relationship between status deficits and war appears to be growing stronger, not weaker, with time. This dovetails with another analysis (in chapter 5) that showed that international norms against the initiation of conflict do not seem to affect this trend: states located in pacific status communities were just as likely to evince the association between status deficits and conflict as those in more violent ones.

The experimental and qualitative chapters combine to suggest at least one microlevel mechanism that might help to explain this broad link between status deficits and conflict. In the two experiments described in those chapters, heightened status concerns led subjects to place a larger value on status and escalate more than those in other experimental conditions. While it would be premature to infer bias from this—we don't know the value of status nor can we fully rule out in the lab experiment that subjects might have seen winning the game as a route to salvaging their status—it does seem as though there is a link between status threats and escalation. Subjects in those experiments, even experienced leaders, seemed more inclined to throw good money after bad following the triggering of status concerns. In the cases, the same pattern appeared, leading, for

[5] Nisbett and Cohen 1996.

example, Nasser to not only intervene in the Yemen Civil War but also to escalate Egyptian involvement until it became what he later referred to as his "Vietnam."

Nevertheless, thinking about "mechanisms," especially those at the individual level, suggests that the findings related to escalation are only a beginning. "Escalation" might be convincing as one potential mechanism that links status concerns to conflict, but what mechanism links status concerns to escalation? Put differently, experimental methods, and randomly assigned status concerns give us confidence in our ability to identify a causal effect (*status threat → escalation*), but don't necessarily tell us anything about mechanisms (*status threat → ? → escalation*). I argued that this was through subjects' increased value for status, but the research was not designed to test whether this was the specific mechanism through which status threats affected escalation.

Other factors, such as emotions, are also plausible. For example, high power might buffer subjects through high-power subjects' ability to regulate emotional reactions. Finally, additional research in case studies or large-*N* data that takes into account factors commonly labeled "real-world conditions"—for instance, higher stakes, organizational incentives, and group dynamics—will help to provide convergent validity for the results described here (though perfectly compatible with experimental methods generally, my experiments did not examine all these factors). This future work will help to fill in critical details, and deepen our understanding of how status and power operate in political decision making.

Another open question relates to the other actions that states might take in response to status deficits. The theoretical requirements are clear: if we assume that states are acting strategically, then any actions taken in response to status deficits must carry the opportunity to improve their international standing. Thus, we can turn back to the initial analysis of the "sources of status" to suggest some routes that states might take in response to status deficits. One of these is the acquisition of nuclear weapons. Anecdotally, this is supported by a number of countries, including India's "peaceful nuclear explosion" of 1974 as well as Iran's recent push to acquire nuclear weapons—a policy that has consistently been linked to a desire for prestige. Other strategies suggested might include those I categorized under the banner of "good citizenship" and include engagement with international organizations. Certainly there appear to be a long list of capabilities and behaviors that states might use to respond to status dissatisfaction and improve their rank within their status community.

IMPLICATIONS FOR IR

The contributions I've discussed are useful on their own, but add even more value in the context of ongoing research programs in IR. Chapter 5 demonstrated that a disjunction between status and material capabilities was a significant predictor of conflict initiation. Put simply, "undervalued" states were more likely to initiate conflict than otherwise-similar but satisfied states. In fact, this prediction follows naturally from the power transition literature, which suggests that war results from a combination of *opportunity* (power transition) and *motive* (dissatisfaction with the status quo). Operationalizing the former is a relatively simple matter, and is easily accomplished by measuring the shifting balance of material capabilities. Thus far, however, there has been much less success in identifying which states are dissatisfied. Most methods developed so far are either post hoc, such as using war initiation to identify dissatisfaction, or several steps removed from actual dissatisfaction (for example, "tau-b," which measures the similarity of alliance portfolios). The measure of status deficits introduced in this book is a far more direct measure of dissatisfaction. And while dissatisfaction *over status* is not the only potential cause of dissatisfaction, it is the one that follows most naturally from power transition theory itself.

More broadly, this book helps provide a foundation for future work on nonmaterial factors in IR. For most of the life span of modern political science, scholars have either lumped these concepts into a residual category to explain otherwise-puzzling results, or used concepts like honor, status, and reputation interchangeably (this tendency is still quite common). Unsurprisingly, neither of those tendencies has aided our understanding a great deal.

Yet a sea change appears to be under way, as a great deal of new work has aimed to disaggregate these concepts as well as provide solid empirical and theoretical foundations for understanding how these concepts affect international politics.[6] This book sets a research agenda for scholarship on status by providing a clear conceptual framework for understanding one way that status concerns may affect international conflict, and evidence from a variety of different sources on the close links between dissatisfaction over status and the initiation of international conflict.

---

[6] See, for example, Mercer 1996; Dafoe and Caughey 2016; Weisiger and Yarhi-Milo 2011; Kertzer 2016.

This work also provides an example of incorporating a factor (status) typically regarded as the exclusive province of political psychologists into a theory compatible with both rationalist and constructivist accounts of international politics. This is a critical step for all "sides" of the field. For those inclined toward rationalist accounts, I have provided evidence that ideational factors can be made to be compatible with those theories. This should help to enrich their theories of politics by incorporating important motives for human behavior, while aiding scholars of status, reputation, and honor by forcing them to clearly specify the trade-offs and boundary conditions of their theories in the process of formalization.

For realists, my book represents a return rather than a departure from orthodoxy. From Thucydides to Morgenthau and Gilpin, status seeking has been widely regarded as a critical motivator of conflict. This work merely returns the focus to a factor already considered important, but severely undertheorized and studied by realists. And finally, for those on the political psychology / constructivism side of the spectrum, this book helps to correct a noted tendency to assume that status seeking is inconsistent with other theories of international politics. Whether that tendency is the result of true beliefs or an understandable desire to carve out a unique niche within political science, it has the pernicious effect of siloing research on psychological factors to a single subfield of political science. Status seeking may sometimes be irrational, but demonstrating this with observational (and even experimental) data is a daunting task, and distracts us from the larger gains to be made by incorporating these nonmaterial factors into broader theories of politics.

POLICY IMPLICATIONS

Many of the most important and influential bodies of research—including the "causes of war" literature that resulted from the aftermath of the two world wars—in IR have flowed directly from the geopolitical problems and tragedies of the times. This suggests the importance of thinking through how our theories of international politics feed back into the political realm.

The first implication for politics concerns how we interpret and react to leaders' demands for status. This is a perennial dilemma of world politics, and while at the time of this writing the countries that come to mind are Iran, China, and Russia, earlier eras have witnessed similar demands from other states. If one lesson of this book is that the initiation of conflict is in some cases motivated by a desire to gain status, this suggests that conflict may be avoided through status concessions before the escalation to violent conflict occurs. This is exactly what France and Britain did in the first decade of the nineteenth century with respect to Germany (though they surely did so grudgingly).

A related point suggests the effectiveness of channeling the desire for greater status toward nonviolent actions. Conflict does bring status benefits to initiators, but other analyses in the book suggested the utility of nonviolent, even prosocial behavior in gaining status rank. Membership in IGOs, for example, seems to be a successful strategy. It's likely that other actions for which we do not have systematic data—such as humanitarian assistance, technological or scientific achievement, and so on—might accomplish the same ends. One can even see some evidence of states pursuing this broader strategy of channeling status demands into constructive or beneficial actions; witness, for instance, US leaders' calls for China to "act like" a member of the "G2." These statements offer the status that US leaders perceive China to desire, but in a manner that does not require militaristic actions, and also constrains Chinese actions through imposition of the norms and responsibilities associated with superpower status.

A second point concerns the importance of norms and beliefs in world politics. I found some evidence that the influence of norms and beliefs was, at the least, constrained: the status benefits of conflict are not confined to only "violent communities" of rogue states, suggesting that norms against violence are not as strong as is sometimes supposed. In another sense, however, there is a powerful role for norms in how status is accorded. The fact that status is socially constructed suggests that if beliefs about what constitutes a valued attribute changes, so too will state behavior. If we argue that one reason states pursued colonial territories had to do with beliefs about beliefs—"you need colonies to be a world power"—then it is obvious that as those beliefs shifted, so too did the actions and policies of most states throughout the world. A more recent example is nuclear weapons. I found strong evidence that nuclear weapons programs were— from 1961 to 2001—associated with higher status. Yet the "global zero" antinuclear proliferation movement may yet be successful in shifting beliefs about whether such capabilities are valued or the subject of opprobrium. If it does, we should expect a corresponding shift in state actions.

A final policy implication concerns the importance of reference groups. Throughout the book, one can see evidence of leaders who have succeeded to varying degrees in understanding their rivals' status concerns and reference groups. French and British leaders, for example, were largely accurate in their inferences about which group Germany cared most about and saw itself as being part of. Similarly, German leaders during the July Crisis also revealed a talent for understanding the status concerns of Russia, and which "clubs" they were most sensitive to membership in. In that latter case, though, the knowledge gleaned concerning Russia's status communities was used to ensure that Russia would not back down since Germany had framed the trade-off in such a way that Russia could either escalate the July Crisis or else lose its seat among the great powers. A large part of many current policy problems concerns exactly these inferences. It is, for example, critical to any policy seeking to accommodate or contain Russian ambitions to understand where the balance of its status concerns lie: in rejoining the ranks of great powers or establishing an unambiguous regional hierarchy with itself at the head of the table.

References

Abeler, J., A. Falk, L. Götte, and D. Huffman. 2011. Reference points and effort provision. *American Economic Review* 101 (2): 470–92.

Abizadeh, A. 2011. Hobbes on the causes of war: A disagreement theory. *American Political Science Review* 105 (2): 298–315.

Achen, C. H. 2000. Why lagged dependent variables can suppress the explanatory power of other independent variables. Working paper.

———. 2002. Toward a new political methodology. *Annual Review of Political Science* 5: 423–50.

Achen, C. H. and D. Snidal. 1989. Rational deterrence theory and comparative case studies. *World Politics* 41 (2): 143–69.

Adler, N., E. Epel, G. Castellazzo, and J. Ickovics. 2000. Relationship of subjective and objective social status with psychological and physiological functioning: Preliminary data in healthy, White women. *Health Psychology* 19 (6): 586–92.

Ahmed, S. 1999. Pakistan's nuclear weapons program: Turning points and nuclear choices. *International Security* 23 (4): 178–204.

Akinola, M., and W. B. Mendes. 2014. It's good to be the king: Neurobiological benefits of higher social standing. *Social Psychological and Personality Science* 5 (1): 43–51.

Alatas, V., L. Cameron, A. Chaudhuri, N. Erkal, and L. Gangadharan. 2009. Subject pool effects in a corruption experiment. *Experimental Economics* 12 (1): 113–32.

Altemeyer, B. 1998. The "other" authoritarian personality. *Advances in Experimental Social Psychology* 30: 47–92.

———. 2003. What happens when authoritarians inherit the earth? A simulation. *Analyses of Social Issues and Public Policy* 3 (1): 161–69.

Anderson, C. A. 1983. Abstract and concrete data in the perseverance of social theories: When weak data lead to unshakeable beliefs. *Journal of Experimental Social Psychology* 19 (2): 93–108.

Anderson, C. A., D. Ames, and S. Gosling. 2008. Punishing hubris: The perils of overestimating one's status in a group. *Personality and Social Psychology Bulletin* 34 (1): 90–101.

Anderson, C. A, and B. J. Bushman. 1997. External validity of trivial experiments. *Review of General Psychology* 1 (1): 19–41.

Anderson, C. A., and A. Galinsky. 2006. Power, optimism, and risk-taking. *European Journal of Social Psychology* 36 (4): 511–36.

Anderson, C. A., O. John, and D. Keltner. 2012. The personal sense of power. *Journal of Personality* 80 (2): 313–44.

Anderson, C. A., M. Lepper, and L. Ross. 1980. Perseverance of social theories: The role of explanation in the persistence of discredited information. *Journal of Personality and Social Psychology* 39 (6): 1037–49.

Anderson, C. A., S. Srivastava, J. S. Beer, S. E. Spataro, and J. A. Chatman. 2006. Knowing your place: self-perceptions of status in face-to-face groups. *Journal of Personality and Social Psychology* 91 (6): 1094–110.

Anderson, M. S. 2014. *The Rise of Modern Diplomacy 1450–1919*. London: Routledge.

Anderson, W. D., and C. H. Summers. 2007. Neuroendocrine mechanisms, stress coping strategies, and social dominance: Comparative lessons about leadership potential. *Annals of the American Academy of Political and Social Science* 614 (1): 102–30.

Andrew, C. 1966. German world policy and the reshaping of the dual Alliance. *Journal of Contemporary History* 1 (3): 137–51.

Ansolabehere, S. D., S. Iyengar, and A. Simon. 1999. Replicating experiments using aggregate and survey data. *American Political Science Review* 93 (4): 901–9.

Ariely, D., U. Gneezy, G. Loewenstein, and N. Mazar. 2009. Large stakes and big mistakes. *Review of Economic Studies* 76 (2): 451–69.

Arkes, H. R., and P. Ayton. 1999. The sunk cost and Concorde effects. *Psychological Bulletin*, 125: 591–600.

Arkes, H. R., and C. Blumer. 1985. The psychology of sunk costs. *Organizational Behavior and Human Decision Processes* 35 (1): 124–40.

Arreguin-Toft, I. 2001. How the weak win wars. *International Security* 26 (1): 93–128.

Baker, R. W. 1978. *Egypt's Uncertain Revolution under Nasser and Sadat*. Cambridge, MA: Harvard University Press.

Baldwin, D. A. 1979. Power analysis and world politics. *World Politics* 31 (2): 161–94.

Ball, S. B., and C. C. Eckel. 1996. Buying status: Experimental evidence on status in negotiation. *Psychology and Marketing* 13 (4): 379–403.

Ball, S. B., and C. C. Eckel. 1998. The economic value of status. *Journal of Socio-Economics* 27 (4): 495–514.

Ball, S. B., C. C. Eckel, P. Grossman, and W. Zame. 2001. Status in markets. *Quarterly Journal of Economics* 116 (1): 161–88.

Barabas, J., and J. Jerit. 2010. Are survey experiments externally valid? *American Political Science Review* 104 (2): 226–42.

Barberis, N., A. Shleifer, and R. Vishny. 1998. A model of investor sentiment. *Journal of Financial Economics* 49 (3): 307–43.

Barkow, J. 1989. *Darwin, Sex, and Status: Biological Approaches to Mind and Culture*. Toronto: University of Toronto Press.

Barnett, M. N., and R. Duvall. 2005. Power in international politics. *International Organization* 59 (1): 39–75.

Barnett, M. N., and J. S. Levy. 1991. Domestic sources of alliances and alignments: The case of Egypt, 1962–73. *International Organization* 45 (3): 369–95.

Barraclough, G. 1982. *From Agadir to Armageddon: Anatomy of a Crisis*. London: Weidenfeld and Nicolson.

Barston, R. P. 2014. *Modern Diplomacy*. New York: Routledge.

Bates, R., A. Greif, M. Levi, J. Rosenthal, and B. Weingast. 1998. *Analytic Narratives*. Princeton, NJ: Princeton University Press.

———. 2000. Analytic narratives revisited. *Social Science History* 24 (4): 685–96.

Bayer, R. 2006. Diplomatic exchange data set, v. 2006.1. Available at the Correlates of War Project Website.

Bazerman, M., T. Giuliano, and A. Appelman. 1984. Escalation of commitment in individual and group decision making. *Organizational Behavior and Human Decision Processes* 33 (2): 141–52.

Beck, N. 2010. Time is not a theoretical variable. *Political Analysis* 18 (3): 293–94.

Beck, N., and J. N. Katz. 1996. Nuisance vs. substance: Specifying and estimating time-series-cross-section models. *Political Analysis* 6 (1): 1–36.

———. 2011. Modeling dynamics in time-series-cross-section political economy data. *Annual Review of Political Science* 14: 331–52.

Beck, N., J.N. Katz, and R. Tucker. 1998. Taking time seriously: Time-series-cross-section analysis with a binary dependent variable. *American Journal of Political Science* 42 (4): 1260–88.

Bennett, A. 2010. Process tracing and causal inference. In *Rethinking Social Inquiry: Diverse Tools, Shared Standards*, edited by H. E. Brady and D. Collier, 207–19. Lanham, MD: Rowman and Littlefield.

Bennett, A., and J. T. Checkel. 2014. Process tracing: From philosophical roots to best practices. In *Process Tracing: From Metaphor to Analytic Tool*, edited by A. Bennett. and J. T. Checkel, 3–38. Cambridge: Cambridge University Press.

Bennett, A., and C. Elman. 2006. Qualitative research: Recent developments in case study methods. *Annual Review of Political Science* 9: 455–76.

Bennett, D. S., and A. C. Stam. 2000. Eugene: A conceptual manual. *International Interactions* 26 (2): 179–204.

———. 2007. Eugene documentation. Available at EUGene Web site.

Berejikian, J. D. 2002. Model building with prospect theory. *Political Psychology* 23 (4): 759–86.

Berinsky, A. J., M. F. Margolis, and M. W. Sances. 2013. Separating the shirkers from the workers? Making sure respondents pay attention on self-administered surveys. *American Journal of Political Science* 58 (3): 739–53.

Bestuzhev, I. 1966. Russian foreign policy, February–June 1914. *Journal of Contemporary History* 1 (3): 93–112.

Birnbaum, M. 2014. There was a rare moment of dissent at Moscow's Soviet-style May Day celebrations. *Washington Post*, May 1.

Blackwell, S. 2004. Pursuing Nasser: The Macmillan government and the management of British policy Towards the Middle East Cold War, 1957–63. *Cold War History* 4 (3): 85–104.

Blondel, V. D., J.-L. Guillaume, R. Lambiotte, and E. Lefebvre. 2008. Fast unfolding of communities in large networks. *Journal of Statistical Mechanics* 2008 (10): 10008.

Boettcher, W., and M. Cobb. 2009. Don't let them die in vain. *Journal of Conflict Resolution* 53 (5): 677–97.

Bolt, J., and J. L. Zanden. 2014. The Maddison project: Collaborative research on historical national accounts. *Economic History Review* 67 (3): 627–51.

Bowen, M. G. 1987. The escalation phenomenon reconsidered. *Academy of Management Review* 12 (1): 52–66.

Brooks, S. G, and W. C. Wohlforth. 2006. Power, globalization, and the end of the Cold War. In *World War I and the End of the Cold War*, edited by G. Goertz, and J. S. Levy, 163–99. Cambridge, MA: MIT Press.

Buzan, B. 1995. The level of analysis problem in international relations reconsidered. In *International Relations Theory Today*, edited by K. Booth and S. Smith, 198–216. University Park: Penn State University Press.

Camerer, C. F. 2004. Prospect theory in the wild. In *Advances in Behavioral Economics*, edited by C. F. Camerer, G. Loewenstein, and M. Rabin, 148–61. Princeton, NJ: Princeton University Press.

Camerer, C. F., and R. Hogarth. 1999. The effects of financial incentives in experiments. *Journal of Risk and Uncertainty* 19 (1): 7–42.

Campbell, D. T., and J. C Stanley. 1963. *Experimental and Quasi-Experimental Designs for Research*. Boston: Houghton Mifflin.

Carlton, D. 1989. *Britain and the Suez Crisis*. New York: Blackwell.

Carnevale, J. J., Y. Inbar, and J. S. Lerner. 2011. Individual differences in need for cognition and decision-making competence among leaders. *Personality and Individual Differences* 51 (3): 274–78.

Carr, E. 1937. *Great Britain as a Mediterranean Power (Cust Foundation Lecture)*. Nottingham: University of Nottingham.

Carretta, T., and R.L. Moreland. 1982. Nixon and Watergate: A field demonstration of belief perseverance. *Personality and Social Psychology Bulletin* 8 (3): 446–53.

Carter, D., and C. Signorino. 2010. Modeling time dependence in binary data. *Political Analysis* 18 (3): 271–92.

Cheng, J. T., J. L. Tracy, T. Foulsham, A. Kingstone, and J. Henrich. 2013. Two ways to the top: Evidence that dominance and prestige are distinct yet viable avenues to social rank and influence. *Journal of Personality and Social Psychology* 104 (1): 103–25.

Chestnut, S., and A. Johnston. 2009. Is China Rising? In *Is China Changing the Rules of the Game?*, edited by E. Paus, P. Prime, and J. Western, 237–60. New York: Palgrave Macmillan.

Chiozza, G., and H. E. Goemans. 2011. *Leaders and international conflict*. New York: Cambridge University Press.

Christopherson, J. A. 1976. Structural analysis of transaction systems vertical fusion or network complexity? *Journal of Conflict Resolution* 20 (4): 637–62.

Clark, C. 2012. *The Sleepwalkers: How Europe Went to War in 1914*. New York: Harper Perennial.

Clark, T. S., and D. A. Linzer. 2015. Should I use fixed or random effects? *Political Science Research and Methods* 3 (2): 399–408.

Clarke, K. A. 2005. Omitted variable bias in econometric research. *Conflict Management and Peace Science* 22 (4): 341–52.

Clauset, A., M. E. Newman, and C. Moore. 2004. Finding community structure in very large networks. *Physical Review E* 70 (6): 066111.

Cline, K., P. Rhamey, A. Henshaw, A. Sedziaka, A. Tandon, and T. J. Volgy. 2011. Identifying regional powers and their status. In *Major Powers and the Quest for Status in International Politics: Global and Regional Perspectives*, edited by T. J. Volgy, R. Corbetta, K.A. Grant, and R.G. Baird, 133–58. Basingstoke, UK: Palgrave Macmillan.

Clunan, A. 2014. Why status matters in world politics. In *Status in World Politics*, edited by T. Paul, D. W. Larson, and W. C. Wohlforth, 365–406. New York: Cambridge University Press.

Colgan, J. D. 2013. Domestic revolutionary leaders and international conflict. *World Politics* 65 (4): 656–90.

Collier, D., 2011. Understanding process tracing. *PS: Political Science and Politics* 44 (4): 823–30.

Collier, D., and J. Mahoney. 1996. Insights and pitfalls: Selection bias in qualitative research. *World Politics* 49 (1): 56–91.

Congleton, R. D. 1989. Efficient Status Seeking: Externalities and the evolution of status games. *Journal of Economic Behavior and Organization* 11 (2): 175–90.

Copeland, D. 2001. *The Origins of Major War*. Ithaca, NY: Cornell University Press.

Corbetta, R., T. J. Volgy, and J. P. Rhamey. 2013. Major power status (in) consistency and political relevance in international relations studies. *Peace Economics, Peace Science, and Public Policy* 19 (3): 291–307.

Craig, G. 1978. *Germany, 1866–1945*. New York: Oxford University Press.

Crampton, R. 1980. *The Hollow Detente: Anglo-German Relations in the Balkans, 1911–1914*. Atlantic Highlands, NJ: Humanities Press.

Csardi, G., and T. Nepusz. 2006. The Igraph software package for complex network research. *InterJournal, Complex Systems* 1695 (5): 1–9.

Dafoe, A. 2015. Prescriptions for temporal dependence: First do no harm. Working paper.

Dafoe, A., and D. Caughey. 2016. Honor and war: Southern U.S. presidents and the effects of concern for reputation. *World Politics* 68 (2): 341–81.

Dafoe, A., J. Renshon, and P. Huth. 2014. Reputation and Status as Motives for War. *Annual Review of Political Science* 17: 371–93.

Davies, J. C. 1962. Toward a theory of revolution. *American Sociological Review* 27 (1): 5–19.

Dawisha, A. I. 1975. Intervention in the Yemen: An analysis of Egyptian perceptions and policies. *Middle East Journal* 29 (1): 47–63.

———. 1977. Perceptions, decisions and consequences in foreign policy: The Egyptian Intervention in the Yemen. *Political Studies* 25 (2): 201–26.

Deaves, R., E. Luders, and M. Schroder. 2010. The dynamics of overconfidence: Evidence from stock market forecasters. *Journal of Economic Behavior and Organization* 75 (3): 402–12.

Deng, Y. 2008. *China's Struggle for Status: The Realignment of International Relations*. New York: Cambridge University Press.

Deutsch, K., and R. Merritt. 1965. Effects of events on national and international images. In *International Behavior: A Social-Psychological Analysis*, edited by H. Kelman, 132–87. New York: Holt, Rinehart and Winston.

DiCicco, J. M., and J. S. Levy. 1999. The evolution of the power transition research program. *Journal of Conflict Resolution* 43 (6): 675–704.

Doran, C. F, K. Q. Hill, and K. Mladenka. 1979. Threat, status disequilibrium, and national power. *British Journal of International Studies* 5 (1): 37–58.

Dore, R. P. 1975. The prestige factor in international affairs. *International Affairs* 51 (2): 190–207.

Druckman, J. N., and C. D Kam. 2011. Students as Experimental Participants. In *Handbook of Experimental Political Science*, edited by J. Druckman, D. P Green, J. H Kuklinski, and A. Lupia, 41–57. New York: Cambridge University Press.

East, M. A. 1972. Status discrepancy and violence in the international System. In *The Analysis of International Politics*, edited by J. Rosenau, V. Davis, and M. A. East, 299–319. New York: Free Press.

Eden, A. 1960. *Full Circle: The Memoirs of Anthony Eden*. Boston: Houghton Mifflin.

Efird, B., J. Kugler, and G. Genna. 2003. From war to integration: Generalizing the dynamic of power transitions. *International Interactions* 29 (4): 293–314.

Elkins, Z., and B. Simmons. 2004. The globalization of liberalization. *American Political Science Review* 98 (1): 171–90.

Ellemers, N., R. Spears, and B. Doosje. 2002. Self and Social Identity. *Annual Review of Psychology* 53 (1): 161–86.

Enough, B., and T. Mussweiler. 2006. Anchoring effects in the courtroom. *Journal of Applied Social Psychology* 31 (7): 1535–51.

Epkenhans, M. 2007. Was a peaceful outcome thinkable? The naval race before 1914. In *An Improbable War? The Outbreak of World War I and European Political Culture before 1914*, edited by H. Afflerbach and D. Stevenson, 130–48. Oxford: Berghahn Books.

Eyre, D. P., and M. C. Suchman. 1996. Status, norms, and the proliferation of conventional weapons. In *The Culture of National Security*, edited by P. Katzenstein, 79–113. New York: Columbia University Press.

Fain, W. T. 2001. "Unfortunate Arabia": The United States, Great Britain, and Yemen, 1955–63. *Diplomacy and Statecraft* 12 (2): 125–52.

Falk, A., and M. Knell. 2004. Choosing the Joneses: Endogenous goals and reference standards. *Scandinavian Journal of Economics* 106 (3): 417–35.

Fast, N., D. Gruenfeld, N. Sivanathan, and A. Galinsky. 2009. Illusory Control. *Psychological Science* 20 (4): 502–8.

Fast, N., N. Halevy, and A. Galinsky. 2011. The destructive nature of power without status. *Journal of Experimental Social Psychology* 48 (1): 391–94.

Fast, N., N. Sivanathan, N. Mayer, and A. Galinsky. 2011. Power and overconfident decision-making. *Organizational Behavior and Human Decision Processes* 117 (2): 249–60.

Fatas, E., T. Neugebauer, and P. Tamborero. 2007. How politicians make decisions: A political choice experiment. *Journal of Economics* 92 (2): 167–96.

Fearon, J. 1997. Signaling foreign policy interests: Tying hands versus sinking costs. *Journal of Conflict Resolution* 41 (1): 68–90.

Fehr, E., and J. List. 2004. The hidden costs and returns of incentives. *Journal of the European Economic Association* 2 (5): 743–71.

Ferguson, C. D. 2010. The long road to zero: Overcoming the obstacles to a nuclear-free world. *Foreign Affairs* 89 (1): 86–94.

Ferguson, N. 1992. Germany and the origins of the First World War: New perspectives. *Historical Journal* 35 (3): 725–52.

Ferris, J. 2008. Soviet support for Egypt's intervention in Yemen, 1962–1963. *Journal of Cold War Studies* 10 (4): 5–36.

———. 2013. *Nasser's Gamble: How Intervention in Yemen Caused the Six-Day War and the Decline of Egyptian Power.* Princeton, NJ: Princeton University Press.

Finkel, S. E., A. Pérez-Liñán, and M. A. Seligson. 2007. The effects of US foreign assistance on democracy building, 1990–2003. *World Politics* 59 (3): 404–39.

Firth, D. 1993. Bias reduction of maximum likelihood estimates. *Biometrika* 80 (1): 27–38.

Fischer, F. 1975a. *War of Illusions: German Policies from 1911 to 1914.* New York: W.W Norton and Company.

———. 1975b. *World Power or Decline: The Controversy over Germany's Aims in the First World War.* London: Weidenfeld and Nicolson.

Florini, A. 1996. The evolution of international norms. *International Studies Quarterly* 40 (3): 363–89.

Flynn, G., and H. Farrell. 1999. Piecing together the democratic peace: The CSCE, norms, and the "construction" of security in Post–Cold War Europe. *International Organization* 53 (3): 505–35.

Fordham, B. O. 2011. Who wants to be a major power? Explaining the expansion of foreign policy ambition. *Journal of Peace Research* 48 (5): 587–603.

Fordham, B. O., and V. Asal. 2007. Billiard balls or snowflakes? Major power prestige and the international diffusion of institutions and practices. *International Studies Quarterly* 51 (1): 31–52.

Foreign Relations of the United States. 1953. Memorandum by the deputy assistant secretary of state for Near Eastern, South Asian, and African affairs (Jernegan) to the Under Secretary of state for administration (Lourie). http://history.state.gov/historicaldocuments/frus1952-54v11p1/d137.

Forsberg, T., R. Heller, and R. Wolf. 2014. Status and emotions in Russian foreign policy. *Communist and Post-Communist Studies* 47 (3): 261–68.

Frank, R. H. 1985. *Choosing the Right Pond.* New York: Oxford University Press.

Frederick, S. 2005. Cognitive reflection and decision making. *Journal of Economic Perspectives* 19 (4): 25–42.

Freedman, D. A. 2008. On regression adjustments to experimental data. *Advances in Applied Mathematics* 40 (2): 180–93.

French, A. M. M. 2010. *United States Protocol: The Guide to Official Diplomatic Etiquette.* Lanham, MD: Rowman and Littlefield Publishers.

Friedman, J. A. 2014. How cumulative dynamics affect military decision making. Working paper.

Friedman, M. 1957. *A Theory of the Consumption Function.* Princeton, NJ: Princeton University Press.

Gaddis, J. L. 1986. The long peace: Elements of stability in the postwar international system. *International Security* 10 (4): 99–142.

Galinsky, A., J. Magee, D. Gruenfeld, J. Whitson, and K. Liljenquist. 2008. Power reduces the press of the situation. *Journal of Personality and Social Psychology* 95 (6): 1450–66.

Galtung, J. 1964. A structural theory of aggression. *Journal of Peace Research* 1 (2): 95–119.

Gartner, S. S. 1999. *Strategic Assessment in War.* New Haven, CT: Yale University Press.

Gartzke, E., and D. Jo. 2009. Bargaining, nuclear proliferation, and interstate disputes. *Journal of Conflict Resolution* 53 (2): 209–33.

Geddes, B. 1990. How the cases you choose affect the answers you get: Selection bias in comparative politics. *Political Analysis* 2 (1): 131–50.

Geiss, I. 1966. The outbreak of the First World War and German war aims. *Journal of Contemporary History* 1 (3): 75–91.

———. 1967. *July 1914: The Outbreak of the First World War; Selected Documents.* New York: W. W. Norton and Company.

———. 1976. *German Foreign Policy, 1871–1914.* London: Routledge.

Geller, D. 1993. Power differentials and war in rival dyads. *International Studies Quarterly* 37 (2): 173–93.

———. 2000. Status quo orientation, capabilities, and patterns of war initiation in dyadic rivalries. *Conflict Management and Peace Science* 18 (1): 73–96.

Gelman, A., and H. Stern. 2006. The difference between "significant" and "not significant" is not itself statistically significant. *American Statistician* 60 (4): 328–31.

George, A., and A. Bennett. 2005. *Case Studies and Theory Development in the Social Sciences.* Cambridge, MA: MIT Press.

Gerber, G. 1996. Status in same-gender and mixed-gender police dyads: Effects on personality attributions. *Social Psychology Quarterly* 59 (4): 350–63.

Gerges, F. A. 1995. The Kennedy Administration and the Egyptian–Saudi Conflict in Yemen: Co-opting Arab nationalism. *Middle East Journal* 49 (2): 292–311.

Gerring, J. 2004. What is a case study and what is it good for? *American Political Science Review* 98 (2): 341–54.

———. 2007. Is there a (viable) crucial-case method? *Comparative Political Studies* 40 (3): 231–53.

Gilady, L. 2002. Naval Procurement, aircraft carriers, and veblen effects. Unpublished manuscript.

———. 2004. Gunboat Diplomacy at the 21st Century: Navies as status symbols. Unpublished manuscript.

Gilpin, R. 1975. Three models of the future. *International Organization* 29 (1): 37–60.

———. 1983. *War and Change in World Politics.* New York: Cambridge University Press.

———. 1988. The theory of hegemonic war. *Journal of Interdisciplinary History* 18 (4): 591–613.

Glaser, C. 1998. The flawed case for nuclear disarmament. *Survival* 40 (1): 112–28.

Glaser, M., T. Langer, and M. Weber. 2005. Overconfidence of professionals and lay men. Unpublished manuscript.

Gochman, C. S. 1980. Status, capabilities, and major power conflict. In *The Correlates of War II: Testing Some Realpolitik Models,* edited by J. D. Singer, 83–123. New York: Free Press.

Goertz, G., and P. F. Diehl. 1992. Toward a theory of international norms: Some conceptual and measurement issues. *Journal of Conflict Resolution* 36 (4): 634–64.

Goldgeier, J., and P. Tetlock. 2001. Psychology and international relations theory. *Annual Review of Political Science* 4: 67–92.

Gordon, M. 1974. Domestic conflict and the origins of the First World War. *Journal of Modern History* 46 (2): 191–226.

Gordon, M., L. Slade, and N. Schmitt. 1986. The "science of the sophomore" revisited. *Academy of Management Review* 11 (1): 191–207.

Gorst, A., and L. Johnman. 1997. *The Suez Crisis*. New York,: Routledge.

Green, D. P. 2009. Regression adjustments to experimental data: Do David Freedman's concerns apply to political science? Working paper.

Greenhill, B. 2008. Recognition and collective identity formation in international politics. *European Journal of International Relations* 14 (2): 343–68.

Gregory, R, S. Lichtenstein, and D. MacGregor. 1993. The role of past states in determining reference points for policy decisions. *Organizational Behavior and Human Decision Processes* 55 (2): 195–206.

Grosenick, L., T. Clement, and R. Fernald. 2007. Fish can infer social rank by observation alone. *Nature* 445 (7126): 429–32.

Gruenfeld, D., M. Inesi, J. Magee, and A. Galinsky. 2008. Power and the objectification of social targets. *Journal of Personality and Social Psychology* 95 (1): 111–27.

Guinote, A., G. Willis, and C. Martellotta. 2010. Social power increases implicit prejudice. *Journal of Experimental Social Psychology* 46 (2): 299–307.

Guisinger, A., and A. Smith. 2002. The interaction of reputation and political institutions in international crises. *Journal of Conflict Resolution* 46 (2): 175–200.

Guldescu, S. 1966. Yemen: The war and the Haradh conference. *Review of Politics* 28 (3): 319–31.

Gunia, B. C., N. Sivanathan, and A. D. Galinsky. 2009. Vicarious entrapment. *Journal of Experimental Social Psychology* 45 (6): 1238–44.

Guzzini, S. 2013. The ends of international relations theory: Stages of reflexivity and modes of theorizing. *European Journal of International Relations* 19 (3): 521–41.

Hafner-Burton, E. M., D. A. Hughes, and D. G. Victor. 2013. The cognitive revolution and the political psychology of elite decision making. *Perspectives on Politics* 11 (6): 368–86.

Hafner-Burton, E. M., B. Leveck, D. Victor, and J. Fowler. 2012. A behavioral approach to international legal cooperation. Working paper.

Hafner-Burton, E. M., and A. H. Montgomery. 2006. Power positions international organizations, social networks, and conflict. *Journal of Conflict Resolution* 50 (1): 3–27.

Halabi, S., J. F. Dovidio, and A. Nadler. 2008. When and how do high status group members offer help: Effects of social dominance orientation and status threat. *Political Psychology* 29 (6): 841–58.

Hall, R. B. 1997. Moral authority as a power resource. *International Organization* 51 (4): 591–622.

Hamilton, K., and R. Langhorne. 2011. *The Practice of Diplomacy: Its Evolution, Theory, and Administration.* Abingdon, UK: Taylor and Francis.

Hamilton, R., and H. Herwig. 2004. *Decisions for War, 1914–1917.* New York: Cambridge University Press.

Haner, C., and P. Brown. 1955. Clarification of the instigation to action concept in the frustration-aggression hypothesis. *Journal of Abnormal and Social Psychology* 51 (2): 204–6.

Harsanyi, J. C. 1976. *Essays on Ethics, Social Behavior, and Scientific Explanation*. Dordrecht: D. Reidel Publishing.

Haslam, N., and S. R. Levy. 2006. Essentialist beliefs about homosexuality: Structure and implications for prejudice. *Personality and Social Psychology Bulletin* 32 (4): 471–85.

Hatemi, P. K., and R. McDermott. 2012. Broadening political psychology. *Political Psychology* 33 (1): 11–25.

Heath, C., R. P. Larrick, and G. Wu. 1999. Goals as reference points. *Cognitive Psychology* 38 (1): 79–109.

Hecht, G., and M. Callon. 2009. *The Radiance of France: Nuclear Power and National Identity after World War II*. Cambridge, MA: MIT Press.

Heffetz, O., and R. H. Frank. 2011. Preferences for status: Evidence and economic implications. In *Handbook of Social Economics*, edited by J. Benhabib, M. Jackson, and A. Bisin, vol. 1A, 69–92. Amsterdam: Elsevier.

Henrich, J., and F. Gil-White. 2001. The evolution of prestige: Freely conferred deference as a mechanism for enhancing the benefits of cultural transmission. *Evolution and Human Behavior* 22 (3): 165–96.

Hertwig, R., and O. Ortmann. 2003. Economists' and psychologists' experimental practices. In *The Psychology of Economic Decisions*, edited by I. Brocas and J. Carrillo, 253–72. New York: Oxford University Press.

Herwig, H. 1986. Imperial Germany. In *Knowing One's Enemies*, edited by E. R May, 62–97. Princeton, NJ: Princeton University Press.

———. 1988. The failure of German sea power, 1914–1945: Mahan, Tirpitz, and Raeder reconsidered. *International History Review* 10 (1): 68–105.

———. 1997. *The First World War: Germany and Austria-Hungary, 1914–1918*. London: Arnold.

Herz, J. 1951. *Political Realism and Political Idealism*. Chicago: University of Chicago Press.

———. 1981. Political realism revisited. *International Studies Quarterly* 25 (2): 182–97.

Hewitson, M. 2000. Germany and France before the First World War: A reassessment of Wilhelmine foreign policy. *English Historical Review* 115 (462): 570–606.

———. 2004. *Germany and the Causes of the First World War*. Oxford: Berg Publishers.

Hillgruber, A. 1982. *Germany and the Two World Wars*. Cambridge, MA: Harvard University Press.

Holmes, J. 2015. The long, strange trip of China's first aircraft carrier. *Foreign Policy*, February 3.

Holsti, K. 1964. The concept of power in the study of international relations. *Background* 7 (4): 179–94.

Holt, C., and S. Laury. 2001. Varying the scale of financial incentives under real and hypothetical conditions. *Behavioral and Brain Sciences* 24 (3): 417–18.

Hopcroft, R. 2006. Sex, status, and reproductive success in the contemporary United States. *Evolution and Human Behavior* 27 (2): 104–20.

Horne, A. 1988. *Harold Macmillan, Volume 1: 1894–1956*. New York: Viking Press.

Horowitz, M. C., R. McDermott, and A. C. Stam. 2005. Leader age, regime type, and violent International relations. *Journal of Conflict Resolution* 49 (5): 661–85.

Horowitz, M. C., and A. C. Stam. 2014. How prior military experience influences the future militarized behavior of leaders. *International Organization* 68 (3): 527–59.

Horowitz, M. C, A. C Stam, and C. M. Ellis. 2015. *Why Leaders Fight*. New York: Cambridge University Press.

Howard, M. 1993. A Thirty Years' War? The two world wars in historical perspective: The prothero lecture. *Transactions of the Royal Historical Society* 3: 171–84.

Huberman, B. A., C. H. Loch, and A. Onculer. 2004. Status as a valued resource. *Social Psychology Quarterly* 67 (1): 103–14.

Hudson, V. 2005. Foreign policy analysis: Actor-specific theory and the ground of international relations. *Foreign Policy Analysis* 1 (1): 1–30.

Huguet, P., F. Dumas, J. Monteil, and N. Genestoux. 2001. Social comparison choices in the classroom. *European Journal of Social Psychology* 31 (5): 557–78.

Hymans, J. 2006. *The Psychology of Nuclear Proliferation*. New York: Cambridge University Press.

Inesi, M. 2010. Power and loss aversion. *Organizational Behavior and Human Decision Processes* 112 (1): 58–69.

Jackson, E. 1962. Status consistency and symptoms of stress. *American Sociological Review* 27 (4): 469–80.

Jaggers, K., and T. Gurr. 1995. Tracking democracy's third wave with the Polity III data. *Journal of Peace Research* 32 (4): 469–82.

Jankowski, J. P. 2002. *Nasser's Egypt, Arab Nationalism, and the United Arab Republic*. Boulder, CO: Lynne Rienner Publishers.

Jarausch, K. 1966. The illusion of limited war: Chancellor Bethmann Hollweg's calculated risk, July 1914. *Central European History* 2 (1): 48–76.

Jervis, R. 1976. *Perception and Misperception in International Politics*. Princeton, NJ: Princeton University Press.

——. 1989. *The Logic of Images in International Relations*. New York: Columbia University Press.

——. 1992. Political implications of loss aversion. *Political Psychology* 13 (2): 187–204.

——. 2012. Fighting for standing or standing to fight? *Security Studies* 21 (2): 336–44.

Jervis, R., and J. Snyder. 1991. *Dominoes and Bandwagons: Strategic Beliefs and Great Power Competition in the Eurasian Rimland*. New York: Oxford University Press.

Jo, D., and E. Gartzke. 2007. Determinants of nuclear weapons proliferation. *Journal of Conflict Resolution* 51 (1): 167–94.

Johnson, C. A. 1962. *Revolutionary change*. Palo Alto, CA: Stanford University Press.

Johnson, D. D. 2009. *Overconfidence and War*. Cambridge, MA: Harvard University Press.

Johnson, D. D., R. McDermott, E. Barrett, J. Cowden, R. Wrangham, M. McIntyre, and S. Rosen. 2006. Overconfidence in wargames: Experimental evidence on expectations, aggression, gender, and testosterone. *Proceedings of the Royal Society B: Biological Sciences* 273 (1600): 2513–20.

Johnson, D. D., and D. Tierney. 2006. *Perceptions of Victory and Defeat in International Politics.* Cambridge, MA: Harvard University Press.

Joll, J. 1968. *1914: The Unspoken Assumptions.* London: Weidenfeld and Nicolson.

Joll, J., and G. Martel. 2007. *The Origins of the First World War.* New York: Longman.

Jones, D. M., S. A. Bremer, and J. D. Singer. 1996. Militarized interstate disputes, 1816–1992: Rationale, coding rules, and empirical patterns. *Conflict Management and Peace Science* 15 (2): 163–213.

Jönsson, C. 2006. Diplomacy, bargaining, and negotiation. In *Handbook of International Relations*, edited by W. Carlsnaes, T. Risse, and B. A. Simmons, 212–34. London: SAGE.

Jönsson, C., and M. Hall. 2005. *Essence of Diplomacy.* Basingstoke, UK: Palgrave Macmillan.

Josephs, R. A., J. G. Sellers, M. L. Newman, and P. H. Mehta. 2006. The Mismatch Effect: When Testosterone and Status Are at Odds. *Journal of Personality and Social Psychology* 90 (6): 999–1013.

Jost, J. T., and D. M. Amodio. 2012. Political ideology as motivated social cognition: Behavioral and neuroscientific evidence. *Motivation and Emotion* 36 (1): 55–64.

Jost, J. T, J. Glaser, A. W. Kruglanski, and F. J. Sulloway. 2003. Political conservatism as motivated social cognition. *Psychological Bulletin* 129 (3): 339–75.

Kacewicz, E., J. W. Pennebaker, M. Davis, M. Jeon, and A. C. Graesser. 2014. Pronoun use reflects standings in social hierarchies. *Journal of Language and Social Psychology* 33 (2): 125–43.

Kagan, D. 1995. *On the Origins of War and the Preservation of Peace.* New York: Random House.

Kahneman, D., and J. Renshon. 2007. Why hawks win. *Foreign Policy*, no. 158: 34–38.

Kahneman, D., and A. Tversky. 1979. Prospect theory. *Econometrica* 47 (2): 263–91.

———. 1984. Choices, values, and frames. *American Psychologist* 39 (4): 341–50.

Kaiser, D. 1983. Germany and the Origins of the First World War. *Journal of Modern History* 55 (3): 442–74.

Kam, C. D. 2007. When duty calls, do citizens answer? *Journal of Politics* 69 (1): 17–29.

Kelman, Herbert C. 1965. Social-psychological approaches to the study of international relations: The question of relevance. In *International Behavior: A Social-Psychological Analysis*, edited by H. C. Kelman, 565–607. New York: Holt, Rinehart and Winston.

Kennedy, P. M. 1972. German colonial expansion: Has the "manipulated social imperialism" been antedated? *Past and Present* no. 54: 134–41.

———. 1973. German world policy and the alliance negotiations with England, 1897–1900. *Journal of Modern History* 45 (4): 605–25.

———. 1974. The development of German naval operations: Plans against England, 1896–1914. *English Historical Review* 89 (350): 48–76.

———. 1980. *The Rise of the Anglo-German Antagonism, 1860–1914.* London: Allen and Unwin.

———. 1982. *Kaiser Wilhelm II: New Interpretations*. New York: Cambridge University Press.

———. 1984. The First World War and the international power system. *International Security* 9 (1): 7–40.

Keohane, Robert O. 1969. Lilliputians' Dilemmas: Small States in International Politics. *International Organization* 23 (2): 291–310.

Kerr, M. 1967. "Coming to Terms with Nasser": Attempts and failures. *International Affairs* 43 (1): 65–84.

Kertzer, J. 2016. *Resolve in International Politics*. Princeton, NJ: Princeton University Press.

Kertzer, J., and J. Renshon. 2015. Putting things in Perspective: Mental Simulation in experimental Political Science. Unpublished manuscript.

King, G. 1997. *A Solution to the Ecological Inference Problem: Reconstructing Individual Behavior from Aggregate Data*. Princeton, NJ: Princeton University Press.

King, G., R. O. Keohane, and S. Verba. 1994. *Designing Social Inquiry: Scientific Inference in Qualitative Research*. Princeton, NJ: Princeton University Press.

King, G., and E. Powell. 2008. How Not to Lie Without Statistics. Unpublished manuscript.

King, G., and M. Roberts. 2015. How robust standard errors expose methodological problems they do not fix. *Political Analysis* 23 (2): 159–79.

King, G., and L. Zeng. 2001a. Explaining rare events in international relations. *International Organization* 55 (3): 693–715.

———. 2001b. Logistic regression in rare events data. *Political Analysis* 9 (2): 137–63.

Kinne, B. J. 2014. Dependent diplomacy: Signaling, strategy, and prestige in the diplomatic network. *International Studies Quarterly* 58 (2): 247–59.

Kissinger, H. 1995. *Diplomacy*. New York: Simon and Schuster.

Koski, J. E., H. Xie, and I. R. Olson. 2015. Understanding social hierarchies: The neural and psychological foundations of status perception. *Social Neuroscience*, 10 (5) 527–50

Koszegi, B., and M. Rabin. 2006. A model of reference-dependent preferences. *Quarterly Journal of Economics* 121 (4): 1133–65.

Kristof, N. D. 1993. The rise of China. *Foreign Affairs* 72 (5): 59–74.

Krupnikov, Y., and A. S. Levine. 2014. Cross-sample comparisons and external validity. *Journal of Experimental Political Science* 1 (1): 59–80.

Kteily, N., A. K. Ho, and J. Sidanius. 2012. Hierarchy in the mind: The predictive power of social dominance orientation across social contexts and domains. *Journal of Experimental Social Psychology* 48 (2): 543–49.

Kugler, J., and D. Lemke. 1996. *Parity and War: Evaluations and Extensions of the War Ledger*. Ann Arbor: University of Michigan Press.

Kühberger, A., M. Schulte-Mecklenbeck, and J. Perner. 2002. Framing decisions: Hypothetical and real. *Organizational Behavior and Human Decision Processes* 89 (2): 1162–75.

Kyle, K. 2003a. Britain and the Crisis, 1955–1956. In *Suez 1956: The Crisis and Its Consequences*, edited by W. Louis, and R. Owen, 103–130. Oxford: Clarendon Press.

———. 2003b. *Suez: Britain's End of Empire in the Middle East, 1991*. London: IP Tauris.

Lake, D. A. 2007. Escape from the state of nature: Authority and hierarchy in world politics. *International Security* 32 (1): 47–79.

———. 2011. *Hierarchy in international relations*. Ithaca, NY: Cornell University Press.

———. 2014. Authority, status and the end of the american century. In *Status in World Politics*, edited by T. Paul, D. W. Larson, and W. C. Wohlforth, 246–70. New York: Cambridge University Press.

Lambert, N. 1995. British naval policy, 1913–1914: Financial limitation and strategic revolution. *Journal of Modern History* 67 (3): 595–626.

Landler, M. 2014. Syrian opposition delegation is given diplomatic status. *New York Times*, May 6, A8

Larson, D. W. 1988. Problems of content analysis in foreign-policy research: Notes from the study of the origins of Cold War belief systems. *International Studies Quarterly* 32 (2): 241–55.

Larson, D. W., T. Paul, and W. C. Wohlforth. 2014. Status and World Order. In *Status in World Politics*, edited by T. Paul, D. W. Larson, and W. C. Wohlforth, 3–32. New York: Cambridge University Press.

Larson, D. W., and A. Shevchenko. 2003. Shortcut to greatness. *International Organization*, 57 (1): 77–110.

———. 2010a. Status concerns and multilateral cooperation. In *International Cooperation: The Extents and Limits of Multilateralism*, edited by I. W. Zartman and S. Touval, 182–208. New York: Cambridge University Press.

———. 2010b. Status seekers: Chinese and Russian responses to US primacy. *International Security* 34 (4): 63–95.

———. 2014a. Managing rising powers: The role of status concerns. In *Status in World Politics*, edited by T. Paul, D. W. Larson, and W. C. Wohlforth, 32–70. New York: Cambridge University Press.

———. 2014b. Russia says no: Power, status, and emotions in foreign policy. *Communist and Post-Communist Studies* 47 (3): 269–79.

Lebovic, J. H., and E. N. Saunders. 2016. The diplomatic core: The Determinants of high-level US Diplomatic visits 1946–2010. *International Studies Quarterly* 60 (1): 107–23.

Lebow, R. N. 2008, *A Cultural Theory of International Relations*. New York: Cambridge University Press.

———. 2010a. Motives, evidence, identity: Engaging my critics. *International Theory* 2 (3): 486–94.

———. 2010b. The past and future of war. *International Relations* 24 (3): 243–70.

———. 2010c, March. *Why Nations Fight*. New York: Cambridge University Press.

Leeds, B. A., J. M. Ritter, S. M. Mitchell, and A. G. Long. 2002. Alliance Treaty Obligations and Provisions, 1815–1944. *International Interactions* 28 (3): 237–60.

Legro, J. W. 1997. Which norms matter? Revisiting the "failure" of internationalism. *International Organization* 51 (1): 31–63.

Leira, H. 2015. The formative years: Norway as an obsessive status-seeker. In *Small State Status Seeking: Norway's Quest for International Standing*, edited by B. de Carvalho and I. B. Neumann, 22–42. Milton Park, UK: Routledge Press.

Lemke, D. 1997. The continuation of history: Power transition theory and the end of the Cold War. *Journal of Peace Research* 34 (1): 23–36.

Lemke, D., and W. Reed. 1996. Regime types and status quo evaluations. *International Interactions* 22 (2): 143–64.

———. 1998. Power Is Not Satisfaction: A Comment on de Soysa, Oneal, and Park. *Journal of Conflict Resolution* 42 (4): 511–16.

Lemke, D., and S. Werner. 1996. Power parity, commitment to change, and war. *International Studies Quarterly* 40 (2): 235–60.

Lenski, G. E. 1954. Status crystallization: A non-vertical dimension of social status. *American Sociological Review* 19 (4): 405–13.

———. 1967. Status inconsistency and the vote. *American Sociological Review* 32 (2): 298–301.

Lener, J. S., D. Small, and G. Loewenstein. 2004. Heart strings and purse strings. *Psychological Science* 15 (5): 337–41

Lerner, J. S., and P. E. Tetlock. 1999. Accounting for the effects of accountability. *Psychological Bulletin* 125 (2): 255–75

Leskovec, J., K. J. Lang, and M. Mahoney. 2010. Empirical comparison of algorithms for network community detection. *Proceedings of the 19th International Conference on World Wide Web.* 631–40.

Levin, S., C. M. Federico, J. Sidanius, and J. L. Rabinowitz. 2002. Social dominance orientation and intergroup bias: The legitimation of favoritism for high-status groups. *Personality and Social Psychology Bulletin* 28 (2): 144–57.

Levite, A. E. 2003. Nuclear Reversal Revisited. *International Security* 27 (3): 59–88.

Levitt, S. D., and J. List. 2007. What do laboratory experiments measuring social preferences reveal about the real world? *Journal of Economic Perspectives* 21 (2): 153–74.

Levy, J. S. 1987. Declining power and the preventive motivation for war. *World Politics* 40 (1): 82–107.

———. 1988. Domestic politics and war. *Journal of Interdisciplinary History* 18 (4): 653–73.

———. 2014. The sources of preventive logic in German decision making in 1914. In *The Outbreak of the First World War: Structure, Politics, and Decision Making*, edited by J. S. Levy, and J. A. Vasquez, 139–66. Cambridge: Cambridge University Press.

Levy, J. S., and J. R. Gochal. 2001. Democracy and preventive war: Israel and the 1956 Sinai campaign. *Security Studies* 11 (2): 1–49.

Lieberman, E. S. 2005. Nested analysis as a mixed-method strategy for comparative research. *American Political Science Review* 99 (3): 435–52.

Lieven, D. 1983. *Russia and the Origins of the First World War.* New York: Macmillan.

———. 2015. *The End of Tsarist Russia: The March to World War I and Revolution.* New York: Viking Press.

List, J. A. 2003. Does market experience eliminate market anomalies? *Quarterly Journal of Economics* 118 (1): 41–71.

Little, D. 1988. The new frontier on the Nile: JFK, Nasser, and Arab Nationalism. *Journal of American History* 75 (2): 501–27.

Lloyd, S. 1978. *Suez 1956: A Personal Account.* New York: Mayflower Books.

Lloyd, T. O. 1996. *The British Empire, 1558–1983.* Oxford: Oxford University Press.

Loch, C. H., B. A. Huberman, and S. Stout. 2000. Status competition and performance in work groups. *Journal of Economic Behavior and Organization* 43 (1): 35–55.

Loeffler, J. C. 1998. *The Architecture of Diplomacy: Building America's Embassies.* Princeton, NJ: Princeton Architectural Press.

Longrigg, S. H. 1958. New groupings among the Arab states. *International Affairs* 34 (3): 305–17.

Lovaglia, M. J., and J. A. Houser. 1996. Emotional reactions and status in groups. *American Sociological Review* 61 (5): 867–83.

Löwenheim, O. 2003. "Do ourselves credit and render a lasting service to mankind": British moral prestige, humanitarian intervention, and the Barbary pirates. *International Studies Quarterly* 47 (1): 23–48.

Lupu, Y., and B. Greenhill. 2014. The networked peace: Intergovernmental organizations, preferences, and international conflict. Working paper.

Lupu, Y., and V. A. Tragg. 2012. Trading communities, the networked structure of international relations, and the Kantian peace. *Journal of Conflict Resolution* 57 (6): 1011–42.

Lupu, Y., and E. Voeten. 2012. A network analysis of case citations by the European Court of Human Rights. *British Journal of Political Science* 42 (2): 413–39.

Lynn-Jones, S. 1986. Detente and deterrence: Anglo-German relations, 1911–1914. *International Security* 11 (2): 121–150.

Ma, N., J. Guan, and Y. Zhao. 2008. Bringing PageRank to the citation analysis. *Information Processing and Management* 44 (2): 800–10.

Macon, K. T., P. J. Mucha, and M. A. Porter. 2012. Community structure in the United Nations General Assembly. *Physica A: Statistical Mechanics and Its Applications* 391 (1): 343–61.

Magee, J., A. Galinsky, and D. Gruenfeld. 2007. Power, propensity to negotiate, and moving first in competitive interactions. *Personality and Social Psychology Bulletin* 33 (2): 200–212.

Mahoney, J., and G. Goertz. 2006. A tale of two cultures: Contrasting quantitative and qualitative research. *Political Analysis* 14 (3): 227–49.

Malone, D. M. 2013. The modern diplomatic mission. In *Oxford Handbook of Modern Diplomacy*, 122–41. Oxford: Oxford University Press.

Mandel, R. 2006. *The Meaning of Military Victory.* Boulder, CO: Lynne Rienner Publishers.

Mandelbaum, M. 1998. Is major war obsolete? *Survival* 40 (4): 20–38.

Maner, J., M. Gailliot, D. Butz, and B. Peruche. 2007. Power, risk, and the status quo. *Personality and Social Psychology Bulletin* 33 (4): 451–62.

Mani, A., S. Mullainathan, E. Shafir, and J. Zhao. 2013. Poverty impedes cognitive function. *Science* 341 (6149): 976–80.

Mansfield, P. 1969. *Nasser's Egypt.* Baltimore: Penguin Books.

Maoz, Z. 1989. Power, capabilities, and paradoxical conflict outcomes. *World Politics* 41 (2): 239–66.

———. 2005. Dyadic mid Dataset (version 2.0). http://psfaculty.vcdvis.edv/zmaoz/dyadmid.html

———. 2010. *Networks of Nations.* New York: Cambridge University Press.

Maoz, Z., L. G. Terris, R. D. Kuperman, and I. Talmud. 2007. Centrality and international conflict: Does it pay to be important? In *Applications of Social Networks Analysis*, edited by Thomas N. Friemel, 121–51. Konstanz, Germany: Universitat Verlag Konstanz.

Markey, D. 1999. Prestige and the origins of war. *Security Studies* 8 (4): 126–72.

———. 2000. The prestige motive in international relations. Ph.D. diss., Princeton University.

Marmot, M. 2005. Social determinants of health inequalities. *Lancet* 365 (9464): 1099–104.

Marsh, A. A., K. S. Blair, M. M. Jones, N. Soliman, and R.J.R. Blair. 2009. Dominance and submission: The ventrolateral prefrontal cortex and responses to status cues. *Journal of Cognitive Neuroscience* 21 (4): 713–24.

Marteau, T., and H. Bekker. 1992. The development of a six-item short-form of the state scale of the Spielberger State—Trait Anxiety Inventory. *British Journal of Clinical Psychology* 31 (3): 301–6.

Mascaro, O., and G. Csibra. 2014. Human infants' learning of social structures the case of dominance hierarchy. *Psychological Science* 25 (1): 250–55.

Maslov, S., and S. Redner. 2008. Promise and pitfalls of extending Google's PageRank algorithm to citation networks. *Journal of Neuroscience* 28 (44): 11103–05.

Mastanduno, M. 1997. Preserving the unipolar moment: Realist theories and US grand strategy after the cold war. *International Security* 21 (4): 49–88.

Maurer, J. 1992. The Anglo-German naval rivalry and informal arms control, 1912–1914. *Journal of Conflict Resolution* 36 (2): 284–308.

———. 1997. Arms control and the Anglo-German naval race before World War I: Lessons for Today? *Political Science Quarterly* 112 (2): 285–306.

Mazur, A. 1985. A biosocial model of status in face-to-face primate groups. *Social Forces* 64 (2): 377–402.

McDermott, R. 2002a. Experimental methodology in political science. *Political Analysis* 10 (4): 325–42.

———. 2002b. Experimental methods in political science. *Annual Review of Political Science* 5: 31–61.

———. 2011. Internal and external validity. In *Handbook of Experimental Political Science*, edited by J. N. Druckman, D. P. Green, J. H. Kuklinski, and A. Lupia, 27–41. New York: Cambridge University Press.

McKeown, T. J. 1991. The foreign policy of a declining power. *International Organization* 45 (2): 257–79.

McMeekin, S. 2011. *The Russian Origins of the First World War*. Cambridge, MA: Harvard University Press.

McNemar, Q. 1946. Opinion-attitude methodology. *Psychological Bulletin* 43 (4): 289–374.

Mearsheimer, J. J. 1994. The false promise of international institutions. *International Security* 19 (3): 5–49.

Mearsheimer, J. J., and S. M. Walt. 2013. Leaving theory behind: Why simplistic hypothesis testing is bad for international relations. *European Journal of International Relations* 19 (3): 427–57.

Meerts, P. W. 2005. Entrapment in international negotiations. In *Escalation and Negotiation in International Conflicts*, edited by I. William Zartman, 111–41. New york: Cambridge University Press.

Mehta, P. H., and R. A. Josephs. 2010. Testosterone and cortisol jointly regulate dominance: Evidence for a dual-hormone hypothesis. *Hormones and Behavior* 58 (5): 898–906.

Mendoza, S. P., and P. R. Barchas. 1983. Behavioral processes leading to linear status hierarchies following group formation in rhesus monkeys. *Journal of Human Evolution* 12 (2): 185–92.

Mercer, J. 1995. Anarchy and identity. *International Organization* 49 (2): 229–52.

———. 1996. *Reputation and International Politics*. Ithaca, NY: Cornell University Press.

Midlarsky, M. I. 1975. *On War: Political Violence in the International System*. New York: Free Press.

Midlarsky, M., and E. Midlarsky. 1976. Status inconsistency, aggressive attitude, and helping behavior. *Journal of Personality* 44 (3): 371–91.

Miller, G. 2003. Hypotheses on reputation: Alliance choices and shadow of the past. *Security Studies* 12 (3): 40–78.

Miller, M. 2013. *Wronged by Empire: Post-Imperial Ideology and Foreign Policy in India and China*. Palo Alto, CA: Stanford University Press.

Miller, N. 1941. The frustration-aggression hypothesis. *Psychological Review* 48 (4): 337–42.

Milner, H. 1991. The assumption of anarchy in international relations theory: A critique. *Review of International Studies* 17 (1): 67–85.

Mintz, A. 2004. Foreign policy decision making in familiar and unfamiliar settings. *Journal of Conflict Resolution* 48 (1): 91–104.

Mintz, A., S. Redd, and A. Vedlitz. 2006. Can we generalize from student experiments to the real world in political science, military affairs, and IR? *Journal of Conflict Resolution* 50 (5): 757–76.

Mommsen, W. 1990. Kaiser Wilhelm II and German Politics. *Journal of Contemporary History* 25 (2): 289–316.

———. 1991. Public opinion and foreign Policy in Wilhelmian Germany, 1897–1914. *Central European History* 24 (4): 381–401.

Moon, H. 2001. Looking forward and looking back: Integrating completion and sunk-cost effects within an escalation-of-commitment progress decision. *Journal of Applied Psychology* 86 (1): 104–13.

Morgan, T. C., N. Bapat, and Y. Kobayashi. 2014. Threat and imposition of economic sanctions, 1945–2005: Updating the ties dataset. *Conflict Management and Peace Science* 31 (5): 541–58.

Morgenthau, H. J. 1948. *Politics among Nations*. New York: Alfred Knopf.

———. 1962. A political theory of foreign aid. *American Political Science Review* 56 (2): 301–09.

Morrison, K. R., N. Fast, and O. Ybarra. 2009. Group status, perceptions of threat, and support for social inequality. *Journal of Experimental Social Psychology* 45 (1): 204–10.

Morrison, K. R., and O. Ybarra. 2008. The effects of realistic threat and group identification on social dominance orientation. *Journal of Experimental Social Psychology* 44 (1): 156–63.

Morrow, I. 1932. The foreign policy of Prince von Bulow, 1898–1909. *Cambridge Historical Journal* 4 (1): 63–93.

Mortimer, J. S. 1967. Commercial interests and German diplomacy in the Agadir Crisis. *Historical Journal* 10 (3): 440–56.

Morton, R., and K. Williams. 2010. *Experimental Political Science and the Study of Causality: From Nature to the Lab*. New York, NY: Cambridge University Press.

Murray, M. 2008. The struggle for recognition in international politics: Security, identity and the quest for power. Ph.D. diss., University of Chicago.

———. 2010. Identity, insecurity, and great power politics. *Security Studies* 19 (4): 656–88.

———. 2012. Recognition, disrespect, and the struggle for Morocco. In *The Struggle for Recognition in International Politics*, edited by T. Lindemann and E. Ringmar, 131–51. Boulder, CO: Paradigm Publishers.

Nayar, B. R., and T. V. Paul. 2003. *India in the World Order: Searching for Major-Power Status*. New York: Cambridge University Press.

Neilson, K. 1995. Russia. In *Decisions for War, 1914*, edited by Keith Wilson, 97–120. London: University College London.

Neumann, I. B., and B. de Carvalho. 2015. Small states and status. In *Small State Status Seeking: Norway's Quest for International Standing*, edited by B. de Carvalho and I. B. Neumann, 1–22. Abingdon, UK: Routledge Press.

Neumayer, E. 2008. Distance, power, and ideology: Diplomatic representation in a world of nation-states. *Area* 40 (2): 228–36.

Newman, M. E. 2004. Fast algorithm for detecting community structure in networks. *Physical Review E* 69 (6): 066133.

Newman, M. L., J. G. Sellers, and R. A. Josephs. 2005. Testosterone, cognition, and social status. *Hormones and Behavior* 47 (2): 205–11.

Nicolson, H. 1937. *The Meaning of Prestige*. London: Cambridge University Press.

Nisbett, R. E., and D. Cohen. 1996. *Culture of Honor: The Psychology of Violence in the South*. Boulder, CO: Westview Press.

Niven, D. 2000. The other side of optimism: High expectations and the rejection of status quo politics. *Political Behavior* 22 (1): 71–88.

Novemsky, N., and D. Kahneman. 2005. The boundaries of loss aversion. *Journal of Marketing Research* 42 (2): 119–28.

Nutting, A. 1967. *No End of a Lesson: The Story of Suez*. New York: Clarkson N. Potter.

Nye, J. S., Jr. 2004. *Soft Power: The Means to Success in World Politics*. Cambridge, MA: PublicAffairs.

Offer, A. 1995. Going to war in 1914: A matter of honor? *Politics and Society* 23 (2): 213–41.

Office of the Historian, U.S. Department of State 1956. Foreign relations of the United States, 1955–1957, Volume XVI, Suez Crisis, July 26–December 31. Online.

———. 1962. Foreign relations of the United States, 1961–1963, Volume xvii, Near East, 1962–1963., Online.

Oldenburg, S. 1978. *The Last Tsar: Nicholas II, His Reign, and His Russia (Volume 4)*. Gulf Breeze, FL: Academic International.

Oldmeadow, J., and S. T. Fiske. 2007. System-justifying ideologies moderate status = competence stereotypes: Roles for belief in a just world and social dominance orientation. *European Journal of Social Psychology* 37 (6): 1135–48.

Onea, T. A. 2014. Between dominance and decline: Status anxiety and great power rivalry. *Review of International Studies* 40 (1): 1–28.

Oneal, J., and B. Russett. 2005. Rule of three, let it be? When more really is better. *Conflict Management and Peace Science* 22 (4): 293–310.

O'Neill, B. 2001. *Honor, Symbols, and War*. Ann Arbor, MI: University of Michigan Press.

———. 2003. Mediating conflicts over honour: Lessons from the Era of dueling. *Journal of Institutional and Theoretical Economics* 159 (1): 229–47.

———. 2006. Nuclear weapons and national prestige. Working paper.

Oppel, B.F. 1972. The waning of a traditional alliance: Russia and Germany after the Portsmouth peace conference. *Central European History* 5 (4): 318–29.

Organski, A.F.K. 1958. *World Politics*. New York: Knopf Press.

Organski, A.F.K., and J. Kugler. 1980. *The War Ledger*. Chicago: University of Chicago Press.

Panke, D., and U. Petersohn. 2012. Why international norms disappear sometimes. *European Journal of International Relations* 18 (4): 719–42.

Papers Relating to Foreign Affairs Accompanying the Annual Message of the President to the First Session of the Thirty-Ninth Congress (Part I). 1866. Washington, DC: US Government Printing Office.

Parker, J. 1962. The United Arab Republic. *International Affairs* 38 (1): 15–28.

Peffley, M., and J. Hurwitz. 1992. International events and foreign policy beliefs. *American Journal of Political Science* 36 (2): 431–61.

Perkovich, G. 2002. *India's nuclear bomb: The impact on global proliferation*.Berkeley: University of California Press.

Pettit, N., and R. Lount Jr. 2010. Looking down and ramping up: The impact of status differences on effort in intergroup contexts. *Journal of Experimental Social Psychology* 46 (1): 9–20.

Pettit, N., and N. Sivanathan. 2012. The eyes and ears of status: How status colors perceptual judgment. *Personality and Social Psychology Bulletin* 38 (5): 570–82.

Pettit, N., K. Yong, and S. Spataro. 2010. Reactions to the prospect of status gains and losses. *Journal of Experimental Social Psychology* 46 (2): 396–401.

Pevehouse, J., T. Nordstrom, and K. Warnke. 2004. The Correlates of War 2 international governmental organizations data version 2.0. *Conflict Management and Peace Science* 21 (2): 101–19.

Pigman, G. 2010. *Contemporary Diplomacy*. Cambridge, UK: Polity.

Plischke, E. 1999. *US Department of State: A Reference History*. Westport, CT: Greenwood Publishing Group.

Plourde, A. 2008. The origins of prestige goods as honest signals of skill and knowledge. *Human Nature* 19 (4): 374–88.

Podeh, E. 1993. The struggle over Arab hegemony after the Suez Crisis. *Middle Eastern Studies* 29 (1): 91–110.

———. 1999. *The Decline of Arab Unity: The Rise and Fall of the United Arab Republic.* Brighton, UK: Sussex Academic Press.

Pope, D., and M. Schweitzer. 2011. Is Tiger Woods loss averse? Persistent bias in the face of experience, competition, and high stakes. *American Economic Review* 101 (1): 129–57.

Porter, M. A., P. J. Mucha, M. E. Newman, and C. M. Warmbrand. 2005. A network analysis of committees in the US House of Representatives. *Proceedings of the National Academy of Sciences of the United States of America* 102 (20): 7057–62.

Powell, R. 1994. Anarchy in international relations theory: The neorealist-neoliberal debate. *International Organization* 48 (2): 313–44.

Pratto, F., J. H. Liu, S. Levin, J. Sidanius, M. Shih, H. Bachrach, and P. Hegarty. 2000. Social dominance orientation and the legitimization of inequality across cultures. *Journal of Cross-Cultural Psychology* 31 (3): 369–409.

Pratto, F., J. Sidanius, L. M. Stallworth, and B. F. Malle. 1994. Social dominance orientation: A personality variable predicting social and political attitudes. *Journal of Personality and Social Psychology* 67 (4): 741–63.

Pratto, F., L. M. Stallworth, and J. Sidanius. 1997. The gender gap: Differences in political attitudes and social dominance orientation. *British Journal of Social Psychology* 36 (1): 49–68.

Pratto, F., L. M. Stallworth, J. Sidanius, and B. Siers. 1997. The gender gap in occupational role attainment: A social dominance approach. *Journal of Personality and Social Psychology* 72 (1): 37–53.

Press, D. G. 2005. *Calculating Credibility.* Ithaca, NY: Cornell University Press.

Prosser, A. 2008, Nuclearization and its discontents: Status, security, and the pathways to nuclear reversal. PhD Graduate Institute of International and Development Studies, Geneva.

Pu, X., and R. L. Schweller. 2014. Status signaling, multiple audiences, and China's blue-water naval ambition. In *Status in World Politics*, edited by T. Paul, D. W. Larson, and W. C. Wohlforth, 141–62. New York: Cambridge University Press.

Putnam, R. D. 1988. Diplomacy and domestic politics: The logic of two-level games. *International Organization* 42 (3): 427–60.

Quester, G. 1995. British, French, and Chinese nuclear forces: Old issues and new. In *Strategic Views from the Second Tier: The Nuclear Weapons Policies of France, Britain and China*, edited by J. Hopkins and W. Hu, 249–69. Piscataway, NJ: Transaction Publishers.

Quint, T., and M. Shubik. 2001. Games of Status. *Journal of Public Economic Theory* 3 (4): 349–72.

Ray, J. L. 1974. Status inconsistency and war-involvement in Europe, 1816–1970. *Peace Science Society Papers* 23: 69–80.

———. 2003. Explaining interstate conflict and war: What should be controlled for? *Conflict Management and Peace Science* 20 (2): 1–31.

Rege, M. 2008. Why do people care about social status? *Journal of Economic Behavior and Organization* 66 (2): 233–42.

Renshon, J. 2006. *Why Leaders Choose War: The Psychology of Prevention.* Westport, CT: Praeger Publishers.

———. 2015. Losing face and sinking costs: Experimental evidence on the judgment of political and military leaders. *International Organization* 69 (3): 659–95.

———. 2016. Status deficits and war. *International Organization.*

Renshon, J., A. Dafoe, and P. K. Huth. 2017. To whom do reputations adhere? Experimental evidence on influence-specific reputations. *American Journal of Political Scince.*

Renshon, J., J. J. Lee, and D. Tingley. 2015. Physiological arousal and political beliefs. *Political Psychology* 36 (5): 569–85.

Renshon, J., J. J. Lee, and D. Tingley. 2016. Emotions and the micro-foundations of commitment problems. *International Organization.*

Renshon, J., and S. A. Renshon. 2008. The theory and practice of foreign policy decision making. *Political Psychology* 29 (4): 509–36.

Renshon, J., and C. Warren. 2015. The complexity of influence: Power and status in the interstate alliance network. Working paper.

Retallack, J. 1996. *Germany in the age of Kaiser Wilhelm II.* New York: Palgrave Macmillan.

Rhamey, J. P., and B. R. Early. 2013. Status-seeking behavior and Olympic performance. *International Area Studies Review* 16 (3): 244–61.

Rich, D. 2003. Russia. In *The Origins of World War I,* edited by R. Hamilton and H. Herwig. New York: Cambridge University Press.

Ridgeway, C. L., and J. Balkwell. 1997. Group processes and the diffusion of status beliefs. *Social Psychology Quarterly* 60 (1): 14–31.

Ridgeway, C. L., and S. J. Correll. 2006. Consensus and the creation of status beliefs. *Social Forces* 85 (1): 431–53.

Ridgeway, C. L., and H. A. Walker. 1995. Status structures. In *Sociological Perspectives on Social Psychology,* edited by K. Cook, G. Fine, and J. House, 281–310. Boston: Allyn and Bacon.

Rohl, J. 1969. Admiral Von Muller and the Approach of War, 1911–1914. *Historical Journal* 12 (4): 651–73.

Rohlfing, I. 2008. What you see and what you get. Pitfalls and principles of nested analysis in comparative research. *Comparative Political Studies* 41 (11): 1492–514.

Ronay, R., and W. Von Hippel. 2010. Power, testosterone, and risk-taking. *Journal of Behavioral Decision Making* 23 (5): 473–82.

Rose, G. 1998. Neoclassical realism and theories of foreign policy. *World Politics* 51 (1): 144–72.

Rosen, S. P. 2007. *War and Human Nature.* Princeton, NJ: Princeton University Press.

Rudman, L., C. Moss-Racusin, J. Phelan, and S. Nauts. 2011. Status incongruity and backlash effects. *Journal of Experimental Social Psychology* 48 (1): 165–79.

Sagan, S. 1996. Why do states build nuclear weapons?: Three models in search of a bomb. *International Security* 21 (3): 54–86.

Saunders, E. N. 2009. Transformative choices: Leaders and the origins of intervention strategy. *International Security* 34 (2): 119–61.

Scheepers, D. 2009. Turning social identity threat into challenge. *Journal of Experimental Social Psychology* 45 (1): 228–33.

Schlesinger, A. M. 2002. *A Thousand Days: John F. Kennedy in the White House.* Boston: Houghton Mifflin Harcourt.

Schmidt, B. M., and M. M. Chingos. 2007. Ranking doctoral programs by placement. *PS: Political Science and Politics* 40 (3): 523–29.

Schott, J. P., L. D. Scherer, and A. J. Lambert. 2011. Casualties of war and sunk costs: Implications for attitude change and persuasion. *Journal of Experimental Social Psychology* 47 (6): 1134–45.

Schroeder, P. 1972. World War I as galloping Gertie: A reply to Joachim Remak. *Journal of Modern History* 44 (3): 320–45.

Schweller, R. L. 1997. New realist research on alliances: Refining, not refuting, Waltz's balancing proposition. *American Political Science Review* 91 (4): 927–30.

Sears, D. O. 1986. College sophomores in the laboratory. *Journal of Personality and Social Psychology* 51 (3): 515–30.

Seawright, J., and J. Gerring. 2008. Case selection techniques in case study research: A menu of qualitative and quantitative options. *Political Research Quarterly* 61 (2): 294–308.

See, K., E.W. Morrison, N. Rothman, and J. Soll. 2011. The detrimental effects of power on confidence, advice taking, and accuracy. *Organizational Behavior and Human Decision Processes* 116 (2): 272–85.

Semple, K., and E. Schmitt. 2014. China's actions in hunt for jet are seen as hurting as much as helping. *New York Times*, April 14, A4.

Shannon, V. P. 2000. Norms are what states make of them: The political psychology of norm violation. *International Studies Quarterly* 44 (2): 293–316.

Sherman, G., J. Lee, A. Cuddy, J. Renshon, C. Oveis, J. Gross, and J. Lerner. 2012. Leadership is associated with lower levels of stress. *Proceedings of the National Academy of Sciences* 109 (44): 17903–7.

Sherman, G., J. Lerner, R. Josephs, J. Renshon, and J. Gross. 2016. The interaction of testosterone and cortisol is associated with elite status in male executives. *Journal of Personality and Social Psychology* 110 (6): 921–29.

Sherman, G., J. Lerner, J. Renshon, C. Ma-Kellam, and S. Joel. 2015. Perceiving others' feelings: The importance of personality and social structure. *Social Psychological and Personality Science* 6 (5): 559–69.

Shleifer, A. 2000. *Inefficient Markets.* New York: Oxford University Press.

Shuckburgh, E. 1986. *Descent to Suez: Diaries, 1951–56.* London: Weidenfeld and Nicolson.

Sidanius, J., F. Pratto, and L. Bobo. 1994. Social dominance orientation and the political psychology of gender: A case of invariance? *Journal of Personality and Social Psychology* 67 (6): 998–1011.

Signorino, C. S, and J. M. Ritter. 1999. Measuring the similarity of foreign policy positions. *International Studies Quarterly* 43 (1): 115–44.

Silk, J. 2002. Practice random acts of aggression and senseless acts of intimidation: The logic of status contests in social groups. *Evolutionary Anthropology: Issues, News, and Reviews* 11 (6): 221–25.

Simonson, I., and P. Nye. 1992. The effect of accountability on susceptibility to decision errors. *Organizational Behavior and Human Decision Processes* 51 (3): 416–46.

Singer, J. D. 1961. The level-of-analysis problem in international relations. *World Politics* 14 (1): 77–92.

———. 1963. Inter-nation influence: A formal model. *American Political Science Review* 57 (2): 420–30.

———. 1988. Reconstructing the correlates of war dataset on material capabilities of states, 1816–1985. *International Interactions* 14 (2): 115–32.

Singer, J. D., S. Bremer, and J. Stuckey. 1972. Capability distribution, uncertainty, and major power war, 1820–1965. In *Peace, War, and Numbers*, edited by B. Russett, 19–48. Thousand Oaks, CA: Sage Publications.

Singer, J. D., and M. Small. 1966. The composition and status ordering of the international system: 1815–1940. *World Politics* 18 (2): 236–82.

Singh-Manoux, A., N. Adler, and M. Marmot. 2003. Subjective social status: Its determinants and its association with measures of ill-health in the Whitehall II study. *Social Science and Medicine* 56 (6): 1321–33.

Small, M., and J. D. Singer. 1973. The diplomatic importance of states, 1816–1970. *World Politics* 25 (4): 577–99.

Smith, A., and A. C. Stam. 2004. Bargaining and the nature of war. *Journal of Conflict Resolution* 48 (6): 783–813.

Smith, P. K., N. B. Jostmann, A. D. Galinsky, and W. W. van Dijk. 2008. Lacking power impairs executive functions. *Psychological Science* 19 (5): 441–47.

Smith, P. K., D. H. Wigboldus, and A. Dijksterhuis. 2008. Abstract thinking increases one's sense of power. *Journal of Experimental Social Psychology* 44 (2): 378–85.

Snyder, J. 1991. *Myths of Empire: Domestic Politics and International Ambition.* Ithaca, NY: Cornell University Press.

Son Hing, L. S., D. R. Bobocel, M. P. Zanna, and M. V. McBride. 2007. Authoritarian dynamics and unethical decision making: High social dominance orientation leaders and high right-wing authoritarianism followers. *Journal of Personality and Social Psychology* 92 (1): 67–81.

Srivastava, S., and C. Anderson. 2011. Accurate when it counts: Perceiving power and status in social groups. In *Managing Interpersonal Sensitivity: Knowing When— and When Not—to Understand Others*, edited by J. L. Smith, W. Ickes, J. A. Hall, and S. D. Hodges, 41–58. Nova Science Publishing.

Staw, B. M. 1981. The escalation of commitment to a course of action. *Academy of Management Review* 6 (4): 577–87.

Staw, B., and J. Ross. 1989. Understanding behavior in escalation situations. *Science* 246 (4927): 216–20.

Steinberg, J. 1966. The Copenhagen Complex. *Journal of Contemporary History* 1 (3): 23–46.

Stevenson, D. 1997. Militarization and diplomacy in Europe before 1914. *International Security* 22 (1): 125–61.

Stoessinger, J. G. 1981. *Nations in Darkness.* New York: Random House.

Stueck, W. 1997. *The Korean War: An international History.* Princeton, NJ: Princeton University Press.

Tajfel, H. 1981. *Human Groups and Social Categories.* New York: Cambridge University Press.

————. 1982. Social psychology of intergroup relations. *Annual Review of Psychology* 33 (1): 1–39.

Taliaferro, J. 1998. Quagmires in the periphery. *Security Studies* 7 (3): 94–144.

————. 2004. Power politics and the balance of risk: Hypotheses on great power intervention in the periphery. *Political Psychology* 25 (2): 177–211.

Tang, S. 2005. Reputation, cult of reputation, and international conflict. *Security Studies* 14 (1): 34–62.

Tausch, N., and M. Hewstone. 2010. Social dominance orientation attenuates stereotype change in the face of disconfirming information. *Social Psychology* 41 (3): 169–76.

Teorell, J., S. Dahlberg, S. Holmberg, B. Rothstein, A. Khomenko, and R. Svensson. 2015. The quality of government standard dataset, version Jan15. http://www.qog.pol.gu.se.

Tetlock, P. 1985. Accountability: The neglected social context of judgment and choice. *Research in Organizational Behavior* 7: 297–332.

Tetlock, P., and J. Goldgeier. 2000. Human nature and world politics: Cognition, identity, and influence. *International Journal of Psychology* 35 (2): 87–96.

Thaler, R. 1980. Toward a positive theory of consumer choice. *Journal of Economic Behavior and Organization* 1 (1): 39–60.

Tomz, M., J. Wittenberg, and G. King. 2003. Clarify: Software for interpreting and presenting statistical results. *Journal of Statistical Software* 8 (1): 1–30.

Traag, V., and J. Bruggeman. 2009. Community detection in networks with positive and negative links. *Physical Review E* 80 (3): 036115.

Trachtenberg, M. 1990. The meaning of mobilization in 1914. *International Security* 15 (3): 120–50.

Turner, J. C., R. J. Brown, and H. Tajfel. 1979. Social comparison and group interest in ingroup favouritism. *European Journal of Social Psychology* 9 (2): 187–204.

Tyszka, T., and P. Zielonka. 2002. Expert judgments: Financial analysts versus weather forecasters. *Journal of Psychology and Financial Markets* 3 (3): 152–60.

US Congress. 1890. *Reports of Committees of the Senate of the United States for the First Session fo the Fifty-First Congress.* Washington, DC: Government Printing Office.

————. 1917. *Hearings before the Committe on Foreign Affairs of the House of Representatives.* Washington, DC: Government Printing Office.

————. 1920. *Diplomatic and Consular Appropriation Bill: Hearings before the Committee on Foreign Affairs, House of Representatives, Sixty-Sixth Congress, Second Session, on the Bill Making Appropriations for the Diplomatic and Consular Service for the Fiscal Year Ending June 30, 1921.* Washington, DC: Government Printing Office.

Van Evera, S. 1994. Hypotheses on nationalism and war. *International Security* 18 (4): 5–39.

————. 1997. *Guide to Methods for Students of Political Science.* Ithaca, NY: Cornell University Press.

Vaughn, S. 1987. Militarizing the last frontier: Technology and the space race. *Review of Politics* 49 (2): 302–9.

Vayrynen, R. 1983. Economic cycles, power transitions, political management and wars between major powers. *International Studies Quarterly* 27 (4): 389–418.

Veblen, T. 1899. *The Theory of the Leisure Class.* New York: Macmillan.

Verba, S. 1964. Simulation, reality, and theory in international relations. *World Politics* 16 (3): 490–519.

Volgy, T. J., R. Corbetta, K. Grant, and R. Baird. 2011. Major Power Status in International Politics. In *Major Powers and the Quest for Status in International Politics: Global and Regional Perspectives*, edited by T. J. Volgy, R. Corbetta, K. Grant, and R. Baird, 1–26. Basingstoke, UK: Palgrave Macmillan.

Volgy, T. J., and S. Mayhall. 1995. Status inconsistency and international war. *International Studies Quarterly* 39 (1): 67–84.

Von Hippel, K. 1996. Sunk in the sahara. *The Journal of North African Studies* 1 (1): 95–116.

von Rueden, C., M. Gurven, and H. Kaplan. 2008. The multiple dimensions of male social status in an Amazonian society. *Evolution and Human Behavior* 29 (6): 402–15.

von Rueden, C., M. Gurven, and H. Kaplan. 2011. Why do men seek status? Fitness payoffs to dominance and prestige. *Proceedings of the Royal Society B: Biological Sciences* 278 (1715): 2223–32.

Wagner, R. H. 2000. Bargaining and war. *American Journal of Political Science* 44 (3): 469–84.

Wallace, M. D. 1971. Power, status, and International War. *Journal of Peace Research* 8 (1): 23–35.

———. 1973. *War and Rank among Nations*. Lanham, MD: Lexington Books.

———. 1982. Armaments and escalation: Two competing hypotheses. *International Studies Quarterly* 26 (1): 37–56.

Walt, S. M. 1987. *The Origin of Alliances*. Ithaca, NY: Cornell University Press.

Walt, S. 2010. Cutting losses in wars of choice. In *The Prudent Use of Power in American National Security Strategy*, edited by S. S. Stephen Van Evera, 131–56. Cambridge, MA: Tobin Project.

Waltz, K. N. 1979. *Theory of international politics*. Long Grove, IL: Waveland Press.

Ward, S. 2012. Status immobility and systemic revisionism in rising powers. PhD diss., Georgetown University.

———. 2014. (Mis)Measuring status? Assessing the influence of economic and military achievement on diplomatic exchange. Working paper.

———. 2015. Lost in translation: The misadventures of social identity and status in IR theory. Working paper.

Watson, D., L. Clark, and A. Tellegen. 1988. Development and validation of brief measures of positive and negative affect. *Journal of Personality and Social Psychology* 54 (6): 1063–70.

Wechsler, D. 1997. *Wechsler Adult Intelligence Scale*. San Antonio, TX: Psychological Corporation.

Wehler, H.-U. 1970. Bismarck's imperialism, 1862–1890. *Past and Present*, no. 48: 119–55.

———. 1985. *The German Empire, 1871–1918*. Oxford: Berg Publishers.

Weisiger, A., and K. Yarhi-Milo. 2011. Revisiting reputation: How past actions matter in international politics. *International Organization* 69 (2): 473–95.

Welch, D. A. 2005. *A Theory of Foreign Policy Change*. Princeton, NJ: Princeton University Press.

Werner, S. 1999. Choosing demands strategically: The distribution of power, the distribution of benefits, and the risk of conflict. *Journal of Conflict Resolution* 43 (6): 705–26.

———. 2000. The effects of political similarity on the onset of militarized disputes, 1816–1985. *Political Research Quarterly* 53 (2): 343–74.

Weyland, K. 1996. Risk taking in Latin American economic restructuring: Lessons from prospect theory. *International Studies Quarterly* 40 (2): 185–207.

Whiting, A. S. 1968. *China crosses the Yalu*. Palo Alto, CA: Stanford University Press.

Wight, M. 1979. *Power Politics*. Gretna, LA: Pelican.

Williamson, S. 1988. The origins of World War I. *Journal of Interdisciplinary History* 18 (4): 795–818.

Williamson, S., and E. May. 2007. An Identity of Opinion: Historians and July 1914. *Journal of Modern History* 79 (2): 335–87.

Williamson, S., and R. Van Wyk. 2003. *July 1914: Soldiers, Statesmen, and the Coming of the Great War: A Brief Documentary History*. Boston: St. Martins.

Wilson, K. 1972. The Agadir Crisis, the mansion house speech, and the double-edgedness of agreements. *Historical Journal* 15 (3): 513–32.

Wilson, S. E., and D. M. Butler. 2007. The sensitivity of time-series cross-section analyses to simple alternative specifications. *Political Analysis* 15 (2): 101–23.

Wohlforth, W. C. 1993. *Power and Perceptions during the Cold War*. Ithaca, NY: Cornell University Press.

———. 1998. Honor as Interest in Russian decisions for war, 1600–1995. In *Honor among Nations: Intangible Interests and Foreign Policy*, edited by E. Abrams, 21–45. Washington, DC: Ethics and Public Policy Center.

———. 1999. The stability of a unipolar world. *International Security* 24 (1): 5–41.

———. 2002. Hierarchy, status, and war. Working paper.

———. 2009. Unipolarity, status competition, and great power war. *World Politics* 61 (1): 28–57.

Wolf, R. 2011a. Recognition and disrespect between persons and peoples. In *The International Politics of Recognition*, edited by T. Lindemann and E. Ringmar, 39–57. Boulder, CO: Paradigm Publishers.

———. 2011b. Respect and disrespect in international politics. *International Theory* 3 (1): 105–42.

Wong, K., M. Yik, and J. Kwong. 2006. Understanding the emotional aspects of escalation of commitment. *Journal of Applied Psychology* 91 (2): 282–97.

Wood, S. 2013. Prestige in world politics. *International Politics* 50 (3): 387–411.

Woodward, E. 1935. *Great Britain and the German Navy*. Oxford: Clarendon Press.

Wooldridge, J. 2002. *Econometric Analysis of Cross-Section and Panel Data*. Cambridge, MA: MIT Press.

World Bank. 2014. World Development Indicators. http://data.worldbank. org/data-catalog/world-development-indicators.

Yergin, D. 1992. *The Prize: The Epic Quest for Oil, Money, and Power*. New York: Free Press.

Zacher, M. W. 2001. The territorial integrity norm: International boundaries and the use of force. *International Organization* 55 (2): 215–50.

Zhang, X. 2008. Status inconsistency revisited: An improved statistical model. *European Sociological Review* 24 (2): 155–68.

Zhang, Y., A. Friend, A. L. Traud, M. A. Porter, J. H. Fowler, and P. J. Mucha. 2008. Community structure in congressional cosponsorship networks. *Physica A: Statistical Mechanics and Its Applications* 387 (7): 1705–12.

Zyphur, M., J. Narayanan, G. Koh, and D. Koh. 2009. Testosterone-status mismatch lowers collective efficacy in groups. *Organizational Behavior and Human Decision Processes* 110 (2): 70–79.

Index